n990045891
3/00
14.95
RAF
(Dav)

The Idea of a
Political Liberalism

HAROLD BRIDGES LIBRARY
ST MARTINS SERVICES LTD.
LANCASTER

0847687937

Studies in Social, Political, and Legal Philosophy
Series Editor: James P. Sterba, University of Notre Dame

This series analyzes and evaluates critically the major political, social, and legal ideals, institutions, and practices of our time. The analysis may be historical or problem-centered; the evaluation may focus on theoretical underpinnings or practical implications. Among the recent titles in the series are:

Can Ethics Provide Answers? And Other Essays in Moral Philosophy
  by James Rachels, University of Alabama at Birmingham
Character and Culture
  by Lester H. Hunt, University of Wisconsin–Madison
Same Sex: Debating the Ethics, Science, and Culture of Homosexuality
  edited by John Corvino, University of Texas at Austin
Approximate Justice: Studies in Non-Ideal Theory
  by George Sher, Rice University
Living in Integrity: A Global Ethic to Restore a Fragmented Earth
  by Laura Westra, University of Windsor
Racist Symbols and Reparations: Philosophical Reflections on Vestiges of the American Civil War
  by George Schedler, Southern Illinois University
Necessary Goods: Our Responsibilities to Meet Others' Needs
  edited by Gillian Brock, University of Auckland, New Zealand
The Business of Consumption: Environmental Ethics and the Global Economy
  edited by Laura Westra, University of Windsor, and Patricia H. Werhane, University of Virginia
Child versus Childmaker: Present Duties and Future Persons in Ethics and the Law
  by Melinda A. Roberts, College of New Jersey
Gewirth: Critical Essays on Action, Rationality, and Community
  edited by Michael Boylan
The Idea of a Political Liberalism: Essays on Rawls
  edited by Victoria Davion and Clark Wolf
Self-Management and the Crisis of Socialism: The Rose in the Fist of the Present
  by Michael W. Howard, University of Maine

The Idea of a
Political Liberalism

Essays on Rawls

EDITED BY
VICTORIA DAVION AND CLARK WOLF

ROWMAN & LITTLEFIELD PUBLISHERS, INC.
Lanham • Boulder • New York • Oxford

ROWMAN & LITTLEFIELD PUBLISHERS, INC.

Published in the United States of America
by Rowman & Littlefield Publishers, Inc.
4720 Boston Way, Lanham, Maryland 20706
http://www.rowmanlittlefield.com

12 Hid's Copse Road
Cumnor Hill, Oxford OX2 9JJ, England

Copyright © 2000 by Rowman & Littlefield Publishers, Inc.
Chapter 9 © 2000 Claudia Card
Chapter 11 © 2000 Bernard P. Dauenhauer
Chapter 14 © 2000 Christoph Fehige

An earlier version of chapter 3, "Rawls's Neglected Children" by Samantha Brennan
and Robert Noggle appeared as "John Rawls's Children" in *The Philosopher's Child*
(Rochester: © University of Rochester, 1998). Reprinted with the permission of the
publisher and authors.

An earlier version of chapter 7, "Reflective Equilibrium and Justice as Political" by
Norman Daniels, appeared in *Justice and Justification* (New York: © Cambridge
University Press, 1996). Reprinted with permission of Cambridge University Press.

All rights reserved. No part of this publication may be reproduced,
stored in a retrieval system, or transmitted in any form or by any
means, electronic, mechanical, photocopying, recording, or otherwise,
without the prior permission of the publisher.

British Library Cataloguing in Publication Information Available

Library of Congress Cataloging-in-Publication Data

The idea of a political liberalism : essays on Rawls / edited by
  Victoria Davion and Clark Wolf.
      p. cm.—(Studies in social, political, and legal
  philosophy)
    Includes bibliographical references and index
    ISBN 0-8476-8793-7 (cloth : alk. paper).—ISBN 0-8476-8794-5
  (paper : alk. paper)
      1. Liberalism.   2. Rawls, John, 1921—Contributions in political
  science. I. Davion, Victoria, 1960– . II. Wolf, Clark, 1962– .
  III. Series.
JC574.I33   2000
320.51—dc21   99-36523
                                                              CIP

Printed in the United States of America

⊗™The paper used in this publication meets the minimum requirements of American National
Standard for Information Sciences—Permanence of Paper for Printed Library Materials, ANSI/
NISO Z39.48-1992.

For Our Families:
Ellen and John
Rebecca, Rachael, and Jonathan

We thank the following, without whom this book would not be possible: James P. Sterba, series editor; the authors in this volume; Mona Freer, our invaluable editorial assistant; Maureen McGrogan and Julie Kirsch, our editors at Rowman & Littlefield; Deborah Lynes of D & D Editorial Services; and the philosophy department at the University of Georgia. Finally, we thank John Rawls, whose work inspired this volume.

CONTENTS

INTRODUCTION:

FROM COMPREHENSIVE JUSTICE

TO POLITICAL LIBERALISM

Victoria Davion and Clark Wolf

1. Rawls and Contemporary Political Philosophy

The publication of this volume marks (approximately) the thirtieth anniversary of the publication of John Rawls's *A Theory of Justice* (1971; hereafter referred to as *Theory* or *TJ*). By any account, the appearance of *Theory* was a turning point for political philosophy. Many observers felt that the entire field was in decline in the 1950s and 1960s (Barry 1996). In 1956, Peter Laslett famously announced that "political philosophy is dead," and Isaiah Berlin once said that he decided to pursue scholarship in intellectual history because he became convinced that philosophy had nothing more to offer to politics. Some people have described this sense of decline in political theory as a field as a gap in the literature: Richard Tuck (1995) notes "the absence of major works of political philosophy of a more or less familiar kind, between Sidgwick and Rawls."[1] Whatever the cause of this perceived gap, the appearance of *Theory* could not have been more cataclysmic in its effect on the field.

What explains the remarkable effect that Rawls's work has had in turning around an entire discipline? Surely there were many factors at play. In *Theory*, Rawls reappropriated for philosophy many subjects that had migrated to other fields—chiefly to economics and political science. Brian Barry reiterates Tuck's comment that since the death of Sidgwick, "nobody until Rawls produced anything that represents a continuation of the canon of political thought, as traditionally conceived" (Barry 1996, 537). But perhaps the most promising counterexamples to this claim are the sophisticated developments in economic theory, especially the development of formal utility theory by Vilfredo Pareto and later by John Von Neumann. These developments made possible a revolution in welfare economics that peaked shortly before the publication of *Theory*, and which can indeed be seen as flowing naturally from the work of turn-of-the-century utilitarians like Sidgwick. But for the most part, those responsible for these developments did not take themselves to be articulating a normative political theory, nor would they have been pleased to have their work identified as philosophical.

For the most part, political philosophers writing in the 1950s and 1960s were not much influenced by developments in economic theory. One of the important features that distinguished Rawls's early work is the careful but critical attention he gives to these developments. Many philosophers were unfamiliar with economic efficiency concepts before encountering these concepts in *Theory*. But although Rawls engaged and employed economic theory in the service of argument, he also articulated and assessed the evaluative assumptions of these theories. This distinguishes his approach from that of many economists, who often regard efficiency concepts as purely positive (nonnormative) but put these concepts to normative use in the context of policy choice. Brian Barry argues that Rawls's work owed little to the work of other twentieth-century political philosophers and notes that the index of *Theory* includes no headings for Arendt, Oakeshott, Popper, Strauss, or Voegelin. But Rawls does consistently refer to recent work by *economists*, and their influence is as clearly present in the index as it is in the text.[2] Perhaps it is more fitting to view Rawls as having reappropriated from economics the central issues of political theory rather than reactivating a field that had been dead since Sidgwick. He managed this reappropriation by giving respectful and informed critical treatment to some of the most current and sophisticated work in political science and economics, and his critical treatment put those works in a new light and brought new depth to discussions of political and economic theory.

In part, the success of *Theory* may also be explained by the persistent but waning philosophical influence of positivism. Many philosophers, like Berlin, were persuaded that philosophy had little to offer politics and that evaluative issues in general were entirely subjective and impervious to philosophical analysis. The argument of *Theory* represents a powerful response to the naive positivist account of justification and analysis. Rawls himself acknowledges the decisive influence of the work of W. V. O. Quine and Burton Dreben and remarks that Dreben persuaded him that "the notions of meaning and analyticity play no essential role in moral theory" (*TJ*, xi). In response to this influence, as well as to influence from the work of Nelson Goodman (*TJ*, 20 n. 7), Rawls developed his account of reason as reflective equilibrium and his coherentist theory of justification (*TJ*, 577–83). Rawls's theory of justification built on contemporary work in philosophy of science and especially on the postpositivist views of Quine and Goodman. Rawls's influence among *philosophers* may be explained, though only partly, by the fact that his account of justification and theory construction offered the most promising postpositivist account of normative theory.

Finally, Rawls's work is simply packed with *arguments*. There is little doubt that this, more than anything else, explains the remarkable influence of his work. Positivists like Ayer had argued that normative theory must, in the end, be nothing more than the expression of affective commitments that are fundamentally inarticulate and not subject to rigorous argument or reasoned discussion. Many were persuaded. The best way to disprove this part of the naive positivist view was by counterexample: Whether one agrees or disagrees with Rawls's conclusions, he demonstrated that normative political theory can be rigorous, argumentative, and reasoned. Offering arguments rather than ideals has its dangers: As the chapters in this volume demonstrate, Rawls has, for the most part, inspired philosophers not as disciples or followers but as critics and opponents. But even Rawls's most articulate critics have adopted argumentative methods that betray his deep influence. Critical attention of this sort is, we believe, the highest form of scholarly compliment. We hope that the essays in this volume will be understood in this spirit.

2. From Comprehensive to Political Liberalism

Whether as raw material for argument or as a critical foil against which other views may be articulated, Rawls's early work has garnered both attention and affection from his critics and critical advocates. It is therefore not surprising to find that many who were attracted to Rawls's early work have sometimes greeted his more recent writings with dismay. Many sympathetic critics of Rawls's early work were attracted to features of his view that Rawls now seems to have abandoned. For example, in a section of *Theory* titled "The Kantian Interpretation of Justice as Fairness" (*TJ*, 251), Rawls writes: "The principles of justice are . . . categorical imperatives in Kant's sense. For by a categorical imperative Kant understands a principle of conduct that applies to a person in virtue of his nature as a free and equal rational being. The validity of the principle does not presuppose that one has a particular desire or aim" (*TJ*, 253). When such a claim is associated with Rawls's statement that "the theory of justice is . . . part of the theory of rational choice" (*TJ*, 16), it is easy to see why so many scholars took Rawls's project to be a promising attempt to show the connection between morality and reason and to show that there are substantive principles that all rational persons must accept as moral constraints or as constraints of justice. It is clear from Rawls's later work that this is not, or perhaps is no longer, what he has in mind.

Scholars who continue to think deepen and change their views over time. Rawls, of course, is no exception. Although he himself argues that, with the exception of a few minor corrections, the view expressed in *Political Liberalism* (1993; abbreviated as *PL*) is *consistent* with that in *Theory*, many of Rawls's critics and friends disagree. Quite a number of commentators seem to believe that Rawls has made unnecessary concessions to his critics, and some even regard these changes as a kind of criticizable moral backsliding. In this spirit, some critics have undertaken to defend "Rawls's earlier self against his later self" (Barry 1995, 876). Rawls himself claims that the only major change has been the development of an account of political stability that, unlike the account articulated in part III of *Theory*, is consistent with the conception of justice as fairness as a whole (*PL* 1996, xvii). It is clear that the work Rawls has produced since *Theory* has had quite a different focus and emphasis, but there is little agreement about the relationship between his early and later writings on political justice. Although one could hardly expect *Political Liberalism* to have the same cataclysmic effect as *Theory*, it is arguable that Rawls's later work has received far less attention than it deserves.

The chapters in this volume treat issues raised by *Political Liberalism* and other recent papers and books. Even with this focus, there is a wealth of material: recent works cover the theory of justice, the problem of pluralism, political legitimacy, the need for political consensus, the basis of political rights, foundations of international law, objectivity in normative theory, and many other issues. While we cannot begin to claim that the chapters in this volume cover the entire range of issues raised by Rawls's recent works, the contributors to this volume have addressed many of the most central. Chapters treat issues of legitimacy, international justice, the moral commitments of liberalism, legitimate entitlements, the problem of stability, and the liberal critique of utilitarianism.

In the following section, we present a brief account of the central argument of *Political Liberalism*. Then in section 4 we briefly describe the chapters in this collection.

3. The Argument of *Political Liberalism*

In *Political Liberalism,* Rawls defends the conception of justice as fairness as a *political* conception of justice. In *Theory,* no distinction was made between comprehensive moral doctrines and freestanding *political* conceptions of justice, but in *Political Liberalism,* this distinction is fundamental. Three features distinguish a political conception of justice. First, it is a moral conception, for the basic structure of society. That is, it is not a conception that applies directly to associations or groups within a society. Second, it assumes no particular comprehensive doctrine but is consistent with reasonable comprehensive doctrines. Third, a political conception, according to Rawls, is formulated solely in terms of certain fundamental intuitive ideas that are taken to be implicit in the public political culture of a democratic society. Rawls argues that such ideas will arise as part of the public culture of any longstanding democratic society. The task of political philosophy, then, is to find a shared basis for settling fundamental political questions by collecting and carefully articulating the principles behind shared moral and political convictions. It does this by articulating these principles as a system and by adjusting and revising them in reflective equilibrium (*PL,* 8–9).

In *Political Liberalism,* Rawls is centrally concerned with issues of stability and legitimacy—issues that did not occupy center stage in *Theory.* These problems are of special importance for pluralistic states in which different citizens do not share the same comprehensive doctrine. Rawls argues that such pluralism should be expected wherever public institutions protect individual liberty and freedom of thought and conscience. In fact, he identifies this pluralism as one of five "general facts" about the political culture of democratic societies, facts that frame the problem of political justice in such societies. According to the first, "the fact of reasonable pluralism," the diversity of comprehensive doctrines is, not a historical contingency, but a natural result of the exercise of human reason under conditions of freedom (*PL,* 36). Second, Rawls argues that a continuing, shared understanding on one comprehensive religious, philosophical, or moral doctrine can be maintained only by an oppressive and unjustifiable use of force (*PL,* 37). He calls this "the fact of oppression." Third, "an enduring and secure democratic regime must be willingly and freely supported by at least a substantial majority of its politically active citizens," else the regime will not be enduring and secure (*PL,* 38).

The fourth general fact is that "the political culture of a democratic society that has worked reasonably well over a considerable period of time normally contains, at least implicitly, certain fundamental intuitive ideas from which it is possible to work up a political conception of justice suitable for a constitutional regime" (*PL,* 38 n. 41). If this were false, then it would be impossible to develop a conception of justice that would gain the willing support of citizens, which (according to fact three) is necessary for stability. Fifth and finally, Rawls argues that "many of our most important moral and political judgments are rendered under conditions such that it is unlikely that conscientious and fully reasonable persons, even after full and free discussion, can exercise their powers of reason so that all arrive at the same conclusion" (*PL,* 58). Rawls refers to this last fact as "the burdens of judgment." He argues that reasonable citizens will recognize that others, like themselves, face the burdens of judgment and that therefore it is unreasonable to expect universal consensus on any comprehensive metaphysical or moral doctrine. Even if our own cherished doctrine is the Final Truth, we cannot expect that others will recognize it as such.

Together, these general facts make the problem of legitimacy extremely pressing. If legitimacy requires, minimally, that a majority of citizens must freely support the democratic regime described by the conception of justice as fairness but the freedoms implicit in that conception ensure that there will be wide pluralism and that different people will have quite different comprehensive doctrines, then it might seem unlikely that liberal political institutions could achieve legitimacy.

According to Rawls, a conception of justice founded on free institutions must embrace *reasonable* pluralism, and *Political Liberalism* is Rawls's attempt to show how this can be done. Political liberalism "applies the principle of toleration to philosophy itself" (*PL,* 10), since it seeks to describe a conception of justice that is consistent with and even supported by a broad plurality of reasonable moral, religious, and philosophical doctrines. *Theory* failed to embrace reasonable pluralism because it required that people endorse justice as fairness based on their adhering to the same comprehensive philosophical doctrine. This is implicit, for example, in the claim that the principles of justice can be seen as "a procedural interpretation of Kant's conception of autonomy and the categorical imperative" (*TJ*, 256). Recognizing reasonable pluralism means realizing that, in fact, people cannot be expected to agree on the same comprehensive doctrine—certainly not a doctrine as difficult and controversial as Kant's. Hence, Rawls argues in *Political Liberalism* that the stability and legitimacy of public institutions cannot be based on general agreement on any particular comprehensive doctrine, including a Kantian conception. The very freedoms that justice as fairness seeks to protect will prevent such agreement, given the expected consequences of the exercise of reason under free institutions. As Rawls put it in the first edition of *Political Liberalism,* the central question to be addressed by a political conception of justice is therefore:

> How is it possible that there may exist over time a stable and just society of free and equal citizens profoundly divided by reasonable though incompatible religious, philosophical, and moral doctrines? Put another way: How is it possible people holding deeply opposed though reasonable comprehensive doctrines may live together and all affirm the political conception of a constitutional regime? What is the structure and content of a political conception that can gain support of such an overlapping consensus? These are among the questions that political liberalism tries to answer. (*PL 1993*, xviii)

To put the question more sharply, consider the predicament of a citizen in a liberal state who is deeply committed to a reasonable but illiberal comprehensive doctrine. Such a person might, for example, be deeply committed to a religious doctrine that places a lower value on freedom of expression or conscience and a higher value on living a life that conforms to God's will. In the preface of the 1996 paperback edition of *Political Liberalism*, Rawls revised his description of the central question to be addressed by a political conception of justice to incorporate the perspective of such a person, noting that

> not all reasonable comprehensive doctrines are liberal comprehensive doctrines; so the question is whether they can still be compatible for the right reasons with a liberal political conception. To do this, I contend, it is not sufficient that these doctrines accept a democratic regime merely as a *modus vivendi*. Rather, they must accept it as members of a reasonable overlapping consensus. Referring to citizens holding such a religious doctrine as citizens of faith, we ask: How is it possible for citizens of faith to be wholehearted members of a democratic society when they endorse an institutional structure satisfying a liberal political conception of justice with its own intrinsic political ideals and values, and when they are not simply going along with it in view of the balance of political and social forces? (*PL* 1996, xxxix –xl)

If "citizens of faith" conform to liberal institutions only because they are too weak to overthrow those institutions and replace them with a theocracy, then they accept liberal principles only as a modus vivendi. Where such an attitude is widespread, argues Rawls, a political regime will be unstable and subject to a shifting balance of power that could be upset if different groups within the society become relatively stronger or weaker. Political liberalism strives to show that a liberal political conception can be endorsed as more than a mere modus vivendi. Even if citizens initially agree to abide by the conception of justice as fairness as a modus vivendi in order to avoid civil strife, Rawls argues that their allegiance to this conception of justice will strengthen over time as they come to understand what justice achieves. In this way, argues Rawls, the conception of justice as fairness reinforces its own foundations, recommending itself to those who are subject to it.

Rawls's aim in *Political Liberalism* is neither to replace reasonable comprehensive doctrines nor to justify them. Rather, the aim is to work out a political conception of justice that reasonable people can all endorse, even if they adhere to widely different comprehensive doctrines. This task requires isolating certain purely political issues and providing justifications for them based on "public reason," justifications that all reasonable people can endorse in overlapping consensus. The project calls for the development and justification of a purely political conception of justice that can be shared by all. This, in turn, requires a distinction between a public basis of justification generally acceptable to everyone and the many nonpublic justifications based on the comprehensive doctrines and acceptable only to those who affirm them. The development of a purely political conception of justice and the public basis of justification for such a conception requires the introduction of a number of new concepts. According to Rawls, these include:

1. The idea of justice as fairness as a *freestanding view* and that of an overlapping consensus as belonging to its account of stability;
2. The distinction between simple pluralism and reasonable pluralism, together with the idea of a reasonable comprehensive doctrine; and
3. A fuller account of the reasonable and the rational worked into the conception of political (as opposed to moral) constructivism, so as to bring out the bases of the principles of right and justice in practical reason. (*PL* 1993, xxx)

In *Political Liberalism*, Rawls develops these concepts by showing how they fit into a political conception of justice that can be the object of an overlapping consensus among the members of a society of people who are *reasonable* but who do not agree on any comprehensive view. "Citizens are *reasonable*," writes Rawls, "when, viewing one another as free and equal participants, they are prepared to offer fair terms of social cooperation and to act on those terms even when this runs contrary to their own narrower interests, provided that others are similarly willing" (*PL* 1996, xliv). Reasonable citizens will agree, argues Rawls, on the following "criterion of reciprocity: Our exercise of political power is proper only when we sincerely believe that the reasons we offer for our political action may reasonably be accepted by other citizens as a justification of those actions" (*PL* 1996, xlvi). A political conception of justice is reasonable in Rawls's sense only if it satisfies this criterion. According to Rawls, the notion of reasonableness underlies the acceptance of this principle of reciprocity. In turn, reciprocity underlies the possibility of a liberal conception of political legitimacy (see *PL*, 217), and the possibility that the stability of a liberal regime may be more than just a balance of power among competing factions. In "favorable circumstances," a political conception of justice will generate its own support, and the institutions to which it leads will be self-enforcing. In such circumstances, stable social cooperation rests on the fact that most citizens accept the political order as legitimate. In such circumstances, they can freely and willingly support a liberal democratic regime governed by a public conception of justice as fairness.

4. Organization of Chapters

We have briefly and, we hope, sympathetically described the project of *Political Liberalism*, the most complete expression to date of Rawls's later views. In this volume, the chapters treat various aspects of Rawls's later work, especially as articulated in *Political Liberalism* and in "The Law of Peoples." All but two of the chapters are published here for the first time.

Part 1, "Reasonable versus Simple Pluralism and the Legitimacy of the State," focuses on questions of exclusion. Marilyn Friedman questions Rawls's exclusion of unreasonable people from what she terms "the legitimation pool." Rawls defines reasonable persons as those who seek fair terms of social cooperation with others and who think reasonable people living under free institutions will disagree about fundamental matters of religion, morality, or philosophy. Unreasonable people lack one or both of these beliefs. Friedman worries that because Rawls argues that we need not take the views of the unreasonable seriously, political liberalism allows the state to impose coercive power on those who reject it, provided that the state has been ratified in the right way by *reasonable* people.

James Sterba deals with the place of religious convictions within the ideal of public reason. Given this ideal, "citizens are to conduct their fundamental discussions within the framework of what each regards as a political conception of justice based on values that others can reasonably be expected to endorse" (*PL*, 226). Because people cannot be expected to agree on religion, it appears that religious considerations have no place in the public debate over fundamental issues. Sterba defends Rawls against critics, arguing that a correct interpretation of the ideal of public reason allows a place for religious convictions after all.

Concluding Part 1, Samantha Brennan and Robert Noggle examine what they take to be a serious gap in Rawls's project: Neither in *A Theory of Justice* nor in *Political Liberalism* does Rawls consider the moral or political status of children. Although Rawls describes his account of justice as designed for a society that is entered only by birth (and exited only by death), he never discusses age or the special vulnerability of children and older people. In fact, some of Rawls's assumptions render the family opaque to political analysis and undermine the ability of his theory to address issues of children's rights. Brennan and Noggle consider several strategies that Rawls might adopt in extending his theory to children. They focus special attention on Rawls's discussion of justice between generations as an avenue to introduce children's rights and interests and on Rawls's discussion of moral development in the later sections of *Theory*. They argue that Rawls's theory would be strengthened, not weakened, if a more sophisticated account of moral development were imported into his discussion of moral psychology.

The chapters in Part 2, "Political Liberalism and International Justice," examine Rawls's attempt to extend the basic considerations of political liberalism to the international arena. In "The Law of Peoples," Rawls argues that political liberalism cannot demand that all societies be liberal, otherwise liberalism's own principles of toleration for other reasonable ways of ordering society would be violated. He then argues that a reasonable law of peoples would require societies to respect only a subset of what liberals usually regard as human rights. Many have noted that Rawls's position in "The Law of Peoples" seems oddly unconnected to other aspects of his project and have argued that Rawls's account of international justice is seriously regressive: Rawls's principles for international law require respect for only a minimal set of basic human rights, which does not include rights of free expression or free association. His account of political legitimacy does not require democracy as a condition for legitimacy. Rawls's law of peoples imposes no requirements of distributive justice beyond the provision of a bare subsistence for all, and it permits serious institutional inequalities.

Allen Buchanan offers a reconstruction of a Rawlsian law of peoples that avoids the regressive features of the view Rawls has expressed—and which Buchanan believes to be more consistent with the political conception of justice Rawls has articulated in his other works. In particular, Buchanan's view may be more "Rawlsian" than Rawls's own view, since it incorporates Rawls's account of reasonable cooperation and the famous argument for the burdens of judgment, and employs them in the service of Rawls's claim that a society is entitled to noninterference as long as it is nonexpansionist and minimally respectful of basic human rights. Buchanan argues that the regressive features of Rawls's view are unmotivated and unnecessary. His own alternative proposal for the extension of the political conception of justice as fairness to the problem of international law is both more coherent with that conception as a whole and more progressive in its implications for international relations.

Roger Crisp and Dale Jamieson discuss Thomas Pogge's reconstruction of a Rawlsian law of peoples. In a widely influential paper, Pogge argues that a plausible account of the law of peoples will include a much more stringent redistributive component than Rawls has recognized and proposes to consider a global resource tax designed to benefit the world's poor. Crisp and

Jamieson consider possible Rawlsian responses to Pogge's proposal. Although they argue that Rawls's own view is less regressive than Pogge has supposed, they do offer support for more extensive international redistribution than Rawls requires. But *pace* Pogge, they argue that alternative institutional arrangements would achieve these goals more efficiently than a resource tax and that Pogge's proposal fails to distinguish between "poor countries" and "poor people." Crisp and Jamieson do argue that international justice should have a redistributive component but reject Pogge's suggestion as to how such redistribution should be accomplished. Although they do not offer a fully articulated alternative, they do identify key properties that any acceptable alternative must possess.

Part 3, "Morality and Political Liberalism," examines the normative assumption of Rawls's view. Clark Wolf considers one of the central arguments for the basic rights and liberties protected by Rawls's first principle of justice, "the equal liberty principle." Rawls argues that our interest in securing basic rights derives in part from what Rawls calls our "higher-order interest" in maintaining the ability to form, rationally revise, and pursue a conception of the good. Wolf considers an articulate reconstruction of this Rawlsian argument in an early paper by Allen Buchanan and uses Buchanan's more formal version of Rawls's argument to illustrate a weakness in Rawls's own account of basic rights and liberties. Wolf argues that the appeal of the first-principle rights and liberties will be narrower than either Rawls or Buchanan has supposed. Wolf shows that this narrower appeal has important implications for Rawls's theory of institutional legitimacy and the justification of political coercion.

Norman Daniels has perhaps done as much as Rawls himself to develop a sophisticated account of reasoning in wide reflective equilibrium to show how this account is connected with traditional problems in moral theory and to connect that account of reason with the liberal conception of justice. In his chapter, Daniels offers a detailed reconstruction of the relationship between Rawls's early and later works. In *Theory,* Rawls argued that the conception of justice as fairness offered an Archimedean point from which to assess the justice of political institutions. In recasting this conception of justice as a political view, Rawls has offered a different perspective on this claim. Some have argued that in his recent work Rawls has relinquished the critical distance that is needed if we are to use this view to assess our institutions. In order to have normative force, a conception of justice must be neither so abstract as to be irrelevant nor so closely bound to existing political institutions that it offers no critical distance.

Critics of *Political Liberalism* have represented the changes in Rawls's view as a kind of philosophical loss. Others have charged Rawls's recent work with a kind of "justificatory schizophrenia," since different citizens must all justifiably accept the liberal conception of justice for quite different reasons and since citizens are expected to apply different normative standards in their personal and their public lives. Daniels defends the political conception of justice as fairness from these charges and offers a detailed analysis and reconstruction of Rawls's account of justification. He argues that the sense that the politicization of justice as fairness represents a "philosophical loss" may reflect nothing more than the persistent appeal of a philosopher's dream that a public conception of justice could be justified in the same way to all rational persons. The charge of justificatory schizophrenia is based on a closely related error, for it is clear that people with different constitutive commitments will have different reasons for their allegiance (or lack of allegiance) to a public political conception. The ability to shift between public and private norms need not imply any kind of schizophrenia, nor does this ability imply a lack of integrity. As long as the rationale for drawing the boundary between public and private values is itself justifiable to an individual in terms of her own system of beliefs and values, she will be able to maintain the distinction between public and private reason without loss of integrity.

In Part 4, "Economics and Entitlements," James Nickel argues that economic liberties should be included among the fundamental freedoms guaranteed by Rawls's first principle of justice, or in any defensible account of the fundamental liberal rights. Like other liberals who are opposed to libertarian conceptions of justice, Rawls consistently underestimates the importance of economic liberties and the connection between economic freedom and personal autonomy. According to Nickel, fundamental economic liberties should include buying and selling labor; engaging in independent economic activity; holding personal and productive property; and buying, selling, and consuming goods and services. Nickel offers both practical and theoretical reasons justifying the protection of a wider range of economic liberties than Rawls has recognized. Although highly critical of Rawls's account of the fundamental liberties, Nickel's contribution offers constructive suggestions for an improved Rawlsian conception of justice.

Rawls devotes most of *Political Liberalism* to issues other than that of distributive justice, but he also makes it clear that he intends that the difference principle must be included as an element of a political conception of justice if that conception is to serve as the object of an overlapping consensus on the part of reasonable persons. In examining two problems regarding individual entitlement, Claudia Card focuses on the second principle element of Rawls's conception of justice as fairness. The first problem Card considers concerns the relationship between the difference principle and the principle of fair equality of opportunity. According to Rawls, the principle of fair equal opportunity has two functions: First, it constrains the scope of the difference principle, and second, it ensures that the system of social cooperation is one of "pure procedural justice" (*TJ*, 87). Card argues that these dual functions are in tension with one another, since some offices cannot meaningfully be identified independent of the advantages attached to them. Rawls briefly redescribes these principles in *Political Liberalism,* but Card argues that his more recent expression of the second principle fails to resolve the problem and seems to eliminate pure procedural justice from the theory.

The second problem on which Card focuses attention is among the deepest and most troublesome features of Rawls's view: the lack of any substantive notion of "desert" in Rawls's conception of justice. From the early discussions of Sandel and Nozick, this has been among the most widely discussed features of Rawls's view, and it is one to which Card has devoted serious attention (Card 1996). Card argues that parties to the original position can and would choose entitlement principles that incorporate a richer conception of personal desert. Because our notion of desert is so deeply historical, Card argues, parties to the original position choice would likely choose entitlement principles that are much more historical than those Rawls proposes.

Rawls claims that political liberalism constitutes a freestanding conception of justice and that this fact distinguishes it from a mere "modus vivendi." A contract would be a mere modus vivendi if it were simply a strategic compromise among existing political interests or a conception of justice tailored to the particular comprehensive doctrines known to exist in society. Rawls argues that those who choose the conception of justice as fairness from the original position need not know anything about the particular political factions that exist in society and that justice as fairness will generate its own support because citizens' allegiance to the liberal conception of justice will gain strength over time. He argues that the moral conception implicit in the conception of justice as fairness recommends itself to those who are subject to it, and thus it reinforces its foundations. In Part 5 ("Modus Vivendi?"), the contributors explore whether Rawls can support these controversial claims and whether the "freestandingness" of a political conception of justice is necessary for stability, as Rawls assumes.

Claudia Mills offers a careful examination of Rawls's account of political consensus and the stability of just institutions. Like Rawls, Mills argues that a political ideal should strive for more than a "mere" modus vivendi. She agrees with both Rawls and his communitarian critics that community is important. But *pace* Rawls, she argues that community may not involve a mutual commitment to shared principles, and she urges that it may be both impossible and unnecessary for citizens to achieve an overlapping consensus on the same political ideal. It is impossible because too many citizens in a liberal state are likely to be "unreasonable" by Rawls's strict measure and unable to join in such a consensus. And it is unnecessary because, as Mills argues, social stability can be achieved even without such a consensus.

The chapters by Bernard Dauenhauer and Scott Hershovitz extend these questions about the stability of modus vivendi agreements. Like Mills, they argue that agreement can be stable even when people do not all accept the same political conception of justice. Dauenhauer argues that the only possible form of political agreement is a modus vivendi and that it is not only unreasonable but potentially unjust to present a conception of justice as anything more substantial. He argues that political ideals should always be presented in a form that leaves them open to future revision and that constitutional ideals can and must be sensitive to historical considerations in a way prohibited by Rawls's theory. According to Dauenhauer, the conception of justice as fairness demands too much when it presents the basic principles of justice as fundamentally unchanging and unchallengeable ideals. He argues that given the historicity of political life, a modus vivendi is the best that can be hoped for. The key task is to distinguish responsible from irresponsible modus vivendi agreements.

Scott Hershovitz argues that Rawls overlooks an important basis for stability and agrees with Dauenhauer's claim that Rawls demands too much consensus. If Hershovitz is right, social stability can be promoted by institutional design even without an overlapping consensus on a public conception of justice. It follows that Rawls's "third general fact" (*PL,* 38) is simply false. Hershovitz draws on James Madison's discussion of power in *Federalist 51,* in which Madison argues that institutions should be constructed so that power is "fractured" and "ambition [can] be made to counteract ambition." As Hershovitz points out, Madison was unwilling to rely on the loyalty of citizens as the anchor to secure social stability but believed that a careful institutional design that divided power through a system of "checks and balances" would protect against an abuse of power if those Rawls would term "unreasonable" were to gain office. As Hershovitz notes, this strategy may be more cynical than Rawls's ideal, but it may also be superior in its ability to provide stability. Stability achieved in this way might be regarded by Rawls as political "in the wrong way," since agreement might reflect only a strategic compromise, a modus vivendi. But if a modus vivendi is sufficiently stable, it may obviate the need for consensus. Since the authors of other chapters in this volume (especially Friedman, Wolf, Mills, and Dauenhauer) have argued that Rawls's overlapping consensus may be an unachievable ideal, this is an important alternate theoretical strategy.

The two chapters comprising Part 6, "Justice, Rationality, and Desires," respond to Rawls's critique of utilitarianism and preferentialism, both in *Theory* and in his later work. Since so many Anglo-American philosophers have found Rawls's critique of these views persuasive, this project has special importance. Richard Arneson offers a detailed account and critique of Rawls's arguments against utilitarianism and the relevance of these changes for Rawls's recent work and argues, *pace* Rawls, that a sophisticated utilitarian theory can accommodate a plausible theory of rights and can adequately account for the "separateness of persons." Rawls's reliance on the "primary goods" standard is crucial to his rejection of utilitarian ideals, but Arneson argues that the primary goods are inadequately supported by Rawls's argument and questions the justification for "the priority rules" that govern relations among the principles of justice. Arneson maintains that the argument of *Political Liberalism* misfires because Rawls fails to show that the conception of justice as fairness is uniquely acceptable for reasonable citizens. In the end, however, Arneson delivers a "mixed verdict" on Rawls's later work: Rawls's arguments against simple aggregate utilitarianism are sound, but crucial elements of his alternative are either unmotivated or poorly supported by the arguments offered in their behalf. It follows that Rawls has not settled the issue between Kantian and utilitarian theory.

In the last chapter, Christoph Fehige articulates a preferentialist theory in terms of three conditions that should be satisfied by an acceptable account of justice. He compares this theory to Rawls's conception of justice as fairness, noting the most important differences. Then Fehige carefully individuates and evaluates Rawls's arguments against preferentialism and utilitarianism. He argues that Rawls's objections to preferentialism are unpersuasive and that Rawls's own conception of justice is therefore inadequately motivated. In an important sense, Rawls's theory fails to take people seriously because it fails to take people's preferences seriously in a wide variety of contexts. Fehige shows that a sophisticated preferentialist theory can adequately respond to Rawls's most serious objections and that some of Rawls's arguments simply fail to address the target at which they are aimed. If Fehige is right, then preferentialism still remains a contender, a serious alternative to Rawls's political conception of justice.

It may seem odd to honor a scholar by publishing a volume in which most of the chapters are highly critical of his work. But clearly it is to Rawls's credit that his books and papers continue to inspire controversy and productive disagreement and to generate articulate reasoned response instead of passive doctrinal adherence. This is an acceptable cost of the general strategy of offering reasons and arguments. And Rawls's own theory explains that such controversy should be expected: "Our most important moral and political judgments are rendered under conditions such that it is unlikely that conscientious and fully reasonable persons, even after full and free discussion, can exercise their powers of reason so that all arrive at the same conclusion"(*PL*, 58). Among political theorists, there is clearly no overlapping consensus on the success of any particular Rawlsian argument, or even on the idea of an overlapping consensus itself. There is much more agreement on the overwhelming significance of Rawls's contribution to the field and on his enduring influence: Rawls's work has redefined the central issues of political philosophy and raised the standard of rigor and argument for the entire field. In important ways, he has set both the agenda for future work in normative political theory and the standard as well. For this, and much more, we owe gratitude that can be expressed in no more earnest form than philosophical engagement with the issues he has put before us.

Notes

1. Barry (1996) cites and quotes both Laslett (1956) and Tuck (1995) in supporting his own argument that Rawls's work transformed the field. Berlin (1978, vii–viii) reports that

H.M. Sheffer persuaded him that logic and psychology were "the only philosophical disciplines in which one could hope for an increase in permanent knowledge."

2. Rawls's index includes, among others, references to Arrow, Baumol, Blaug, Buchanan, Downs, Georgescu-Roegen, Harrod, Harsanyi, Hicks, Jevons, Kaldor, Keynes, Knight, Koopmans, Luce, Marglin, Marshall, Myrdal, Nash, Olson, Pareto, Pigou, Raiffa, Ramsey, Samuelson, Savage, Sen, Simon, Solow, Tawney, Tinbergen, Tobin, Trivers, Tullock, Vickrey, Walras, and Wicksell. It also includes references to numerous economic concepts.

References

Barry, Brian. 1995. John Rawls and the Search for Stability. *Ethics* 105, no. 4: 874–915.

———. 1996. Political Theory Old and New. In *A New Handbook for Political Science,* edited by Robert E. Goodin and Hans-Dieter Klingemann. Cambridge: Oxford University Press, 531–48.

Berlin, Isaiah. 1978. *Concepts and Categories.* New York: Penguin.

Card, Claudia. 1996. *The Unnatural Lottery: Character and Moral Luck.* Philadelphia: Temple University Press.

Laslett, Peter. 1956. *Philosophy, Politics, and Society.* First series. Oxford: Basil Blackwell.

Rawls, John. 1971. *A Theory of Justice.* Cambridge: Harvard University Press.

———. 1993. *Political Liberalism.* New York: Columbia University Press.

———. 1996. *Political Liberalism.* Pbk. ed. Cambridge, Mass.: Harvard University Press.

———. 1999. *Collected Papers.* Edited by Samuel Freeman. Cambridge, Mass.: Harvard University Press.

Tuck, Richard. 1995. History. In *A Companion to Contemporary Political Philosophy,* edited by Robert Goodin and Phillip Pettit. Oxford: Basil Blackwell, 72–89.

1

JOHN RAWLS AND THE POLITICAL COERCION

OF UNREASONABLE PEOPLE

Marilyn Friedman

Political power is always coercive power according to John Rawls.[1] *Political Liberalism* is Rawls's study of how to justify the use of that coercive power against citizens. Coercive state power is legitimate, for Rawls, so long as reasonable and rational persons reasoning under certain constraints would agree to its exercise.

More specifically, political coercion is justified so long as it accords with a political conception of justice that free and equal citizens would endorse in their capacity as reasonable and rational persons, in an overlapping consensus that spans their diverse moral, religious, and philosophical commitments, their "comprehensive doctrines."[2] Reasonable and rational persons constitute, for Rawls, what I will call "the legitimation pool," the pool of persons whose endorsement would confirm the legitimacy of Rawls's political liberalism—or whose rejection would confirm its illegitimacy.

Suppose that someone contends that she cannot accept Rawls's conception of political liberalism from the standpoint of her comprehensive doctrine. Rawls's response to this contention would differ substantially depending on whether or not that person were reasonable. If the person were reasonable, then Rawls would regard her rejection of his political liberalism as a serious reason to consider revising it. Not so, however, if the person were unreasonable. Rawls's method of legitimation takes no account of how unreasonable people would react to political liberalism. Their rejection appears to carry no theoretical weight.

If a state's legitimacy depends only on the endorsement of reasonable and rational persons, that means that a state that is endorsed only by its reasonable citizens is thereby sufficiently entitled to exercise its coercive power over *un*reasonable citizens *without* their consent. In that case, how do those citizens remain free and equal? And in what sense are they politically autonomous?

The mere fact of someone's unreasonableness does not by itself create this tension for political liberalism since an unreasonable person might nevertheless endorse the system. Granted, her actual endorsement, on Rawlsian grounds, would be irrelevant to the legitimacy of the liberal state. Nevertheless, her political autonomy is, in some liberal sense, not violated by liberalism's exercise of its political power over her since she consents to it. My focus of concern is directed to those unreasonable persons who *withhold* consent from political liberalism. It is *their* political autonomy that seems to be violated by Rawls's legitimation methods.

Rawls, of course, is not the only philosopher who seeks political legitimacy in the consent of reasonable persons only. Thomas Scanlon and Thomas Nagel, for example, also frame the problem in these terms.[3] Rawls, however, gives the concept of reasonableness a very elaborate explication. Thus, his exclusion of the unreasonable merits special attention.

It is crucial to be clear about what Rawls means by "reasonableness" since he uses this word as a term of art. Reasonable persons are those who seek fair terms of social cooperation with others and who expect people living under free institutions to disagree about fundamental matters of religion, morality, or philosophy. *Un*reasonable persons are those who lack one or both of these attitudes. We are not required by Rawls to take seriously the political views of unreasonable persons. He would also impose on them the coercive power of a state that they reject, provided only that the state has been ratified in the right way by reasonable persons. Indeed, as I point out later, the legitimate Rawlsian state may even infringe on some of the basic rights and liberties of unreasonable persons. Such persons thus appear to lose political autonomy in several ways. This is a foundational concern for any theory that calls itself "liberal."

To be sure, given the enormous diversity among human viewpoints, the exclusion of unreasonable people from the legitimation pool makes the search for legitimacy more manageable than it otherwise would be. This consideration, however, is a practical one only and is not a principled reason for excluding anyone. Rawls, by contrast, elevates the exclusion of the unreasonable into a matter of principle in his quest for political legitimacy. The question is whether that principled exclusion is inconsistent with any of the aims or values of the system that Rawls seeks thereby to defend. Since Rawls views a social contract as "a hypothetical agreement . . . between all rather than some members of society,"[4] the prospects for internal consistency are not promising. This problem will form my primary concern.

1. Rawls on Reasonableness and Rationality

First, let us consider more fully what Rawls means by reasonableness and rationality. In Rawls's ideal society, citizens are both reasonable and rational. Rational persons adapt means to their given ends and adjust their ends in light of their overall life plans. Rationality alone is not sufficient to make citizens just since rational agents do not necessarily seek fair cooperation "as such" nor "on terms that others as equals might reasonably be expected to endorse."[5] Those concerns are comprised instead by the virtue of reasonableness.

Reasonable persons are willing to "propose and honor fair terms of cooperation" and "to recognize the burdens of judgment and to accept their consequences."[6] The "burdens of judgment" are the sources of possible limitation and error involved in the exercise of human reason. These sources include the variability and finitude of human experience, the ways in which those experiences underdetermine our judgments about them and permit differing interpretations, the chance influence of divergent norms, and so on.[7]

Reasonableness is public in a way that rationality is not. Our reasonableness is our readiness to participate in the public world and therein negotiate, and abide by, the fair terms of social cooperation with others that will ground our social relationships with them.[8] The distinctive moral power of reasonableness is a sense of justice, and the distinctive moral power of rationality is a conception of the good.[9] "Someone who has not developed and cannot exercise [those] moral powers to the minimum requisite degree," writes Rawls, "cannot be a normal and fully cooperating member of society over a complete life."[10]

Rawls's method of political legitimation is developed in regard to his idealized account of liberal society. Does it tell us anything about actual, imperfectly liberal societies? There may well be reasonable and rational people in actual societies who reject their own would-be liberal systems because, from the standpoint of their comprehensive doctrines, those systems are unacceptable. In an imperfectly liberal society, one might learn something about the imperfections of the system from reasonable and rational persons who reject it. Rawls apparently thinks, however, that the opinions of *un*reasonable persons do *not* tell us anything informative about whether a system is legitimate or not. It seems that regardless of whether an actual society is ideally liberal, imperfectly liberal, or illiberal, the political opinions of unreasonable people simply do not count.

In the real world, of course, people might be unreasonable because they have grown up under unjust institutions rather than under the free institutions postulated in Rawls's ideal society. Real world unreasonableness has a different sociohistorical context than does the ideal-world variety, and this fact surely *diminishes* the justification for excluding unreasonable persons from the legitimation pool. People who become unreasonable because they have grown up under unfair institutions certainly constitute good evidence of the unfairness of those institutions. This would still not mean, however, that their opinions as such revealed anything reliable about what was wrong with their imperfect institutions. If bad institutions make people fascists, this might be good evidence that something is wrong with their institutions but it would not confirm the truth of their fascism.

In this chapter, I focus mainly on unreasonableness and only occasionally on irrationality. I interpret Rawls's view of reasonableness as requiring both of the attitudes that Rawls sets out—the quest for fair terms of social cooperation and the belief that reasonable persons might disagree about fundamental comprehensive matters. Someone is unreasonable if he or she rejects either (or both) of these two attitudes.

The twofold nature of the notion of reasonableness does raise a curious question of detail, however. What if the two attitudes that comprise reasonableness part company? What about those who are reasonable in one way but not in the other? Could someone who seeks fair terms of social cooperation nevertheless reject the idea that reasonable people can disagree about fundamental comprehensive matters? Alternatively, could someone who believes that reasonable people can disagree about fundamental matters nevertheless not seek fair terms of social cooperation? If these two variations are possible, then we might need a ranking of these attitudes so as to determine which was more central to the liberal concern for political legitimacy. Reasonableness is, in any case, surely a matter of degree, and we should want to delineate the minimal threshold level of reasonableness that entitles someone to be free of any state coercion except that to which they would consent. I leave these questions about degrees of reasonableness for another occasion.

2. Liberalism, Consent, and Political Autonomy

My focus is on Rawls's exclusion of unreasonable people from the legitimation pool, that group of persons whose support, or its lack, tests his conception of political liberalism. It is useful to recall why anyone's consent matters to political legitimacy. In the liberal tradition, the legitimacy of state power is linked to the value of the political autonomy of citizens. Free and equal citizens have political autonomy, among other things, when they themselves specify the fair terms of their own social cooperation.[11]

In real life, citizens rarely congregate to formulate from the ground up the terms of their social cooperation. Mindful of this reality, liberalism settles for the mere *consent* of the governed to arrangements that have been worked out by a very few among them. In principle, these arrangements must still be justifiable from the standpoint of each citizen. In the words of Jeremy Waldron, liberalism requires "that all aspects of the social world should either be made acceptable or be capable of being made acceptable to *every last individual.*"[12] Waldron continues, "If there is some individual to whom a justification cannot be given, then so far as *he* is concerned the social order had better be replaced by other arrangements, for the status quo has made out no claim to *his* allegiance."[13] In Thomas Nagel's view, the quest for universal citizen consent to a political system is definitive, not simply of *liberal* political philosophy, but of political theory in general. The "ultimate aim of political theory," writes Nagel, is to find a way "to justify a political system to everyone who is required to live under it."[14] Thus, liberalism in particular, and perhaps political theory in general, seek to make us an offer that no one can refuse.

The aim of liberalism, however, is not merely to win allegiance. The mere allegiance of citizens might be the product of compulsion or indoctrination, and from a liberal perspective, such consent would not by itself demonstrate or constitute the legitimacy of a political order. The requisite allegiance must be warranted, and that warrant must furthermore be recognizable from the standpoint of the consenting citizen. Each citizen must be able to consent to the social order by virtue of her *recognition* of its justification. Thereby a citizen exercises genuine political autonomy.[15] Thus Nagel writes:

> The pure ideal of political legitimacy is that the use of state power should be capable of being *authorized* by each citizen—not in direct detail but through acceptance of the principles, institutions, and procedures which determine how that power will be used. This requires the possibility of unanimous agreement at some sufficiently high level, for if there are citizens who can legitimately object to the way state power is used against them or in their name, the state is not legitimate.[16]

The idea that all citizens of a large-scale political system would ever consent to their system, however, is a hopeless nonstarter. Few people in the real world have consented in any significant sense to the societies in which they live. Even with the exponential growth of cybersociety and technologies of communication, it would still be a daunting prospect to get every adult citizen in a large modern society to consider political liberalism (or any other political philosophy) and express an opinion on it. (Let us not forget how many people still lack computer literacy, not to mention good old-fashioned reading and writing literacy.) In practice, only the consent of *some* persons is a realistic possibility.

As is well known, liberal theorists have devised various notions to cope with this practical problem. The recent favorite is the notion of hypothetical consent, its current popularity owing much to Rawls's first book, *A Theory of Justice*.[17] Hypothetical consent is the consent someone *would* give to something under appropriate, and specified, conditions. For Waldron, the concept of hypothetical consent is very important, for it can decrease the wrongness of illegitimate state intervention in someone's life.[18] Waldron argues that if someone, who happens not to have consented to being treated in a certain manner, *would* have consented had she been in a position to do so, then treating her in that manner is *less wrong* than it would have been if she would not, even hypothetically, have consented to it.[19]

For most modern liberals, hypothetical consent is construed in terms of the *reasons* for accepting one political arrangement rather than another. As Waldron notes, "Liberalism is also bound up in large part with respect for rationality."[20] The idea of *rationally reconstructed* hypothetical consent solves the problem created by the practical impossibility of sampling the political opinion of every adult citizen. The rational reconstruction need only be devised and endorsed by a few intellectuals who take the liberty of determining entirely on their own what an entire citizenry would endorse if its members, implausibly, were all reasonable, rational, and had the leisure to enter the dialogue.

That last sentence is, of course, ironic. The strategy of imagining rationally reconstructed hypothetical consent faces well-known difficulties. "Real people," suggests Waldron, "do not always act on the reasons we think they might have for acting: the reasonableness of the actors in our hypothesis may not match the reality of men and women in actual life."[21] That to which people actually consent may well not match that to which a handful of intellectuals *thinks* it would be rational for them to consent. Waldron suggests, nevertheless, that the liberal probably has to assume some minimum of "reasonableness" on the parts of people "if the project of social justification is to get off the ground at all."[22] This modified approach, we should note, is not a matter of liberal principle but rather a pragmatic concession to the practical limitations of our ability to test political conceptions.

Rawls's conception of reasonableness, in particular, does not apply to everyone. Some people, for example, do not accept the burdens of judgment and believe instead that "reasonable" people will *not* disagree on conceptions of the good or other comprehensive moral, religious, or philosophical matters.[23] Perhaps concomitant with this view, some people believe that the one true faith should be forcibly imposed on all persons as part of the political system itself, even on those persons who do not accept its tenets. Rush Limbaugh, for example, urges the political enforcement of specifically Judeo-Christian values.[24]

As Waldron notes, attitudes such as this pose a problem for liberals. Modern liberal democracies are, as the current mantra goes, pluralistic. They contain persons with varying political values. Some citizens of liberal democracies believe that the system ought to be "acceptable to every last individual" (to reiterate Waldron's words). Others, by contrast, believe that the system ought to impose certain values on all citizens, regardless of whether or not those values are acceptable to every last individual. One and the same political doctrine is not likely to satisfy both of these groups simultaneously.

Waldron recommends that liberals acknowledge that their "conception of political judgment will be appealing only to those who hold their commitments in a certain 'liberal' spirit."[25] Those who lack the liberal spirit are not likely to find such a system acceptable. Such persons would only consistently consent to political liberalism if they were to abandon what Rawls would call their illiberal comprehensive doctrines. This creates a problem for liberal theories that rely on a notion of hypothetical consent, *even if* rationally reconstructed. It seems viciously circular to try to justify a liberal doctrine in terms of the hypothetical consent of a citizenry if the condition grounding that hypothesis is that citizens do not hold the illiberal commitments they do in fact hold. Such illiberal commitments can be deeply important to people, enough so to shape their very identities. Disregarding those commitments in the rational reconstruction would be like saying that all citizens *would* consent to political liberalism if only they were not the illiberals they actually are. This sort of hypothetical consent rings hollow.

The quest for liberal legitimacy thus raises a problem analogous to other liberal paradoxes. If one values liberal tolerance, for example, one must nevertheless not tolerate those expressions and modes of living that would undermine toleration itself as a social practice. If one values liberal free expression, one must nevertheless withhold it from those whose expressions would undermine the very practice of free expression. It appears, similarly, that if one is seeking fair terms of social cooperation among persons who are free and equal and who are assumed to disagree reasonably on fundamental comprehensive matters, then one must not allow persons who *reject* this goal or that assumption to hijack the legitimation process. In each case, a liberal principle comes up against its limiting case: The freedom given readily to those who do not threaten the system must be withheld from those who would use it to destroy the system.

Yet this very necessity seems inconsistent with the liberal goal of resting on the consent of *all* the governed. In Rawls's view, the legitimacy of a political system is sufficiently established even if it is endorsed by only the reasonable and rational among its citizens. Reasonableness, however, is defined in terms of the very values and assumptions from which Rawls derives his political liberalism. How satisfactory or meaningful is the consent of a citizenry if the process of representing or obtaining consent excludes the opinions of those persons who, because they start with nonliberal attitudes, are the very ones who might vote "no"? By excluding from the legitimation pool exactly those persons who do not accept the political values and basic tenets on which Rawls grounds political liberalism, Rawls rigs the election in advance.

The exclusion of unreasonable persons from the legitimation pool thus seems to beg important questions in the defense of liberalism. And the liberal commitment to political autonomy appears to be undermined by withholding political autonomy from precisely those persons who reject the system that advocates it.

3. The Fate of Unreasonable People

Let us now clarify the fate that awaits those who are unreasonable in Rawls's political liberalism, for there is more at stake than simply being excluded from the legitimation pool. Rawls distinguishes between "the fact of pluralism as such and the fact of reasonable pluralism."[26] His emphasis is on the latter. Reasonable pluralism is the diversity of *reasonable* views about fundamental matters of religion, morality, and philosophy. Rawls is particularly concerned to exclude from the legitimation pool those who hold *un*reasonable views. Under this heading, Rawls includes "doctrines that reject one or more democratic freedoms." In a footnote that is crucial for our purposes, he suggests that the way to treat unreasonable doctrines is to *contain* them "like war and disease—so that they do not overturn political justice."[27]

How does one "contain" a doctrine? Doing so requires regulating and controlling the media in which it is expressed and promulgated—books, magazines, cyberspace, and so on. More significantly, it requires suppressing those who hold the doctrine, in particular, suppressing their expression and/ or enactment of it. At the same time, however, Rawls contends that "it is unreasonable for us to use political power . . . to repress comprehensive views that are *not* unreasonable."[28] Rawls's recommendation to "contain" the unreasonable doctrines that reject democratic freedoms thus contrasts markedly with the basic rights and liberties that his system accords to reasonable doctrines.

Thus, while supporters of reasonable doctrines will enjoy basic rights and liberties, supporters of certain unreasonable doctrines, in particular those that reject democratic freedoms, will be treated like the bearers of a pestilence. Their political autonomy will be denied in two ways. First, they will be excluded from the legitimation pool, that collection of citizens whose consent to the political system confirms its legitimacy. Second, in daily life, they will be denied the full protection of the system's basic rights and liberties, particularly freedom of expression.

4. Who Are the Unreasonable?

Mindful of what lies in store for unreasonable people, let us now attempt to evaluate the full theoretical and practical significance of Rawls's view. One useful initial strategy is to try to determine *who* the unreasonable persons are. There are at least two relevant possibilities here, and they foreshadow contradictory intuitions.

First, one should worry about a liberalism that ignores, from the outset, the political views of certain groups among a citizenry. Despite some manner of commitment to the notion of free and equal persons, liberal democracies have historically used unwarranted grounds, such as race and sex, for excluding various groups of adults from political participation and full civil rights. This practical inconsistency in the history of the tradition should make us wary of any seemingly principled reason for yet again excluding certain groups of persons from something so important as the legitimation pool.

Second, however, one should also worry about those persons among a citizenry who seek *on their own,* independent of the formal political process, to dominate others or to impose a social order that degrades, marginalizes, or oppresses others. There is no reason to suppose that all oppressive tendencies in human relationships originate with bad government. One must also beware of *individuals* who harbor their own oppressive tendencies or convictions and for whom political freedom would provide an opportunity to act oppressively. Indeed, part of the valuable potential of a formal political process is its capacity both to curb any possible human proclivities toward dominating or oppressing other persons and to deny political influence to those who manifest such tendencies.[29] One important form of political influence is to be publicly considered as someone whose opinion helps to decide the legitimacy of a political system, in other words, to be a publicly recognized member of a legitimation pool.

To summarize these two initial concerns: It appears at the outset that there are both *bad and good* reasons for excluding particular persons from a legitimation pool. Race and sex are bad reasons, and no one should be excluded, either intentionally or inadvertently, on grounds such as these. Our legitimation strategy should invoke only good reasons, if any, for excluding people. On the other hand, being someone who wants to dominate others looks like a good reason for being excluded from the legitimation pool. We must also ensure that the *application* of the good reasons is not over inclusive, that is, that it does not exclude by mistake any persons who do belong in the legitimation pool.

How do Rawls's legitimation methods apply to those groups that have historically been excluded unjustly from real-world liberal political processes? The category of "reasonableness" should alert us to possible dangers in such application. Some of the groups historically denied the rights and privileges of liberal citizenship were disenfranchised at least partly because they were regarded as poor reasoners, as people who could not achieve the detached impartiality needed to reflect on the common good. Women, for example, fell into this camp.

Does Rawls's exclusion of unreasonable persons mean that women's voices once again count for little or nothing in the search for liberal legitimacy? Part of the answer depends on the extent to which the stereotype of women being poor reasoners persists today. Even if it does persist, there has been a marked improvement in the public regard for women's reasoning capacities by the end of the twentieth century in the United States. Compared to former decades, the public now widely acknowledges a substantial level of female achievement in many fields that are regarded as involving reason, for example, the professions.

Recall that by "reasonableness" Rawls means two things: first, the willingness to seek fair terms of social cooperation and, second, the acknowledgment that reasonable people can disagree on fundamental matters of religion, morality, and philosophy. Our question must be, Do these particular sorts of attitudes have anything to do with the various public images and conceptions of women?

The gender stereotypes studied by psychologists are rarely as specific as the traits that comprise Rawls's conception of reasonableness. As is well known, men have been stereotyped in terms of agency and instrumentality; desirable adjectives for men include independent, forceful, ambitious, aggressive, competitive, dominant. Women have been stereotyped, by contrast, in terms of emotionality and social relationships; desirable adjectives for women include affectionate, compassionate, warm, gentle, understanding, and tender.[30] These common feminine stereotypes do not obviously support the view that women are unreasonable in either of Rawls's senses.[31]

Indeed, rather than supporting the idea that women are unreasonable in Rawls's sense, conventional gender stereotypes seem instead to support the idea that they are quite *reasonable.* Consider, for example, the stereotype of women as relational. This idea seems to suggest that women would cooperate with those to whom they relate socially and would want the forms of cooperation to be acceptable to all concerned. In more specialized contexts, such as psychoanalysis and political theory, women have sometimes been stereotyped as less conscience-driven than men, as having a weaker sense of justice.[32] This suggests that they might be more capable of tolerating, and regarding as reasonable, those who hold religious, moral, or philosophical doctrines different from their own. This idea is reinforced by the stereotype of women as compassionate and understanding.

My suggestions about how women would fare under Rawls's approach to unreasonable people are based on mere associations of ideas. They are by no means logically entailed by the stereotypes in question—not that stereotypes are ever very logical in their operations. However, even if the common stereotypes of women suggested that women were *quite* reasonable, this would not directly tell us anything about real women. Stereotypes are hardly the best guide to empirical truth.

Do *real* women deny the burdens of judgment any more than men? Do real women, any more than men, think that reasonable people will *not* disagree about fundamental matters of religion, morality, or philosophy? Do real women reject fair terms of social cooperation any more than men? Without doubt, there are individual women who avoid fair terms of social cooperation. It does not seem, however, that women outnumber men in the ranks of savings-and-loan swindlers, junk-bond peddlers, hostile corporate raiders, and so on. If any gender group shows widespread tendencies to eschew fair terms of social cooperation, it is not women.

There is still another way in which women might be unreasonable in Rawlsian terms. "Womankind," according to one old school of philosophical thought, is "the everlasting irony in the life of the community [that] changes by intrigue the universal purpose of government into a private end . . . and perverts the universal property of the state into a possession and ornament for the family."[33] According to this Hegelian view, women are incapable of impartial political participation because they cannot rise above loyalty to their own family members. Women simply favor "their own" and do not treat all citizens as abstract equals. If women really are, to a great degree, guided politically by such partial loyalties, then they would scarcely seek fair terms of social cooperation with other citizens. They would try instead to promote the welfare of their own loved ones through the political process. If women really favored "their own" substantially more in the political process than men, while men much more readily attained an impartial civic attitude, then women might indeed be more unreasonable than men and might merit exclusion from the legitimation pool.

What can be said about this possibility? Lacking empirical evidence on the question, I offer an unsystematic, uncontrolled personal observation. As women now participate in the public political cultures of many nations, they do not appear (to me) to do so with any more partiality then men. Yes, some women have been involved in self-serving political scandals. Yet anyone familiar with politicians such as Chicago's legendary first Mayor Richard Daley knows that many men have attained levels of nepotism and cronyism in public life that are unrivaled by any woman.[34] When it comes to self-serving partiality and taking care of one's own, the myth of men's public *im*partiality should be consigned to the ranks of the tooth fairy.

The overall relevance of gender to Rawls's conception of reasonableness thus seems to me to be as follows. There is no overt or covert gender bias built into his conception. Nothing about the ways in which Rawls defines reasonableness excludes real women as a group from the legitimation pool—any more or any less than it excludes men as a group. Granted, some persons might misapply Rawls's views because they mistakenly stereotype women as unreasonable. The philosophical tradition, as Genevieve Lloyd has argued, traditionally defined reason by excluding *whatever* were, or were considered to be, feminine traits.[35] Someone could, for example, interpret Rawls's requirement of cooperative fairness so as to exclude whatever it is that women do when relating socially with others. Anyone who is predisposed to think that all the interesting forms of fair social cooperation are the products of male collaboration will simply find a way to interpret the interest in fair terms of social cooperation in such a way that women's cooperative endeavors have nothing to do with it.[36] In such cases, however, the fault would lie with the mistaken gender stereotype and not with Rawls's method for confirming the legitimacy of political liberalism.

Thus, the case of women does not give good reason to worry about Rawls's exclusion of unreasonable persons from the legitimation pool. Other examples are not so sanguine. According to a common attitude in traditional political theory, members of the poorer classes are so absorbed with their own plights that they cannot be trusted to consider the wider public good when participating in the political process. The assumption has often been made that wealthier classes are able to surmount self-interest and base their political decisions on the common good. Although this line of reasoning could easily support welfare rights and greater efforts to better the lot of the poor, it has also been used simply as an excuse for excluding the poor from the political process by means of property qualifications as a requirement for participation. This latter strand of thought in the liberal tradition simply dismisses the poorer classes as incapable of possessing the attitudes required by liberal citizenship.[37] On this view, the poor seek only self-serving and unfair terms of social cooperation and are, therefore, by Rawls's criteria, unreasonable.

Thus, Rawls's conception of unreasonableness has, at best, mixed results when applied to real groups of people. At least one of the groups historically disenfranchised by liberal democracies, namely, the poorest classes in a society, might qualify as unreasonable in Rawls's sense. Accordingly, they would be excluded from Rawls's legitimation pool, and that would be an intuitively disturbing outcome of his theory.

The other intuitive point I wish to raise about the sorts of real people who might be excluded from Rawls's legitimation pool pertains to persons who want to dominate or oppress others. By contrast with the previous result, if oppressive people were excluded from the legitimation pool, this would be an intuitively *welcome* outcome of Rawls's exclusion of unreasonable people. Let us see if Rawls's views do carry this implication.

Rawls's criteria of reasonableness would exclude those persons in a liberal democracy, for example, who (1) insist as part of the public culture that their comprehensive beliefs are true; (2) want to impose their comprehensive doctrines on others; (3) reject the basic, liberal democratic political values, such as the liberal ideal of persons as free and equal; and (4) do not believe that the fundamentals of the political system need to be justified to all. In more Rawlsian terms, the last people in particular would lack a full sense of justice; they would lack the willingness "to act in relation to others on terms that [those others] can endorse." Such persons would lack a sense of justice sufficient to make them "fully cooperating members of society."[38]

What about people with comprehensive doctrines that devalue women and subordinate them to men? Such doctrines do not construe all persons as free and equal. Some of those doctrines, as interpreted by some of their supporters, would deny to women the same measure of political freedom and equality that is granted to men. According to Rawls's criteria, the adherents of such doctrines appear to be unreasonable and should, accordingly, be excluded from the legitimation pool. Rawls himself, however, does not spell out these implications of his views, and he does not apply them consistently. Susan Moller Okin argues that when the doctrine in question is a familiar religion, Rawls actually vacillates in his reaction to those who believe women should be subordinated to men.[39] Thus, despite his strong statement about the containment of doctrines that themselves would deny basic freedoms, Rawls appears willing to include the real-world adherents of some of those doctrines in his legitimation pool.

Despite Rawls's vacillation on this issue, his principles, in the context of his ideal theory at least, do imply that the believers of male-dominant religions, for example, should be excluded from the legitimation pool. Such doctrines conflict with the idea of persons—*all* persons, women as well as men—as being free and equal. The same would apply to those who hold comprehensive doctrines that privilege some racial, ethnic, or religious group above others. Rawls does note that comprehensive doctrines that require the "repression or degradation of certain persons on . . . racial or ethnic" grounds conflict directly with the principles of justice and are apparently unreasonable.[40] If it is unreasonable on Rawlsian grounds to believe in racial inequality, then it is surely also unreasonable to believe in gender inequality. By holding Rawls to his own principles, we would be able to exclude sexists (along with racists) from the legitimation pool.

These various thoughts about who the unreasonable persons are thus yield mixed results. On the one hand, there is the happy prospect that persons committed to certain systems of social domination will be excluded from the legitimation pool. On the other hand, there is also the worrisome risk that long-standing group stereotypes might lead many thinkers to exclude some of the very sorts of persons who have historically been unjustifiably disenfranchised by liberalism. There is, therefore, no clear-cut set of intuitions telling us that the impact of Rawls's exclusion of unreasonable people will be wholly benign or wholly malign.

In addition, these thoughts about application do not settle fully the question of whether or not any unreasonable persons *should* be excluded from the legitimation pool. Even if the rubric of "unreasonable people" did turn out to fit the right-wing religious fundamentalists who worry many philosophers,[41] this by itself does not show that denying political autonomy to the unreasonable ones is internally consistent with politically liberal principles. It is to that problem that I now return.

5. The Main Problem

In a nutshell, the problem is that the unreasonable persons who are excluded from Rawls's legitimation pool are defined as such by the rejection of certain ideas and attitudes. Those ideas are themselves basic conceptions and values that define a liberal democratic tradition. They include, to reiterate once again, first, the view that reasonable persons are affected by the burdens of judgment and will therefore disagree over fundamental comprehensive matters and, second, the concern to seek fair terms of social cooperation. The problem is that anyone lacking these ideas or political values is not merely unreasonable; more specifically, they are also *illiberal.*

Thus, Rawls's legitimation pool for political liberalism is defined precisely in such a way as to exclude those whose prior (illiberal) commitments would lead them to reject political liberalism. As Samuel Scheffler has noted, this attempt to justify liberal principles "appears to presuppose a society in which liberal values are already well entrenched. It is not clear that political liberalism provides any reason for establishing liberal institutions in societies that do not already have liberal traditions."[42] If Rawls is not to engage in serious question-begging, he needs a conception of reasonableness that is politically neutral, one that is not defined in terms of the politically liberal values he seeks to defend. The challenge for Rawls is to find good but politically *independent* reasons for eliminating so-called unreasonable people from the legitimation pool. Can this be done?

Let us consider more closely one of the defining attitudes of a reasonable person, the quest for fair terms of social cooperation. What exactly does this rule out? Rather obviously, it rules out seeking *un*fair terms of social cooperation. More specifically, it rules out seeking terms of cooperation that give some persons undeserved advantages while making others bear undeserved burdens.

The problem is that matters of fairness and deservedness are themselves political notions. Few people would seriously say they wanted social systems that gave them unfair or undeserved advantages. Most people would characterize the terms of social cooperation they seek as fair. (I here employ a principle of normative charity.) Most of the people who believe that women should be subordinated to men either believe that men are smarter and stronger than women, and therefore deserve to rule, or believe that the traditional female social roles which many of us regard as socially subordinated to men's social roles are equally valued and not subordinated to them at all.[43] When I describe these views as aiming at women's (undeserved) subordination, I am using *my* terms, not those of their exponents. Thus, the terms of social cooperation that I regard as inegalitarian or hierarchical might well seem, to some other persons, as quite fair indeed.

These differences of opinion precisely exemplify the sorts of diversity out of which *Political Liberalism* seeks the emergence of an overlapping political consensus. Persons raised under the so-called free institutions of actual liberal democracies frequently arrive at not only moral or religious diversity but political diversity as well. Many religious, moral, and philosophical doctrines themselves harbor political content. (Political philosophy is, after all, a type of philosophy.) Indeed, most of the important and intractable cultural battles of recent years have emerged from the clash of incommensurable political views entailed by diverse moral, religious, and philosophical doctrines.

Rawls recognizes that comprehensive doctrines often have political implications. Indeed, he discusses the comprehensive doctrines that would be discouraged or excluded altogether within his ideal society.[44] It seems, however, that he does not recognize how this insight undermines the very legitimacy of his legitimation method. It does so, to repeat, in two ways. First, it reveals that Rawls's conception of unreasonableness, which is used to exclude certain persons from the legitimation pool, is question-begging because it is already biased in favor of persons with basic liberal values; second, it reveals that one of the very features making a doctrine "unreasonable" in Rawls's conception of it, namely, that it is coercively imposed on persons who reject it, turns out to be a feature of the very political liberalism that is supposedly legitimized using Rawls's methods.

To be sure, for those of us steeped in the political culture of liberalism, the people who reject some of its basic political values are an unsavory lot indeed. I myself fear people who insist dogmatically that their religious "truths" apply to my life contrary to my own convictions. I distrust people who seek terms of social cooperation that simply enhance their prospects at my expense. I, frankly, would be overjoyed to find good reasons for keeping these sorts of people out of *my* legitimation pool. Unfortunately, I cannot find principled but politically neutral reasons for doing so.

In Rawls's view, the public culture of a liberal democratic society lacks any "public and shared basis of justification" that could establish for all citizens the truth of any particular comprehensive doctrine. Accordingly, in liberal public culture, no one can make good the claim that her comprehensive beliefs are true. Thus, when someone attempts to impose her beliefs on others in the public sphere of a liberal pluralist society, she is thereby attempting to impose them on some at least for whom those beliefs are not publicly justifiable. Those who are reasonable, according to Rawls, must count anyone who would attempt to do this as *un*reasonable.[45] Thus, another trait that indicates unreasonableness is the readiness to impose one's comprehensive beliefs on others to whom those beliefs are unjustified and unjustifiable, given the available, publicly shared resources for justifying doctrines.

It is ironic that if we substituted the word "political" for that of "comprehensive" in the description of the trait that I have just given, we would have a description of what Rawls himself is trying to do on behalf of political liberalism. That is, Rawls's ideal society would impose its coercive power consensually only on reasonable persons at best, but for unreasonable people, including all those with illiberal prior commitments, political liberalism would be an unjustifiable and nonconsensual imposition. Unreasonable persons are to feel the coercive power of the liberal state despite their possible lack of consent, its legitimacy having been, for Rawls, established without their consent or even their participation in the legitimation dialogue.

Rawls's approach is therefore similar in one respect to the very viewpoints that he regards as unreasonable, namely, it seeks to justify the use of coercive (liberal) power over some of the individuals who reject its tenets. From their points of view, it is *Rawls* who appears, by analogy with his own characterization of it, to be unreasonable.

Rawls imagines an ideal society with genuinely free institutions in which maturing persons will come to endorse the political values and principles that underlie those institutions. Rawls's ideal society aims for political stability and the stable perpetuation of its distinctive sorts of institutions. The goal of political stability has long attracted political philosophers who had dreams of a better social world. In most cases, however, political philosophers have believed that no society could achieve stability without noble lies and not-so-noble forms of censorship or coercion that would impede the destabilizing influence of dissident ideas and social movements.

Liberalism promised to surmount those restrictive tendencies by grounding itself on a political philosophy that no one could refuse—not because they were coerced into endorsing it but because they were convinced of its justification. Unfortunately, most of the methods for showing that liberal principles are indeed convincing seem hedged with provisos that exclude from the outset exactly those persons whose prior convictions *would* lead them to refuse.

Let me be thoroughly clear about the nature of this outcome. According to my interpretation of it, one appealing implication of Rawls's conception of unreasonableness is the exclusion from the legitimation pool of some of the very sorts of people whose comprehensive doctrines should trouble those of us who are committed to equalities of gender, race, and so on. This heartening outcome rests unfortunately on starting points that contradict the political conception the method is supposed to justify. The political autonomy that liberalism promises to all persons and the social contract that Rawls wants, namely, a "hypothetical agreement . . . between all rather than some members of society,"[46] are both restricted in the end only to those who begin with liberal political values.

There is no Archimedean point, as we all know, from which to begin the search for political legitimacy. We begin this endeavor as persons defined by commitments that are often *both* religious, moral, or philosophical *and* political. Political liberalism wins consent only by excluding from the outset those very persons whose illiberal convictions would lead them to reject the system. Political liberalism, furthermore, would impose its coercive power on the nonliberal persons who reject its legitimacy—just as those persons, if they had the chance, might seek to impose their own political conceptions on dissenters from their own doctrines, including liberals.

Nor can political liberalism claim that one of its distinctive values is a respect for the political autonomy of *all* its citizens. Each political doctrine, including political liberalism, would suppress the political autonomy of some of the citizens who lived under it, in particular, all those whose opposition threatened to destabilize the system. Political liberalism would do so in part by excluding those dissidents from the legitimation pool and in part by suppressing their free expression in daily life. In Rawls's political liberalism, the suppressed persons are the "unreasonable" ones who, therefore, seem to deserve their fate. Yet this epithet masks the fundamentally political and contested nature of the notion.

My melancholy conclusion is that political liberalism is simply one more political doctrine among many, freestanding or not, with no greater politically independent, *consent-based* claim to anyone's allegiance than many of its political rivals.[47]

Notes

1. John Rawls, *Political Liberalism,* pbk. ed. (New York: Columbia University Press, 1996), 216. In this chapter, all references to *Political Liberalism* are to this 1996 edition.

2. The exact wording varies with different passages. See, for example, *Political Liberalism,* 217, where Rawls states that political power is justifiable "only when it is exercised in accordance with a constitution the essentials of which all citizens may reasonably be expected to endorse in the light of principles and ideals acceptable to them as reasonable and rational. This is the liberal principle of legitimacy."

3. See, for example, Thomas Scanlon, Contractualism and Utilitarianism, in *Utilitarianism and Beyond,* ed. Amartya Sen and Bernard Williams (Cambridge: Cambridge University Press, 1982), and Thomas Nagel, *Equality and Partiality* (New York: Oxford University Press, 1991).

4. Rawls, *Political Liberalism,* 258.

5. Rawls, *Political Liberalism,* 51.

6. Rawls, *Political Liberalism,* 49 n. 1, 49–51.

7. Rawls, *Political Liberalism,* 54–58.

8. Rawls, *Political Liberalism,* 53–54.

9. Rawls, *Political Liberalism,* 52.

10. Rawls, *Political Liberalism,* 74.

11. Rawls, *Political Liberalism,* 72.

12. Jeremy Waldron, *Liberal Rights: Collected Papers 1981–1991* (Cambridge: Cambridge University Press, 1993), 36–37; emphasis added.

13. Waldron, *Liberal Rights,* 44.

14. Nagel, *Equality and Partiality,* 8, 33.

15. Joseph Raz argues that consent to a political authority is binding only in case the authority is independently justifiable on certain specified sorts of grounds; see Joseph Raz, *The Morality of Freedom* (Oxford: Oxford University Press, 1986), 88–94.

16. Nagel, *Equality and Partiality,* 8.

17. John Rawls, *A Theory of Justice* (Cambridge, Mass.: Harvard University Press, 1971).

18. This issue, however, reveals a difference between the legitimacy of a government's exercise of its coercive power and a citizen's obligation to obey that government. Waldron argues that, even though it makes the coercive action of government more legitimate, hypothetical consent does *not* increase the degree of someone's obligation to *obey* the dictates of her government (*Liberal Rights,* 49–50). Hobbes recognized this distinction between legitimacy and obligation when arguing that the state might rightfully attempt to execute someone who, at the same time, had no obligation to submit to this treatment and could, furthermore, rightfully attempt to escape (see Thomas Hobbes, *Leviathan,* ed. Michael Oakeshott [New York: Collier Books, 1962], 164. For Waldron's reference to this passage, although to a different edition of *Leviathan,* see *Liberal Rights,* 50).

19. Waldron, *Liberal Rights,* 49.

20. Waldron, *Liberal Rights,* 41–42.

21. Waldron, *Liberal Rights,* 55.

22. Waldron, *Liberal Rights,* 56.

23. According to Leif Wenar, Catholic doctrine is premised on this view; see Leif Wenar, *Political Liberalism:* An Internal Critique, *Ethics* 106, no. 1 (October 1995): 32–62, especially 42–48.

24. Rush Limbaugh, *The Way Things Ought to Be* (New York: Pocket Star Books, 1993), especially chap. 25, Religion and America: They Do Go Together. Strictly speaking, Limbaugh's view is not unreasonable in Rawls's sense. Limbaugh believes that "America was founded as a Judeo-Christian country" (278), and like Rawls, Limbaugh bases his politics on traditional values. The difference between them lies in what they believe the basic values of that tradition to be.

25. Waldron, *Liberal Rights,* 57.

26. Rawls, *Political Liberalism,* 63–64.

27. Rawls, *Political Liberalism,* 64 n. 19.

28. Rawls, *Political Liberalism,* 61; emphasis added.

29. This potential, as we all know, is often unrealized in practice.

30. Susan Golombok and Robyn Fivush, *Gender Development* (Cambridge: Cambridge University Press, 1994), 7, 18. Golombok and Fivush refer here to the Bem Sex Role Inventory; see S. Bem, The Measurement of Psychological Androgyny, *Journal of Consulting and Clinical Psychology,* 42 (1974), 155–62.

31. For Rawls, rationality is self-interested, instrumental rationality. It involves finding means to one's ends and adjusting one's ends in light of still broader aims and goals for one's life. There might well be people who think that women are incapable of doing this, or less capable of doing it than men. Once again, that view is not a part of Rawls's theory as such, so the only question is whether the stereotype of women will lead to widespread *mis*application of Rawls's conception of rationality when applied to women. Even this may not be a problem. Although the stereotypes of agency and instrumentality are applied to men more often than to women, women are still thought to be capable of finding the means to the ends that *they* are supposed to seek, namely, promoting social relationships and expressing emotion.

It is true that women have been specifically characterized as irrational. In the end, however, I can ignore this stereotype, since all the interesting philosophical problems for Rawls's political liberalism turn on his notion of reasonableness.

32. On this point, see the discussion by Carole Pateman, "The Disorder of Women": Women, Love, and the Sense of Justice, *Ethics* 91 (1980): 20–34.

33. G. W. F. Hegel, *The Phenomenology of Mind,* trans. J. B. Baillie, intro. by George Lichtheim (New York: Harper Torchbooks, 1967), 496.

34. See Mike Royko, *Boss: Richard J. Daley of Chicago* (New York: New American Library, 1971).

35. Genevieve Lloyd, *The Man of Reason: "Male" and "Female" in Western Philosophy* (Minneapolis: University of Minnesota, 1984).

36. This would be reminiscent of the persistent anthropological idea that in hunter-gatherer societies, men are the hunters and women are the gatherers, an idea that persists despite recent evidence showing that women's frequent capture of small game contributed more to the protein needs of such societies than did men's occasional capture of big game.

37. See the discussion of this issue in Waldron, *Liberal Rights,* 283–92.

38. Rawls, *Political Liberalism,* 19.

39. Susan Moller Okin, *Political Liberalism,* Justice and Gender, *Ethics* 105, no. 1 (October 1994): 31–32.

40. Rawls, *Political Liberalism,* 196, 210.

41. Discussions of *Political Liberalism* sometimes use the example of right-wing religious fundamentalism as a test case for political liberalism; see, for example, Okin, *Political Liberalism,* Justice, and Gender, and Michael Huemer, Rawls's Problem of Stability, *Social Theory and Practice* 22, no. 3 (fall 1996): 375–95.

42. Samuel Scheffler, The Appeal of Political Liberalism, *Ethics* 105, no. 1 (October 1994): 20.

43. Some of my opponents on women's issues might not hold such elaborate theories and might simply be hypocrites who mask with high-sounding rationales what they themselves secretly recognize to be the subordination of women. I do not suppose, however, that all my opponents are hypocrites. In my view, there are people who believe sincerely in the inferiority of women or in the "equal" value of those female roles that appear to me to involve subordination. These sincere disputes exemplify the sort of pluralism that Rawls attempts to surmount, unsuccessfully I believe.

44. Rawls, *Political Liberalism,* 195–211.

45. Rawls, *Political Liberalism,* 61.

46. Rawls, *Political Liberalism,* 258; also cited at note 4 above.

47. For a nonconsensual approach to the justification of liberalism, see Gerald F. Gaus, *Justificatory Liberalism* (New York: Oxford, 1996).

2

RAWLS AND RELIGION

James P. Sterba

In *Political Liberalism,* John Rawls sets out an ideal of public reason according to which "citizens are to conduct their fundamental discussions within the framework of what each regards as a political conception of justice based on values that others can reasonably be expected to endorse."[1] Since all citizens in pluralistic societies, like our own, cannot reasonably be expected to share the same religious values, Rawls's ideal of public reason generally rules out any role for religious considerations in public debate over fundamental issues in such societies. Accordingly, philosophers who hold that religious considerations should play such a role in public debate have criticized Rawls's ideal for being too restrictive.[2] In response, Rawls has modified his ideal to explicitly allow a role for religious considerations in public debate over fundamental issues.[3] In addition, other philosophers, like Robert Audi, who are attracted to Rawls's ideal of public reason have offered their own accounts of public reason that also allow religious considerations to play a role in public debate.[4] Nevertheless, some critics of Rawls's ideal of public reason, such as Nicholas Wolterstorff, remain unsatisfied.[5] These philosophers want an even greater role for religious considerations than either Rawls or Audi allows. In this chapter, I argue that once Rawls's ideal of public reason is correctly interpreted, it will be possible to reconcile that ideal with much of the role its critics want religion to have in public debate.

1. The Ideal of Public Reason

Originally, Rawls ruled out any role for religious considerations in public debate whenever "matters of constitutional essentials and questions of basic justice" are at issue in pluralistic societies, like our own. Because religious considerations are typically drawn from comprehensive conceptions of the good, which are not shared by all the citizens of pluralistic societies, Rawls argued that normally such considerations should not be used in public debate.

Yet, Rawls allowed that there could be exceptions to this restriction. In certain cases, Rawls allowed that an appeal to religious considerations could

34

be justifiably used in support of a political conception of justice in pluralistic societies. As examples of such justifiable uses, Rawls cites the American abolition movement that began in the 1830s and the civil rights movement led by Martin Luther King in the 1960s. In each of these examples, Rawls allowed that "the abolitionists or the leaders of the civil rights movement did not go against the ideal of public reason; or rather, they did not provided they thought, or on reflection would have thought (as they certainly could have thought), that the comprehensive reasons they appealed to were required to give strength to the political conception to be subsequently realized."[6] Nevertheless, Rawls contended that normally citizens must be "able" and "ready" to explain to one another how the principles and policies they advocate and vote for can be supported by considerations of public reason.[7] Apparently responding to criticisms, Rawls subsequently modified this requirement, allowing that citizens may propose whatever considerations they like for public policy, including religious considerations, provided they are also prepared "in due course" to offer considerations that comply with public reason.[8]

Robert Audi also defends a view of public reason that is quite similar to Rawls's.[9] According to Audi, the following principles govern public discourse:

The Principle of Theo-Ethical Equilibrium
Those who are religious should embody a commitment to a rational integration between religious deliverances and insights and secular ethical considerations.

The Principle of Secular Rationale
Everyone has a prima facie obligation not to advocate or support any law or public policy that restricts human conduct, unless he or she has, and is willing to offer, adequate secular reasons for this advocacy.

The Principle of Secular Motivation
Everyone also has a prima facie obligation to abstain from advocacy or support of a law or public policy that restricts human conduct unless he or she is sufficiently motivated by some normatively adequate secular reasons.

The Institutional Principle of Theo-Ethical Equilibrium
Religious institutions, at least insofar as they are committed to citizenship in a liberal democratic society, have a prima facie obligation to seek an equilibrium between religious deliverances and secular ethical considerations when advocating or supporting laws or public policies that restrict human conduct.

The Principle of Ecclesiastical Political Neutrality
In a free and liberal democratic society, churches committed to being institutional citizens in such a society have a prima facie obligation to abstain from supporting candidates for public office or pressing for laws or public policies that restrict human conduct.

The Principle of Clerical Neutrality
Clergy in a liberal democratic society have a prima facie obligation 1) to observe a distinction between their personal political views and those of their
office or otherwise held by them as clergy, especially in making public statements, 2) to prevent any political aims they may have from dominating their
professional conduct as clergy, and 3) to abstain from officially (as religious
leaders) supporting candidates for public office or pressing for laws or policies
that would restrict human conduct.

Obviously, compared to Rawls's view, Audi's view is much more detailed in
its requirements, and when compared with Rawls's earlier view, which only
allowed religious considerations to play a role in public debate in certain
exceptional cases, Audi's view allows for a greater role for religious considerations in public debate. This assessment is reversed, however, when Audi's
view is compared with Rawls's later view. In that comparison, Audi's view is
more restrictive than Rawls's later view since Rawls now has an even more
relaxed requirement about providing public reasons.[10] Nevertheless, critics
have contended that all versions of these views are still too restrictive, holding
that religious considerations should play a still greater role in public debate.

2. Criticisms of the Ideal

A basic criticism that has been raised to the views of Rawls and Audi focuses
on the public reasons that each would make centrally important to public
discourse. In general, critics question whether such reasons are actually available to the extent that defenders of the ideal of public reason say they are.[11]
Obviously, if such reasons are not generally available, the question of whether
to require their presence along with religious reasons will not generally arise.
If public reasons are not generally available, then, either religious reasons, or
other reasons drawn from our comprehensive conceptions of the good, will
turn out to be the only reasons that we will generally have on which to ground
our coercive public policies.

But what are these public reasons on which Rawls and Audi claim that
coercive public policies should be grounded? As Rawls characterizes them,
they are reasons that everyone can reasonably be expected to endorse in a
liberal democratic society.[12] As Audi characterizes them, they are reasons that
all fully rational citizens in possession of all the relevant facts (and so fully
informed) would affirm. Both Rawls and Audi agree that citizens should be
capable of appealing to such public reasons when advocating restricting human conduct, at least with respect to matters of constitutional essentials and
questions of basic justice.

Audi also provides a metaethical theory that he thinks helps explain why
fully rational and fully informed citizens would reach the agreement that is
presupposed by public reasons. This metaethical theory makes two claims:
First, that moral properties supervene on natural properties so that no two

people or acts that are alike in all their natural properties will differ in their moral ones; second, that moral properties are possessed by virtue of natural ones so that, for example, an act is obligatory by virtue of being a way of avoiding running over a small child. Appealing to this theory, Audi argues that since we already know what sorts of natural properties are relevant to moral decisions, for example, the properties affecting people's pleasure and pain, freedom of movement, and human capacities, and since we already know, for example, that being truthful with people is essential to treating them with respect and that brutality to children makes them suffer unjustly and tends to make them abusive themselves, thereby continuing the infliction of suffering, and since these natural properties determine moral ones,[13] it follows that fully rational people should come to endorse moral principles such as those prohibiting murder, assault, theft, and dishonesty and those requiring some degree of beneficence toward other people.[14] According to Audi, such principles generate the public reasons on which coercive public policies should be based.

As I have noted, for Rawls, public reasons are the principles and ideals that are justifiable to every citizen in a liberal democratic society. More specifically, Rawls suggests that they include the ideal of citizens as free and equal, the ideal of a well-ordered society, the ideal of the original position, and possibly his two principles of justice, which Rawls claims can be derived from his original position. But the ideal of citizens as free and equal and the ideal of a well-ordered society are widely understood to be very formal ideals, from which little, if anything, can be derived with regard to matters of constitutional essentials and questions of basic justice. Thus, political ideals as different as libertarianism and socialism can both be interpreted as regarding citizens as free and equal and society as well ordered. By contrast, Rawls's ideal of the original position is clearly a substantive rather than a formal ideal. From it, either Rawls's two principles of justice or principles similar to them can be derived, but given the contentiousness of this ideal and its derived principles, it is not clear that it belongs to the domain of public reason as one of those values that everyone can reasonably be expected to endorse. Even Rawls acknowledges this when he writes:

> Accepting the idea of public reason and its principle of legitimacy emphatically does not mean . . . accepting a particular liberal conception of justice down to the last details of the principles defining its content. We may differ about these principles and still agree in accepting a conception's more general features. We agree that citizens share in political power as free and equal, and that as reasonable and rational they have a duty of civility to appeal to public reason, yet we differ as to which principles are the most reasonable basis of public justification.[15]

Although Rawls admits in this passage that his two principles of justice cannot be derived from the ideal of public reason alone, he still contends that all citizens in a liberal democratic society, by virtue of being reasonable and rational, are required to endorse the ideal of public reason.

But is this the case? Are all citizens in a liberal democratic society, by virtue of being reasonable and rational, required to endorse the ideal of public reason and thus to conduct public debate by appealing to values that everyone can reasonably be expected to endorse? Surely, this is one interpretation of what it means for citizens to be reasonable and rational in a liberal democratic society, but is it the only one?

Nicholas Wolterstorff in his critique of Rawls's ideal of public reason purports to offer another. According to him:

> In a democracy, we discuss and debate, with the aim of reaching agreement. We don't just mount the platform to tell our fellow citizens how we see things. We listen, and we try to persuade. . . . Seldom, even on unimportant issues, do we succeed in reaching consensus, not even among reasonable and rational citizens. . . . But we try.
>
> Then, finally, we vote. It cannot be the case that in voting under these circumstances, we are violating those concepts of freedom and equality which are ingredient in the Idea of liberal democracy, since almost the first thing that happens when societies move toward becoming liberal democracies is that they begin taking votes on various matters and living with the will of the majority—subject to provisos specifying rights of minorities.
>
> . . .We aim at agreement in our discussions with each other. . . . Our agreement on some policy need not be based on some set of principles agreed on by all present and future citizens and rich enough to settle all important political issues. Sufficient if each citizen, for his or her own reasons, agrees on the policy today and tomorrow—not for all time. It need not even be the case that each and every citizen agrees to the policy. Sufficient if the agreement be the fairly-gained and fairly-executed agreement of the majority.[16]

So, according to Wolterstorff, citizens are reasonable and rational in a liberal democratic society if, after all sides have the opportunity to express their views, they abide by the results of majority voting, provided that the will of the majority is constrained by certain minority rights.

3. Starting a Reconciliation

One of the rights that Wolterstorff thinks minorities do not have in a liberal democratic society is the right to have matters of constitutional essentials and questions of basic justice decided in a way that everyone can reasonably be expected to endorse. To grant minorities this right would be to endorse Rawls's ideal of public reason, and Wolterstorff objects to Rawls's ideal of public reason on grounds of fairness:

> Is it equitable to ask of everyone that, in deciding and discussing political issues, they refrain from using their comprehensive perspectives . . . ?
>
> [This] seems to me not equitable. [For it] belongs to the *religious convictions* of a good many religious persons in our society that *they ought to base* their

decisions concerning fundamental issues of justice on their religious convictions. They do not view it as an option whether or not to do so. It is their conviction that they ought to strive for wholeness, integrity, integration, in their lives; that they ought to allow the Word of God, the teachings of the Torah, the command and example of Jesus, or whatever, to shape their existence as a whole, including, then, their social and political existence. Their religion is not, for them, *something else* than their social and political existence; it is also about their social and political existence. Accordingly, to require of them that they not base their decisions and discussions concerning political issues on their religion is to infringe inequitably on their free exercise of their religion. If they have to make a choice, they will make their decisions about constitutional essentials and matters of basic justice on the basis of their religious convictions, and make their decisions on more peripheral matters on other grounds—exactly the opposite of what Rawls lays down in his version of the restraint.[17]

Thus, Wolterstorff thinks that he has provided another interpretation of what it means for citizens to be reasonable and rational in a liberal democratic society—one that happily lacks the unfairness that he believes characterizes Rawls's interpretation with its demand for public reason.

Wolterstorff contends that without the unfairness of Rawls's interpretation of what it means for citizens to be reasonable and rational in a liberal democratic society, religious reasons will function more freely in public debate. Yet, notice that Wolterstorff's interpretation of what it means for citizens to be reasonable and rational in a liberal democratic society still constrains how religious reasons are to function in public debate. First, before religious reasons can be enacted in public policy, their advocates must muster a majority of votes, and second, the enactment of such reasons is further constrained by minority rights, which Wolterstorff leaves unspecified here, beyond saying that Rawls's ideal of public reason should not be incorporated into such rights because it is unfair.

But is it unfair to impose Rawls's ideal of public reason on public debate? Presumably, Wolterstorff thinks there are good religious reasons to support the constraints that he himself wants to impose on public debate—the requirement of majority rule and minority rights—whereas, by contrast, he thinks that Rawls's ideal of public reason is an unfair constraint on those who regard religious reasons as fundamental to their lives. So one might conclude that Wolterstorff regards his view of public debate as supported by religious reasons and regards Rawls's view as, at best, supported by only secular reasons.

Yet, when Wolterstorff goes on to illustrate the difference between his view and Rawls's and Audi's views, he associates his view with what he calls a parliamentary model, which operates by majority rule, but then associates Rawls's and Audi's views with what he calls a Quaker model, which requires some form of consensus to reach decisions.[18] By characterizing Rawls's and Audi's views in this way, however, Wolterstorff implicitly concedes that their views, as well as his own, can be supported by religious reasons—at least he implicitly concedes that their views can be supported by the religious reasons that characterize a Quaker tradition. This means that the choice between his view of public debate and Rawls's and Audi's views can be understood as being a choice between views that are all supported by religious reasons. That could explain why Wolterstorff argues for the choice of his own view, not by appealing to specifically religious reasons, but by appealing to an ideal of fairness. Given that Rawls's and Audi's views, as well as his own, can all be supported by religious reasons, Wolterstorff appears to recognize the need to appeal to something that is neutral or common to them all in order to support his religious view over views such as theirs. Accordingly, he appeals to an ideal of fairness.

But are Rawls's and Audi's views of public reason an unfair requirement to impose on public debate? Let us grant that Wolterstorff has made a prima facie case that Rawls's and Audi's views are unfair to religious majorities by limiting their use of religious reasons. What needs to be determined is whether this is the only unfairness that is at issue here. It would not do to correct one unfairness by imposing a similar or even greater unfairness. We need to determine, therefore, whether a minority, religious or otherwise, that loses out to a religious majority might also be unfairly treated, and if it is unfairly treated, whether that unfairness needs to be addressed as much, or even more so, than the unfairness to which Wolterstorff has drawn our attention.

Presumably, if the imposition of the majority will on the minority is to be fair, it must be possible to morally blame the minority for failing to accept that imposition. If that were not the case, then the minority could justifiably resist that imposition, and the will of the majority would lack moral legitimacy.[19] But if the imposition of the will of the majority is to be fair, there must, then, be sufficient reasons accessible to the minority, religious or otherwise, to morally require it to accept that imposition. For the members of a group cannot be morally required to do something if they cannot come to know and so come to justifiably believe that they are so required. Fairness here requires that there be reasons accessible to a minority that are sufficient to require the acceptance of the will of the majority by that minority.

Surprisingly, or not so surprisingly, Wolterstorff accepts this requirement of fairness; that is, he accepts the need for there to be reasons accessible to a minority that are sufficient to morally require acceptance of the will of the majority in the relevant cases. Moreover, Wolterstorff thinks that he has provided just the kind of reasons that are needed to morally require the minority's submission to the will of a religious majority in a liberal democratic society. As he puts it: "It need not even be the case that each and every citizen agree to the policy. Sufficient if the agreement be the fairly-gained and fairly-executed agreement of the majority."[20] According to Wolterstorff, then, the fact that an agreement is fairly gained and fairly executed by a religious majority should provide the minority with sufficient reasons to morally require its submission to the will of the majority in such cases. Moreover, such a fact should be accessible to a minority in a legitimate state, and its accessibility would render the minority morally blameworthy for failing to submit to the rule of the majority in such cases. Thus, by putting his justification for rule by a religious majority in terms of fairness, Wolterstorff must think that he is providing a moral justification that everyone in a liberal democratic society should regard as sufficient to justify that rule.

Yet, notice that if Wolterstorff is successful in providing a sufficient moral justification for both secularly and religiously committed minorities to accept the rule of religious majorities in such cases, he would have succeeded in more ways than he realizes since he would have also succeeded in satisfying Rawls's ideal of public reason. This is because Rawls's ideal of public reason requires a justification that everyone can reasonably be expected to endorse in a liberal democratic society. Moreover, the sense of reasonable in Rawls's requirement is not epistemological (it is not that we can reasonably predict that everyone will endorse something), nor is it morally neutral (it is not that everyone is required by minimal rationality to endorse something). Rather it is moral (it is that everyone is required by fair terms of cooperation to endorse something).[21] So when Rawls's ideal of public reason is correctly understood in this way, it clearly coincides with what Wolterstorff is claiming. For Wolterstorff is claiming that everyone, religious or otherwise, morally ought to accept the requirements of fair majority rule in a liberal democratic society.[22]

4. The Reconciliation

Although Wolterstorff's ideal for public debate in a liberal democratic society can thus be seen to coincide with Rawls's own ideal of public reason, Wolterstorff and Rawls may still be disagreeing about what their ideals, now recognized to be substantially equivalent, require. This is because they are each focusing on different aspects of the application of their ideals. Wolterstorff is focusing on the unfairness of denying members of a religious majority the right to base their decisions on religious reasons, or the unfairness of requiring them to bifurcate their lives between what they are committed to religiously and what they are, or could be, committed to nonreligiously. I have granted the prima facie unfairness of such requirements. Surely, fairness would allow religious people to base their decisions on their religious reasons, provided that other requirements of fairness are satisfied. Certainly, fairness would also not require religious people to bifurcate themselves between what they are committed to for religious reasons and what they are committed to for nonreligious reasons, provided that other requirements of fairness are satisfied.

By contrast, Rawls and Audi are each focusing on a different requirement of fairness for majority rule. They are focusing on the issue of whether minorities, religious or otherwise, would have sufficient reasons accessible to them for submitting to the rule of the majority. Wolterstorff seems aware of this problem, and that is why he put the case for rule by a religious majority in terms of an ideal of fairness. But fairness can have both procedural and substantive requirements.[23] Fairness can procedurally require that a minority submit to a majority only after the minority members have had a chance to speak their minds and been outvoted.[24] But fairness can also substantively require that a minority submit to a majority only when there are certain additional reasons accessible to the members of the minority that support the will of the majority.

If a majority is constrained only procedurally, its impositions on a minority can turn out to be quite severe. For example, a religious majority could require a minority to financially support its religious activities or to participate in its religious services. The majority also, for example, could impose significant restrictions on women or on homosexuals as demanded by its religious doctrines. Moreover, such impositions typically would be much more constraining than the requirements that Rawls and Audi seek to impose on public discourse. So, if fairness is to be secured, particularly with respect to matters of constitutional essentials and questions of basic justice, there must be substantive reasons as well as procedural reasons that are accessible to the minority for accepting the will of the majority. And while these substantive reasons need not, by themselves, be sufficient to require abiding by the will of the majority, they must, when joined together with the procedural reasons that are also accessible to the minority, provide a sufficient justification to require abiding by the will of the majority. So, it turns out that the requirements of fairness go further than Wolterstorff explicitly allowed. To meet the requirements of fairness, procedural reasons that are accessible to the minority are not enough; at least with respect to matters of constitutional essentials and questions of basic justice, there must be substantive reasons that are also accessible to the minority, and taken together, these procedural and substantive reasons must constitute a sufficient justification to require the minority to abide by the will of the majority.

Nevertheless, fairness does not require that each and every advocate of the majority view be willing to offer, or be motivated by, these procedural and substantive reasons. Although these reasons must be accessible to the minority, they can be accessible to the minority without it being required that each and every majority advocate not only have these reasons but also be sufficiently motivated by them. So, fairness does not impose on majority advocates the particular requirements that Rawls and Audi endorsed, and Wolterstorff is correct in maintaining that those particular requirements constitute an unfair imposition on a religious majority.

Even so, collectively, the majority does have an obligation to ensure that sufficient procedural and substantive reasons for going along with the majority are accessible to the minority, at least with respect to matters of constitutional essentials and questions of basic justice. To meet this obligation, it generally suffices that the majority has taken sufficient steps to ensure freedom of speech, quality public education, and open debate for people of all persuasions. The idea is that through these institutional structures, the needed public reasons will be made accessible. From time to time, however, this obligation will also require that some well-placed majority advocates help make accessible sufficient procedural and substantive reasons for the minority to go along with the will of the majority. By ensuring the accessibility to the minority of sufficient procedural and substantive reasons for their going along with the majority, this collective obligation of the majority is thereby discharged.

5. Conclusion

I have argued that once Rawls's ideal of public reason is correctly interpreted, critics of that ideal, like Wolterstorff, can actually be seen to be endorsing that very ideal while possibly disagreeing with Rawls concerning its practical consequences. I further argue that when the practical consequences of the ideal of public reason are correctly specified, we need to reject Rawls's and Audi's requirement that each and every majority advocate be able to provide the minority with sufficient reasons to necessitate its going along with the will of the majority, and to reject Audi's additional requirement that each and every majority advocate be motivated by those reasons. I contend that when such requirements are correctly judged by the ideal of public reason, they can be seen to be an unfair imposition on the majority. It follows that much of the role that critics of Rawls and Audi have wanted religious reasons to have in public debate can be justified. However, I have also argued that when the practical consequences of the ideal of public reason—now seen as shared by Rawls, Audi, and Wolterstorff—are correctly specified, they require that the minority have more reasons accessible to them for accepting the will of the majority than the purely procedural reasons that Wolterstorff seems to favor. What is additionally required, I have argued, is that there be both procedural and substantive reasons accessible to the minority that, taken together, are sufficient to require the minority's acceptance of the will of the majority and that collectively, the majority has an obligation to ensure that such reasons are accessible to the minority. In brief, I have shown that Rawls, his defenders, and his critics, like Wolterstorff, all have good reason to modify the practical requirements that they have endorsed in favor of requirements that are actually demanded by the ideal of public reason they all can be seen to accept.

Acknowledgments

An earlier version of this chapter was presented at the Fourteenth International Social Philosophy Conference held in Kingston, Ontario, Canada, July 18–21, 1996. I am grateful to Robert Audi, Shyli Karin-Frank, Janet Kourany, Jan Narveson, Robert Van Wyk, and Nicholas Wolterstorff for their comments on this version.

Notes

1. John Rawls, *Political Liberalism* (New York: Columbia University Press, 1993), 226. (Unless otherwise noted, in this chapter references to *Political Liberalism* are to the 1993 edition.) Throughout this discussion, I assume that all citizens are morally competent, that is, sufficiently capable of understanding and acting upon moral requirements.

2. Robert Audi and Nicholas Wolterstorff, *Religion in the Public Square* (Lanham, Md.: Rowman & Littlefield, 1997); 67–120; Philip Quinn, Political Liberalisms and Their Exclusions of the Religious, *Proceedings and Addresses of the American Philosophical Association* 69, no. 2 (1995): 35–56; Paul Weithman, The Separation of Church and State: Some Questions for Professor Audi, *Philosophy and Public Affairs* 20 (1991): 52–65; and the contributors to *Religion and Contemporary Liberalism*, ed. Paul Weithman (Notre Dame, Ind.: University of Notre Dame Press, 1997).

3. John Rawls, *Political Liberalism*, pbk. ed. (New York: Columbia University Press, 1996), li–lii.

4. Robert Audi, The Separation of Church and State and the Obligations of Citizens, *Philosophy and Public Affairs* 18 (1989): 259–96; Robert Audi, Religion and the Ethics of Political Participation *Ethics* 100 (1990): 386–97; Robert Audi, Religious Commitment and Secular Reason: A Reply to Professor Weithman, *Philosophy and Public Affairs* 21 (1991): 66–76.

5. Audi and Wolterstorff, *Religion in the Public Square*, 67–120.

6. Rawls, *Political Liberalism*, 251.

7. Rawls, *Political Liberalism*, 217–18.

8. Rawls, introduction to *Political Liberalism*, pbk. ed. (1996), li–lii.

9. Audi and Wolterstorff, *Religion in the Public Square*, 1–47, 122–44, 167–73.

10. For example, Rawls's constraint on the use of religious reasons in public discourse applies only to matters of constitutional essentials and questions of basic justice whereas Audi's constraint on the use of such reasons applies wherever laws and public policies restrict human conduct.

11. Audi and Wolterstorff, *Religion in the Public Square*, 67–120, 145–66; Quinn, Political Liberalisms and Their Exclusions of the Religious.

12. Rawls, *Political Liberalism*, 24. On one occasion, Rawls characterizes the policies that are favored by public reasons to be policies that are at least not unreasonable in the sense that those who oppose them can nevertheless understand how reasonable people can affirm them (see Rawls, *Political Liberalism*, 253). This seems to be an appropriate way of understanding the ideal of public reason in contexts where public reasons are very difficult to come by.

13. Audi and Wolterstorff, *Religion in the Public Square*, 19–20.

14. Audi and Wolterstorff, *Religion in the Public Square*, 17. Of course, given Audi's theory, fully rational people who know the relevant natural facts will know the moral principles such facts determine, but whether they will endorse such principles and abide by them is another issue. They will do that only if in addition to being fully rational, they are also sufficiently moral.

15. Rawls, *Political Liberalism*, 226–27.

16. Wolterstorff, *Religion in the Public Square*, 108, 114. In another place, Wolterstorff further elaborates: "Suppose that some law or policy with coercive import is under consideration. We each state our view on the matter—saying whatever we want to say. We each listen to the other, and make our final decision in light of what we have heard. Then we vote. If I lose in the vote, then though I don't agree, I acquiesce—unless I find the decision truly appalling. I don't like the decision; I prefer that it have gone the other way. But I've been allowed to say whatever I wanted to say, and I've been heard, genuinely heard. Is there anything more that I can ask of you by way of respect?" (p. 160).

17. Audi and Wolterstorff, *Religion in the Public Square,* 104–5. And in another place, Wolterstorff again takes up the fairness issue: "There's a common pattern to the impression of the person who embraces the liberal position that his insistence on [public reason] deals fairly with religion, and to his impression that his insistence on the separation interpretation [of church and state] deals fairly with religion. The common pattern is this: the liberal assumes that requiring religious persons to debate and act politically for reasons other than religious reasons is not in violation of their *religious* convictions; likewise he assumes that an educational program which makes no reference to religion is not in violation of any parent's *religious* convictions. He assumes, in other words, that though religious people may not be in the *habit* of dividing their life into a religious component and a nonreligious component, and though some might not be *happy* doing so, nonetheless, their doing so would not be in violation of anybody's religion. But he's wrong about this. It's when we bring into the picture persons for whom it is a matter of religious conviction that they ought to strive for a religiously integrated existence—it's then, especially, though not only then, that the unfairness of the liberal position to religion comes to light" (Audi and Wolterstorff, *Religion in the Public Square,* 116).

18. Audi and Wolterstorff, *Religion in the Public Square,* 152.

19. To be morally legitimate, the will of the majority must be backed up with more than power. The minority must have a moral duty to accept the imposition of the majority, but that could only be the case if the minority would be morally blameworthy for failing to accept that imposition. Moreover, as I noted in note 1, I am assuming throughout this discussion that everyone is morally competent, that is, sufficiently capable of understanding and acting upon moral requirements.

20. Audi and Wolterstorff, *Religion in the Public Square,* 114.

21. Rawls, *Political Liberalism,* 48ff.

22. I do not think the same holds for Audi's view of public debate because "rational" in his ideal of what fully informed and fully rational people would endorse is not understood in any moral sense. But then it does not follow that fully rational but nonmoral people, even when fully informed, will always endorse (even verbally) the requirements of morality, and certainly they will not always abide by them.

23. Procedural constraints are usually opposed to nonprocedural constraints, and substantive constraints are usually opposed to formal constraints. So it is possible for a procedural constraint to be a substantive one (for example, Rawls's original position) and for a formal constraint to be a nonprocedural one. Nevertheless, typically procedural constraints will be formal, and substantive constraints will be nonprocedural, and at this point my analysis is only trying to cover typical cases.

24. Except for his important provisos concerning minority rights, Wolterstorff might seem to be committed only to a procedural constraint on majority rule. But what if a majority decides to significantly limit the use of religious reasons in public debate (the outcome of U.S. constitutional history)? Would Wolterstorff rest content, or would he still object that such limitations are substantively unfair to the minority? My guess is that he would still object on grounds of substantive unfairness, and he would be right.

3

RAWLS'S NEGLECTED CHILDHOOD:

REFLECTIONS ON THE ORIGINAL POSITION,

STABILITY, AND THE CHILD'S SENSE OF JUSTICE

Samantha Brennan and Robert Noggle

Rawls's attitude toward children displays a rather ironic sort of neglect. Though he spends several chapters of *A Theory of Justice* exploring the empirical details of the development of moral reasoning in childhood, he pays almost no attention to the moral status of children. This neglect of questions of children's rights and justice within families in a 586-page book that aspires to articulate a complete theory of distributive justice, and in *Political Liberalism,* the 371-page sequel that was meant to correct and further develop the initial theory, is really quite remarkable.[1] In this chapter we argue that Rawls's omission is a serious one, both in terms of concern for children and in terms of the status of the proposed theory of justice. Section 1 examines the problems for children that follow from Rawls's omission of them in his version of the social contract, and section 2 examines the one place in Rawls's work where children do have a role, his account of moral development.

1. Reflections on the Original Position

A theory of justice is incomplete to the extent that it does not address the question of the moral status of children and obligations we have toward them. This is not to say that it is a criterion for a theory of justice to be a complete theory of justice that it develop a *particular* view about the moral status of children and of our associated obligations. Rather, a theory of justice, to be a complete theory, must acknowledge and address the issues.[2] Yet, in the case of Rawls, it seems reasonable to expect more, to expect an account that pays special attention to the welfare of children. After all, there is much sympathy on Rawls's part for the people who are the least advantaged in society, and surely the children of the least advantaged adults are even more vulnerable than the other members of their families.

How is it that Rawls leaves children out of his conclusions about the just society? This chapter argues that the neglect of children in Rawls's theory of justice is no accident. Instead, the paucity of conclusions about justice and children follows from Rawls's version of the social contract as it is presented in *A Theory of Justice* and later revised in *Political Liberalism*. Although the neglect of children is a feature of both books, we argue that changes made to the theory in *Political Liberalism* make possible answers to the problem of children's moral status that were not possible for Rawls's theory as articulated in *A Theory of Justice*.

In *A Theory of Justice*, Rawls assumes that the individuals in "the Original Position" are "heads of families" or, alternatively, are "representatives of family lines."[3] As feminist critics such as Susan Moller Okin have noted, the result of Rawls's characterizing the contractors in this way is that the question of justice within these families goes unnoticed.[4] Although this may be an effect of Rawls's assumption, Rawls's motivation for "The-Heads-of-Families Assumption" is not to make the family immune to questions of justice. Rather, Rawls has as his goal solving the problem of justifying justice-based obligations to future generations. Just how the heads-of-families assumption is supposed to accomplish this will be taken up later. In *Political Liberalism*, Rawls abandons that assumption in favor of another solution to the problem of justice for future generations, making theoretical room to put forward a view about justice for children. Rawls does not put forward a view about children in *Political Liberalism*, but one that is compatible with his more general view is suggested in this chapter.

As has been noted, Rawls has remarkably little to say about children and the requirements of justice. It may be that in *A Theory of Justice* there is not much he can say, given the heads-of-families assumption. The first task, then, in evaluating Rawls's theory for its potential as a theory of justice that speaks to the question of justice for children will be to see whether the heads-of-families assumption is indeed required. In *Political Liberalism*, Rawls himself gives up the assumption, yet he does not go on to give an account of justice for children. And so our second task will be to see whether there are the positive resources in *A Theory of Justice* or *Political Liberalism* to develop a Rawlsian account of justice for children, even if it is not one that Rawls himself puts forward. Following the development of Rawls's theory chronologically, we focus our attention first on *A Theory of Justice*.

1.1. The Problem of Justice for Future Generations

Rawls famously argues that the principles of justice for the basic institutions of our society are those that would be chosen by contractors in the original position from behind a veil of ignorance. The veil of ignorance ensures that the parties to the contract do not know their place in society, class position or social status, their fortune in the distribution of natural assets and abilities, their level of intelligence, and strength or even special features of their own psychology, the particular circumstances of their society, and what generation they will be in.[5] The purpose of the veil is to ensure that each person, not knowing what his or her circumstances will be when the veil is lifted, will be unable to choose principles tailored to her or his advantage.

But Rawls thinks that the neutralizing effect of the veil of ignorance fails in one important respect: It cannot secure justice for all persons. What group of persons is left out? Rawls thinks that the veil of ignorance is insufficient to eliminate bias against future persons, those people who will exist only as members of future generations. Why does the veil fail to make the choice impartial with regard to them? Rawls reasons as follows: "Since the persons in the original position know that they are contemporaries (taking the present time of entry interpretation), they can favor their generation by refusing to make any sacrifices for their successors; they simply acknowledge the principle that no one has a duty to save for posterity. Previous generations either have saved or they have not: there is nothing the parties can do now to affect that."[6]

1.2. The Solution According to *A Theory of Justice*

Despite the fact that rational, self-interested agents reasoning behind the veil of ignorance would not choose to save future generations, Rawls believes that we do have justice-based obligations to future generations. To ensure that parties to the original position would choose principles that would mandate just savings for future generations, Rawls changes the motivational assumption of strict self-interest in the case of future generations. Instead of being mere *individuals,* the parties in the original position are to be thought of as *heads of families.* Rawls writes, "The parties are regarded as representing family lines, say, with ties of sentiment between successive generations."[7] In short, the parties choose a just-savings principle over a no-saving principle because, just as good parents care about their offspring, the parties in the original position care about the generations to come.

1.3. Criticisms of the Heads-of-Families Assumption

By assuming that the individuals behind the veil of ignorance are not mere individuals but, rather, heads of families, Rawls weakens his theory in two important respects. First, he restricts its scope, for his theory of justice cannot address questions of justice among members of the same family. Second, it loses normative force because it bases obligations of justice on ties of sentiment.

How does it leave out issues of justice within the family? If the parties in the original position are seen as head of families, there will be no need for discussion about rules of justice that apply *within* the family. Even if we think of the contractors as family *representatives* concerned with the overall good of their families, rather than as simply the source of authority in the family as Rawls's term "head" might suggest, there is still no motivation for the contractors to discuss rules that apply within their families. In knowing that they are the family representatives, the contractors do not have to worry that they will turn out to be less powerful family members when the veil is lifted. And so children drop out of Rawls's contract picture entirely. At best, the interests of children are represented by a parent (in the case of circumstances external to the family, say, in school), and at worst (in the case of their life within the family), issues concerning them are not part of the subject matter of justice at all.

In the course of comparing Rawls's theory to that of Hegel, Jane English comments, "Apparently affection, intuitions and identification with the interests of others are supposed to obviate clearly defined principles for balancing conflicting interests within a sphere of love. By making the parties in the original position heads of families, rather than individuals, Rawls makes the family opaque to claims of justice."[8] To see the danger of this result for children, consider the following statistics regarding family violence. In Canada during the 1980s, more than two-thirds of the child victims of homicide, for whom a killer was identified, were killed by a parent. Almost one-third of the children killed were under the age of one, and more than 70 percent were under five years of age.[9] This statistic focuses our attention on children as victims of homicide, but there are myriad other less severe harms to children that occur primarily within the family, such as physical, sexual, and emotional abuse. Although most families provide loving, caring, and safe environments for their children, that is not always the case. Further, it seems that insofar as a society fails to protect its children from harm, it will be *unjust*. This point deserves further elaboration. Children are persons, and a just society cannot be one that allows a particular group of persons to be systematically harmed by other persons. The status of children as living within families should not exempt them from the protections of Rawls's own principles of justice.

Concerns about the heads-of-families assumption and the motivational assumption to which it is connected come from other quarters as well. Philosophers concerned with the moral status of women and children dislike the assumption because it makes the family opaque to questions about justice. But one might also dislike the assumption because it weakens Rawls's claim to have secured a just-savings principle and justice for future generations.

Rawls attempts to ground obligations of justice toward all future persons from the care that actual heads of families feel for their descendants. But this attempt is problematic for three reasons. First, it is one thing to justify obligations of justice from actual caring, quite another to do so when that caring is absent. Recall the analogy made between good parents who care about their offspring and the parties in the original position who care about the generations to come. But, not all parents are good, and not all heads of families care about other family members. Likewise, not all family representatives care about saving for future descendants. Second, even if the average person does care for his or her descendants, we can go on to ask about the limits of that care. How many generations into the future does the caring extend? It seems it will probably not be enough to ground obligations to persons in the distant future. These first two points raise questions about what follows from the heads-of-families assumption, but one can also reasonably raise worries about the motivational pull of the assumption. Third, even if most people do care about their descendants, what about those people who do not, either because they have descendants and do not care or because they do not have descendants? Why should they accept requirements of justice that follow from the heads-of-families assumption?[10]

In short, if guaranteeing justice for future generations means we must assume that we already care about the fate of future generations, then Rawls's argument fails to achieve its task. Arguably, to the extent that we do care about future generations, no requirements of justice are needed. To the extent that we do not care about future generations, we have no reason to assume that family heads or representatives behind the veil choosing principles of justice will care either. For a wide range of reasons (including the claim that it cannot be justified from self-interest), many moral theorists have rejected Rawls's view that justice-based obligations are owed to future generations.[11] Yet, the claim that justice demands that we not use all of the earth's resources, leaving future generations with a planet unable to support human habitation, is compelling.

1.4. Connections between Justice for Future Generations and Justice for Children

It is important to pause and clarify the relationship between the problem of justice for future generations and the problem of justice for children. According to Rawls's view in *A Theory of Justice,* the heads-of-families assumption is thought to solve the problem of justice for future generations. Unfortunately, solving the problem of future generations by making the contractors be heads of families makes it impossible for Rawls to address the problem of justice for children. Given this way of thinking about the relationship between the problem of justice for future generations and the problem of justice for children, it is clear that the problems are distinct. Indeed, they tug in different directions since Rawls's method for solving one problem makes it more difficult to solve the other.

But there is another way of thinking about the relationship between the problem of justice for children and the problem of justice for future generations, and it draws our attention to what the two problems have in common. The problem of justice between generations and the problem of the moral status of children are related in that the most immediate members of the next generation are one's children. Although one can note this interesting overlap in the membership of the two groups under discussion, it is important to realize that guaranteeing justice for one group does not help the other.[12] One could believe that future generations have moral status but that this moral status is attained only at adulthood. Thus, justice for future generations is consistent with the denial of children's moral status. Alternatively, one might believe that future generations do not count morally but that existing children do have moral status. Thus, granting moral status to children is consistent with a denial of moral status for future generations.

What, then, are the options? It seems they are as follows: First, we might keep the heads-of-families assumption and leave aside the question of justice and children. Second, we might remove the heads-of-families assumption, leaving room available to pose questions about justice and children at the cost of leaving aside the answer to the problem of justice for future generations provided by Rawls in *A Theory of Justice*. Third, we might see if the problem of justice for future generations could be solved without the heads-of-families assumption. Using Rawls's method of reflective equilibrium, and considering our theories in light of our intuitions about their implications, one might well choose to abandon his solution to the problem of justice for future generations in favor of solving the problem of justice for children. But if we can find a way to address the problem of justice for future generations that does not involve the heads-of-families assumption, then it might be possible for a Rawlsian theory of justice to address both issues. What follows is a discussion of this third option.

1.5. Doing without the Heads-of-Families Assumption

A number of attempts have been made to secure justice for future generations from contractarian foundations without the heads-of-families assumption. We will not attempt to review or examine all of them but will present three options: the first suggested by Jane English, the second suggested by D. Clayton Hubin, and the third put forward by Rawls himself in *Political Liberalism*.[13]

Jane English notes a number of possible difficulties with Rawls's version of the social contract, including the one we focus on here, Rawls's present time of entry interpretation of the contract. English argues that if Rawls gave up the present as the time of entry, then he need not have the parties be heads of families in order to justify long-term savings.[14] Rather, self-interested individuals, not knowing what time in human history they are from, would choose principles of savings to equalize the earth's resources between generations.[15]

Rawls's reason for the present time of entry assumption is that he intends the standpoint of the original position to be useful in moral debate. It would "stretch fantasy too far" and exceed the limits of our imaginative abilities to consider ourselves as possibly being from any time in human history.[16] Rawls worries that if the contractors did have the full range of points of entry as possibilities, the contract device would cease to be "a natural guide to intuition."[17] But given the other leaps in imagination Rawls's proposal requires us to make (to imagine ourselves ignorant of our sex, for example), it is not clear that Rawls need resist this amendment to his theory. When we are considering the wrongness of using resources now, rather than saving for later, one way we do so is by imaginatively occupying the point of view of members of future generations and asking what they would think of us. And so it would seem that as Rawlsian moral agents we are capable of projecting ourselves imaginatively into the future.

D. Clayton Hubin's suggestion is less extravagant, but it also has the result of securing a weaker savings principle than Rawls believes is required. Hubin argues that rational, self-interested individuals, reasoning behind the veil of ignorance, will choose a savings principle in recognition of the fact that they may be parents when the veil is lifted. Writes Hubin, "They will recognize that the possibility of their having children (and caring about their children in this way) makes it possible that in real life they will have a direct and vital interest in the conditions under which the subsequent generation lives."[18] It is worse not to have saved for future generations and wind up as someone who cares about their children's inheritance of resources than it is to have saved and wind up as someone who doesn't care about future generations. Rawlsian contractors acting to avoid the worst outcome will choose a savings principle, argues Hubin. However, Hubin notes that a savings principle justified by his argument will be weaker than one justified by Rawls's argument since Hubin's argument relies on the actual concern of parents for their children and grandchildren and that concern probably does not extend beyond a few generations.

Some people may object that Hubin's answer reintroduces the heads-of-families assumption since it relies on the contractors reasoning as heads of families would. But this is to misunderstand Hubin's suggestion. All Hubin needs is for the contractors to consider the *possibility* that they may be heads of families once the veil is lifted. This is consistent both with the contractors also considering that they may not be heads of households and with the function the veil is supposed to serve. It does not reintroduce the heads-of-families assumption.

In *Political Liberalism,* Rawls's characterization of the contractors changes dramatically. Rather than being "us" in any sense, we are told to think of the contractors in the original position as "our representatives." Rawls writes, "The parties in this position are described as rationally autonomous representatives of citizens in society."[19] He removes the stipulation that the representatives care for their descendants, or more properly, the descendants of those whom they represent, while retaining the present time of entry interpretation of the original position.[20] Instead, Rawls adopts a solution to the problem of justice for future generations that he credits to Jane English, Derek Parfit, and Thomas Nagel. Rawls claims that the contractors must choose a principle of just savings that they would want previous generations to have adopted.[21]

1.6. Counting Children In

Which solution to the problem of justice for future generations is correct? We do not attempt to resolve this question in this chapter. Instead, we assume in what follows that one of the above solutions is correct and that Rawls can secure some level of savings for future generations without the heads-of-families assumption. The next move is to see what can be gained in terms of accounting for children by not conceiving of the parties in the original position as heads of families. We can now ask whether there are answers to the problem of children that come from within Rawls's theory or that are at least consistent with Rawls's theory.

What are some alternatives to conceiving of the contractors as parents? If the contractors are representatives of individuals (as Rawls says in *Political Liberalism*) rather than representatives of families (as he says in *A Theory of Justice*), can children be included as parties to the social contract? The contrast between Rawls's theory with other contractarian theories is sharp when the characterization of individuals in the original position is considered. According to many other contemporary contractarian theories, the contractors reach agreement by bargaining in full knowledge of their abilities and powers. In these theories, the options for dealing with children are clear: Either children count as parties to the contract, or they do not. And in most cases they do not. The chief difficulty in including children in a contractarian account without the benefit of the veil of ignorance is motivational. Why would we (adults) need to make deals with children? From a purely self-interested point of view, what do they have to offer us? Suppose they did have something to offer that outweighed the costs of feeding and clothing them (say, their future investment in a pension plan to fund our retirements) and that this alternative was superior to other arrangements we might pursue (say, investing directly into our own pension plans), why would we believe that they are rationally able to follow through on their deals?

But for Rawls the issue is murkier. With the contractors conceived of as individuals stripped of their individual identities (according to *A Theory of Justice*) or as representatives ignorant of certain facts about the parties they represent (according to *Political Liberalism*), it is not so clear what it would even *mean* for Rawls to include children. Consider the contrast with including women as contractors. Okin suggests that Rawls leave aside the assumption that the parties in the original position are heads of families. Instead, they are to be individuals, both men and women. For Rawls, one's sex is assumed to be something about which a contractor in the original position would be ignorant. And so it would appear that there is no difficulty thinking of women as parties in the original position. However, Okin notes that some feminist theorists have argued that women are different from men in their moral reasoning. If this view of differences in moral reasoning is correct, making the contractors ignorant of their sex will not be sufficient for using Rawls's contract device to deal with justice between the genders. We can either allow both styles of reasoning to be present, which would defeat the purpose of the veil of ignorance, or we can allow only one style of reasoning and assuming that standard is the male standard, leave women out. One might think that this problem is resolved when we move to thinking of the contractors as representatives. But it is not. The same problem re-arises, only this time it concerns the gender of the representatives or their knowledge of which genders they represent.

Adding children as parties to the contract is even more difficult. The claim usually made about children and rationality is not simply that they reason differently but that they are not fully rational. If we imagine some of the parties to the contract being children, when we put them behind the veil and take away knowledge of their age, what we are left with are less than fully rational agents. Without rationality it seems we are also without the normative force of the contract argument, for we do not generally think that decisions made by irrational agents have standing. Adding an idealizing assumption that they are fully rational while abstracting facts about their age negates any positive impact of adding children as parties in the original position.[22]

A related problem is that for Rawls, the role the contract plays in his theory is not strictly foundational.[23] Rather, the original position is put forward as a heuristic devise designed to formalize our thinking about justice. It is meant to support, rather than replace, the intuitive argument for his preferred principles of justice. The constraints on the original position are meant to be ones that we would recognize as legitimate constraints on moral reasoning. Rawls describes the original position as a "natural guide to intuition" and writes that "it is important that the original position be interpreted so that one can at any time adopt its perspective."[24] We are to use the original position as a tool of moral reasoning by adopting the standpoint of a party in the original position. What would it mean to adopt the standpoint of a child contractor or to think of oneself as the representative of a child in the original position?

Perhaps what is required is, not that one reason as a child, but that one consider now what one would want if one were a child, using the reasoning powers one possesses as an adult, or in the case of the representative, consider what the child would want were he or she to reason as an adult. In this model, an adult reasoner is considering what is in a child's interests but is not reasoning as a child to find that out. Is this a standpoint that could be imported into Rawls's original position? In *A Theory of Justice*, Rawls assumes that the point of entry for the contractors is "during the age of reason."[25] So in his view, the parties in the original position know they will be adults when the veil is lifted. If we take away this assumption (for which Rawls himself offers no arguments), then once the veil is lifted, the parties might be at any stage in their life, from baby to teenager, from young parent to senior citizen.[26] The contractors would be forced to consider a whole-life, cradle-to-grave, view of their lives. In this revised Rawlsian version of the social contract, we think about what the world would be like, under various principles of justice, if we were at any stage in the life of any member of our society.[27] The result is that the contractors would have to consider the possibility that they might be children, or even newborn babies, once the veil is lifted. Considering this possibility will motivate the contractors to make sure that such people are cared for properly.

One objection to this position might be that persons in the original position would figure out that they are not really children by noticing how sophisticated the reasoning was that they were engaging in. But this would be to misunderstand the veil of ignorance; the veil is really no more than a way of dramatizing a logical constraint on the kinds of arguments that can be properly used in determining whether or not a proposed principle of justice is in one's interest when this determination is taking place in the original position. The reasoning, "This principle benefits children and I am an adult so this principle is not in my interest," is excluded by the veil because of the "I am an adult" premise.[28] In the representative model, this is even simpler to understand. The representative is a rational agent who does not know whose interests are represented, those of a child or those of an adult.

Clearly, the answer to the problem of justice for children proposed here is not Rawls's view. But could a consistent Rawlsian accept this change in the construction of the original position? Something like this way of thinking seems to be behind Rawls's reasoning about appropriate restrictions on liberty. In a discussion of paternalism, Rawls writes that "we must choose for others as we have reason to believe they would choose for themselves if they were at the age of reason and deciding rationally."[29] That is to say, the right choice for a child is the choice a rational adult would have wanted made for himself or herself as a child were he or she in a position to so choose.

Some who are concerned with children's moral status will not be satisfied. If the moral rules governing children are those decided on by rational agents, is this not equivalent to saying that children do not count and that adults do? To put the question differently, Are contractarian theories that assume the contractors to be rational inherently paternalistic?

To respond to this objection we need to distinguish between paternalism at the level of moral principles and at the foundational level.[30] A theory can be based on the deliberations of fully rational agents while containing requirements of justice that protect those who are less than fully rational. Such a theory may, in one sense and on one level, exclude children while offering the best treatment of children's concerns on another level. In the parties as representatives interpretation of the original position, the same foundational paternalism applies as well, since our representatives not only do not know who we are but presumably are more rational than we are. There is no fundamental asymmetry between the Rawlsian account of adults and that of children: There is a sort of foundational paternalism with regard to each which is embodied in the idea that parties to the original position are rational (either because they are idealizations of us or because they are rational representatives of us). And so to the extent that such a theory is paternalistic, the paternalism is a good thing, getting right one of the most important insights of contractarian thinking, namely, that there is an important connection between what rational agents would choose for themselves and the requirements of justice. Using the revised version of the original position, we can make sense of what this claim means for children.

In conclusion, while Rawls leaves children out of his conclusions about justice, it seems that a consistent, alternative Rawlsian account can count them in. We have said nothing about what would follow as requirements of justice were the contractors to reason the way we have suggested. Working out the details and implications of such an account is, of course, a much larger project, which we cannot pursue here. Instead, we turn now to the part of Rawls's theory where children are discussed, his account of stability.

2. Stability, the Child's Sense of Justice, and the Parochialism of *Political Liberalism*

Rawls's argument for justice as fairness has two parts. In the first, he argues that the two principles of justice (the principle of greatest equal liberty and the difference principle) are fair because they would be chosen by free and equal persons from a fair and equal starting point. In the second part, he argues that the two principles are "stable," that they are psychologically workable and appropriate for real persons outside the original position. Part of this argument rests on a conception of childhood and the moral development of children. This part of the chapter examines the theory of childhood moral development Rawls endorses in *A Theory of Justice* and asks three questions about it. First, what is the role of this material in *A Theory of Justice?* Second, is it neglected in *Political Liberalism?* Third, would it have been worth emphasizing it more rather than less?

In the first part of his argument, Rawls uses the original position to show that the two principles would be chosen from a fair initial starting point by rational free and equal beings who are not motivated by envy. He claims, however, that this is not enough to show that the two principles are superior to competing conceptions of justice. In addition, we need to ask "whether the well-ordered society corresponding to the conception adopted [by the parties to the original position] will actually generate feelings of envy and patterns of psychological attitudes that will undermine the arrangements it counts to be just."[31]

To understand the second part of Rawls's argument,[32] one must understand two crucial theoretical notions: stability and a sense of justice. Roughly, a conception of justice is stable in Rawls's sense only if people would have a disposition to adhere to it and to support the institutions that it endorses. To be stable, a conception of justice must be capable of gaining our allegiance, of providing us with motivation to support the institutions it endorses. Rawls defines a "sense of justice" as "a normally effective desire to apply and to act upon the principles of justice." If we can internalize and become willing to act upon a conception of justice, then we have acquired a sense of justice corresponding that conception.

Rawls wants to show that actual persons could acquire a conception of justice corresponding to the two principles of justice. That is, he wants to argue that they could accept the two principles of justice both as just constraints on their actions and as part of their own good. It is in the context of this part of the project that Rawls discusses the moral development of children. If children would in fact acquire this sense of justice, this desire to act on the two principles of justice, then a society founded on those principles would be stable.

Rawls endorses an approach to child moral development that is inspired by the cognitive-development theories of moral development advocated by Jean Piaget and Lawrence Kohlberg.[33] According to Rawls, children in a just society will normally go through three distinct stages in the development of their sense of justice.[34] He calls the first stage "the morality of authority." In this stage, the child is utterly helpless and completely dependent on the parent. This dependency has at least two aspects. First, the child depends on the parent for his or her very existence, so that it is necessary to secure the good graces of the parent for survival.[35] The child also depends on the parent for guidance,[36] for the parent is the sole source of information as to what is and is not advisable and prudent, about how the world works and how to get along in it. At this point, the child has no basis on which to question the injunctions of the parent, and this dependence is one fundamental fact about early childhood.

A second fundamental fact about (typical) childhood is that the child is loved by the parent. Rawls posits the psychological principle—a "first psychological law"—that a child who is loved will respond with love.[37] This love is an important new factor in the life of the child, and it has three important effects. First, because the child recognizes that the person on whom she depends does in fact love her, she comes to trust the parent. This trust strengthens her tendency to respect and obey the commands of the parent, presumably because she comes to realize that the parent's commands are for the benefit of the child. Second, and perhaps more important, the child comes to desire to be like the parent, and part of being like the parent consists of using the parent's standards to judge herself.[38] The familiar childhood propensity to try to "act grown up" involves (among other things) internalizing the standards of behavior of the adult whom she loves and on whose guidance and protection she relies. Third, when the child disobeys the parent's commands (which, as Rawls notes, is inevitable), she will feel guilt at having disappointed the parent, whom she loves. The content of the morality of the child at this stage is simply a collection of the commands of the parent, which often seem arbitrary from the child's limited point of view and which are obeyed in an effort to please and to be like the parent. For Rawls, the essence of this morality of authority is that "there is typically an authoritative person who is loved and trusted, or at least who is accepted as worthy of his position, and whose precepts it is one's duty to follow implicitly. . . . The prized virtues are obedience, humility and fidelity to authoritative persons; the leading vices are disobedience, self-will, and temerity."[39]

Readers of Piaget will recognize that Rawls's morality of authority is extremely close to Piaget's "morality of heteronomy." Piaget describes this first stage as consisting of "unilateral respect of the little child who receives a command without even the possibility of disagreement."[40] Yet this respect is also tinged with affection, so that the child feels that "a mutual sympathy surrounds relationships that are most heavily charged with authority."[41] Indeed, he claims that this "spontaneous mutual affection" between child and parent "no doubt is the starting point for that morality of the good" that is the product of cooperation in the second stage.[42] Rawls also borrows Piaget's emphasis on imitation[43] and his observation that from the point of view of young children much of the totality of the parent's commands will seem arbitrary.[44] Rawls's first principle of moral psychology also looks very similar to a rule that Piaget endorses: "The feeling of obligation only appears when the child accepts a command emanating from someone he respects."[45] Finally, compare Rawls's summary of the virtues and vices of this stage with Piaget's: "Right is to obey the will of the adult. Wrong is to have a will of one's own."[46]

Both Rawls and Piaget endorse the same basic picture of the child's nature. The child has certain dispositions, most notably, the disposition to love someone who loves her, and the disposition to imitate, obey, and judge oneself by the standards used by the one who is loved and respected. These dispositions are all postulated as more or less basic facts about young children rather than dispositions that must be "trained into" them through conditioning, reward, and punishment.[47] These basic dispositions are the stuff of later moral development. Morality (or, for Rawls, at least the sense of justice) is not a set of sui generis dispositions forced onto an otherwise amoral child, but, rather, it is something that is built out of these already existing dispositions. The trick for such accounts of children's moral development is to show how a moral sense (or, in Rawls's case, a "sense of justice")[48] can arise from these basic dispositions.

Rawls and Piaget accomplish this trick by appealing to the experience of being a part of a cooperative association with others. This occurs in what Rawls calls "the morality of association" and what Piaget calls "the morality of cooperation." Association, Rawls notes, pervades the life of a child. There are associations involved in activities such as games as well as those with fellow students once the child is in school. And as the child matures and passes out of the first stage, she comes to see the family itself as an association. These associations, and the cooperative activities in which they engage, spark the development of the child's sense of justice; the skills the child learns as she cooperates are the building blocks of the morality of association. To explain how this occurs, Rawls postulates a second psychological law: "As individuals enter the association . . . they acquire . . . attachments when others of longer standing membership do their part and live up to the ideals of their station." In this way, "bonds of mutual trust and friendship develop among them."[49]

Once these ties are established, the same dynamics that caused the child to obey the commands and internalize the standards of the parent are transferred to the group. Because the group's activities benefit its members, the members acquire a desire to "honor one's obligations and duties . . . as a form of good will."[50] This process is much the same as the one that produces in the child the desire to obey the commands of the parent. In addition, just as the parent becomes a role model for the child, so too will the child find role models within the group, persons who do an exemplary job of filling the role assigned to them by the group. These role models arouse the child's innate desire to imitate, causing the child to further internalize the standards of the group by imitating those who conform to them.

The imitation of role models, both in the family and in other social groups, does more than simply account for the internalization of the group's standards. It also develops certain cognitive skills that are necessary for a sense of justice. Imitating a role model requires that the child learn to view the world from the perspective of another person. Initially, the child's "ability to put himself in [others'] places is still untutored," but this "lack is gradually overcome as we assume a succession of more demanding roles with their more demanding schemes of rights and duties [which] require us to view things from a greater multiplicity of perspectives."[51]

The ability to see things from the point of view of another, along with the attachment to the group, creates a "morality of association in which the members of society view one another as equals, as friends and associates, joined together in a system of cooperation known to be for the advantage of all and governed by a common conception of justice."[52] This morality consists of "the cooperative virtues: those of justice and fairness, fidelity and trust, integrity and impartiality" and denounces the vices of "graspingness and unfairness, dishonesty and deceit, prejudice and bias."[53] It is a direct and apparently inevitable result of cooperation within an association; it is "*bound to exist* once we become attached to those cooperating with us in a just (or fair) scheme."[54]

Again, the similarities with Piaget are worth noting. Piaget emphasizes that cooperation drives the development of genuine morality (which he calls the morality of autonomy): "Adult authority . . . is not in itself sufficient to create a sense of justice. This can develop only through the progress made by cooperation and mutual respect"[55] Indeed, the basic idea of what goes on in this stage is virtually the same in Rawls and Piaget. For both Rawls and Piaget, learning to cooperate develops the child's ability and desire to participate in cooperative associations. Piaget develops and supports this idea through an extensive study of one of the primary cooperative activities of children: the playing of games. According to Piaget, children's game playing produces a crucial effect, the transformation of the idea of a rule as an arbitrary command to the idea of a rule as a "necessary condition for agreement."[56] Furthermore—and this is highly relevant for Rawls's project—the development of the consciousness of rules as being necessary for agreement (and therefore cooperation) is correlated with respect for and compliance with those rules.[57] Apparently, as children see that the rules of games make cooperation possible, and as they develop the desire to cooperate with others, they come to respect the rules that make cooperation possible. In other words, the conception of rules as governing "systems of cooperation" (as Rawls would say) seems to play a part in the child's coming to have a desire to abide by those rules.

Rawls goes on to postulate a third and final stage in which the child comes to desire to comply with the principles of justice purely out of respect for them "as principles" rather than because of "ties of friendship and fellow feeling for others, and . . . concern for the approbation of the wider society."[58] To explain this transfer of motives, Rawls postulates a third psychological law: "We develop a desire to apply and to act upon the principles of justice once we realize how social arrangements answering to them have promoted our good and that of those with whom we are affiliated."[59] This third stage, then, involves the generalization of the sense of justice acquired in the second stage. It allows for the building of much larger cooperative arrangements than could be possible simply on the basis of fellow feeling. Rawls writes: "While every citizen is a friend to some citizens, no citizen is a friend to all. But their common allegiance to justice provides a unified perspective from which they can adjudicate their differences."[60]

The basic picture that emerges from Rawls, which we can fill out by looking at the work of Piaget and Kohlberg (from which it is clearly drawn), is that cooperation brings about two main psychological developments: the ability to see things from the point of view of others and the ability and desire to participate in fair systems of cooperation and to do one's part as a member of such a system. This is exactly what Rawls needs if he is to demonstrate how the sense of justice, the ability and willingness to abide by principles that are fair, would arise in a just society. The ability to transcend one's own perspective and adopt another perspective is necessary for the kind of reasoning for which the original position is a metaphor. And the ability and desire to participate in fair systems of cooperation are necessary for stability.

The cognitive-development picture of moral learning that Rawls endorses has been the subject of much controversy. Kohlberg, in particular, has come under attack both by psychologists and by philosophers. Kohlberg's most well-known critic is, of course, Carol Gilligan.[61] She claims that Kohlberg's work was male biased both experimentally (because he used only male subjects) and conceptually (because it was based on what she sees as a masculine conception of morality). Many philosophers and psychologists have also questioned Kohlberg's assumption that the later stages are "better," or more adequate, or more accurately reflect moral reality.

These attacks on Kohlberg's work—as important and powerful as they are—do not call into question the basic tenets of the cognitive-development approach to moral development theory that Rawls needs for his purposes. Thus, these attacks need not force Rawls to abandon his approach to childhood moral psychology. The parts of cognitive-development theory on which Rawls relies are not the parts that have become so controversial.[62] All Rawls *really* needs to claim is that there is a pattern of development that includes the morality of cooperation[63] and that this morality of cooperation is the foundation of the sense of justice.

Apparently, then, Rawls can take the least controversial (and some would add, the best) ideas of Piaget and Kohlberg and put them to work in his theory. For Rawls's purposes, the most important part of Kohlberg's work is his empirical claim that the development of the willingness and ability to cooperate is a normal part of childhood. Rawls could draw little else from Kohlberg's theory. For Rawls's purposes, Piaget's most crucial idea is the conceptual analysis of what cooperation requires. This comes out most clearly in Piaget's conceptual analysis of the reasoning that must go on in games in order for there to even be a game. One of Piaget's most important insights about moral development is that the kinds of reasoning necessary for morality are present in games. The basic results of this conceptual analysis are twofold. First, in games, one must learn to participate cooperatively with others even if they have different, perhaps even opposing, goals. Second, what counts as fairness in a game is what could be endorsed from an impartial perspective rather than what is good from one's own perspective. In the end, Rawls really needs only the empirical observation that children play games, coupled with Piaget's insights as to what kinds of reasoning are necessary to play a game, in order to give his theory the kind of stability argument he needs.

These two crucial but fairly plausible claims from cognitive-development psychology are all Rawls needs to support his claim that cooperation naturally leads to a sense of justice, which includes that ability to engage in the kind of impartial reasoning that is the cornerstone of the original position and the desire to act on the basis of that impartial (fair) reasoning. In short, these two basic claims imply that it is indeed possible for children to develop a disposition to engage in and abide by arrangements that embody fair systems of cooperation. This, in turn, provides good evidence that the conception of justice as the principles appropriate for governing a fair system of cooperation is indeed stable, that it could, in fact, generate support in the form of motives among the citizens to support the institutions it counts as fair.

Now that we've explored the role that childhood plays in *A Theory of Justice,* let us turn to *Political Liberalism.* The first thing to notice is that *Political Liberalism* contains no discussion whatsoever about childhood. This is surprising for two reasons. First, the main aim and raison d'être of *Political Liberalism* is to correct what Rawls had come to see as flaws in the stability argument.[64] Since the material on child moral development played a key role in that argument, it is surprising not to see much mention of it in *Political Liberalism.* Second, since the theory of child development on which Rawls relies in *A Theory of Justice* became extremely controversial, it is rather surprising that Rawls did not feel compelled to comment on the controversy.

To see why the account of the moral development of children does not figure prominently in *Political Liberalism,* we have to look carefully at the question of stability. It turns out that the issue of stability involves *two* questions. The first is whether and how we become motivated to support the institutions that justice as fairness endorses. Rawls's solution involves the story about how we acquire our sense of justice (that is, the motivation to support just institutions), and that story involves the moral psychology of childhood. The second question is whether the motivation supplied by our sense of justice would be overpowered by competing motivation supplied by our conception of the good. The theory of the child's development of the sense of justice is intended to show that we would have *some* motivation to endorse just institutions. But we are also (often very strongly) motivated to pursue our conception of the good. What keeps this motivation from overpowering the motivation supplied by the sense of justice? This question has two answers, one in *A Theory of Justice* and one in *Political Liberalism.* The *Theory of Justice* answer is that justice is "congruent" with "our" good. The new answer, in *Political Liberalism,* is that the principles of justice are subject to an overlapping consensus of comprehensive doctrines.

Political Liberalism, in fact, was written largely to work out problems with the older version of the answer to this second question about stability. The new answer (and thus *Political Liberalism* itself) is driven by what Rawls calls "the fact of pluralism of reasonable comprehensive doctrines."[65] Roughly, this is the fact that there are and always will be a variety of religious, philosophical, and moral doctrines in any modern pluralistic liberal democracy. This fact forces Rawls to develop a new solution to the second problem of stability, for he cannot appeal to the fact that we recognize that justice as fairness is "congruent" with "our" good because we do not agree about what that good is: There is no single conception of the good that we all share. But the fact of reasonable pluralism has little obvious effect on the first question about stability, the one involving the development of the sense of justice.

In a passage concerning the first question about stability (the one to which the sense of justice and the moral development of children is relevant), Rawls characterizes stability as a condition in which "citizens act willingly so as to give one another justice over time. Stability is secured by sufficient motivation of the appropriate kind acquired under just institutions." In a footnote to this passage, Rawls adds: "How this happens I have discussed in *Theory,* esp. chap. VIII. I hope that account suffices, for our purposes here, to convey the main idea."[66] Clearly, then, Rawls does not actually reject his theory of childhood moral development to answer this first question about stability; in fact, he reendorses it. But while it is true that *Political Liberalism* is largely concerned with stability, and while it is true that the child development material is a key to the stability problem, the material plays no significant role in *Political Liberalism.* The reason for this apparent neglect is that there are two parts to the stability question and *Political Liberalism* is concerned with the second. This, then, is why there is only the slightest reference to child development in this later work: *Political Liberalism* is an attempt to work out a new answer to the *second* question about stability, and the material about child psychology is relevant only to the first question.

Or is it? Is Rawls's account of child development relevant *only* to the first question of stability? Could it also be deployed to help solve the second stability problem as well as the first?

To answer the second question about stability, Rawls appeals to the notion of an overlapping consensus of reasonable comprehensive doctrines.[67] For a conception of justice to be subject to such an overlapping consensus is for each of those doctrines to affirm it for its own reasons and in its own way. It may seem at first glance that the way to figure out whether some political conception could be the focus of an overlapping consensus would be to look at all the reasonable comprehensive doctrines and see what they could affirm. But Rawls rejects this methodology. He claims that we must derive the necessary materials, not from the particular reasonable comprehensive doctrines themselves, but from general facts that will apply to all those who hold *reasonable* doctrines in the societies toward which *Political Liberalism* is addressed: "We do not look at the comprehensive doctrines that in fact exist and then draw up a political conception that strikes some kind of balance of forces between them. . . . Rather, it [political liberalism] elaborates a political conception as a freestanding view working from the fundamental idea of society as a fair system of cooperation. . . . The *hope* is that this idea . . . can be the focus of a reasonable overlapping consensus."[68]

In other words, Rawls assumes that each reasonable comprehensive doctrine will, in fact, affirm certain core ideas (most notably the idea of society as a system of fair cooperation between free and equal persons). He conceives his project in *Political Liberalism* as one of building up a political conception of justice out of those core ideas. If he succeeds, the conception of justice should be capable of winning an overlapping consensus, since it will be an articulation of values that each reasonable comprehensive doctrine endorses.

How does Rawls know what core values the reasonable comprehensive doctrines will endorse? The answer to this question reveals much about Rawlsian methodology and the parochialism of the theory of justice, especially as presented in *Political Liberalism:* "Justice as fairness starts *from within a certain political tradition* and takes as its fundamental idea that of society as a fair system of cooperation."[69] The fundamental ideas from which *Political Liberalism* is built are "implicit in the political culture of a democratic society."[70]

Rawls assumes (or, perhaps, hopes) that the history of a pluralistic society will be the source of these shared ideas on which an overlapping consensus is built: As people learn that they have little choice but to live together with people with whom they disagree, they will often over time come genuinely to espouse the virtues of toleration, free faith, reasonableness, and, in effect, the idea of society as a cooperative venture between free and equal people on fair terms.[71] It is this history of toleration in a pluralistic society that Rawls sees as the source of the shared ideas which *Political Liberalism* develops into a conception of justice that he hopes will be the focus of an overlapping consensus of reasonable comprehensive doctrines.

In effect, then, Rawls's answer to the stability problem involves a kind of bootstrapping. He sets out to solve the stability problem, that is, to explain how a well-ordered democratic society can exist given reasonable pluralism. To do this, he appeals to the fund of shared public culture of a democratic pluralistic society. Apparently, he aims to solve the stability problem by reference to the shared understandings of a society that has already achieved some sort of stability.[72] This near circularity makes the theory parochial because it is appropriate for and directed toward a very particular kind of society—namely, constitutional liberal democracies with shared traditions of toleration. Indeed, Rawls is quite candid in his admission of this parochialism. This admission will no doubt please some communitarian critics who have (probably incorrectly) seen *A Theory of Justice* as attempting to articulate universally valid political principles.[73] But those who think of liberalism as a political system that is good for more than just liberals are likely to find this parochialism rather disappointing.

Rawls assumes, then, that the basic concepts on which his theory is based will be generally available only to members of a certain kind of society with a certain kind of history. But this seems rather pessimistic, for there is good reason to hope that the basic concepts necessary for Rawlsian liberalism might be derivable from *universal* features of society and human psychology, including the psychology of childhood moral development. If so, then political liberalism may not be nearly as parochial as Rawls seems to think. If there is something universal (or at least very widely applicable) in Piaget's basic theory, then Rawls's theory could be founded on concepts that psychology (virtually?) *guarantees* that we will all have (and find motivating) rather than on concepts that only members of certain societies will have. Cooperation is surely a universal aspect of human life, and learning to cooperate is a universal part of childhood. If the earliest experiences of cooperation lead a child to develop a certain kind of moral outlook, and if that outlook is the fundamental idea of the theory of justice, then that theory may not be nearly as parochial as Rawls claims.

Whether or not cooperation is in fact universal, and whether or not it has the effects on the child's moral outlook that Piaget, Kohlberg, and Rawls claim, are surely empirical questions. This is not the proper forum to settle such questions, but if the data turn out the way Piaget and Kohlberg hope, then cognitive-development theory may provide the sort of grounding necessary for a Rawlsian overlapping consensus *without* having to assume the existence of shared liberal traditions, the stability of which is precisely what we are trying to explain.

There is good reason to think that cooperation requires—as a *conceptual* matter—certain abilities and attitudes on which a moral theory of justice might be grounded. Cooperation can take place only with the agreement of those involved. This seems just to be a conceptual fact about what it is to cooperate. If all normal children learn to cooperate, then the idea of agreement being necessary for a cooperative enterprise is a concept all normal children acquire. This is a key concept on which the Rawlsian theory is based, so it seems fairly promising to attempt to ground justice as fairness in features of child development that are common to all children. This is not the same as grounding the theory in universal principles appropriate to all rational beings. Nor is it the same as grounding the theory in value-neutral premises. But it is far less parochial than building the theory on the public culture of a specific sort of society with a specific kind of history. If Piaget's conceptual analysis of cooperation and Kohlberg's data are even approximately correct, then there is reason to be optimistic about the prospect of grounding political liberalism in facts about typical, if not universal, human psychological development.

There is another way to see how a theory of child moral development might be far more useful to the Rawlsian project than Rawls may realize. Rawls's account of stability depends on the reasonableness of the people in the society, that is, on their willingness to cooperate even with those who hold comprehensive doctrines different from their own. Reasonable people will have reasonable comprehensive doctrines, and those will endorse, each in its own way in an overlapping consensus, the political conception of justice. This conception of justice, claims Rawls, will embody a conception of society as a fair system of cooperation among free and equal persons who may or may not share one's comprehensive doctrine. Whether an overlapping consensus affirming this conception is possible depends on whether the people are reasonable.

Rawls addresses the relatively simple problem of getting "reasonable" people—people who realize that it is unreasonable to attempt to coerce others to accept their comprehensive doctrines—to endorse the principles of justice as fairness, which articulate the value of cooperation even among those who hold differing comprehensive views. But the *hard* problem is to get unreasonable "true believers" to subscribe to a tolerant system. Rawls sidesteps this problem by limiting his theory to societies dominated by persons holding reasonable comprehensive doctrines.[74]

But perhaps the theory of moral development can help. Suppose that children develop a conception of cooperative fairness early on. If an ideal of reasonableness could be articulated to them as being a consequence of a basic kind of cooperative fairness that they already endorse, then they might tend to develop reasonable versions of their comprehensive doctrines. Indeed, Piaget's work on games provides us with a model for the reasonable response to cases in which fair and impartial judgments from the point of view of the original position clash with our own comprehensive doctrines. Piaget points out that in (competitive) games, what I want qua competitor has to be subordinated to what I want qua person who wants to play the game. This sort of situation is parallel to the second stability problem: What I want qua reasoner in the original position conflicts with what I want qua proponent of some comprehensive doctrine. This sort of lesson, one might hope, could be applied to the wider social context, making children more likely to realize that they can endorse a cooperative arrangement with people whose goals differ from their own, much as one does when one plays a game.

This possibility could have enormous theoretical and practical implications. It might help extend Rawls's work on stability from the easy problem of getting reasonable people to endorse justice as fairness to the hard problem of getting unreasonable people to do so. It also might help set an agenda for public civic education: If the conception of reasonableness as cooperating even with those who have differing beliefs and goals and of society as a cooperative endeavor can be articulated and reinforced in the school and in the community, then the influence of unreasonable comprehensive doctrines could perhaps be moderated.

If this is right, then Rawls may not have needed to qualify his theory of moral development to apply only to children in a just society. For even in unjust societies there will be cooperative arrangements. If the basic building blocks for liberalism are present in cooperation, then there is reason to hope that a liberal sense of justice could in fact arise in children, even in unjust societies. Whether or not such a hope is justified is an interesting and potentially vital question. In part, though, the answer depends on empirical facts that we do not yet have.[75] The importance of the answer is such, however, that we should press ahead both in moral psychology and in moral and political philosophy until we do know the answer. Until we do, it seems somewhat pessimistic to assume, as Rawls seems to, that a liberal sense of justice could arise only in liberal societies.

It is probably true that the particular institutions and rules Rawls argues for are best suited to societies with a certain history and certain traditions. But does that mean that the basic idea of the original position, that justice is founded on the fair conditions of cooperation, is culture bound? If (virtually) all children learn to cooperate, then in what sense is a theory that builds on the universal features of cooperation culture specific? Of course, the outcome of the original position procedure, and perhaps some of the details of its formulation, might be culture specific, but why think that the basic idea of a pluralistic society as a fair system of cooperation must be? If the basic principles at the heart of liberalism appeal to values that we all learn as children, then there is good reason to hope that the idea of liberal society is not culturally specific, that it can appeal to those who are not already liberals. A popular book holds that everything one needs to know one learns in kindergarten. That is no doubt an overstatement, but perhaps the basic values to which liberalism appeals are, in fact, learned then. This, of course, is not to directly repudiate anything that Rawls says in *Political Liberalism*. It is to ask whether *Political Liberalism* would be a more powerful, less parochial theory if Rawls had not neglected childhood.

Acknowledgments

Although this chapter is a joint project, Samantha Brennan is primarily responsible for section 1, and Robert Noggle is primarily responsible for section 2. Brennan thanks Jim Ketchen and Elaine Brown for research assistance and the University of Western Ontario, London, Ontario, for financial support during the time this chapter was written. She also thanks colleagues Michael Milde, Tracy Isaacs, and Bob Binkley for helpful comments on earlier drafts. Portions of the second section were presented at the 1997 meeting of the American Philosophical Association (APA) at Berkeley, California, and the 1996 meeting of the Florida Philosophical Association. Noggle thanks Nancy Snow for her comments at the APA presentation, as well as members of both audiences for comments and suggestions.

Notes

1. Although the moral status of children and the duties we owe to them are different issues than the issue of family justice, they are linked in more ways than the obvious connection that many families contain children. The more interesting connection is that the same feature of Rawls's argument in *A Theory of Justice* (1971) that makes it impossible for him to address family justice also makes it impossible for him to account for children. For a critical discussion of Rawls and family justice as it relates to *A Theory of Justice*, see Okin 1989, chapter 5. For a discussion of these themes in Rawls's later work, especially *Political Liberalism* (1993), see Okin 1994.

2. For an alternative contractarian account of justice, see Narveson 1988. The contrast is interesting because Narveson recognizes the importance of the challenge children pose for contractarianism. Devoting an entire chapter, "The Problem of Children," to the issue, Narveson comes down on the side of denying that children have any moral status. One can disagree with Narveson's conclusions while at the same time applaud his recognition of the question as important and pressing.

3. Rawls 1971, 128, 146. Although Rawls uses these terms interchangeably, one might think that there are important differences between them. The connotation of "head of family" is that an authority figure (usually male), whereas "family representative" has no gendered connotation and suggests a more democratic model of the family. For the purposes of this chapter, the similarity between the terms matters more than the differences and so "heads of families" has been adopted as Rawls, and his commentators, use it more often.

4. Writes Okin, "Thus the 'heads of families' assumption, far from being neutral or innocent, has the effect of banishing a large sphere of human life . . . from the scope of the theory" (Okin, 1989, 95).

5. Rawls 1971, 137.

6. Rawls 1971, 140.

7. Rawls 1971, 292.

8. English 1977, 95.

9. Wright and Leroux 1991.

10. One can raise the motivational worry more generally with Rawls's requirement that reasoning in the original position take place behind a veil of ignorance.

11. For a defense of the claim that any duties we may have to future persons are not requirements of justice because they cannot be *correlative duties,* see Steiner 1994, 259–61.

12. This error is reinforced by popular politics. A great deal of sloganeering in favor of various environmental measures goes on in the name of concern for children.

13. English 1977 and Hubin 1976.

14. This simplifies English's position somewhat. According to English, Rawls could justify a short-term savings principle from the original position since among those currently living are people from three or four generations. She also worries that a short-term savings principle is all that the heads-of-families assumption can justify since the natural ties of concern between generations do not extend beyond three or four generations.

15. English 1977, 99.

16. Rawls 1971, 138.

17. Rawls 1971, 138.

18. Hubin 1976, 76.

19. Rawls 1993, 305.

20. Rawls 1993, 20 n. 22 and 274 n. 12. It is ironic that Rawls drops this assumption without ceremony given the amount that has been written by feminist political philosophers and others critical of the assumption and its implications.

21. Dropping the heads-of-families assumption does not lead to Rawls's addressing the issue of justice in and for families. Okin 1994 argues that although Rawls explicitly includes the family as one of the basic institutions of society, and hence, part of the proper subject matter of justice, he retains the idea that the family is more properly governed by affection than justice. This issue is pursued further here. What matters for our purposes is that without the heads-of-households assumption, he *could* have addressed the question of justice and children even if he, in fact, does not.

22. See O'Neill 1993.

23. This is made especially clear in the articles written by Rawls after the publication of *A Theory of Justice* and in his more recent book *Political Liberalism*.

24. Rawls 1971, 139.

25. Rawls 1971, 146.

26. Rawls himself writes in *Political Liberalism* that we should think of the terms of social cooperation as applying to members of society over "a complete life" (Rawls 1993, 20). So while he nowhere considers children explicitly, childhood is clearly part of everyone's complete life.

27. Further, given the account in English 1977, we must consider that we might be alive at any time in the history of our community.

28. I owe this objection and the response to my colleague Bob Brinkley.

29. Rawls 1971, 209.

30. For a useful discussion of the various levels in moral theory, see Kagan 1992.

31. Rawls 1971, 531; see also Rawls 1971, 144; compare Rawls 1993, 140ff., esp. 140 n. 7 where he makes the second part of this two-step procedure a bit clearer: "In the second part they ask whether a society well ordered by the principles selected in the first part would be stable: that is, generate in its members a sufficiently strong sense of justice to counteract tendencies to injustice." The connection between envy and stability seems to be that if a person's sense of justice provides her with motives to adhere to the institutions of a just society in spite of any envy that might arise, and if the conception of justice on which society is founded is congruent with her conception of the good, then envy should not arise since she will see the society ordered as it is by the principles of justice as being in one's own interest.

32. Rawls 1971, 505; see also 312. Technically, the decision about whether the conception is workable takes place in the original position, the idea being that workability is one of the things that the parties to the original position would want in a conception of justice. Quotation in this paragraph is from Rawls 1971, 505.

33. Rawls also explicitly acknowledges an intellectual debt to Piaget and Kohlberg in *A Theory of Justice* (Rawls 1971, 460 n. 5).

34. Rawls frames the stability problem as a problem about keeping a just society going rather than getting an unjust society to be just, so he only needs the claim that development will occur this way, at least in already just societies. However, it is certainly possible that this kind of development goes on in all societies, whether or not they are just. This point is elaborated later.

35. See Rawls 1971, 463, where Rawls notes in passing that the child is initially motivated by rational self-interest.

36. Rawls 1971, 463.

37. Rawls 1971, 463.

38. See Rawls 1971, 464–65.

39. Rawls 1971, 466.

40. Piaget 1932, 90.

41. Piaget 1932, 90.

42. Piaget 1932, 195.

43. See also Piaget 1932, 49–50, for the importance of imitation in the early stages of rule-consciousness. There, Piaget notes that children learning to play games first imitate those who know how to play. Kohlberg also shares this emphasis on imitation. In fact, he makes the notion of imitation of a respected and loved model central to his theory (see Kohlberg 1984, 105–65).

44. See Piaget 1932, 178. Piaget draws on this fact in his characterization of this stage as heteronomous.

45. Piaget 1932, 53; see also 195.

46. See Piaget 1932, 195. Piaget's conception of this stage has more to it, for according to Piaget, this stage is marked by two other additional features. First, there is a sort of superstitious attachment to the rules as unalterable and sacred features of the universe. Second, there is a very strict view of responsibility that does not allow mitigation for anything, even intention (see Piaget 1932, chap. 2). Rawls does not follow this part of Piaget, but nearly everything he does say is traceable all or in part to Piaget.

47. The dispositions to love, imitate, and obey and internalize the standards of the loved one are basic in the sense that all normal children have them. They appear more or less automatically, rather than having to be deliberately "trained into" the child by parents or society. They may or may not be basic in the theoretical sense of not being explainable by other factors. Indeed, Kohlberg postulated a reinforcement mechanism that, together with a basic motivation for competence, helps explain the disposition to imitate (see Kohlberg 1984, 191ff). He is careful to claim, though, that the motivation is intrinsic. The story is roughly that there is a basic motivation for competence, and since the child has no source of knowledge about whether she has done things competently, she ends up imitating adults (who, presumably by virtue of their superior power, are assumed to be competent). Thus, imitation is explained by the fact that imitation and seeking reinforcement from adults are the best ways to satisfy the basic motivation for competence. Rawls also hints at a similar position in *A Theory of Justice* (see Rawls 1971, 495).

48. The distinction will become crucial when we turn to *Political Liberalism*. Piaget and Kohlberg (at least initially) believed themselves to be investigating the development of morality in toto (though Kohlberg has backed off a bit from this position in response to the work of Carol Gilligan (see Kohlberg 1984, 224–36). But in *Political Liberalism*, at least, Rawls is only talking about a much more limited notion, namely, a *political conception of justice.*

49. Rawls 1971, 470, 471.

50. Rawls 1971, 471.

51. Rawls 1971, 469. Rawls does not say exactly how role-taking leads to the ability to view things from other people's perspectives. For Kohlberg's account, as well as a survey and critique of some alternatives, see Kohlberg 1984, 94–169.

52. Rawls 1971, 472.

53. Rawls 1971, 472.

54. Rawls 1971, 472; emphasis added. It is worth noting that Rawls limits this claim to just or fair cooperative arrangements, which raises a number of important and interesting questions. First, what counts as a just (nonstate) cooperative arrangement? Susan Moller Okin has criticized Rawls for not adequately addressing this question (see Okin 1989, 97–101). Second, could the sense of justice arise in an unjust cooperative arrangement? Rawls does not claim that it could. Okin seems to assume that it cannot. It is not clear that this is the correct assumption to make, however. For according to the theory that Rawls presents, and certainly

in Piaget and Kohlberg, it is not so much that the family qua family is the school of justice but, rather, that the family qua cooperative arrangement is the school of justice. Children, in this view, do not learn justice by observing just institutions but by cooperating. If this is correct, then it is at least possible that children could learn the necessary foundations for a sense of justice even from an unjust family, so long as it still qualified as a cooperative arrangement. Even an unjust family, so long as it is a cooperative association, could play the role Rawls needs it to play in the transformation from the morality of authority to the morality of cooperation. Saying this, however, does not get Rawls off the hook for failing to take account of gender issues within the family. But it does raise the possibility that the sense of justice may be much easier to acquire—and thus a just society be much more stable—than Rawls realizes.

55. Piaget 1932, 319–20; see also 348 and numerous other places as well.

56. Piaget 1932, 71.

57. Piaget 1932, 71.

58. Rawls 1971, 473.

59. Rawls 1971, 473–74.

60. Rawls 1971, 474. Piaget does not exactly postulate this stage, but he seems to assume that its processes occur at some point. Though he only talks about the development of the morality of cooperations in reference to particular schemes of cooperations (for example, the game of marbles), he assumes that this is the source of the adult's sense of fairness in general. Thus, he assumes some sort of process of the sort that Rawls envisages here that transforms the sense of fairness-in-a-particular-cooperative-scheme (for example, the game of marbles) to a sense of fairness in general. This sense of fairness in general is not tied to particular affections for the members of the group but can stand alone to govern one's interactions with a group of people, not all of whom one has ties of affection toward. Thus, what Rawls splits into stages two and three may better be thought of as corresponding to Piaget's second stage. For both of them, this endpoint of moral development involves respect as a motive for the sense of justice. For respect for persons as such can be a motive to behave justly toward persons even if one has no particular affection toward them. In this respect, much of Piaget's work ties in quite nicely with the Kantian remarks Rawls makes in *A Theory of Justice* (Rawls 1971, 476–78). A possible disagreement between Rawls and Piaget may lie in the role of affection in moral development. Piaget does not postulate a stage in which affection drives cooperation. Though Rawls is not as clear as we might want, he does seem to imply in the description of the third stage that the morality of cooperation in the second stage is driven by affection (see Rawls 1971, 473–74). Piaget, on the other hand, constantly emphasizes the importance of respect as a motive for cooperation (see Piaget 1932, 94–108).

61. Most notably in Gilligan 1982.

62. Indeed, one might be tempted to think that it is this very controversy that led Rawls to virtually ignore his own theory of moral development in *Political Liberalism*. But as is shown later, Rawls does not in fact abandon this theory at all.

63. It is also worth noting in this connection that Piaget (unlike Kohlberg) did make an explicit effort to study girls to make sure his theory was not gender biased. Though he found some differences in detail, the basic move from the heteronomous "morality of authority" to the morality of cooperation was essentially the same. This is not surprising, since, in effect, what Piaget does is simply to provide a sort of conceptual analysis of cooperative endeavor and to show how it can be the basis for certain moral attitudes (namely, fairness). Since it is the fact of cooperation rather than the actual content of the game that is important, these results should hold for all sorts of cooperative endeavors. Thus, if it turns out that little girls play different sorts of games than little boys do, this should not matter, since the important fact is that games of whatever sort are cooperative endeavors.

64. See Rawls 1993, xv–xx.

65. Rawls 1993, xvi.

66. Both quotations are from Rawls 1993, 43.

67. A "comprehensive doctrine" is a complete or relatively complete moral, philosophical, and religious view that includes, among other things, one's conception of the good (see Rawls 1993, 13).

68. Rawls 1993, 39–40; emphasis added. On the hopeful but uncertain nature of the Rawlsian enterprise, see Rawls 1993, 150–58 and 14–15.

69. Rawls 1993, 14.

70. Rawls 1993, 13–14. Rawls elaborates as follows: "This public culture comprises the political institutions of a constitutional regime and the public traditions of their interpretation, as well as historic texts and documents that are common knowledge. . . . In a democratic society there is a tradition of democratic thought, the content of which is at least familiar and intelligible to the educated common sense of citizens generally. Society's main institutions, and their accepted forms of interpretation, are seen as a fund of implicitly shared ideas and principles" (Rawls 1993, 14).

71. See Rawls 1993, xxv and 158–68.

72. This is perhaps a bit too harsh: Rawls does present what he admits is a rather rough sketch about how an overlapping consensus might come into being (Rawls 1993, 158–68), and it may well be that an explanation of the forces of a stable system can be informative even if they do not explain how a system became stable (I take it this is true, for instance, in physics). Thus, while the theory seems circular, it does not seem viciously circular. Rawls's story about how the overlapping consensus appears essentially involves two components. First, events such as religious wars lead to constitutional consensus as a modus vivendi. Second, this modus vivendi leads to overlapping consensus via a moral psychological principle that says that those who benefit from a system will do their part if others do theirs and if they see the system as just (Rawls 1993, 163). This picture is based on two assumptions, both of which are quite problematic. The first is that the overlapping consensus will occur only in societies in which there is a history of modus vivendi. The second is that there is a psychological principle that essentially guarantees that people living in a modus vivendi they see as just will come to affirm its principles in their comprehensive doctrine, thus enabling an overlapping consensus to occur. The problem with the first assumption is that it makes *Political Liberalism* very parochial. The problem with the second is that it essentially answers our question simply by asserting a psychological law that answers it. That is not much of an answer.

73. Indeed, this sort of bootstrapping methodology is implicit in *A Theory of Justice* as well, for the method of reflective equilibrium has to have some initial intuitions to equilibrate with the theory. Apparently, then, *Political Liberalism* is in part a declaration of the source of those initial intuitions: They come from our shared public culture as a constitutional democracy and from the fact that we, or at least most of us, have comprehensive doctrines that are "reasonable," that is, which we affirm while at the same time recognizing that a reasonable person may hold some other comprehensive doctrine.

74. Rawls does say a bit in *Political Liberalism* about how, over time, a modus vivendi will lead to more toleration on the part of even the intolerant.

75. One of the most important of these is how some children manage to learn the "right" lesson from cooperation, that is, the lesson that the sorts of reasoning and willingness to cooperate can be generalized from the limited context of a particular cooperative association to society as a whole.

References

Daniels, Norman, ed. 1989. *Reading Rawls: Critical Studies on Rawls'* A Theory of Justice. Stanford, Calif.: Stanford University Press.

English, Jane. 1977. Justice between Generations. *Philosophical Studies* 31: 91–104.

Flanagan, Owen. 1984. *The Science of the Mind.* Cambridge, Mass.: MIT Press.

———. 1991. *The Varieties of Moral Personality.* Cambridge, Mass.: MIT Press.

Gilligan, Carol. 1982. *In a Different Voice: Psychological Theory and Women's Moral Development.* Cambridge, Mass.: Harvard University Press.

Hobbes, Thomas. 1651. *The Leviathan.*

Hubin, D. Clayton. 1976. Justice and Future Generations. *Philosophy and Public Affairs* 6, no. 1: 70–83.

Jecker, Nancy S. 1992. Intergenerational Justice and the Family. *Journal of Value Inquiry* 26: 495–509.

Kagan, Shelly. 1992. The Structure of Normative Ethics. *Philosophical Perspectives* 6: 223–42.

Kohlberg, Lawrence. 1984. "Stage and Sequence" and "A Current Formulation of the Theory." In *The Psychology of Moral Development,* vol. 1 of *Essays on Moral Development.* San Francisco: Harper and Row, 7–169 and 212–318, respectively.

Kukathas, Chandran, and Philip Pettit. 1993. *Rawls: A Theory of Justice and Its Critics.* Stanford, Calif.: Stanford University Press.

Minow, Martha. 1986. Rights for the Next Generation: A Feminist Approach to Children's Rights. *Harvard Women's Law Journal* 9: 1–24.

Narveson, Jan. 1988. *The Libertarian Idea.* Philadelphia, Pa.: Temple University Press.

Okin, Susan Moller. 1989. *Justice, Gender, and the Family.* New York: Basic Books.

———. 1994. Political Liberalism, Justice, and Gender. *Ethics* 105 (October): 23–43.

O'Neill, Onora. 1993. Justice, Gender, and International Boundaries. In *The Quality of Life,* edited by Martha Nussbaum and Amartya Sen. Oxford: Clarendon Press, 303–23.

Piaget, Jean. 1932. *The Moral Judgment of the Child.* New York: Harcourt Brace.

Rawls, John. 1971. *A Theory of Justice.* Cambridge, Mass.: Harvard University Press.

———. 1993. *Political Liberalism.* New York: Columbia University Press.

Steiner, Hillel. 1994. *An Essay on Right.* Oxford: Blackwell.

Thompson, Janna. 1993. What Do Women Want? Rewriting the Social Contract. *International Journal of Moral and Social Studies* 8, no. 3: 257–72.

Wright, Christine, and Jean-Pierre Leroux. 1991. Children as Victims of Violent Crime. Service Bulletin of the Canadian Centre for Justice Statistics, vol. 11, no. 8.

4

JUSTICE, LEGITIMACY, AND HUMAN RIGHTS

Allen Buchanan

1. The Distinction between Justice and Legitimacy

It has been said that while *A Theory of Justice* is about justice, *Political Liberalism* is about legitimacy—about the conditions that must be satisfied if it is to be morally justifiable to use force to secure compliance with principles of justice.[1] This is almost correct. *Political Liberalism* is about the role that considerations of legitimacy should play in theorizing about justice. By bringing the relationship between justice and legitimacy to center stage, Rawls has launched his second revolution in thinking about justice.

Once the distinction between justice and legitimacy is noticed, it is hard to understand how it could have been so neglected by most who have written about justice until the appearance of *Political Liberalism*. In *A Theory of Justice*, Rawls, like most theorists of justice before and after the book's publication, proceeded as if the task of the political philosopher was to articulate and support principles of justice on the basis of the best moral view available, on the assumption that it is morally justifiable to enforce those principles if need be (for example, to solve the assurance problem—to provide reasonable assurance to those disposed to comply with principles of justice that others will reciprocate or to prevent free riding). Rawls's assumption in *A Theory of Justice* was that one can first determine what justice requires and then ask what the circumstances are that permit enforcement of justice (such as the need to solve collective action problems that would result in noncompliance).

In contrast, in *Political Liberalism*, Rawls shows how a conception of legitimacy can in part determine the content of the principles of justice rather than merely serve as an external constraint on the enforceability of principles of justice that are derived independent of considerations of legitimacy. The significance of this view—which might be called "the primacy of legitimacy"[2]—is perhaps clearest in Rawls's application of his principle of legitimacy to the idea of an international legal order in his paper "The Law of Peoples."[3] Rawls notes that

> not all regimes can reasonably be required to be liberal, otherwise the law of
> peoples would not express liberalism's own principle of toleration for other

reasonable ways of ordering society nor further its attempt to find a shared basis of agreement among reasonable peoples. Just as a citizen in a liberal society must respect other persons' comprehensive religious, philosophical, and moral doctrines provided they are in accordance with a reasonable political conception of justice, so a liberal society must respect other societies organized by comprehensive doctrines, provided their political and social institutions meet certain conditions that lead the society to adhere to a reasonable law of peoples.[4]

In other words, one of Rawls's chief tasks in "The Law of Peoples" is to determine how the constraints of legitimacy determine the content of principles of international justice.

Some have taken strong exception to the results of this endeavor. A number of critics, including some who were generally sympathetic to *A Theory of Justice* and *Political Liberalism,* have charged that the principles for an international legal order derived in "The Law of Peoples" are unacceptably inegalitarian, even regressively illiberal.[5] In particular, they have objected to his conclusion that a reasonable law of peoples would require only that societies respect a proper subset of what liberals usually regard as human rights, that societies should be regarded as fully legitimate even if they lack democratic institutions, make no provisions for distributive justice beyond the guarantee of subsistence for all members, do not recognize freedom of expression or of association, and include serious institutionally sanctioned inequalities between men and women or even between different castes or races. If this criticism should turn out to be valid, it would raise serious questions about the revolutionary strategy of which it is a part, the attempt to take legitimacy seriously in the process of arguing for substantive principles of justice. In order to evaluate this criticism it is necessary to reconstruct Rawls's arguments to make clearer the basis for his claim that a reasonable law of peoples would require only this truncated set of rights.

2. The Reasonableness Criterion as a Principle of Legitimacy

In the passage cited above, Rawls states that liberalism must recognize reasonable pluralism in formulating a law of peoples: Toleration must be shown to hierarchical, that is illiberal, societies so long as they are ordered by comprehensive conceptions of the good that are reasonable. Thus, a reasonable law of peoples will be a law for reasonable peoples.

In "The Law of Peoples," Rawls says little explicitly about how the notion of reasonableness is to be applied to the comprehensive conceptions of the good that order hierarchical societies. In *Political Liberalism,* in contrast, Rawls explicitly first characterizes reasonableness as applied to persons: "Rather than define the reasonable directly, I specify two of its basic aspects as virtues of persons. Persons are reasonable in one basic aspect when, [(a)] among equals, say, they are ready to propose principles and standards as fair terms of cooperation and to abide by them willingly, given the assurance that others will likewise do so. . . . and [(b)] they are willing to recognize the burdens of judgment."[6] To recognize the burdens of judgment is to appreciate that there are a number of factors that can lead to reasonable disagreements among persons on matters of value, including questions of justice. Rawls says little about what this appreciation amounts to practically speaking, that is, in efforts to determine whether a conception of the good is reasonable. He does not articulate a set of minimal epistemic conditions—standards of minimal rationality that any acceptable argument for organizing a society according to a conception of the good must satisfy—and then argue that appreciation of the burdens of judgment entails that one not attempt to impose on others any principles of social order that one cannot support by arguments that satisfy those standards.

After characterizing reasonableness as applied to persons, Rawls goes on to connect the idea of the reasonable as applied to persons with that of a society organized by reasonable principles: "The reasonable is an element of the idea of society as a system of fair cooperation and that its fair terms be reasonable for all to accept is part of its idea of reciprocity."[7] It would seem to follow that a society organized according to a comprehensive conception of the good would meet the criterion of reasonableness if, and only if, that comprehensive conception could be consistently held by a reasonable person, one who is willing to propose and accept fair terms of cooperation with others as equals, assuming they are so willing, and who properly acknowledges the burdens of judgment. (We will see that the inclusion of the phrase "as equals" creates difficulties for this interpretation, but more of that later.)

According to this interpretation, Rawls's task in "The Law of Peoples" is to articulate the minimal conditions that any society must satisfy if it is to fall within the domain of the reasonable and hence be entitled to toleration, that is, to noninterference by societies organized according to different principles. And this will require showing that the society is organized according to principles that could be accepted by persons who are reasonable according to the two aspects of reasonableness (a) and (b) noted previously.

There is a striking difficulty with this line of interpretation, however, namely, the inclusion of the phrase "as among equals" in the first aspect of reasonable persons stated in the reasonableness criterion. For Rawls's point in "The Law of Peoples" is that some societies can be reasonable—ordered according to principles that reasonable persons could accept—and yet be quite inegalitarian. Indeed, at times in *Political Liberalism* Rawls seems to restrict the characterization of reasonableness to reasonable persons in a *liberal society,* as when, for example, he equates recognizing the burdens of judgment with accepting the consequences of the burdens of judgment "for the use of public reason in a constitutional [i.e., liberal] regime."[8] Similarly, Rawls sometimes refers to the principle that it is unjustifiable to impose principles upon persons who can reasonably reject them (that is, principles that are inconsistent with their reasonable conceptions of the good) as "the liberal principle of legitimacy."[9]

The difficulty is that if the notion of reasonableness (as including aspects

[a] and [b] previously) is only applicable to liberal societies, then that notion cannot be used by Rawls in "The Law of Peoples" to determine which societies are entitled to be regarded as members in good standing of the society of peoples, and hence to noninterference. In other words, if the notion of reasonableness applies only to liberal societies, then it cannot be invoked to distinguish between those illiberal societies that are entitled to toleration and those that are not. But if this is the case, then we may ask, How is the latter distinction to be drawn?

In fact, in "The Law of Peoples" direct references to the notion of reasonableness, understood as including the idea of fair terms among persons as equals, are not in evidence. Instead, in that work Rawls simply sets out two conditions that a society must meet if it is to be entitled to noninterference: respect for what Rawls calls human rights properly speaking and nonexpansionism (refraining from attempting to impose its own conception of the good on other societies). Societies that are illiberal but that meet these two conditions he refers to as "well-ordered hierarchical societies."[10]

If one assumes that "The Law of Peoples" builds consistently on *Political Liberalism,* one will assume that well-ordered societies are entitled to noninterference because they are organized according to comprehensive conceptions of the good which, though illiberal, are reasonable. And one would expect that "The Law of Peoples" would argue that hierarchical comprehensive conceptions of the good can be reasonable. However, this is not how Rawls proceeds in "The Law of Peoples." As I have already suggested, the notion of the reasonable recedes into the background, or drops out of the picture altogether, in the latter work. Instead, Rawls sets out the two conditions that a hierarchical society must meet if it is to be well ordered. These questions naturally arise, then: Where do these two conditions come from? and If they are not supposed to be derivable from the two-aspects criterion of reasonableness set out in *Political Liberalism* (on the assumption that that criterion, with its emphasis on fair cooperation *among equals,* only applies to liberal societies), what reason is there to accept Rawls's two conditions? In particular, what reason is there to conclude that a society that is quite inegalitarian in its treatment of women, say, is entitled to be regarded as a member in good standing in the society of peoples so long as it respects Rawls's truncated set of human rights? The problem is that the notion of reasonableness specified in *Political Liberalism* seems inapplicable to the task of the "Law of Peoples" yet no alternative notion of reasonableness on which to base Rawls's conditions for well-ordered hierarchical societies is presented in that work.

Consider first the nonexpansionism condition. It would be natural to say that reasonable societies will be nonexpansionist because reasonableness includes as one of its aspects a recognition of the burdens of judgment and recognizing the burdens of judgment entails not attempting to impose one's own society's conception of the good on others. But if the reasonableness criterion is only to be applied in liberal societies, then this way of supporting the claim that hierarchical societies are entitled to noninterference is not available. So the question remains: If the reasonableness criterion is only a *liberal* principle of legitimacy, what grounds the nonexpansionism condition?

Next consider Rawls's second condition for well-ordered hierarchical societies in "The Law of Peoples": respect for what he deems human rights proper. This is a much leaner list of rights than those that are generally regarded as human rights. According to Rawls, hierarchical society is entitled to noninterference if (in addition to being nonexpansionist) it respects its members' rights to material subsistence; rights against religious persecution (though this is compatible with there being an established religion); rights against slavery, involuntary servitude, and forced occupations; a right to hold personal property; a right to emigrate; and a limited right to dissent at an appropriate level within what Rawls calls a "consultation hierarchy."[11] For Rawls, the list of human rights proper does not include a right to democratic governance or democratic participation, nor does it include liberal-style rights to freedom of religion, expression, or association.

In "The Law of Peoples," Rawls does offer a reason why these particular rights, and only these, must be respected by a society if that society is to be well ordered and, hence, entitled to noninterference. He asserts that hierarchical societies that are well ordered are those that are organized according to a "common good conception of justice." A common good conception of justice includes three elements: (1) "the system of laws imposes moral duties and obligations on all members of society"; (2) the conception of the good according to which the society is organized "takes impartially into account what it sees not unreasonably as the fundamental interests of all members of society"; and (3) "there is a sincere and not unreasonable belief on the part of judges and other officials who administer the legal order" that the law is indeed guided by a common good conception of justice.[12]

The idea of a common good conception of justice can provide the basis for Rawls's assertion that a hierarchical society is entitled to noninterference if we make the following assumption: The institutional embodiment of a common good conception of justice includes what Rawls calls the human rights properly speaking. The idea is that a society that did not respect those fundamental rights would not be organized by a common good conception of justice. Respecting those rights is necessary, in particular, if everyone's essential good is to be impartially taken into account. This interpretation merely pushes the puzzle back another step, however, for we can now ask, Why should we assume that a society is entitled to noninterference (assuming it is nonexpansionist) if and only if it is organized according to a common good conception of justice?

At this point there seem to be only two candidates for interpreting the structure of Rawls's view: According to interpretation one, there is a radical discontinuity between *Political Liberalism* and "The Law of Peoples." The notion of reasonableness employed in the latter plays no significant role in determining the limits of toleration in the latter, in spite of Rawls's statement at the beginning of "The Law of Peoples" that the task is to develop principles of international order which recognize that societies can be illiberal yet reasonable. Instead, an entirely new notion, that of a common good conception of justice, is foundational for determining which nonliberal societies are entitled to toleration and noninterference. In this first interpretation, the idea of a common good conception of justice and the idea of the human rights proper as the institutional embodiment of a common good conception are not grounded in the notion of reasonableness that is so central to *Political Liberalism.* One gap in Rawls's view, understood according to interpretation one, is that we still have no account of why the nonexpansionist condition is to be included in the conditions for well-ordered hierarchical societies. It appears to be simply stipulated, because there is nothing in the notion of a common good conception of justice that constrains the external relations of a society that embodies it in this or any other way.

According to interpretation two, Rawls's argument in "The Law of Peoples" goes like this:

1. A society is entitled to noninterference (and to be regarded as a member in good standing in the society of peoples) if and only if it is organized by reasonable principles.
2. Principles for organizing a society are reasonable if and only if they could be accepted by reasonable persons, that is, by those who (a) acknowledge the burdens of judgment and (b) are willing to propose and accept fair terms of cooperation.
3. Those who acknowledge the burdens of judgment will not attempt to impose their conception of the good on other societies (i.e., are nonexpansionist).
4. A society is organized on the basis of fair terms of cooperation if and only if it is organized by a common good conception of justice.
5. If a society is organized by a common good conception of justice, it will respect the human rights proper.
6. Therefore, a society is entitled to noninterference (and to be recognized as a member in good standing in the society of peoples) if and only if it is nonexpansionist and respects the human rights proper.

There is much to be said for argument 1–6, whether or not it is supported by the Rawlsian texts. The intuitive idea is that although there are and can be disputes about what counts as fair terms of cooperation, the latter notion has some minimal content that is not reasonably disputable and this minimal content is captured by the idea of a common good conception of justice, whose institutional embodiment in turn requires the human rights proper.

On the face of it, interpretation two is preferable. It not only connects "The Law of Peoples" with its predecessor *Political Liberalism* in a coherent way but also, in so doing, provides an argument (1–6) for the conclusion that there can be reasonable, though illiberal, societies and that reasonable persons will tolerate such societies. In addition, interpretation two, unlike interpretation one, accounts for both the human rights proper condition and the nonexpansionist condition.

Interpretation one, in contrast, portrays a radical discontinuity between *Political Liberalism* and "The Law of Peoples" by severing the idea of reasonableness, so central to the former, from the attempt to derive a law of peoples while supporting only one of the two conditions, respect for the human rights proper, and that only by the seemingly ad hoc stipulation that societies which satisfy the minimal standards of a common good conception of justice are entitled to noninterference. Because interpretation one fails to connect the idea of a common good conception of justice to the notion of reasonableness, it renders mysterious Rawls's introductory remark in "The Law of Peoples," cited above, that his task is to reveal the basis for an agreement "among [the] reasonable peoples of the world," for unless all societies that meet his two conditions for noninterference fall within the domain of the reasonable, this remark would make no sense.

The only difficulty with interpretation two is that it seems to be inconsistent with those passages in *Political Liberalism* in which Rawls appears to regard the "two-aspect" reasonableness criterion as a principle that applies only within liberal societies, as a distinctively liberal principle of legitimacy. If the reasonableness principle's first aspect is understood to include not only the willingness to accept and impose fair terms of cooperation but also the further liberal-sounding specification that cooperation is to be regarded as cooperation "among persons regarded as free and equal," then there is an inconsistency. However, as my formulation of the reasonableness criterion in argument 1–6 indicates, we might instead conclude that what is relevant to the law of peoples is what might be called Rawls's fundamental reasonableness criterion, one that characterizes a more general sense of reasonableness that omits this specification.

On the interpretation I am suggesting, Rawls in effect has two reasonableness criteria: a general one, or the reasonableness criterion proper, and one that includes the particular way reasonableness gets specified within the distinctive political culture of a liberal society. The former speaks only of fair terms of cooperation; the latter, of fair terms of cooperation among persons considered as free and equal. The idea of a common good conception of justice is then understood as providing the minimal content for the idea of fair cooperation—that is, fair cooperation as such, not fair cooperation among persons as free and equal.

The advantages of attributing this distinction between a general and a liberal-specific notion of reasonableness to Rawls are great. It allows us to reconstruct the central argument of "The Law of Peoples" as 1–6 while avoiding any inconsistency with those passages in *Political Liberalism* that seem to restrict the notion of reasonableness to liberal societies. And in so doing, this interpretation both presents the two works as a coherent whole and defends Rawls against the charge that his conditions for legitimate hierarchical societies are ad hoc.

For these reasons, I will proceed on the assumption that interpretation two is correct and that argument 1–6 captures the main outlines of Rawls's central argument in "The Law of Peoples." We are now in a position to see whether Rawls's attempt to introduce considerations of legitimacy into the heart of theorizing about justice is successful.

3. The Duality of Justice

Perhaps the most striking conclusion Rawls reaches in the execution of this second revolution is what I shall call "the duality of justice thesis," the assertion that there are very significant differences between the principles of justice it is legitimate to enforce in a liberal democratic society and those that may be enforced in an international legal system. More specifically, as we have seen, in "The Law of Peoples" Rawls concludes that while the liberal egalitarian principles of justice he argued for in *A Theory of Justice* and in *Political Liberalism* may be justifiably enforced in a liberal democratic society such as the United States, it would be wrong to attempt to enforce them in international law because they cannot be justifiably imposed on illiberal societies. According to the duality of justice thesis, to require hierarchical societies to comply with the liberal egalitarian principles of justice that comprise Rawls's theory of justice as fairness would be to act illegitimately. The proper standard of justice for the international legal system is far less demanding: Instead of the full list of civil and political rights set out in Rawls's "Equal Liberty Principle" (which includes rights to participate in democratic government and rights to freedom of expression and freedom of religion), "the Principle of Fair Equality of Opportunity," and "the Difference Principle," all that a legitimate international legal order can require of any state is that it be nonaggressive in its foreign relations and that it respect the human rights proper.

It is worth dwelling, for a moment, on just how conservative (or regressive) Rawls's view of international law is. In "The Law of Peoples," Rawls concludes that a proper application of the notion of legitimacy yields the result that it would be wrong to try to use international legal institutions or unilateral action to compel any state to do more than respect the human rights proper in its dealings with its own citizens. This means that even states that prevent women or members of a particular racial or ethnic minority from getting an education, from voting, or from holding public office are to be regarded as fully legitimate so long as they do not threaten the physical security of such persons, provide them with a minimal of material means for subsistence, do not persecute them for their religion, and allow them to voice their views at some "appropriate" level of a consultation hierarchy (and are nonexpansionist). In Rawls's view, a state that used public resources to support a hereditary elite in luxury would be quite legitimate as long as everyone were provided with the means of subsistence.

Rawls would no doubt emphasize that the only hierarchical societies he regards as legitimate are *well-ordered* ones. Well-ordered societies are stable in the sense that their basic principles of justice are public and, when implemented over time, generate their own support. In brief, in a well-ordered society the public order is regarded as legitimate by the members of that society.

"Well-orderedness" rules out gross inequalities that can be sustained over time only by sheer brute force, but it is still compatible with gross inequalities. A sufficiently clever regime, if it lasted long enough, might gradually replace the enforcement of its principles by brute force with popular support for them by effective policies of indoctrination. Such a process would be greatly facilitated by the lack of a right to democratic participation and the lack of the liberal rights of freedom of religion and expression.

The charge that Rawls's view counts as legitimate unacceptably inegalitarian social orders is serious. However, in general, liberal critics of "The Law of Peoples" have done a better job of pointing out what they take to be the regressive implications of Rawls's duality of justice view than in showing how these implications can be avoided while at the same time taking seriously the crucial distinction between justice and legitimacy. In fact, they have neither argued that Rawls is wrong to make so much of the distinction between justice and legitimacy nor provided an alternative account of legitimacy that avoids what they take to be the regressive implications of Rawls's account. Most important, these critics have not challenged—or apparently even noticed—the fundamental theoretical stance on which Rawls's duality of justice view rests, what I have called "the primacy of legitimacy thesis." To that extent, they simply have not engaged the central features of Rawls's current view.[13]

My strategy, in contrast, is to take Rawls's distinction between justice and legitimacy seriously but to argue that Rawls is mistaken as to the implications of this distinction for a morally defensible international legal order. I argue that Rawls's view on the primacy of legitimacy as well as his particular principle of legitimacy (the general reasonableness criterion) can be preserved without the regressive implications concerning human rights that critics of "The Law of Peoples" find so disturbing. To do so, I will have to show that at least the more inegalitarian of what Rawls regards as well-ordered hierarchical societies do *not* pass the test prescribed by his legitimacy principle—or at least I will have to show that it is unwarranted to assume, as Rawls does, that such societies fall within the domain of the reasonable.

4. Reasonableness and Human Rights

To pursue this strategy, we must examine argument 1–6 more closely. Rawls is on solid ground, I believe, when he says that reasonableness requires a common good conception of justice, for it is hard to see how terms of social cooperation that do not include the three elements of a common good conception could be regarded as fair terms of cooperation, even if fairness is understood in the most minimal way. A system of law that exempted some persons from having any moral duties or obligations would not treat those individuals as being minimally equal in the sense required for even the most austere notion of fair cooperation: They would either be above others, occupying a position of godlike privilege, or they would be beneath others (as when slaves are said to be "morally dead"—beings who are not understood to have moral obligations because they are assumed to lack moral personality). Similarly, a comprehensive conception of the good that did not impartially take into account everyone's essential interests would not be a fair basis for cooperation in even the most minimal sense; in such a system the good of some would not count at all, and hence to require their cooperation would not be fair.

Rawls's argument for the crucial premise 5 is rather terse.

> The requirement we laid down [under the idea of a common good conception of justice] was that a society's stem of law must be such as to impose duties and obligations on all its members and be regulated by what judges and other officials reasonably and sincerely believe is a common good conception of justice. We then say that for this condition to hold, the law must at least uphold such basic rights as the right to life and security, to personal property and the elements of the rule of law, as well as the right to a certain liberty of conscience [the right against religious persecution] and freedom of association [within the strictures of the social hierarchy] and the right to emigration. These we refer to as human rights.[14]

Nevertheless, the following seems plausible enough: What Rawls calls human rights appear to be institutional embodiments of the conviction that everyone's essential interests are to count in the organization of society where this, in turn, is understood to be required by the idea of fair terms of cooperation. It would be difficult to argue that a society which did not honor these basic rights could be described as being organized according to a comprehensive conception of the good that is reasonable in the sense of being acceptable to persons who are willing to accept fair terms of cooperation, even according to the least robust interpretation of fair cooperation. The question, then, is, not whether respect for Rawls's truncated list of human rights (along with nonexpansionism) is necessary for a hierarchical society to be justified in enforcing its principles of social order, and to be free from interference by other societies, but whether it is *sufficient*.

If 1–6 is the correct reconstruction of Rawls's argument, then it appears that there are only three ways one can argue that Rawls's standard for membership in the society of peoples is not sufficiently demanding, that it legitimizes unacceptably inegalitarian societies. First, one can argue that a proper acknowledgment of the burdens of judgment is compatible with rejecting as unreasonably inegalitarian some social orders that meet Rawls's minimal requirements. Second, one can argue that Rawls has construed the idea of fair terms of cooperation *too* minimally, that some extremely inegalitarian societies that meet Rawls's minimal requirements do not exemplify fair terms of cooperation. Third, one can argue that even if Rawls is correct in holding that fair terms of cooperation, as such, only require his truncated list of human rights, the secure institutional realization of those rights requires a richer set of rights, including a right to democratic government (not just a consultation hierarchy) as well as liberal-style rights to freedom of expression and freedom of association. Each of these arguments for expanding Rawls's requirements for being a member in good standing of the society of peoples will be considered in turn.

4.1. The Burdens of Judgment

Surprisingly, Rawls does not consider arguments, familiar from discourse about human rights, that gender, racial, ethnic, or caste discrimination is unjust wherever it occurs. Instead, Rawls seems simply to assume that those who offer those arguments fail to recognize the burdens of judgment—that a proper appreciation of the sources of disagreement among reasonable persons entails that all arguments against these forms of discrimination are not compelling. Or, to put the same point differently, Rawls seems to assume, without argument, that those who advocate forms of discrimination that are compatible with his truncated human rights list can support their inegalitarian views by arguments that are not unreasonable, once the burdens of judgment are properly acknowledged.

At this juncture it is important to remember that in the real world of human rights discourse, those who advocate regimes of extreme inequality are quite reasonably expected to provide arguments for those inequalities. Although I cannot of course canvass all of them here, I can indicate some of the more familiar arguments offered by the advocates of extreme inequality and suggest why I think one can criticize them effectively without failing to recognize "the burdens of judgment." On the contrary, I will suggest that the arguments typically given in favor of regimes that discriminate on the basis of race, ethnicity, caste, or gender fail to meet minimal standards for rational argumentation.

Consider a standard argument frequently offered by spokespersons for dictators or authoritarian ruling elites in developing countries: There is no universal, that is, human right to democratic governance because in some societies (like this one), democratic government is incompatible with the kind of social discipline needed for effective economic development. This argument, like most if not all arguments for undemocratic institutions, rests on empirical generalizations about what does and what does not facilitate economic development or other dimensions of the common good. The effective reply to such arguments is to challenge the relevant empirical generalizations, and they are very implausible generalizations indeed. For example, there is substantial evidence that undemocratic regimes are plagued by corruption, that corruption severely retards economic development, and that undemocratic states are therefore more prone to economic disasters, such as famines.[15]

To make this point clearer, consider Rawls's conjecture that the reasonableness criterion does not rule out social orders that are deeply sexist, which systematically deprive women of rights that men enjoy without providing anything like compensating privileges for women. Consider the fate of women under the Taliban theocratic regime in Afghanistan. Reportedly, women are not allowed anything beyond the most basic education, if that, nor are they allowed to participate in political processes, to move freely outside the home, or to travel, except under very restrictive conditions. They also have virtually no rights regarding divorce, though men have substantial rights in this regard.

Surely, a proper recognition of the burdens of judgment does not preclude us from requiring that a positive defense of these inequalities be provided, nor from criticizing such a defense by pointing out that it rests either on dubious assumptions to the effect that "the essential interests" of women differ from those of men or that women are not equal to men except in the very minimal sense that their good is to count for something. My surmise is that in general, the defenders of gender, racial, ethnic, or caste inequalities tend to make just these sorts of assumptions and that the assumptions are eminently criticizable—that they fail to meet the minimal standards for moral argument that are quite compatible with, and indeed required by, a proper recognition of the burdens of judgment.

The example of racial inequalities is highly illustrative. It is sometimes said that advocates of racial inequalities believe persons should be treated differently simply because of the color of their skin. This is a gross misunderstanding of racism. Racists believe that a darker skin is merely the external mark of an inward inferiority. When pressed to justify Apartheid or Jim Crow laws, the racist appeals to a web of empirical generalizations about the moral and intellectual inferiority of blacks, assertions about the nature of black people. These generalizations can and ought to be challenged.

This is not to say that the disagreement between racists and antiracists is always purely empirical, only that it invariably includes a significant empirical element without which the racists' justifications fail in their own terms. The racist also may be wrong, not only about his generalizations concerning the intellectual inferiority and moral viciousness of blacks, but about which sorts of differences among individuals or groups are capable of providing a plausible basis for unequal treatment.

As noted earlier, Rawls supplies no account of what a proper recognition of the burdens of judgment requires when it comes to assessing the reasonableness of comprehensive conceptions of the good. He provides no set of epistemic standards for empirical claims used in arguments to justify inequalities nor any minimal standards for reasonable inferences. However, reflections on the sorts of justifications actually given for extremely inegalitarian regimes suggest that any plausible account of the burdens of judgment is likely to rule out much more than Rawls assumes.

It might be objected that some who advocate gender, racial, ethnic, or caste inequalities (or undemocratic regimes) do not defend them in these ways. They simply claim that the inequalities are required by the revealed doctrines of their comprehensive religious conceptions of the good. To this I would reply that however the burdens of judgment are to be understood, it would be implausible, especially for a Rawlsian, to hold that rejecting such a "purely religious" justification for serious inequalities constitutes a failure to recognize the burdens of judgment. On the contrary, it is the person who refuses to give reasons to support such inequalities—beyond claiming that they are required by his religious doctrines—who cannot be regarded as having properly recognized the burdens of judgment and, hence, who cannot be regarded as reasonable.

Properly recognizing the burdens of judgment, in a world containing not only different religious conceptions of the good but secular ones as well, requires that argumentation concerning what counts as "fair terms of cooperation" *among human beings* be framed primarily in terms of the interests of *human beings,* considered in their own right. By asserting that reasonableness requires at least that a comprehensive conception of the good that is to serve as the basis for organizing society must recognize the minimal freedom and equality of persons captured by the idea of a common good conception of justice, Rawls himself admits as much. But once we go this far, the burden of justification lies on those who support inequalities beyond this minimum, and that burden cannot be born simply by making religious claims that are not accessible to those who hold reasonable secular views. Given that what is at issue is fair terms of cooperation among human beings, defenders of ethnic, racial, caste, or gender inequalities must support their views with reasons that engage directly with the interests of those who are expected to participate in such a cooperative scheme.

Rawls's notion of acknowledging the burdens of judgment is unfortunately one-sided. It counsels humility—a clear-eyed recognition that, for a number of reasons, there can be disagreement about values and justice among reasonable persons. Humility is not the only relevant virtue, however. In fact, it is at best only half the story; there is also the need for an acknowledgment of justificatory *responsibility,* for acknowledging that justifications for coercively backed principles of social order must meet minimal standards of argumentation. In other words, reasonableness requires humility as well as responsibility, a recognition that reasonable people can agree but also a recognition that reasonable peoples' arguments meet minimal critical standards. This second, equally crucial, dimension of reasonableness is not discussed by Rawls.

There is another difficulty with Rawls's assumption that well-ordered hierarchical societies that respect his list of human rights proper are reasonably organized. Rawls maintains that all that is necessary for a hierarchical society to be legitimate, so far as religious freedom goes, is that it not persecute religious minorities. It is permissible for there to be a state religion: "A hierarchical society may have an established religion with certain privileges. Still, it is essential to its being well-ordered that no religions are persecuted or denied civic and social conditions that permit their practice in peace and, of course, without fear."[16] The problem is that this limited right to religious freedom appears to be compatible with arrangements that seem to violate the reasonableness criterion—that involve the coercive imposition of rules of public order upon persons who cannot accept them from the standpoint of their reasonable comprehensive religious conceptions.[17] Suppose, for example, there are compulsory holidays according to the state religion or that it is illegal to engage in business activities on Saturday. Or suppose that all women, whether they are Muslim or not, are required by law to wear a veil in public. Such arrangements are compatible with members of minority religions being free to practice their religion without fear (we are assuming that their religious doctrines do not make refraining from work on Saturday or wearing a veil in public *impermissible*). Nonetheless, these tenets of another religion are being imposed by the coercive power of the state. Here, then, is another area in which Rawls has failed to show that social orders that respect what he takes to be the human rights pass his reasonableness test.

4.2. Fair Terms of Cooperation

I have already noted that Rawls is on firm ground when he asserts that respect for his truncated list of human rights is necessary for meeting the standard of fair terms of cooperation. The question, however, is whether it is also sufficient, as he assumes.

It is very important at this point to understand upon whom the burden of argument lies. Given that fair terms of cooperation at least require the minimal equality and freedom embodied in the idea of a common good conception of justice—that everyone's basic interests are to count for something and that everyone is to have moral obligations and duties—the proper question to ask is, How are inequalities (regarding gender, race, ethnicity, caste, or the distribution of political power) compatible with the terms of cooperation being fair?

Notice that Rawls's account of reasonableness is not directed toward those who would deny that they are bound to take the requirements of fair cooperation into account—those who instead say that fairness has nothing to do with it, that only the revealed will of God, or the pursuit of some perfectionist ideal, counts. Rawls is assuming that reasonableness, at least as it applies to conceptions of justice, requires a commitment to finding fair terms of cooperation. This point is extremely important since it implies that if inequalities are to fall within the domain of the reasonable, they must be consistent with the idea of fair cooperation.

However, Rawls seems to be insufficiently appreciative of how difficult it would be to justify the extreme inequalities of the Taliban regime or of the traditional Hindu caste system by appeal to the idea of fair cooperation. It is interesting to note that in general, it is efficiency, or the maximization of social good, that is typically appealed to in order to justify such inequalities when anything beyond purely religious "reasons" are offered in support of them. I have already suggested that such appeals to efficiency or the optimal social good appear invariably to rest on false empirical claims (about what is needed for economic stability or for development or about the natural differences between those at the top and those at the bottom of the social hierarchy). Quite apart from this, however, the crucial point is that if we take Rawls's reasonableness criterion seriously, any attempt to justify inequalities by appeals to efficiency or the maximization of the common good is ruled out as irrelevant if the inequalities in question cannot be shown to be compatible with the terms of cooperation being fair. Rawls is on very shaky ground when he assumes that the extreme forms of discrimination that are compatible with his account of a well-ordered hierarchical society can be reconciled with a commitment to fair terms of cooperation.

Showing that an extremely inegalitarian social order is compatible with fair terms of cooperation would require more than supporting claims about the natural differences between men and women or blacks and whites or untouchables and Brahmins in a way that meets the minimal epistemic standards that are properly included in the idea of acknowledging the burdens of judgment. Thus, for example, even if reasonable empirical support could be mustered for generalizations to the effect that certain racial groups or women rank lower according to objective measures of some desirable "natural" characteristics, the burden would still be on the advocate of racial or gender inequality to show why it is that *these* differences warrant unequal treatment in the social system. And this, in turn, would entail showing how a social system that based unequal treatment on these differences would meet the requirement of being a *fair* system of cooperation—not just one that maximized the good or was efficient or attained some perfectionist ideal.

It is worth emphasizing that nowhere in *Political Liberalism* or in "The Law of Peoples" does Rawls engage actual or possible defenses of inegalitarian social orders. He merely assumes or conjectures that those who recognize the burdens of judgment must concede that such inequalities fall within the domain of the reasonable, that they count as fair terms of cooperation.

I do not presume to have shown that all arguments for hierarchical arrangements are so defective that no departures from the liberal rights Rawls advocates in his theory of justice as fairness can count as reasonable in Rawls's sense. I believe I have shown, however, two things: First, Rawls's assumption that seriously inegalitarian, undemocratic societies fall within the realm of the reasonable is an unsupported conjecture; second, the burden of argument lies on those who contend that such societies can be supported by reasonable comprehensive conceptions of the good. I have also *suggested* that in general, that burden of argument has not been met successfully, though I do not pretend to have justified that generalization.

4.3. The Insecurity of Rawlsian Human Rights

Rawls assumes that his truncated list of human rights makes institutional sense without the addition of other rights typically regarded as human. But this assumption is dubious. Rawls does not address the familiar and plausible view that one cannot consistently advocate what he calls the human rights properly speaking and at the same time deny the right to democratic governance. The familiar claim is that in general and in the long run, the only reliable way to secure Rawlsian human rights is to make the government that is responsible for enforcing them subject to the controls that democratic processes provide.

Rawls assumes, without argument, that a society that includes what he calls a consultation hierarchy will reliably secure what he calls the human rights properly speaking, even in the absence of a multiparty political system, liberal-style freedom of expression and association, and a universal or even broad franchise that empowers citizens to vote at least on who will represent them in the making of the most basic laws. It is hard to evaluate this assumption, in part because Rawls says so little about what a consultative hierarchy includes. He does say that judges and other officials in a consultation hierarchy are bound to listen to voices of dissent. However, the idea that consultation is hierarchical seems to imply that persons are not allowed to address officials at the upper end of the hierarchy directly, and the qualifier "consultative" presumably implies that dissenters have no institutionally recognized power to try to influence social policy, as they would have if they had the right to vote and to form political parties. If this is so, then it appears that the government of a society that includes only a consultative hierarchy is less likely, other things being equal, to be held accountable by its citizens than one that is democratic. Therefore, it would also appear that, other things being equal, Rawlsian human rights will tend to be more secure in a democratic society than in a society that includes only a consultation hierarchy.

Earlier I noted that some who have been sympathetic to Rawls's views have expressed alarm over the apparently regressive character of his current views about human rights, but if my arguments are sound, this concern may be misplaced or at least exaggerated. Critical to my account is a distinction between what Rawls's notion of legitimacy requires and what he assumes it to require. In my view, the notion of reasonableness on which Rawlsian legitimacy rests places more substantial constraints on inequalities than Rawls himself believes it does. A plausible understanding of the burdens of judgment and the idea of fair terms of cooperation carries us beyond the truncated list of Rawlsian human rights and much closer to what might be called the mainstream of contemporary human rights doctrine.

5. The Law of Peoples Reconsidered

If my analysis is correct, then Rawls's formulation of a rather austere (or regressive) law of peoples is premature at best. He is not entitled to conclude that his principle of legitimacy (the reasonableness criterion) bars international enforcement of anything beyond the extremely lean set of rights he calls the human rights proper. He is not entitled to this conclusion because he has done nothing to show that respect for the "basic" human rights is sufficient, not just necessary, for reasonableness. If this is the case, then recognizing what I have called the primacy of legitimacy may be compatible with a law of peoples that is much more egalitarian than Rawls supposes.

Acknowledgments

I am grateful to Thomas Christiano for his helpful comments on an earlier draft of this chapter.

Notes

1. David Estlund, The Survival of Egalitarian Justice in John Rawls's *Political Liberalism, Journal of Political Philosophy* 4, no. 1 (1996): 68.

2. The phrase "primacy of legitimacy" is not intended to mean that considerations of legitimacy have priority over considerations of justice; it is simply a denial of the claim that what is just can be determined independent of considerations of legitimacy.

3. John Rawls, The Law of Peoples, in *On Human Rights: The Oxford Amnesty Lectures 1993,* ed. Stephen Shute and Susan Hurley (New York: Basic Books, 1993), 42–82. Rawls has now expanded his views in a work entitled *The Law of Peoples* to be published by Harvard University Press.

4. Rawls, The Law of Peoples, 43.

5. Fernando R. Teson, *A Philosophy of International Law* (Boulder, Colo.: Westview Press, 1998), 107–21; Darrel Moellendorf, Constructing the Law of Peoples, *Pacific Philosophic Quarterly* 77, no. 2 (1996): 135–44; Kok-Chor Tan, Liberal Toleration in Rawls's Law of Peoples, *Ethics* 108 (January 1998): 283–85.

6. John Rawls, *Political Liberalism* (New York: Columbia University Press, 1993), 49 (unless otherwise noted, in this chapter references to *Political Liberalism* are to the 1993 edition).

7. Rawls, *Political Liberalism,* 49–50.

8. Rawls, *Political Liberalism,* 54.

9. John Rawls, *Political Liberalism,* pbk. ed. (Cambridge, Mass.: Harvard University Press, 1996), xlvi, 136.

10. Rawls, *Political Liberalism,* 60–61.

11. Rawls, The Law of Peoples, 62–68.

12. Rawls, The Law of Peoples, 53.

13. This evaluation applies to the criticisms in Teson, *A Philosophy of International Law;* Moellendorf, Constructing the Law of Peoples; and Tan, Liberal Toleration, as well as by others.

14. Rawls, The Law of Peoples, 57.

15. See, for example, Amartya Sen, *Poverty and Famines: An Essay on Entitlement and Deprivation* (Oxford: Oxford University Press, 1981).

16. Rawls, *Political Liberalism,* 53.

17. I am indebted to Thomas Christiano for clarifying this point.

5

EGALITARIANISM AND A GLOBAL RESOURCES TAX:

POGGE ON RAWLS

Roger Crisp and Dale Jamieson

The publication of Rawls's *A Theory of Justice* (hereafter *Theory* or *TJ*) in 1971 was the culmination of nearly twenty years' work in moral and political philosophy.[1] Yet Rawls confessed to important limitations in the scope of *Theory:* Justice as fairness forms only part of a complete moral theory; it applies only to societies in which the circumstances of justice obtain; and, most important for our purposes, it is a theory of justice that applies within but not among nation-states. Almost immediately after completing *Theory,* Rawls set to work reformulating the foundations of his theory. The resulting book, *Political Liberalism* (hereafter *Liberalism* or *PL*) was another impressive achievement, but it did little to extend the scope of Rawls's theory.[2]

In the meantime, other philosophers and political theorists were busy extending Rawls's theory in ways he never intended, applying it to everything from the distribution of organs for the purposes of transplant to international relations. Thomas Pogge offered one of the most powerful extensions of Rawls's theory in his *Realizing Rawls (RR).*[3] He argued that if Rawls's theory were instantiated in the real world, it would have powerful egalitarian implications. In part III of *Realizing Rawls,* Pogge began to develop a globalized version of Rawls's theory.

In his 1993 Amnesty International lecture "The Law of Peoples" (LP), Rawls, for the first time, addressed the question of how his theory might apply across national boundaries.[4] He rejected Pogge's "maximalist" reading of his theory, instead giving an apparently "minimalist" account of duties across national boundaries. Pogge replied in an influential paper, "An Egalitarian Law of Peoples" (ELP).[5] In this chapter, we examine the Rawls-Pogge debate.

1. The Global Resources Tax

Thomas W. Pogge has recently offered some powerful arguments in favor of a global resources tax (GRT). According to Pogge, the most plausible version of "the law of peoples" will, contrary to Rawls in *Liberalism,* include an egalitarian distributive component. The basic idea is that each people must, via its government, pay a tax on any resources it chooses to extract from its own territory, the proceeds from which are to be used to benefit the world's poor (ELP, 200–201). Since the cost of these taxes would be passed on by producers, they would ultimately be paid by consumers.

Pogge claims that a 1 percent GRT could be imposed at once, and that the idea is supported by both forward-looking and backward-looking moral arguments (200–202). In particular, he suggests, a GRT would be chosen in Rawls's "second session" of the original position, in which principles to govern the relations between states are being selected (205–8). Pogge says that each delegate in the session would be interested not only in justice but in the well-being of the people she represents (208–11) and that delegates with an interest only in justice would wish to incorporate measures of egalitarian distribution in the law of peoples (211–14).

Pogge argues that Rawls has shied away from such egalitarianism through a mistaken understanding of what liberalism is required to tolerate (ELP, 214–19). Liberals must accept that justice may demand that certain human rights to well-being be met despite the views held in what Rawls has called "hierarchical societies," that is, societies which may be "well ordered" but have nonliberal, hierarchical institutions. Finally, Pogge claims that economic sanctions will motivate states to pay their share of the GRT (219–24). We should not forget that states can act for moral reasons: "We must be realistic, but not to the point of presenting to the parties in the original position the essentials of the status quo as unalterable facts" (224).

Pogge's proposal is powerful and suggestive, and there is much to be said in its favor. First, it is undoubtedly well intentioned, since Pogge means the GRT to redress inequalities between the world's poor and rich, to establish transfers as matters of entitlement rather than charity, and, by taxing consumption, to ease pressure on the earth's resources. Second, Pogge is attempting to offer a genuinely feasible and practical alternative to the current largely laissez-faire attitude of rich to poorer countries. Finally, he makes more plausible than Rawls the notion that discussion of such issues is best carried on in terms of a law of peoples.

Nevertheless, there are some problems with Pogge's arguments. More can be extracted from Rawls's account of the law of peoples than Pogge believes (see section 2). Pogge's proposal can be seen as "ideal" or "nonideal," and there are problems with it interpreted in either way (see section 3). There are also straightforward practical difficulties with the GRT (see section 4). Finally, even if these difficulties are resolved, the GRT may fail to respond to the needs of those in countries such as China which are in a transitional stage of development, and it may also have damaging effects on the global environment (see section 5). We conclude with some suggestions about how the problems Pogge has identified might best be approached.

2. Rawls, Global Egalitarian Distribution, and the GRT

According to Pogge, each delegate in the Rawlsian global original position is to assume that the people she represents is concerned only with its society's being a liberal one and not with the well-being of the members of that society (ELP, 206, 208).

There are two responses Rawls might make to this challenge. As Pogge notes, Rawls says that the delegates will represent "the fundamental interests" of the people they represent (206–7). Rawls speaks also of the representatives' doing the best they can for their people's "essential interests as persons" (ELP, 53). In light of this, Rawls's first response could be to accept that there is indeed a contrast between the political interest in a just society and an interest in economic well-being but claim that the delegates will represent both kinds of interest. In his brief discussion of the extended original position in *A Theory of Justice* (*TJ*, 378), Rawls speaks of the contracting parties, the representatives of states, as being concerned with "interests." Rawls does not signal here in *Theory* that he is using the notion of interests differently from the way he used it earlier in that book in elucidating the domestic original position. There, interests were explained in terms of "primary goods" (for example, *TJ*, 142). One of the primary social goods is income and wealth (*TJ*, 92). So it may be that income and wealth will also be a concern of the delegates in the global original position.

An alternative strategy for Rawls would be to deny any stark contrast between political and economic interests. Rawls says that one important element of the liberal idea of justice is "measures assuring for all citizens adequate all-purpose means to make effective use of their freedoms" (LP, 51; see ELP, 207). In the global original position, then, we may assume that delegates will take steps to ensure that their people's economic well-being is sufficient for them to exercise their freedoms.

Pogge appears to recognize that the exercise of freedom requires an economic base when he writes, "Each delegate assumes that her people has no interest at all in its standard of living (beyond its interest in the minimum necessary for just domestic institutions)" (LP, 209). The parenthesis implies that this minimum will be insufficient to meet Pogge's concerns. But Rawls is nowhere explicit about what this minimum consists in. Would it not be possible for him to suggest that it will differ little from the level achieved by a 1 percent GRT? After all, the poverty that so moved Pogge in *Realizing Rawls* is severe and chronic and goes hand in hand with a lack of "effective civil and political rights" (*RR*, 273). As Thomas Nagel and others have suggested, egalitarian concern begins to diminish when the worse-off are absolutely fairly well-off.[6] So Rawls may perhaps claim that once all are at his minimum level, justice is assured, leaving open the possibility of other moral demands for further assistance.

This brings us to Pogge's second important claim about Rawls's law of peoples, namely, that it has no egalitarian distributive component. Pogge gives the incomplete list of principles Rawls includes within the law of peoples, claiming that the complete list would not include an egalitarian principle of distribution (LP, 205 n. 14).

The passage Pogge cites as evidence (LP, 75–76) comes in Rawls's discussion of nonideal theory and unfavorable conditions, that is, of situations of only partial compliance in which some societies, for economic, social, or political reasons, cannot themselves become well ordered. What does Rawls's nonideal theory say about these situations? Rawls does indeed reject any liberal principle of distributive justice, including the difference principle, for use at the global level. His reasons are the constructivist ones that the difference principle "is not framed for our present case" and, perhaps more plausibly, the recognition that hierarchical societies reject all liberal principles of distributive justice. Rawls is seeking common ground between liberal and hierarchical societies, and therefore avoids explicitly liberal principles of distribution. But that is not to say that the law of peoples is silent on global distribution. Having rejected liberal principles of distribution, Rawls continues:

> Although no liberal principle of distributive justice would be adopted for dealing with unfavorable conditions, that certainly does not mean that the well-ordered and wealthier societies have no duties and obligations to societies burdened by such conditions. For the ideal conception of the society of peoples that well-ordered societies affirm directs that in due course all societies must reach, or be assisted to, the conditions that make a well-ordered society possible. This implies that human rights are to be recognized and secured everywhere, and that basic human needs are to be met. (LP, 76; cf. 55, 75)

This passage makes it clear that, *pace* Pogge (ELP, 209), Rawls does not wish to restrict the meeting of basic needs only to liberal societies.

Pogge suggests that meeting basic needs may not enable a people to achieve domestic justice. This is undeniable, but Pogge himself cannot be offering any cast-iron guarantee of the success of GRT in meeting this goal. However, given the close link in both directions between domestic justice and the meeting of basic needs,[7] it is hard to imagine a case in which meeting basic needs would not be thought important to improving the prospect of justice.

It might be claimed that Rawls is open to Pogge's charge that Rawlsian global justice does not protect those living in badly ordered societies where there is no prospect of change since Rawls does not provide much in the way of argument for the link between justice and the meeting of needs. But Rawls might claim that politics is just not sufficiently predictable to allow us to wash our hands of any particular society. He might say that we should always act on the assumption that a society can come to satisfy the conditions that make a well-ordered society possible.

Rawls explicitly refrains from discussing how economic and technological aid may best be given (LP, 76–77), but he has not ruled out the idea of a GRT. Delegates may believe not only that such a tax is the best way to ensure the internal economic conditions for a well-ordered society but that, as Pogge points out (ELP, 214), large global inequalities may affect domestic justice in poorer societies. So a GRT may be part of Rawlsian theory, even if it enters at a lower level than in Pogge's proposal.

All of this sits well with Rawls's view that the conception of the common good of justice will secure for everyone in a hierarchical society "minimum rights to means of subsistence and security (the right to life)," and that these rights in particular are basic (LP, 62, 225 n. 26; cf. 43). This right is a human right (68) and one of the principles of the law of peoples is that such rights be honored (55, 80).

3. Ideal or Nonideal?

Now we move to some problems with Pogge's own positive position. In *Theory*, Rawls draws an important distinction between ideal theory and nonideal theory (*TJ*, 8–9, 245–46). When constructing an ideal theory of justice, or the ideal part of a theory of justice, one assumes that everyone complies with the demands of justice. In so doing, one works out the principles that govern a well-ordered society in favorable circumstances. According to Rawls, one can then move on to nonideal theory, which concerns those principles that govern situations of scarcity or unfortunate historical circumstance, and situations of injustice. At which theoretical level is Pogge operating? We shall suggest that his views can be understood in either way and that there are problems with each.

Pogge speaks of an "ideal world" (ELP, 201), and his putting GRT alongside the views of Rawls (ELP, 211–12) suggests that his proposal can be seen as ideal (see also ELP, 205). If it is so understood, the following difficulties arise.

Pogge rightly notes that present national borders are not only historically but morally arbitrary, distancing himself from what Charles Beitz calls the "morality of states" (ELP, 198–99).[8] No egalitarian can accept, without a great deal of argument, the difference between the life prospects of those born a few miles from one another on either side of the U.S.-Mexico border. The best way to ensure that equality of life chances is not skewed by morally arbitrary borders would be not to allow moral weight to such borders. That, we suspect, is what would be decided behind the veil of ignorance in the global original position. The purpose of the GRT is to provide those who are very poor with that to which they are entitled. But it is far from clear that the morality of states provides the best, or even an acceptable, conceptual and institutional framework in which that can be done.[9]

Pogge speaks approvingly of Rawls's argument for property: "Unless a definite agent is given responsibility for maintaining an asset and bears the loss for not doing so, that asset tends to deteriorate" (LP, 57; quoted in ELP, 200 n. 6). Would this support the notion even at the ideal level that each people owns its territory? In fact, it is not clear why Rawls is entitled to this claim in ideal theory. It may well be that in a world in which individuals do not comply with the demands of morality, nonowned assets will deteriorate. But that is no reason to think that the same will happen in an ideal world. For political morality may demand from everyone, for example, care of the environment for the sake of future generations. There may be other arguments for property, based perhaps on effectiveness and coordination. But these may not go so far as to justify, in an ideal world, nation-states with almost total control of the assets within their borders. This suggests that there will be no ideal law of peoples at all; rather, there will be a law of persons. We take it that this chimes with Pogge's own moral individualism (ELP, 210–11, 215, 218).

Pogge suggests that there is an incoherence between Rawls's conceptions of domestic justice and of global justice (ELP, 210–11). We believe that Pogge is right to suggest that there is a problem in Rawls's views here but that it is better characterized as a *tension,* not an incoherence. It is not a question of Rawls's being nonindividualistic at the global level, as we hope to have shown in section 2; it is rather that Rawls is too ready to take the opportunity offered by constructivism for not extending the difference principle.

Rawls's main argument for not extending the difference principle seems to rest on a failure to distinguish ideal from nonideal theory. He argues for his two-stage procedure thus: "Peoples as corporate bodies organized by their governments now exist in some form all over the world. Historically speaking, all principles and standards proposed for the law of peoples must, to be feasible, prove acceptable to the considered and reflective public opinion of peoples and their governments" (LP, 50).

As Pogge rightly points out (ELP, 197), the notion of "a people" is unclear. But also odd is Rawls's reference to "feasibility," for that notion is part of nonideal theory. The kind of feasibility required for ideal theory is much weaker, and one might have thought that a global difference principle which ignored national boundaries is almost as feasible today as the application of the difference principle within any country of the world. As Pogge puts it in *Realizing Rawls* (26), "Realism hardly requires that principles of justice must conform to the prevailing sordid realities." The tension in Rawls's thought, then, consists in the different feasibility requirements at each level.

What will the law of persons require? It may still impose a GRT on anyone who uses world resources, but why should it? Why should it not merely require transfers from those who are better-off through no doing of their own to those similarly worse-off? In this respect, transfers would be analogous to contemporary development aid. Pogge claims that GRT has the advantage of offering the poor that to which they are entitled, instead of charity (ELP, 202). But if, as seems plausible, the poor have entitlements to aid, then present "charity" is in fact better described as justice. And the same would go for transfers in an ideal world.

So the main problem with Pogge's suggestion understood as ideal is that arrangements other than the GRT would be better grounded. Most of the time, however, Pogge writes as if he is proposing the adoption of a GRT in our "non-ideal world" (ELP, 202), that is, "the world as we know it" (ELP, 224). So, let us now consider Pogge's suggestion as nonideal.

It is true that adoption by all of a GRT scheme might be argued to be likely to improve matters considerably from the point of view of global justice. But so would increased transfers or many other schemes. So the GRT proposal must be thought to have some special backing in philosophical argument or political rhetoric.

Pogge claims that it has the support of philosophical argument in abundance (ELP, 200–201). From the forward-looking point of view, it is supported by consequentialism and contractualism, and from the backward-looking point of view by a Lockean theory of appropriation. But neither consequentialism nor any plausible form of contractualism will support anything as moderate as the GRT; both will be far more demanding. Much larger transfers will increase overall well-being and would be selected from behind any plausible veil of ignorance. Lockean theories rely on a theory of just acquisition. Since most Lockean theories, including Nozick's, will allow that present possession is based on unjust acquisition and transfer, these also may require much larger transfers, this time for rectificatory purposes.[10]

What about political rhetoric? One problem concerns the rights of ownership, which Pogge himself wishes not to question. It is generally held that states have complete rights of ownership over their own resources. If doubt about the completeness of this right can be made to arise, then why should states not just transfer wealth rather than go through the administrative hoops of GRT?

Another problem for the GRT as a practical political proposal concerns political motivation. To a great extent the nations of the world act on the basis of their perceived self-interest, and it is difficult to imagine nations collectively agreeing that a GRT is in their interests. If the GRT functioned in the way in which Pogge envisions, the main beneficiaries would be the poorest people in the poorest countries. At a time when countries such as the United States are reducing overseas aid and major donors are writing off the entire continent of Africa as "a basket case," it is difficult to imagine that nations would be motivated to act in the interests of the poorest of the poor. This suggests either that it would be practically impossible to impose a GRT using moral argument or that such a GRT would be shaped so as to subvert its main purpose. The policy most likely to succeed would have to be based on the argument that the interests of politicians' own states, and therefore their own self-interest, will be furthered by increasing the amount of development aid, or by proper use of it (depending on which hemisphere the politician is from).[11]

We may be too pessimistic. And as Rawls says (LP, 73), these issues of political wisdom are matters to which political philosophy has little to add. But we doubt whether moral argument can achieve very much at the global political level. Most politicians are unfortunately unlike Shaftesbury or Wilberforce (see ELP, 222). States, like most individuals, will not respond well to a demanding morality without sanctions; in a nonideal world, appeals to self-interest are morally preferable to morally backed proposals such as GRT.

This raises a final question about individual obligations. Pogge is in favor of extending domestic liberal theory to the level of global justice. He has argued previously that this move, because of its comprehensiveness, unity, and elegance, is more in line with constructivism than Rawls's own method (*RR,* 258). Pogge speaks only of our "collective responsibilities." But one should be able to extend liberal theory inward as well as outward in order to ascertain its implications for individual morality. Doing this causes a problem for Pogge. Given the extent of present inequalities in the world, a moral view which requires each wealthy person, in a nonideal world like ours, to surrender only 1 percent of their income seems too undemanding. To retain comprehensiveness, unity, and elegance may require a more demanding principle at the individual level and, hence, the global level. But a proposal for a demanding GRT would be extremely unlikely to succeed.

4. Efficiency, Conscientiousness, and Individual Entitlement

Let us now assume that the GRT is in place and consider some of the more straightforwardly practical problems with the proposal. First, there would be problems of efficiency. Countries with GRT obligations must have in place systems of collecting and transferring revenue, and recipient countries must have institutions that permit them to spend money effectively and efficiently. Several rich countries, including the United States, are already in arrears in their payments to international organizations. Free market societies often claim that they have difficulties in collecting broad-based taxes on producers. Even a relatively simple tax like the proposed tax on the British thermal unit (BTU) content of energy came under fire in the United States for the administrative difficulties its collection would entail. On the recipient side, the poorest countries of the world often have extremely inefficient governmental institutions. There are many reasons for this, including poor infrastructure, badly educated government employees, and low salaries. But often countries are poor in part because of social conflict or war. Delivering benefits in such conditions may be close to impossible.

In addition to practical problems of delivering GRT revenues to those who are most in need, many recipient governments would simply not try. As the history of foreign assistance programs shows, some governments would use GRT revenues to benefit urban elites, to build military machines, or simply for personal enrichment.

Pogge is sensitive to these concerns, which is why he leaves open the possibility that some or all GRT revenues could be distributed through United Nations (UN) or nongovernmental organizations (ELP, 202). But this also raises some difficulties.

GRT funds are supposed to be used to improve the position of the poor. If a government is conscientious and efficient, it may administer GRT funds on behalf of the poor. If it is not, then these funds may be administered by UN or nongovernmental organizations (NGOs), or they may not be transferred at all. Mixes are possible. Pogge writes that "a country might receive 60 percent of the GRT funds it is eligible for, one third of this through the government and two thirds of it through other channels" (ELP, 202).

We should notice first that while Pogge had earlier written that "payments would be a matter of entitlement rather than charity" (ELP, 202), here he speaks of countries being "eligible for" GRT funds. One way of trying to make this language consistent would be to say that it is the poor who are entitled to GRT funds while governments and other institutions are eligible for such funds only insofar as they are likely to be efficient and conscientious in delivering them to those who are entitled. But if that is the view, then it is not clear why national governments should be privileged institutions for the disbursement of funds at all. It may be that NGOs are generally more efficient and conscientious in delivering resources to the poor than national governments. If that is the case, then it would appear that the GRT should transfer its revenue to NGOs rather than to the national governments of poor countries.

But this raises another issue. If it is poor people who have entitlements and transfers are made only to their governments, insofar as they are efficient and conscientious, then it is unclear why Pogge speaks of payments being made "to the governments of the poorest societies, based on their per capita income . . . and population size" (ELP, 201). This view seems to suggest that governments have some entitlement independent of the entitlements of the poorest people. Some of the poorest people do not live in the poorest societies. The GRT does not seem to be geared up to answer to their needs, and in that respect is inconsistent with Pogge's assumption of moral individualism.

Pogge wants the GRT to be a matter of entitlement rather than charity, to directly benefit the poorest of the poor, and he wants the GRT to work through national governments whenever possible. But it is difficult to reconcile these demands. Once the GRT is conceptualized as a transfer mechanism from rich to poor countries, then withholding these funds for whatever reason counts against these transfers being entitlements rather than charity. If it is poor people themselves who are entitled to these funds, then where such a person lives should have nothing to do with whether he or she is benefited, and there should be no presumption that national governments should figure in these transfers. Either Pogge should give up the morality of states, or he should give up the view that it is poor people themselves who are entitled to the proceeds of the GRT.

In addition to this problem of internal consistency, there is also the difficulty of who decides whether GRT money is to be distributed by national governments, the UN or NGOs, or not at all. Pogge suggests that "these rules are to be designed, and possibly revised, by an international group of economists and international lawyers" (ELP, 203). But this raises the questions of who these people are, how they are chosen, and who they represent. Since they will decide how money taken from the rich countries is to be spent, it is difficult to believe that they would not represent the interests of those countries. Virtually every international organization that transfers money to poor countries guarantees strong representation for donors. Even if this were not the case, economists and lawyers, whatever their citizenship, are members of the global professional class. It is the poor who are supposed to be entitled to the funds, but they are nowhere around when it comes to making the decisions about how and even whether the money will be spent.

5. Regressiveness and Environmental Effects

The practical problems outlined in section 4 might be thought to be technical difficulties concerning how a particular GRT is conceptualized and established. The principle, it might be said, is surely a good one, both for the poor and for the environment. While this may be true, it is far from obvious.

Pogge's GRT would be instituted in a world characterized by enormous inequality. Because different countries are at different stages of development, they have different resource needs. In general, developing countries use resources much less efficiently than developed countries. The efficient use of resources is in part a product of capital—both because energy efficient technologies require large capital investments and because better-educated populations are likely to use resources more efficiently. The GRT might be beneficial for very poor countries because they use so little in the way of resources, but transitional countries might well be disadvantaged by the GRT.

Consider the case of China. That country is as inefficient in its use of energy as Poland or the old USSR, with its major industries consuming "30 to 90 percent more energy than similar industries in developed countries."[12] According to the World Bank, the United States produces more than four times as much gross domestic product (GDP) per unit of energy input as does China while countries such as Italy, Austria, Switzerland, Denmark, and Japan produce more than ten times as much GDP per unit of energy consumed.[13] In order to develop an economy in which it can use resources as efficiently as the countries of the Organization for Economic Cooperation and Development (OECD), China will have to become richer, which will involve using large amounts of resources in a relatively inefficient way during the transition. Thus, at least for the foreseeable future, a GRT would seem to be harder on China than on OECD countries precisely because China produces less GDP per unit of energy consumed. It may be that China would be a beneficiary country or outside of the GRT regime altogether. But since Pogge gives no very detailed principles for inclusion in one category rather than another, it is unclear where China would fall. Moreover, this is only one example of how a GRT could have paradoxical distributional effects.

There are several reasons why the GRT, as Pogge conceives it, is likely to have only marginal positive effects on global environmental problems and perhaps some unexpected negative effects as well. Let us consider an example of the latter.

Despite concerns about safety and long-term environmental damage, it appeared during the 1970s that much of the world would eventually rely on nuclear power for electricity generation. With a few exceptions (e.g., France), that scenario has not come to pass. A GRT of the sort that Pogge proposes would appear to make nuclear power desirable relative to fossil fuel–fired generating plants. Nuclear power is not very resource intensive; the main costs it imposes involve risks of catastrophic accident and disposal of nuclear wastes. Oil- and coal-fired plants are resource intensive, although they do not carry the risks or disposal costs associated with nuclear power. Because of the risk of climate change, there is reason to be concerned about generating electricity from fossil fuels. But the problem with the GRT is that is that it favors nuclear power over fossil fuels by taxing extraction but not disposal. Thus, it deals with only one dimension of the environmental problems involved with electricity generation.

A more important reason why the GRT is likely to be ineffective in addressing environmental problems is that its focus is on nonrenewable rather than renewable resources but it is the latter that are most endangered. In the 1970s, there was widespread concern about the exhaustion of nonrenewable resources—oil, coal, minerals, and so on. Economists argued that as these resources became increasingly scarce, rising prices would lead to more efficient allocation, the discovery of new deposits, and the development of alternatives. Thus far, this line of argument has been correct. With respect to most nonrenewable resources, prices are lower, and reserves are greater now than they were in the 1970s. Environmentalists then paid relatively little attention to renewable resources—species, plants, soils, air, water—because nature continually reprovisions us with these goods. But the most serious environmental problems we now face involve the disruption of the natural systems which maintain these renewable resources. Pogge writes that "this tax could be extended, along the same lines, to reusable resources: to land used in agriculture and ranching, for example, and, especially, to air and water used for the discharging of pollutants" (ELP, 200). While there are proposals for carbon taxes and already existing markets in pollution permits, these involve different principles from Pogge's GRT. In part, this is because the GRT addresses private (or at least national) goods while the other policy instruments address public goods. It is difficult to see how Pogge's GRT can be extended to renewable resources such as soils. Even less clear is how the GRT can help us preserve such (non-) resources as wilderness and biodiversity.

6. Conclusion

We have been very critical of Pogge's proposal for a GRT. This should not obscure the fact that he has done a great service by sketching a specific proposal about how we might address global inequality and environmental degradation. In conclusion, we will briefly mention what would be required in a more adequate approach to the problems that Pogge has identified.

First, in our view, the problem of global inequality should be thought of in terms of the claims and entitlements of individuals. While Pogge appears to agree with this, his attempt to work within the conceptual structure of Rawls's law of peoples was problematic from the beginning. Instead of thinking of duties and obligations as linking only governments, we should think of them as joining people at all levels of social organization.

Second, once we have rejected the morality of states, it is easy to see that almost any plausible principle of justice will have very serious distributive implications. Pogge's GRT, if not regressive, does not begin to constitute a truly egalitarian law of peoples. "Demandingness" is itself demanded of any theory of justice.

Finally, any attempt to think seriously about global environmental problems will have to pay at least as much attention to renewable resources, which are global public goods, such as climate stability, ozone, and biodiversity, as privately held nonrenewable resources. Designing policies that satisfy all these demands and are feasible is a challenging task, but, in our view, morality demands nothing less.

Notes

1. John Rawls, *A Theory of Justice* (Cambridge, Mass.: Harvard University Press, 1971).

2. John Rawls, *Political Liberalism* (New York: Columbia University Press, 1993) (unless otherwise noted, references in this chapter to *Political Liberalism* will be to the 1993 edition).

3. Thomas W. Pogge, *Realizing Rawls* (Ithaca, N.Y.: Cornell University Press, 1989).

4. John Rawls, The Law of Peoples, in *On Human Rights,* ed. S. Shute and S. Hurley (New York: Basic Books, 1993), 41–82, 220–30.

5. Thomas W. Pogge, An Egalitarian Law of Peoples, *Philosophy and Public Affairs* 23, no. 3 (Summer 1993): 195–224.

6. Thomas Nagel, *Equality and Partiality* (New York: Oxford University Press, 1991), 70.

7. See, for example, the work of Amartya Sen, noted by Rawls in LP, 229 n. 53.

8. Charles Beitz, *Political Theory and International Relations* (Princeton, N.J.: Princeton University Press, 1979).

9. On page 199 of An Egalitarian Law of Peoples, Pogge says that he will entertain "Rawls's fantasy that the world's population neatly divides into peoples cleanly separated by national borders" in sections I–V of his article. We might then expect him—especially given his emphasis on the point that to understand Rawls one has to assume that existing distributions have no normative force merely through being in place (ELP, 212)—explicitly to distance himself from this fantasy in his concluding section VI. He does not, of course, since the GRT itself rests on the fantasy.

10. There may be some tension between Pogge's attempts to ground GRT on both the Lockean proviso and a rectification principle (ELP, 220–21).

11. Pogge does offer some self-interest arguments in favor of GRT (ELP, 222–23), but these could be redeployed to support many other schemes.

12. World Resources Institute, *World Resources 1994–95* (New York: Oxford University Press, 1994).

13. International Bank for Reconstruction and Development, *World Development Report 1994* (New York: Oxford University Press, 1994), 170.

6

FUNDAMENTAL RIGHTS, REASONABLE

PLURALISM, AND THE MORAL

COMMITMENTS OF LIBERALISM

Clark Wolf

1. Liberalism and Fundamental Constitutional Rights

Virtually all liberal theories incorporate a version of fundamental rights constitutionalism, the view that the scope of democratic rule must be radically limited where its exercise would compromise vital liberties (Murphy 1995, 78). In fact, the view that some rights deserve constitutional protection from the democratic process is sometimes regarded as the essential identifying feature that distinguishes liberal theories as *liberal.* In this spirit, Allen Buchanan writes:

> The liberal political thesis, as I define it, is the thesis that the state should enforce certain basic civil and individual rights and liberties—roughly speaking, those which are found in the U.S. Constitution's Bill of Rights, and in John Rawls's first principle of justice. These rights include rights to freedom of religion, expression, thought, and association, the right of political participation, and the right of due process. This first thesis is closely related to, and may be argued to imply another thesis that is also associated with liberalism, namely that the proper role of the state is to protect basic individual liberties, not to make its citizens virtuous or to impose upon them any particular or substantive conception of the good life. The connection between these theses should be clear: if the state enforces the basic civil and political liberties, it will leave individuals free, within broad limits, to pursue their own conceptions of the good and will preclude itself from imposing upon them any one particular conception of the good or of virtue. (Buchanan 1989, 854)

But while many liberals will agree on the claim that fundamental rights deserve special constitutional protection, different liberal theories give different accounts of the origin or justification of these rights, and not all such theories regard the same rights as having the fundamental importance that justifies special constitutional protection. Both in Rawls's early work and in his more recent papers, the fundamental rights are theory of justice. Rawls's first principle of justice sti to have an equal right to a fully adequate scheme which is compatible with a similar scheme of liber 291). Rawls argues that this principle has lexical pr of the conception of justice as fairness, including t equal opportunity and defining the limits of dist also emphasizes the fundamental liberties as the primary goods—goods that are to be understood as all-purpose by all rational people regardless of any of their other wants or values.

In this chapter, I examine the basis for Rawls's theory of fundamental rights and its role in *Political Liberalism*. I argue that Rawls's account of these rights has changed in important ways from his early work in *A Theory of Justice* to his later work in *Political Liberalism* and recent papers. But the core of Rawls's argument for the value and identification of these rights remains unchanged: Rawls views the fundamental rights as those rights that are necessary for the exercise of basic human capacities, which he calls "the two moral powers." It is because the fundamental rights are necessary conditions for the exercise of these fundamental capacities that these rights are taken to reflect "the higher-order interests" of all rational persons. This stable core in Rawls's account of fundamental rights leaves his argument open to some persistent problems. I argue that these problems do not constitute conclusive objections to Rawls's project but that an understanding of them should lead us to modify our acceptance of Rawls's larger project, and to qualify acceptance of the account of political legitimacy Rawls offers in his recent work. Such an understanding may also help to explain the transition from Rawls's earlier work in *A Theory of Justice* to his later work in *Political Liberalism*. Even more important than this exegetical objective, an examination of Rawls's arguments will, I hope, help in the articulation of a modest but plausible understanding of the nature and limits of fundamental constitutional rights.

2. Rawls on Rational Revisability and Fundamental Liberal Rights

Rawls's argument for the fundamental liberal rights, the content of his first principle of justice, has been the focus of much less scholarly attention than other features of his view. It is not difficult to see why this should be so: Liberal theorists are more in agreement about the fundamental rights than they are about distributive and redistributive aspects of the theory of justice. The difference principle and its implications for the structure of basic social institutions are the source of most of the interesting conflict between Rawls and his libertarian critics. The original position justification of the difference principle has been similarly controversial: Rawls's argument for the claim that parties to the original position should employ maximin reasoning in their choice among conceptions of justice is widely regarded as perhaps the

argument in *Theory*. Those who find Rawls's project attractive
d it necessary either to find some alternate supporting argument for
erence principle or to articulate an alternate and less controversial
iple of distributive justice.

It is fair to say that the distributive features of Rawls's conception of justice
have been at the center of attention both from Rawls's critics and his supporters and that this flurry of activity has overshadowed the argument for the
basic liberal rights. But if this imbalance of critical attention is due to a mistaken belief that liberals can all agree about the fundamental rights, then
Rawls's argument for the first principle deserves more serious critical examination. I first present what I hope is a plausible and sympathetic reading of
Rawls's argument for the fundamental rights. It is both interesting and important that this argument can be expressed in a way that is largely independent of many of the more controversial features of Rawls's view, including the
original position construction and the notoriously unpersuasive argument
for maximin reasoning.

Rawls supports the first principle rights and liberties by connecting these
rights to his account of moral psychology, specifically to what he calls the
"two moral powers." These two powers are fundamental human capacities
that explain why human beings are both appropriate moral subjects and agents,
and Rawls takes them to be relatively uncontroversial assumptions about
human moral psychology. These powers are, first, the capacity for a sense of
justice and, second, the capacity for a conception of the good. The former,
Rawls tells us, implies "a capacity to understand, apply, and act from (and
not merely in accordance with) the principles of political justice that specify
fair terms of cooperation." The latter is the capacity to "have, to revise, and
rationally pursue a conception of the good" (Rawls 1990, §7).

A conception of the good is a system of values that defines our first-order
aims and objectives. According to Rawls: "Such a conception is an ordered
family of final ends and aims which specifies a person's conception of what is of
value in human life; or alternatively, of what is regarded as a fully worthwhile
life. The elements of such a conception are normally set within, and interpreted by, certain religious, philosophical, or moral doctrines in the light of
which various ends and aims are ordered and understood" (Rawls 1990, 14).

It is important for Rawls that one's conception of the good is likely to
change over time. Such change may be the result of rational self-reflection,
interaction with others, or new information. Acceptance of an evaluative conception will imply acceptance of certain aims and interests. But because one's
evaluative conception is likely to change over time, the interests one has as a
result of acceptance of a particular conception of the good cannot be taken to
be the constitutive identifying features of individuals: When a person rationally reconsiders her fundamental values and comes to accept a different or
revised conception of the good, she is still the same person. In this sense, the
capacities implicit in the moral powers define higher order interests: Our
interest in maintaining the ability to critically revise our conception of the

good is separate from and prior to the interests implicit in our acceptance of a particular conception of the good. Our interest in maintaining the ability to exercise the two moral powers is therefore a "higher-order" interest that is, in this sense, fundamental to our conception of ourselves as agents who act and deliberate over time. Citizens in a liberal society identify themselves as independent of and not identified with any particular conception of the good. It will not do for public institutions to identify citizens with specific evaluative conceptions, because ideas of value change over time as individuals subject their ideals to rational scrutiny. It is in this sense that the higher-order interests implicit in the two moral powers are said to have priority over our first-order interests: It may be good for us when we get what we value and want. But it is even more important, argues Rawls, for us to be in a position to evaluate our wants and values.

The two moral powers are crucial elements of Rawls's conception of citizens as "free and equal." The fact that all citizens have these powers to at least a minimum degree is, "the basis for equality among citizens as persons" (Rawls 1971, § 77; 1990, § 7). The capacity for a sense of justice is necessary since it is one of the capacities that makes social cooperation possible. The "freedom" of persons is embodied first in the notion that persons as members of a liberal society will regard themselves as self-authenticating sources of claims on the basic institutions of society: They regard themselves as *entitled* to make claims on the basic institutions so that they may advance and pursue their conception of the good within the bounds of a public conception of justice. And the capacity to adopt, rationally revise, and pursue a conception of the good is among the most important constituents of the conception of citizens as free. Such rational review is sometimes associated with the Kantian conception of freedom of the will, which presupposes the ability to frame one's choices reasonably instead of acting on first-level wants and desires. In the political context, the ability to revise and pursue our values is associated with freedom of conscience and other personal freedoms.

Throughout his work, Rawls employs his account of the two moral powers in identifying and justifying the fundamental liberal rights. Although he identifies the content of the first principle in terms of what he calls "basic liberties," it is quite clear that he understands the first principle of justice to include both liberties and *rights,* understood as Hohfeldian claims. First principle protections for freedom of expression, thought, and conscience, for example, are understood to embody claims against others, quite similar to First Amendment protections for freedom of speech guaranteed in the U.S. Constitution.

In drawing up a list of basic "liberties" of this sort, Rawls notes that we might proceed in either of two different ways:

> One way is historical: we study the constitutions of democratic states and put together a list of liberties normally protected, and we examine the role of these liberties in those constitutions which have worked well. While this kind of information is not available to the parties in the original position, it is available

to us—to you and me who are setting up justice as fairness—and therefore this historical knowledge may influence the content of the principles of justice which we allow the parties as alternatives. A second way is to consider which liberties are essential social conditions for the adequate development and exercise of the two powers of moral personality over a complete life. Doing this connects the basic liberties with the conception of the person used in justice as fairness. (Rawls 1993, 292–93)

Which are the liberal rights? They are just those rights that are necessary for the exercise of the capacity to understand, apply, and act from principles that specify fair terms of cooperation and the capacity to adopt, rationally revise, and pursue a "conception of the good." Why should we care about the basic liberal rights? It is because our conception of ourselves as autonomous persons embodies a conception of ourselves as possessing the two moral powers. The fundamental rights are necessary for our exercise of these powers, so we value these rights as necessary for our autonomy. Since Rawls regards autonomy as a higher-order value that takes priority over other values we may have, the rights that protect autonomy are given priority over other elements of the conception of justice as fairness.

3. The Plausibility of Rawlsian Moral Psychology

What are the evaluative assumptions of this Rawlsian argument? As presented here, the argument for fundamental rights is more or less independent of the original position and many other controversial elements of Rawls's broader view. The argument from the two moral powers does involve substantive assumptions about human moral psychology; it also assumes that those who possess these powers will have certain higher-order interests and that these interests should be understood as being *prior* to other lower-order interests. Are these assumptions plausible? Do we think of ourselves as possessing the moral powers described in Rawls's argument, and if so, do we (necessarily?) have the higher-order interests Rawls describes? Do we, or should we, regard these interests as prior to our other values and interests?

As a first step toward answering these questions, we may rehearse familiar arguments for them: Anyone who has a sense that some pursuits are more valuable than others has a conception of the good, and anyone who hopes to shape her life around goals given by this evaluative conception hopes rationally to pursue her conception of the good. Because rational individuals will want to shape their lives around their values, they will also have reason to ensure, as far as possible, that social institutions do not prohibit them from rationally pursuing their ends. This is sufficient to support the claim that rational agents have a strong *prima facie* reason to value the rights and liberties that are necessary for the exercise of their capacity reflectively to evaluate their fundamental evaluative commitments.

It is significant for liberal theorists not only that different persons have different conceptions of the good but also that a thoughtful person's conception of what is valuable in a human life will change as a result of life experience or as a result of rational self-reflection. Because thoughtful persons will recognize that the evaluative conception they now accept may change over time, they will also recognize that they have the higher-order interest Rawls describes: an interest in protecting the capacity for critical self-reflection about commitments. This implies an interest in promoting and preserving political institutions that are flexible enough to accommodate changes in current commitments and values. This argument can even be accepted within a narrow preferentialist framework: A person's interest in preserving the ability to satisfy her *preferences* generates a reason to arrange her life so she will not be thwarted in her ability to satisfy the preferences she will have in the future.[1] This argument from the value of the two moral powers is also the basis for a limited argument against perfectionist institutions, which attempt to impose a conception of human value by limiting individual liberty to pursue alternate conceptions. Recognizing that current commitments may change over time, rational individuals will recognize that they have an interest in maintaining circumstances of political liberty that allow rational reflection and reconsideration of current fundamental commitments.

Some have mistakenly argued that commitment to the value of the second moral power, the ability to critically revise and rationally pursue a conception of the good, involves a kind of value skepticism or relativism—the belief that evaluative systems are all equally good so that in the end it doesn't really matter which evaluative system we accept. But the ability to revise beliefs is especially important for value realists, not for skeptics. One important reason to want to preserve the ability to rationally revise our evaluative commitments is that we may believe that some evaluative schemes are better justified or morally superior to others. Realists will want to get their values right and will value the ability to revise their conception of the good because, as Mill and others have insisted, they cannot be fully justified in the acceptance of the values they hold unless they are in a position to consider their basis and justification.

But neither is the value of rational reconsideration bound to value realism or objectivism: Even noncognitivists can acknowledge that evaluative *change* may have a cognitive component and that we have good reason to value our ability rationally to reconsider our evaluative assumptions. Noncognitivists like Simon Blackburn, Allan Gibbard, and even A. J. Ayer believe that their metaethical theories are true and justified, and well supported by the careful arguments they offer. If they regard their arguments as rationally persuasive, then they must be open to the possibility that some error-bound realists might eventually see the light and come to understand the rational grounds for noncognitivism. According to Allen Buchanan:

> All the principle of revisability commits one to is the view that valuation is a rational enterprise. By [this] I mean the very minimal view that value judgments, and hence conceptions of the good, are subject to rational assessment.

On the weakest interpretation of this view, rational assessment is limited to considerations of the consistency or coherence of one's value judgments with each other and with one's other beliefs. . . . So even if the justifiability of a life plan is only a matter of achieving and maintaining the consistency or coherence of one's own system of belief, this is quite enough to commit one to the principle of revisability. (Buchanan 1975, 399)

As Buchanan notes, the value of rational reconsideration increases if one regards values as objectively discoverable and supported by reason. Rawls's assumption that people can rationally assess their conceptions of value seems fully acceptable as an assumption about human moral psychology, if not entirely uncontroversial. And rational persons who have an evaluative conception and regard valuation as (minimally) subject to rational assessment have reason to value and protect their ability to exercise the second moral power.

Even minimalist assumptions about the relationship between reason and value imply that there is good reason to accept Rawls's account of the first moral power, the capacity to understand, apply, and act from principles that specify fair terms of cooperation. If our values can be the springs of action, and if values are subject to rational assessment, then our ability to assess our values may importantly explain the possibility that we can act from the principles we come to accept after rational consideration. If Rawls can support the claim that the principles of justice embody fair terms of cooperation, and the claim that reflective persons have sufficient reason to value fairness in themselves as well as in the institutions of society, then the value of the first moral power may be partly explained in terms of the second: The capacity for a sense of justice is partly explained by our ability to assess and rationally revise our conception of the good. And this is a capacity that will be highly valued by all rational beings who have beliefs about what makes a human life go well. If we are to some extent rational, if we have a conception of the good, and if we regard valuation as subject to rational assessment, then we will value our capacity to exercise the two moral powers. But if we value our capacity to exercise these powers, then we will also value highly any other things that are necessary for their exercise. The basic rights and liberties described in the first principle of justice are necessary for the exercise of these powers, so we will highly value these rights and liberties.

This reconstructs an important part of Rawls's argument for the first principle of justice. It is important once again to emphasize the extent to which this argument can be articulated in a way that makes it independent of the original position and other controversial features of Rawls's view. In the account of Rawls's argument I have offered, there is no reference to the more controversial features of Rawls's view.[2] If Rawls's assumptions about moral psychology and human interests employed are plausible, this is a strong and interesting argument for the basic liberal rights. In section 4, I examine an early attempt by Allen Buchanan to extend Rawls's argument to show that all practically rational persons have reason to value the fundamental liberal rights.

4. Fundamental Rights, Revisability, and Rational Choice

In his early work, Rawls was tempted by the notion that liberalism might be a uniquely rational political conception. In *A Theory of Justice,* for example: "The merit of the contract terminology is that it conveys the idea that principles of justice may be conceived as principles that would be chosen by rational persons, and that in this way conceptions of justice may be explained and justified. The theory of justice is a part, perhaps the most important part, of the theory of rational choice" (Rawls 1971, 16). This claim links Rawls's early project with a long line of traditional liberal theorists who have tried to show that a liberal conception of the state is uniquely choice worthy and rationally superior to all alternative views. Such rationalist foundations stretch back to Condorcet's pure dream that perfect democracy would eventually lead to the most perfect use of the different knowledge of different individuals and that this would gradually lead us toward the most perfectly rational political institutions. More recent strains of this rationalist theme can be found in Vilfredo Pareto's ideal of a mathematical politics, David Gauthier's *Morals by Agreement,* James Buchanan's work on constitutional economics, and John Harsanyi's rational-contractarian defense of utilitarianism.

Rawls has now abandoned the claim that the theory of justice is part of the theory of rational choice. In 1989, he wrote that his earlier claim was "simply a mistake. What should have been said is that the account of the parties [to the original position] and their reasoning uses the theory of rational choice (decision), but that this theory is itself part of a political conception of justice, one that tries to give an account of reasonable principles of justice. There is no thought of deriving those principles from the concept of rationality as the sole normative concept" (Rawls 1989, 60). It is important to understand both why Rawls was initially attracted to the notion that liberalism might be uniquely rational and the reasons for his later rejection of this claim. In this interest, it is worthwhile to examine one of the most interesting and promising attempts to make good Rawls's early case for liberal rationalism. Allen Buchanan's (1975) reconstruction of Rawls's argument is of special interest because of its formal clarity and because it relies centrally on the argument from the two moral powers and the value of rational revisability. It is also significant because Buchannan's work has influenced Rawls and many other contemporary liberal theorists.[3] The partial failure and limited but decisive success of Buchanan's argument is significant in its own right but also because it brings into sharp relief an important limitation in Rawls's recent account of political liberalism.

Buchanan articulates the substance of the second moral power as a formal principle: "*Revisability Principle R*: One ought, ceteris paribus, to maintain an attitude of critical revisability toward one's own conception of the good (or life plan) and of openmindedness toward competing conceptions" (Buchanan 1975, 399). Buchanan argues that this principle is a principle of practical rationality. He argues that one can reject this principle only if one holds that

(a) One's theoretical judgment is infallible.
(b) One's judgment about the goodness of ends is infallible.
(c) One's judgment about the ranking of ends is infallible.
(d) One is infallible in one's judgment that (a), (b), and (c) are true. (Buchanan 1975, 400)

Since changing theoretical judgments, changing judgments about the value of ends, or changing judgments about the ranking of ends would each imply revisions in one's conception of the good, only an agent who holds each of these can rationally reject the revisability principle. But few people regard themselves as infallible, and surely no one could be justified in regarding herself as infallible in so many domains. If not, one may argue, then no rational person can be justified in rejecting the revisability principle itself. Buchanan hammers home his claim that no one can be justified in rejecting the revisability principle by arguing that its rejection could be rational only if one believes, in addition to items a–d above, that

(e) Both the factual circumstances which one's theoretical beliefs represent and the values expressed in one's judgments about ends and their rankings are immutable, and
(f) One is infallible with respect to one's belief that assumption (e) is true. (Buchanan (1975, 401)

If Buchanan is right, then it would seem that only an omniscient god could be justified in rejecting Principle R: "It is difficult to imagine a less plausible set of epistemological theses than (a)–(f). Yet if one is to reject the principle that one ought to maintain an attitude of critical revisability toward one's life plan, one must embrace all of them. If this is so, then R is at least as plausible as these epistemological theses are implausible" (Buchanan 1975, 401).

But the revisability principle has two corollaries, and acceptance of R implies acceptance of these as well. The first is "*Epistemic Corollary Re:* One ought, ceteris paribus, to attempt to satisfy the epistemic conditions necessary for the effective expression of an attitude of critical revisability" (Buchanan 1975, 401). The second corollary is practical and specifies a rational interest in implementing and preserving the conditions necessary for flexible changes in one's evaluative commitments: "*Implementation Corollary Ri:* One ought, ceteris paribus, to attempt to provide for the implementation of those new or revised conceptions of the good which one may develop as a result of one's commitment to R and Re" (Buchanan 1975, 402).

If one follows the argument this far, it is difficult to avoid the next precipitous step: It is argued that the political and civil liberties listed in Rawls's first principle of justice are necessary constituents of any political society that hopes to allow citizens the liberty to form and to rationally revise and pursue a conception of the good. Liberties of thought and discussion are necessary to satisfy the epistemic corollary while liberties of movement and other civil liberties are necessary for the implementation of revised evaluative conceptions.

Even the distributive features of Rawls's conception of justice as fairness can be supported with this argument: The primary goods are described as all-purpose means, necessary for the pursuit of any reasonable conception of the good.[4] An adequate provision of such goods must then be necessary for those who wish to maintain the freedom to implement their evaluative conception. Universal provision of at least a basic minimum of primary goods may be defended as the material conditions necessary for the exercise of the two moral powers. It is noteworthy that this argument supports a more minimal distributive principle than Rawls's difference principle: The implementation corollary requires only that one have access to a basic minimum provision of primary goods.

Buchanan's account of the revisability argument sets in sharp relief the specific claims that must be defended by advocates of Rawls's conception of justice as fairness. If the argument works, it provides the strongest kind of support for liberalism: If R is a principle of rationality, then all rational agents must accept it. If acceptance of R implies rational acceptance of Re and Ri, then rational agents must accept them as well. And if acceptance of these corollaries implies an interest in creating and protecting liberal rights, then all rational agents have an interest in promoting those rights and the institutions that protect them. If successful, the revisability argument would imply that liberalism is uniquely rational—that it is not only rationally permissible to accept a liberal theory of the state, it is irrational to reject it. Just as important, if this argument works, it provides a foundation for liberalism that bypasses Rawls's appeal to the original position as a morally credentialed perspective from which to chose principles of justice. Many have rejected Rawls's theory because they cannot accept Rawls's account of the original position choice. If liberalism can be defended without appealing to the original position.

What form of liberalism should we accept, and which are the fundamental liberal rights? Given this understanding of the theoretical foundations of liberalism, we can define the set of fundamental liberal rights with a formal membership condition: The fundamental liberal rights are just those rights that are necessary for the protection of people's ability to adopt and to rationally revise and pursue their conception of the good. The dispute between libertarians and liberals then gains context and content as a dispute about whether welfare rights are necessary for these projects. This provides a context for other tricky questions like the question whether economic rights should be included among the Rawlsian "basic liberties." This becomes a question about the relationship between these rights and the ability to be flexible and self-reflectively rational with respect to our evaluative commitments.

5. A Problem with Rational Revisability

If we accept Buchanan's argument that R, Re, and Ri are principles of practical rationality for imperfect agents like ourselves, then it seems that we must also be committed to rationally supporting the basic liberties that constitute the core of a liberal political theory. But there are two ways to call this argument into question. First, we might try to show that Buchanan's principles are not, in fact, principles of practical reason. Second, we might show that rational agents would sometimes be justified in rejecting these principles even if these principles were principles of practical reason.

How would we argue that Buchanan's principles are not principles of practical reason? Buchanan bases his claim that they *are* principles of practical reason on his argument that they are principles that every rational agent has sufficient reason to accept. If it can be shown that there are circumstances in which rational agents would be justified in rejecting the revisability principle and its corollaries, this would effectively undermine this portion of Buchanan's argument. Interestingly, showing that rational agents sometimes have sufficient reason to reject these principles will not show that they are *not* principles of practical reason: Derek Parfit has argued that practically rational agents sometimes have sufficient reason to reject even fundamental principles of practical rationality (Parfit 1984, part I). But if some rational agents have sufficient reason to reject the revisability principle, then they can also have reason to reject the liberal rights that protect our ability to rationally revise our evaluative commitments. This would be sufficient to show that Rawls's and Buchanan's argument does not show that liberalism is uniquely rational.

I will argue that Buchanan's principles are *not* principles of rationality even though they are principles most of us surely have good reason to accept and employ most of the time. But some people in some circumstances have sufficient reason to reject these principles and to adopt more inflexible and nonrevisable guides. The way in which Buchanan's argument fails is instructive not only for those interested in rationality but also for those interested in understanding the relationship between rationality and liberalism, for if some people are justified in rejecting Buchanan's principles, they may lack adequate reason to promote liberal institutions that protect their ability to rationally revise their current evaluative conception.

When is it rational to reject Principle R? Whenever I have reason to believe that my future judgment about "the good" may be inferior to my present and past judgment. Consider the situation of a youthful idealist who self-reflectively endorses her current conception of value. This person recognizes, however, that people often forsake youthful ideals and mistrusts her own ability to maintain her current ideals. If she suspects that she might later backslide on her current commitments, it might be rational for her to try to limit her opportunities to revise her conception of the good. In a famous passage, Derek Parfit describes such a predicament:

> Let us take a nineteenth century Russian who, in several years, should inherit vast estates. Because he has socialist ideals, he intends, now, to give land to the peasants. But he knows that in time his ideals may fade. To guard against this possibility, he does two things. He first signs a legal document, which will

automatically give away the land, and which can only be revoked with his wife's consent. He then says to his wife, "If I ever change my mind and ask you to revoke the document, promise me that you will not consent." (Parfit 1973, 145)

In binding his future choice with a present commitment, Parfit's Russian nobleman restricts his ability rationally to pursue the new conservative ideals he may acquire later, after he reconsiders his present socialist ideals from the new perspective he will have when he inherits his wealth. Since he regards his present judgment as superior to the judgment he may have later, he restricts his ability to rationally reconsider his present commitment. If he is right to doubt his ability to remain loyal to his ideals, and justified in regarding these ideals as the right ones nonetheless, then the course of action he chooses seems to be a rational response to his expectation of backsliding. But in binding his future judgment to his present judgment, he implicitly rejects the revisability principle. If he is justified in his expectation that he will become selfish and reactionary, then his choice to reject this principle seems quite justified and rational. But if so, then it can sometimes be rational to reject the revisability principle even when one does not believe oneself infallible in the ways that Buchanan describes.

This undermines Buchanan's argument for the claim that the revisability principle and its corollaries are principles of rationality. By implication, it undermines his strong claim that all practically rational agents have reason to support the fundamental liberal rights. The revisability argument fails as a rationalist foundation for liberalism since it does not succeed in showing that it is irrational to reject the liberal conception of the state.

Perhaps recognition that the strong version of this argument fails partly explains Rawls's rejection of his early claim that the theory of justice is part of the theory of rational choice. More recently, Buchanan himself has recognized that this early argument fails to recognize the importance of rational commitment and that there may be circumstances in which a rational agent might reject the revisability principle. But as he also recognizes, this partial failure of the argument from revisability and rational choice does not imply its irrelevance: Most of us still have sufficient reason to accept the revisability principle in all but exceptional circumstances. Because of this, we also have sufficient reason to support the political rights and liberties that make possible our own exercise of the two moral powers. The argument is important even if it shows that most people have reason to accept liberalism at least most of the time, and even if it fails to show that liberalism is uniquely rational. We can learn much about the limits of liberalism by considering the circumstances in which people's rational rejection of the revisability principle may justify their rejection of the fundamental liberal rights.

6. Two Objections to Rational Revision and Fundamental Rights

When is it rationally permissible to refrain from critical self-reflection about our evaluative commitments, or even to take steps to cut off our ability to engage in rational reconsideration? There are at least five different kinds of circumstances that can make it rational for a person to reject the revisability principle. First, a person might firmly and justifiably believe that her current commitments are the *right* ones and that further deliberation is likely to raise doubt and shake faith in "the truth." Second, some people may trust an authority more than they trust themselves. Once again, there are circumstances in which this trust could be justifiable. Such a person may view rational reconsideration as likely to lead her to accept views that are worse, in the relevant respect, than the view she now accepts on trusted authority. Third, one might have reasons to mistrust one's own future reasoning powers and might, as a way to compensate for this, take steps to limit later freedom to deliberate and reconsider. In this mode, Kant considers the predicament of a person who knows that he has contracted hydrophobia and may endanger others when the disease affects his ability to make rational decisions (Kant 1797/1991, 220). Fourth, we may regard deliberation as a costly process and rationally decide that we will most likely have better ways to spend our time. When deadlines approach, for example, we may have good reason to limit our options for deliberative reconsideration as a way of forcing ourselves to focus on the task at hand. Fifth and finally, one might plausibly regard the *stability* of one's evaluative commitments as possessing a value that is to some extent independent of their being maximally justified from the epistemic point of view. If we want others to regard us as *reliable,* we may be concerned to maintain our internal evaluative status quo whether or not it is the one we would adopt at the end of an exhaustive process of rational revision.

Recent critics have attacked liberal political theories by arguing that liberalism incorporates substantive evaluative assumptions—that liberalism itself contains or embodies a specific nonneutral conception of the good. One form of this objection focuses on the value of rational reconsideration and its association with personal autonomy: This connection is quite clear in Rawls's identification of the two moral powers as preconditions of individual autonomy and in Buchanan's implicit association between autonomy and the rational reconsideration of values. In sections 6.1 and 6.2, I examine two versions of this objection.

6.1. Objection One

Some critics have argued that the liberal emphasis on critical self-reflection is likely to leave citizens of a liberal state rootless and uncommitted, separated from any constitutive values that could give shape to their lives. On this view, often associated with the communitarian critique of liberalism, liberal theories fail to accommodate the fact that individuals typically have deep commitments that are not subject to rational revisability. Fortunately, this claim can be evaluated in partial abstraction from other features of the liberal-communitarian debate. According to Alisdair MacIntyre, the liberal emphasis on autonomy and rational reconsideration of values embodies a conception of the person as a set of open possibilities, with no necessary attachments or fixed ends. But this understanding of political community, argues MacIntyre, denudes the community of common virtues and ideals (MacIntyre 1984, 145). MacIntyre and other communitarian and postcommunitarian critics describe liberal citizens as rootless social atoms, incapable of concrete or long-standing commitments and attachment to community and place. Even some *defenders* of liberalism seem to accept this critique. Steven Macedo writes:

> [A liberal society] would probably pay for [its] diversity, tolerance, and experimentation with a degree of superficiality, the consequence of a lack of depth or persistence in commitments. There might be a certain amount of feigned or affected eccentricity. And with all the self-critical, self-shaping introspection, perhaps also a degree of self-absorption or even narcissism. . . .
>
> Liberalism holds out the promise, or the threat, of making all the world like California. By encouraging tolerance or even sympathy for a wide array of lifestyles and eccentricities, liberalism creates a community in which it is possible to decide that next week I might quit my career in banking, leave my wife and children, and join a Buddhist cult. (Macedo 1990, 278)

The connection between the claim that liberal citizens will be rootless and the revisability principle is clear: If liberal rights are intended to protect people's ability to rationally revise and perhaps reject even their deepest values, then these rights might be thought to promote the superficiality and narcissism Macedo describes. This is hardly an attractive picture of a citizen in a liberal state. But are liberal citizens really likely to be wishy-washy and undirected in this way? Certainly it is *open* to them to be uncommitted and to lack constitutive commitments, but just as certainly it does not follow that freedom for critical self-examination will leave people uncommitted. One possible outcome of the process of critical self-examination might be that a person will renew and strengthen her commitment to her deepest values and will emerge better able to pursue those values effectively. We only need to look around us to confirm that liberal citizens can and do have stable commitments, even if such commitments arise through a process of rational reflection and reconsideration instead of being simply adopted from the prevailing social and community standards.[5] One may participate in and even be *immersed* in the life of a community without sacrificing one's critical capacity to evaluate that community's values.

But of course rational self-reflection sometimes will lead people to change their conception of value, and people's values may be less stable where the right to engage in rational reconsideration is protected and valued. As critics like MacIntyre and Macedo might emphasize, it is plausible to believe that there is independent value in the stability of one's evaluative beliefs: A person who revised her evaluative commitments in response to every street-corner fanatic, who took on a new evaluative ideology every other day (or year), would be wishy-washy and uncommitted in just the way Macedo describes.

But the value of stability in one's values is not absolute and cannot be entirely independent of the content of the values to which one is stably committed. If our values are bigoted, then stability will be no great virtue. Liberal rights may protect our ability to engage in rational reconsideration, but they cannot guarantee that we will use our capacity for self-critical reflection well. Liberals can argue, following Mill, that this is an acceptable price to pay for the liberty that fundamental rights afford. But critics may still emphasize the cost implicit in evaluative change. Perhaps liberals are to be identified as those who regard these costs as an acceptable price to pay for fundamental liberties.

6.2. Objection Two

If liberals must recognize the value of rational reconsideration, then Daniel Bell is not a liberal. Bell emphasizes the personal and psychological cost of rational self-reflection when this reflection leads us to reject values that are or have been fundamental guiding forces in our lives. He is unpersuaded that the benefits we gain by protecting our right to reconsider our fundamental commitments outweigh the potential cost we may incur if rational reconsideration undermines our commitment to values that define us as persons:

> If the choice is between a picture of a self totally immersed in its social world and incapable of any critical distance whatsoever, and one partially immersed but also able to distance itself from any one particular attachment it chooses to focus on, the liberal suggestion admittedly appears more plausible. But is there not another alternative, one that perhaps better captures the way we think of ourselves and our core commitments? I have in mind the idea that we are indeed able to re-examine some attachments, but that there are others so fundamental to our identity that they cannot be set aside, and that an attempt to do so will result in serious and perhaps irreparable psychological damage. (Bell 1993, 10)

If Bell is right, then some people may be *harmed* by too much critical self-examination. The attempt to set aside or reconsider their most basic constitutive commitments will be so wrenching that it will cause "irreparable damage." It is not difficult to imagine the kind of situation that Bell has in mind: A person whose identity is deeply bound up with the community in which she lives will indeed suffer if she makes an effort to wrench herself from that community and from her identity in it. For example, a woman who finds herself in a sexist marriage may, after critical reflection, decide that she can no longer play the role of a passive housewife. The only available remedy may be entirely to redefine the terms of family interaction. In many cases, the only remedy may be divorce or separation—a dissolution of the family community that is sure to be painful and difficult for all members. It is not difficult to agree with Bell that the attempt to set aside this previous identity may cause irreparable psychological damage.

But even if Bell is right that rational reconsideration sometimes involves serious risks, even if we incur these risks if we accept Buchanan's Principle R or protect our ability to exercise Rawls's two moral powers, this may not be enough to persuade us to forbear from critical self-reflection or to reject the liberal rights that protect our ability to critically evaluate our values. Even when shedding unsupportable constitutive values is painful and wrenching, even damaging, it may still be a valuable thing to do. It may be wrenching and dislocating to extricate one's self from a bad marriage, but it is not obviously better to remain in it. In a dialogue written by Will Kymlicka, the character Louise says to her communitarian friend Anne:

> We were "damaged" and "disturbed" by trying to escape patriarchy, but we were even more damaged and disturbed within patriarchy. You never once . . . consider how people can be damaged by their constitutive attachments, how these attachments can systematically undermine people's sense of self-respect, and make them subordinate to others. Feminists will insist that we be free to question our constitutive attachments, not just when they break down, but even when they are working as expected, for the subordination of women is built into our everyday expectations about men's and women's behavior. . . . What we need is a conception of the self that recognizes that we have constitutive attachments, and that they are damaging to give up, but that these attachments can themselves be damaging, and hence that we must be free to question and possibly reject them even when they don't "break down." (Kymlicka, in Bell 1993, 210)

We can connect this example with the problem of stability that occupied us in section 6.1: If people are free to reconsider their commitments, then they will be free to reconsider commitments like marriage and community membership. In a liberal society in which people have the freedom to reconsider and redefine their commitments, people are more likely to suffer the psychological pain involved in divorce or the anguish that might come from breaking traditional community ties. But in an illiberal society, people are more likely to suffer from the pain and disadvantage incurred when they are *unable* to dissociate themselves from institutions that no longer reflect their values as those values change over the course of a lifetime. It is not at all clear that this latter risk is less serious than the risks associated with freedom for critical self examination, and if not, then Bell's observation that critical self-reflection may have costs cannot constitute a telling objection against liberalism.

7. Toward a Modest Defense of Liberal Rights

In my response to the two objections above, I have argued in favor of liberalism. But the character of this argument is quite different from the character of Buchanan's argument for the unique rationality of liberal institutions or from Rawls's early argument associating the theory of justice with the theory of rational choice. Instead of trying to show that liberalism is uniquely rational, I have argued that the risks associated with liberalism are not greater than the risks associated with the rejection of liberalism, so Bell's argument, for example, does not identify a disadvantage that is peculiar to liberalism alone. But some people may regard the dangers of critical self-reflection as more worrisome than the danger of being trapped by one's constitutive commitments.

For example, one can imagine that the members of an Amish community might take steps to prevent members from engaging in the kind of critical self-reflection that might cause them to renounce their community membership. Lacking a rationalist argument of the kind Buchanan and Rawls once hoped to articulate, we cannot condemn such people as irrational or unreasonable. This limitation has far-reaching implications for the legitimacy of liberal institutions, especially when the maintenance of such institutions requires that we use the coercive power of the state to limit the rights of illiberal minorities, like the Amish, to preserve their communities by limiting the ability of community members to engage in rational reconsideration of community values.

Rawls's claim that the first principle liberties have "lexical priority" over other elements of the conception of justice as fairness depends on his claim that the higher-order interests these rights protect have priority over the first-level interests we have because of the particular conception of the good that we accept. If some people are justified in rejecting the revisability principle, and their reasons for rejecting it reflect first-order values that they have because of the conception of the good they accept, then the revisability principle cannot be *prior* to these first-order interests. This undermines the claim that the first principle of justice must have lexical priority over other principles and aims. If liberalism must be defended by showing that the risks associated with nonliberal institutions are greater (even for nonliberals) than the risks associated with liberal institutions, then it becomes important to know specifically what the risks are, and to whom they are risks. If advocates of a nonliberal theological state are persuaded that liberalism is not the political conception favored by God, then no matter how rational they may be, they will be unpersuaded by risk-balancing arguments for liberalism. Those who reject the revisability principle may be *rationally justified* in rejecting the lexical priority of justice over other social ends. The problem of pluralism is especially pressing when there is a significant minority of people who are rationally justified in accepting an illiberal conception of justice, and who have sufficient reason to reject the fundamental liberal rights.

If the argument I have given here is sound, it will not follow that liberalism is unacceptable. Nor will it follow that we should place a higher value on our first-order aims than on our ability to exercise the two moral powers. For similar reasons, it will not follow that we have reason to reject the revisability principle. Most of us surely have excellent reasons to preserve our ability to rationally revise and pursue a conception of the good, and our support for fundamental constitutional rights may reflect this in much the way that Rawls and Buchanan describe. But it is instructive to focus on those who, because of their constitutive commitments, may have good reason to reject liberal rights and liberal institutions. This focus will help us see the limits of liberal argumentation and discover some of the limits of liberalism itself.

8. Rawls on Constitutive Commitments and Critical Self-Reflection

There is a persuasive liberal response to the objections discussed above: liberalism does not require or impose rational reconsideration of basic evaluative commitments on unwilling and otherwise unreflective citizens, it simply requires that people must not be denied the freedom to critically revise and pursue their conception of the good. Because of this, citizens whose constitutive commitments are consistent with the liberal principles of justice need not call their fundamental ideals into question and need not experience the psychological harms that are supposed to result from rational self-reflection. Rawls himself acknowledges that people have constitutive commitments, and he does not regard this as inconsistent with the conception of justice as fairness, or the argument from revisability:

> Citizens may have, and normally do have at any given time, affections, devotions and loyalties that they believe they would not, and indeed could and should not, stand apart from and objectively evaluate from the point of view of their purely rational good. They may regard it as simply unthinkable to view themselves apart from certain religious, philosophical, and moral convictions, or from certain enduring attachments and loyalties. These convictions and attachments . . . help to organize and give shape to a person's way of life, what one sees oneself as doing and trying to accomplish in one's social world. We think that if we were suddenly without these particular convictions and attachments we would be disoriented and unable to carry on. In fact, there would be, we might think, no point in carrying on. (Rawls 1993, 31)[6]

It is evident that Rawls himself sees no conflict between the value of rational revisability and the notion that people may have constitutive commitments and that they may be unable or unwilling to stand apart from their deepest values. There is no assumption that people will be perfectly rational in their *exercise* of the rights that protect the capacity for critical self-reflection, or that they will be self-transparent in their efforts to criticize their deepest commitments.

I have argued that some people may be justified in rejecting the revisability principle (and the fundamental liberal rights) because they are in the grip of *specific* constitutive commitments. These are people who will be rationally unpersuaded by the liberal argument under discussion here. In section 9, I argue that the existence of such people presents a problem for Rawls's account of political legitimacy.

9. Constitutive Commitments and Liberal Legitimacy

If the argument presented just above is right, then there may be citizens in a liberal state who are rationally committed to values that justify their rejection of liberal rights and institutions. Some of these will be individuals who are committed to values that many of us may regard as repulsive. Macedo gives the example of Nazi citizens in a liberal state who

> must respect the property, the political rights, and freedoms of Jewish Americans. They may, occasionally, march in Jewish communities, but they must get permits, keep order, and otherwise respect the peace and quiet of these neighborhoods. They can gather in uniforms, with broadsheets, slogans, music, and other paraphernalia, in legally rented private halls, as long as they do not make too much noise. Nazis must pay taxes to support the liberal institutions they detest, including public schools. The liberal polity requires that the Nazis be law-abiding Nazis and that is not easy. They cannot be "gung-ho" Nazis, in fact they cannot *be* Nazis at all, but only play at it. (Macedo 1990, 260)

One might not think that this is much of a problem: If it's only Nazis, fascists, and monarchists who can't support liberal political institutions, then, one might think, so much the worse for them. If the only people who can't be comfortable liberal citizens are those who reject this principle of moral equality, this may not constitute a serious problem for liberal political theory. But Margaret Moore argues that there are other more inoffensive groups who will be unable to accept the values implicit in the liberal conception of justice:

> It is not only groups such as the Nazis whose lives are coercively structured by liberal principles. Other groups, such as the Amish in the mid-western United States and the Old Russian Believers in northern Alberta, find the liberal emphasis on individual autonomy and critical reflection threatening to their more communally oriented and simple religious existence. Their cultural survival depends on isolating their children from the many possibilities for choice that surround them: it depends, in other words, on devaluing the exercise of autonomy and emphasizing instead living according to the word of God. (Moore 1993, 178)

Notice the connection between rejection of Buchanan's revisability principle and rejection of the liberal rights: Those like Macedo's "liberal Nazis" and Moore's "Old Russian Believers" who have reason to reject the liberal conception of the state are just those who have reason to reject the revisability principle and its implications concerning the justification of fundamental rights. The existence of such people has sometimes been thought fatally to undermine the justification for fundamental liberal rights. Again according to Moore:

> If liberalism cannot claim to be derived in a way which is neutral among the competing conceptions of the good prevalent in contemporary society, how does it justify coercing those who do not accept liberalism to live according to its principles? This is a particular problem for liberalism because it is committed to the view that institutions or principles are legitimate only if they secure the consent of those subject to them. . . . This confines valid consent or rational consent to those who accept the liberal starting point. But [liberal apologists] . . . cannot

show that not accepting the liberal starting point is irrational. And this means that it is unjustifiable to confine valid consent to those who accept the liberal doctrine of equal respect for persons and the liberal concept of morality. To confine valid consent to those who accept liberal assumptions is on all fours with the communist who claims that her theory is legitimate because acceptable to those who are not blinded by false consciousness (and is unable to give a non-circular explanation of what this is) or the fascist who claims legitimacy for her theory because grounded in an unargued-for hierarchical conception of morality and society. (Moore 1993, 137–38)

If there are some people who have no compelling reason to accept the liberal commitment to basic civil and political rights and liberties, this is a problem for liberalism, since liberals have generally argued that institutions and associations are legitimate only if they can be rationally justified to those who are subject to them. Indeed, Jeremy Waldron (1993) has identified this idea of the rational defensibility of institutions as the core of the liberal view, and in one of the most famous passages in *Political Liberalism,* Rawls writes:

> When may citizens . . . properly exercise their coercive political power over one another when fundamental questions are at stake? To this question, political liberalism replies: our exercise of political power is proper and justifiable only when it is exercised in accordance with a constitution the essentials of which all citizens may reasonably be expected to endorse in the light of principles and ideals acceptable to them as reasonable and rational. (Rawls 1993, 217)

But what if there are citizens in a liberal state who cannot reasonably be expected to endorse these "constitutional essentials" in light of principles acceptable to them as reasonable and rational? What if these citizens are led by their deeply and rationally held evaluative commitments to violate the strictures of the liberal state, perhaps by restricting their children's opportunities by preventing their exposure to liberal ideals? Like the Supreme Court in *Yoder* v. *Wisconsin,* many liberals may regard this as a violation of children's right to an adequate education.[7] What if it is necessary to use "the coercive political power" of the state to prevent rational but illiberal citizens from conscientiously violating the rights of others? In such circumstances, Rawls's principle of legitimacy seems to imply that our use of force against them is illegitimate. But surely the liberal state will protect the rights of others even in circumstances such as these. The response that "such people accept a conception of the good that is not reasonable" will be small comfort to those members of liberal states who are subject to the state's coercive power but who have no reason to accept the principles that govern the use of that power.

If there are citizens in a liberal state to whom the basic rights and liberties cannot be justified, this undermines the legitimacy of liberal institutions, and recognition that there can be such persons provides important insight into the limits of liberal justice. I do not believe that this should lead us to accept Moore's claim that the liberal who is willing to use coercion for protection of rights and to guarantee that interaction is consensual is "on all fours with" the fascist or the "ethnic cleanser" who wants an ethnically pure state and who is unconcerned about the violation of rights. But it is clear that the liberal principle of legitimacy depends on more fundamental commitments, and involves a more substantive moral conception, than either critics or advocates of liberalism have typically acknowledged. The problem of rational illiberal minorities yields two important questions: First, what is a liberal state to do with rational but illiberal citizens? Second, what are the more fundamental moral underpinnings to the liberal view?

Rawls's answer to the first question is clear and uncompromising: He insists that the liberty of intolerant persons and groups should be restricted "only when the tolerant sincerely and with reason believe that their own security and that of the institutions of liberty are in danger" (Rawls 1971, 220). This answer provides the ground for the claim that liberal institutions will impose the lightest possible burden on those who conscientiously dissent, and it may be unreasonable to expect more from any political theory. Surely there are good reasons to think that political regimes that *deny* the fundamental liberal rights will be much harder on rational and conscientious dissenters and that illiberal minorities may still prefer to be minorities in a liberal state than in an authoritarian state built around values that are neither liberal nor their own. Thus, theocratic Christian fundamentalists may prefer living under liberal institutions rather than living in a theocratic Muslim state. This provides at least some justification for the claim that liberal values are not "on all fours" with those of illiberal regimes.

To find the answer to the second question, to articulate the basic evaluative underpinnings of liberalism, we must look further. According to Margaret Moore (1993), the fundamental evaluative assumption of liberalism is the identification of the "person" with the capacity for autonomy. According to Buchanan, at least in the early article considered here, it is the higher-order value of rational reconsideration of our fundamental commitments. According to early Rawls, it is a commitment to the moral equality of citizens. In Rawls's later work, the fundamental claim is that liberal institutions will be acceptable at least to those who are reasonable and who accept a reasonable conception of the good. Brian Barry once claimed that liberals are committed to a much more substantive Faustian conception of persons:

> Liberalism rests on a vision of life: a Faustian vision. It exalts self-expression, self-mastery . . . ; the active pursuit of knowledge and the clash of ideas; the acceptance of personal responsibility for the decisions that shape one's life. For those who cannot take the freedom, it provides alcohol, tranquilizers, wrestling on the television, astrology, psychoanalysis, and so on, endlessly, but it cannot by its nature provide certain kinds of psychological security. (Barry 1973, 127)

I am not persuaded by Barry's claim that liberals must embrace this Faustian vision. It seems unlikely that there is any unique set of fundamental evaluative assumptions that all liberals must have in common—different people may have quite different reasons for accepting and promoting fundamental rights. If there is no common evaluative core shared by all liberals, then the attempt to articulate the necessary evaluative assumptions of liberalism is hopeless. The best we can hope for, perhaps, is to describe a range of evaluative assumptions that are individually sufficient for acceptance of the fundamental liberal rights. If we find that liberalism can be defended on the basis of an exceptionally wide range of evaluative assumptions, this may be regarded as an advantage of the liberal conception of justice. Clearly, this is what Rawls has in mind when he says that political liberalism can be the object of an overlapping consensus on the part of individuals who have widely divergent but reasonable conceptions of the good.

Another modest way to defend the liberal conception of the state would be to show that evaluative assumptions that justify this conception are minimal and that many or most people have good reason to accept these assumptions. Understood in these more modest terms, Buchanan's reconstruction of Rawls's argument for the fundamental liberal rights may be decisively successful. Most of us, surely, do have good reason to accept the revisability principle and may have good reason to defend our commitment to the fundamental liberal rights in much the way Buchanan describes.

In the spirit of this more modest project for the defense of fundamental liberal rights, I propose that we may defend liberal institutions in terms much less contentious than those described by Barry. Although some may find Barry's Faustian liberalism appealing, I would argue that one should find Buchanan's and Rawls's argument for the fundamental rights persuasive if one is committed to two theses that, if not uncontroversial, are probably acceptable to most people.

1. *Thesis of Moral Equality:* No competent adult has natural authority over any other.
2. *Social Space Thesis:* There are valuable forms of life that can be pursued within liberal institutions.

From the first commitment comes the liberal concern for consent and for the necessity of a set of rights that protect individuals from unwarranted interference. But one must also accept the more substantive social space thesis, which states that there is sufficient space within liberal institutions so that it is possible to develop and rationally pursue valuable forms of life. As we have seen, some people doubt that this second thesis is true, and some who doubt may be *justified* in doubting that it is true. We can call such people "true believers." The Amish, the Old Russian Believers, and other members of fragile communities may have reason to reject the social space thesis, since liberal institutions may undermine the values they hold dear. If members of these groups believe that their way of life is uniquely sanctioned by God, they will not believe that the alternative forms of life people can pursue in a liberal state are valuable; rather, they will view these alternatives as dangerous temptations that lead people away from "the one true path." Amish children growing up in a liberal state are much more likely to reject the constitutive values that bind Amish communities together. This explains why members of such groups may reject and may be rational in their rejection of the fundamental rights liberals hold dear.

Such people will not be entirely reasonable in Rawls's special sense of that term, but as Rawls emphasizes, reasonable members of a liberal state must recognize the extent to which pluralism will flourish under free institutions. Such reasonable liberal citizens may have no reasons that will or rationally should persuade true believers that the exercise of political power in defense of liberal rights is justifiable. This may not imply that the exercise of coercive political power is wrong in such circumstances, at least where it is necessary to protect and enforce fundamental rights. But perhaps our attitude toward the enforcement of fundamental rights should be both firm and humble once we recognize that these rights may not be rationally justifiable to all.

If we cannot show that all rational persons have reason to support and uphold liberal institutions, we will have to rely on a more minimal account of the justification of liberal institutions. This is just what Rawls has done, in his more recent work, where liberal institutions are defended, not as uniquely rational, but as appropriate for and justifiable to a limited group of people whose values are reasonable in Rawls's special sense of that term. If the argument of this chapter is sound, Rawls has not gone far enough in qualifying the view expressed in *A Theory of Justice*. The liberal conception of legitimacy must also be revised to explain how it can be proper and justifiable to exercise political power when there are rational (though perhaps not entirely reasonable) illiberal minorities whose members have no good reason to endorse the constitutional essentials that govern the exercise of power.

Many critics are unsatisfied with the more qualified and limited argument Rawls offers in his later work. Some theorists who liked Rawls's earlier views seem to regard the argument of *Political Liberalism* as a case of morally criticizable backsliding. But if liberal institutions cannot be adequately defended in terms that all rational persons must accept, then Rawls was right to move toward a more modest account of political justification. Even when liberalism is defended in these more modest terms, most of us have good reason to promote and uphold institutions that protect fundamental rights. This more modest philosophical defense of liberalism may be the best available defense. And in the end, this more modest and less rationalist defense of liberal rights is enough. If arguments for a stricter and more traditional liberal rationalism fail, then they offer only false hopes for the justification of fundamental rights.

Notes

1. See Fehige (chapter 14 of this volume) for a preferentialist argument against Rawls's account of the value of rational revisability.

2. I do not mean to imply that the original position is unnecessary or that Rawls could

eliminate without cost these controversial elements of the conception of justice as fairness.

3. Notably the work of Norman Daniels (1996).

4. There is, of course, reason to question this account of the primary goods. On the one hand, one might question whether the specific goods Rawls identifies fit this condition (whether they are in fact all-purpose means). This tack is famously taken in Schwartz (1973). On the other hand, one may question whether all-purpose means can be described in terms of goods. This strategy has been productively pursued by Sen (1992), Nussbaum (1992, 1995), and Arneson (1989), among many others.

5. Will Kymlicka emphasizes this point in Kymlicka (1989).

6. See also Rawls (1993, 31).

7. In *Yoder,* the court ruled that it was permissible for the Amish to remove their children from school for the last years of high school. This was consistent with the judgment that it would violate the rights of children to deny them access to education *tout court.*

References

Arneson, Richard. 1989. Equality and Equality of Opportunity for Welfare. *Philosophical Studies* 56: 77–93.

Barry, Brian. 1973. *The Liberal Theory of Justice.* Oxford: Clarendon Press.

———. 1995. *Justice as Impartiality.* Oxford: Clarendon Press.

Bell, Daniel, ed. 1993. *Communitarianism and Its Critics.* Oxford: Clarendon Press.

Blackburn, Simon. 1984. *Spreading the Word.* Oxford: Clarendon Press.

Buchanan, Allen. 1975. Revisability and Rational Choice. *Canadian Journal of Philosophy* 5: 395–408.

———. 1989. Assessing the Communitarian Critique of Liberalism. *Ethics* 99, no. 4: 852–82.

Daniels, Norman. 1996. *Justice and Justification: Reflective Equilibrium in Theory and Practice.* New York: Cambridge University Press.

Gibbard, Allan. 1990. *Wise Choices, Apt Feelings.* Cambridge, Mass.: Harvard University Press.

Kant, Immanuel. 1797/1991. *The Metaphysics of Morals.* Translated by Mary Gregor. New York: Cambridge University Press.

Kymlicka, Will. 1989. *Liberalism, Community, and Culture.* Oxford: Clarendon Press.

———. 1993. Some Questions about Justice and Community. In *Communitarianism and Its Critics,* edited by Daniel Bell. Oxford: Clarendon Press, 1993, 208–21.

———. 1996. *Multicultural Citizenship.* Oxford: Clarendon Press.

Macedo, Stephen. 1990. *Liberal Virtues: Citizenship, Virtue, and Community in Liberal Constitutionalism.* Oxford: Clarendon Press.

MacIntyre, Alisdaire. 1984. *After Virtue.* 2d ed. Notre Dame, Ind.: University of Notre Dame Press.

Mill, John Stuart. 1859/1987. *On Liberty.* Indianapolis, Ind.: Hackett.

Moore, Margaret. 1993. *Foundations of Liberalism.* Oxford: Clarendon Press.

Murphy, Jeffrie G. 1995. Legal Moralism and Liberalism. *Arizona Law Review* 37 no. 1: 73–93.

Nagel, Thomas. 1970. *The Possibility of Altruism.* Princeton, N.J.: Princeton University Press.

———. 1986. *The View from Nowhere.* New York: Oxford University Press.

———. 1997. *The Last Word.* New York: Oxford University Press.

Narveson, Jan. 1988. *The Libertarian Idea.* Philadelphia: Temple University Press.

Nussbaum, Martha. 1992. Human Functioning and Social Justice: In Defense of Aristotelian Essentialism. *Political Theory* 20: 202–46.

———. 1995. Human Capabilities, Female Human Beings. In *Women, Culture, and Development,* edited by Martha Nussbaum and Jonathan Glover. New York: Oxford University Press.

Okin, Susan Moller. 1989. *Justice, Gender, and the Family.* New York: Basic Books.

Parfit, Derek. 1973. Later Selves and Moral Principles. In *Philosophy and Personal Relations,* edited by Alan Montefiore. Montreal: Basic Books, 137–69.

———. 1984. *Reasons and Persons.* Oxford: Clarendon Press.

Rawls, John. 1971. *A Theory of Justice.* Cambridge, Mass.: Belknap Press of Harvard University Press.

———. 1980. Kantian Constructivism and Moral Theory. *Journal of Philosophy* 77, no. 9: 515–72.

———. 1989. Justice as Fairness: A Briefer Restatement. Unpublished manuscript.

———. 1993. *Political Liberalism.* New York: Columbia University Press.

Schwarz, Adina. 1973. Moral Neutrality and Primary Goods. *Ethics* 83: 294–307.

Sen, Amartya. 1992. *Inequality Reexamined.* Cambridge, Mass.: Harvard University Press.

———. 1999. *Development as Freedom.* N.Y.: Knopf.

Waldron, Jeremy. 1993. *Liberal Rights: Collected Papers 1981–1991.* New York: Cambridge University Press.

Young, Iris. 1990. *Justice and the Politics of Difference.* Princeton, N.J.: Princeton University Press.

7

REFLECTIVE EQUILIBRIUM AND

JUSTICE AS POLITICAL

Norman Daniels

1. Politicizing Justice: Pluralism and Stability

In *A Theory of Justice* (hereafter *Theory*), Rawls argues that justice as fairness provides an Archimedean point from which to assess the justice of social institutions (Rawls 1971, 260–63). If a contractarian agreement on principles of cooperation were tied too closely to the actual interests and desires of persons, for example, if no veil of ignorance were present, then it would not provide such an Archimedean point. People are shaped by the institutions under which they live, and a contract reflecting their known interests would be mired too much in the effects of those institutions to provide critical leverage. Traditional alternative ways of anchoring that Archimedean point, such as a priori or perfectionist assumptions about the nature of persons and the social order, are also unattractive for several reasons. For one, such assumptions usually are too general to yield a useable contract. Alternatively, idealized contractors may seem so unreal to us that we cannot identify with them or their choices. Finally, the assumptions may be too narrowly held to provide a basis for common agreement. How, then, is that Archimedean point to be established?

If Rawls's original position had been based on only on the weakest assumptions about human rationality—that is, if justice were derivable from rationality alone—then it would be clear how the Archimedean point was secured. The original position, however, rested on more robust assumptions: "Reasonable" people had to agree it was an appropriate device for selecting principles of justice because the contract procedure was fair to all participants. In the decade after *Theory* was published, partly in response to claims that justice as fairness rested on a "deep theory" (see Dworkin 1973), Rawls fleshed out the set of beliefs or ideals that one must accept in order to consider the original position an appropriate device for selecting among alternative conceptions of justice.

By the time the Dewey Lectures were published in the *Journal of Philosophy* (1980), Rawls had clarified the importance of several key background

127

ideas that had been insufficiently emphasized in *Theory,* even though they were modeled in the original position. These included the ideal of a "free and equal" moral agent with two basic moral powers, a capacity to form and revise a conception of the good and a sense of justice. Persons so conceived have a "higher-order interest" in securing the development of those powers. The background ideas, which also included the ideal of a well-ordered society and a conception of procedural justice, were necessary to motivate the construction in justice as fairness. The Archimedean point was rooted in acceptance of these beliefs or ideals, and people who find these ideas unacceptable "will be unmoved by justice as fairness even granting the validity of its arguments" (Rawls 1974, 637; see Daniels 1980, 85).

What would lead people to accept these ideas in the "deep theory"? The answer seemed to be this: Philosophical arguments involving the comparison of alternative conceptions of justice and their underlying ideas would persuade us to converge on these beliefs in wide reflective equilibrium. Although these beliefs were not a priori (indeed, they were revisable), they would, after due reflection, be considered acceptable to a wide majority of people. Ultimately, justification for a conception of justice consisted of that view being contained within a wide reflective equilibrium of an individual's beliefs. The wide reflective equilibrium was a coherent set of considered moral judgments about justice at all levels of generality, principles of justice, deeper background beliefs or ideals of the person and of the role of morality in society, and even general social theory. To achieve wide reflective equilibrium, an individual worked back and forth among all these elements, testing principles against cases, considering philosophical arguments defending different theoretical perspectives, and revising wherever necessary to produce the most acceptable set of beliefs.

Rawls confirms this picture of the task in *Theory* and its focus on the individual undertaking a philosophical task:

> TJ *[Theory]* does not address persons as citizens but rather as individuals trying to work out their own conception of justice as it applies to the basic political and social institutions of democratic society. For the most part their task is solitary as they reflect on their own considered judgments with their fixed points and the several first principles and intermediate concepts and the ideals they affirm. TJ is presented as a work individuals might study in their attempt— admittedly never fully achieved and always to be striven for—to attain the self-understanding of wide reflective equilibrium. (Rawls 1995b, 6)

As we shall see, this characterization and its contrast with the task in *Political Liberalism* (hereafter *Liberalism)* contribute to the feeling some people have that the role of philosophical activity changes between the two books and that the politicization of justice and justification involves "philosophical loss" in a sense to be explained in section 2.

In retrospect, it seems quite striking that little attention was paid at this stage of the development of Rawls's thinking (or mine [see Daniels 1979 (chap. 2 in Daniels 1996) and Daniels 1980 (chap. 4 in Daniels 1996)], following and elaborating on his) to the great diversity in beliefs about philosophical, religious, and even moral matters that would have to be incorporated in such wide reflective equilibria. Perhaps the narrowed focus of attention came from the fact that so much of *Theory* was concerned with defeating utilitarianism and the arguments needed to do so drew on a narrow spectrum within a shared philosophical tradition. But whatever the explanation, little attention was paid to the kinds of diversity present in our own society.

Once we focus on that diversity in background beliefs, it seems less plausible to think that the same philosophical arguments about the acceptability of justice as fairness and its deeper components would be persuasive to all, regardless of their starting points. The very criteria for what would count as a good philosophical argument would be affected by some of those background beliefs. The point was made by a number of critics, of course, that people holding certain fundamentalist religious views, for example, would find themselves unable to commit themselves to the principles of justice (see White 1991). Such cases might have been dismissed as marginal. For example, one important adequacy test that a conception of justice must pass, according to *Theory*, is that it be feasible in this sense: It must be possible in general for people who grow up under social institutions governed by it to be motivated to comply with it. But stability does not require the compliance of everyone, regardless of how far out of the mainstream their views might be. Insofar as these exceptions are thought relevant to the stability test, then perhaps they could just be ignored (cf. Barry 1995). This dismissal means not taking seriously enough the implications of the more general problem of pluralism.

The fact of pluralism is pervasive and deep and cannot be simply ignored. Especially under conditions of freedom of thought and expression, the very conditions protected by the principles characterizing justice as fairness, people are likely to develop quite varied solutions to the complex moral and philosophical issues that humans seek answers to. Suppose we restrict our concerns in worrying about convergence or stability to people who are reasonable in the sense that they are concerned to live with others on fair terms, assuming that the others are so willing; they also understand that to be fair, the terms of cooperation must be ones that other free and equal persons can accept (Rawls 1993, 48–54; cf. Cohen 1994a, 1537). Reasonable people, we should also suppose, will then recognize that others who share this concern to cooperate on acceptable terms will be led to disagree on many issues because of what Rawls calls "the burdens of judgment" (1993, 54–58). These burdens include the following conditions: the conflicting and complex evidence that bears on issues, the disagreements about how to weight considerations, the vagueness of some of our concepts, the effects of the totality of a person's experience on how she weights considerations, the multiplicity of normative considerations that are relevant and from which a selection must be made in

any specific case. We are driven, Rawls concludes, to accept *reasonable pluralism* about many matters of importance. This is a basic fact of political life,
and even among reasonable people, we will find disagreements that threaten
the original suggestion that philosophical argument could produce convergence on the same wide reflective equilibrium.

The specific feature of his theory that, by the late 1980s, seemed to Rawls
most incompatible with the fact of pluralism was his account of stability, one
of two conditions of adequacy he imposes on theories of justice in *Theory*
(the other is acceptability in wide reflective equilibrium). As noted earlier, a
theory of justice must yield a stable social arrangement, at least compared to
alternative conceptions. People raised in a well-ordered society governed by a
conception of justice must be able to abide by the commitments of that conception without unacceptable strain. Justice must engage their motivations.

Rawls is not concerned here about the general fact that acting morally will
sometimes involve a sacrifice of individual self-interest. He is not worried
about the traditional skeptic who asks, Why should I be just rather than
pursue my own rational advantage? Rather, he has in mind the moral person
who will say, Why should I be just, since justice is not as important as salvation? or Why should I be just, since justice is not as important as establishing
a caring community? Such persons are presumably willing to sacrifice their
self-interest on occasion to the demands of morality. The problem is that they
also sacrifice justice to other moral concerns, since they do not give the priority to justice over other values that justice as fairness requires. Over time,
given the burdens of judgment, people will be raised in and attracted to diverse moral conceptions of this sort, even though they also share a common
framework of institutions governed by, say, justice as fairness. Stability is threatened if concerns about justice are overridden in these ways by enough people
who are influenced by these comprehensive moral and religious views.

In *Theory,* Rawls (1971, § 86) argued that there was a "congruence" between acting in accordance with justice and the good for people. This argument seems to have invoked particular views about the good of autonomy
that are characteristic of certain comprehensive liberal views, such as Mill's or
Kant's (see Freeman 1994; Cohen 1994a; Rawls 1995a; but see Barry 1995
for reservations about the scope of this appeal to a comprehensive view).
People holding other comprehensive moral views, or views that do not share
this particular assessment of the good of autonomy, would have a different
view of the strains of commitment. For example, liberal Catholics would not
accept the Kantian view of the importance of autonomy. They might, nevertheless, have other reasons for accepting the principles of justice, for example,
that the principles manifest God's natural law (see Freeman 1994, 632).

How, then, can the Archimedean point be secured? How can it be maintained as a stable point? If we cannot assume that (even reasonable) people
with diverse comprehensive views can be led by reasoned philosophical argument, or rather, by some specific set of such arguments, to stable convergence
on justice as fairness, how can convergence, including stability, be achieved?

What is the deepest form of stability that can be achieved, given reasonable pluralism? This is the central question raised by *Liberalism*.

Rawls's answer to this problem is to recast justice as fairness as a freestanding *political* conception of justice. The key ideas out of which justice as fairness (or other, alternative reasonable political conceptions of justice) is constructed, for example, the idea that citizens are free and equal, are now taken to be shared elements of our political life, that is, of a public, democratic culture. These ideas are already held or accepted by most people who share that culture, whatever other views they diverge on. In effect, it is not philosophy alone—aided by universal reason—that has led people to converge on these ideas but a shared set of institutions and history.

Rawls (1993, 145; 1995a, 149) suggests that we think of the political conception of justice as fairness as a "module" with its own internal principles, reasons, and standards of evidence. For example, justice as fairness includes the two principles of justice ordered in a particular way. Together these ordered principles, illuminated by the shared background ideas and publicly defendable standards of evidence and reasoning, specify the content of "public reason" as it is used to deliberate about matters of justice. This module should be complete: It should give reasonable answers to a broad range of questions about "constitutional essentials and basic questions of justice" (Rawls 1995a, 142). These answers are "reasonable" in light of the kinds of reasons to which the political conception is restricted. In effect, the justification for these answers only goes so far: It appeals only to reasons contained in the public view. Rawls calls this "pro tanto justification." To say that a claim about what is just is justified "pro tanto" is not to say that it is a fully justified belief for a particular person. The criterion for full justification ultimately remains acceptability in wide reflective equilibrium (Rawls 1995a, 141–43), and pro tanto justification deliberately refrains from seeking such deeper justification. (Later, I introduce the term "political reflective equilibrium" to characterize the limited results of pro tanto justification as compared to full justification.) By not seeking or alluding to deeper justification, pro tanto justification does not alienate those who have different reasons for accepting the module.

The module is ultimately justified for people in quite different ways, depending on other aspects of the comprehensive views they hold in wide reflective equilibrium. Rawls calls this "full justification" (1995a, 143). No uniform or universal philosophical argument produces a shared rationale for, and convergence on, the module. Instead, it is incorporated for different reasons within the distinct wide reflective equilibria that coexist in a pluralist society. Within the public domain, where we debate matters of justice, we need not—indeed we should not—appeal to those deeper justifications at all. We simply build on people's agreement with the basic ideas and restrict their reasoning about matters of justice to the kinds of considerations internal to the political conception of justice. We restrict them to "public reason."

We obtain the greatest stability we can for a political conception of justice,

Rawls argues, answering his central question in *Liberalism,* when there is the right type of "overlapping consensus" on it, that is, when there is overlapping consensus for the right reasons. People with different comprehensive moral views must justify for themselves, by their own lights, that is, in their own wide reflective equilibria, the acceptability of the module. Their rationales will thus differ in ways that reflect their other philosophical, moral, and religious beliefs. Some may insist, for example, that there is "moral truth," others may deny it. Some might see the principles of justice as forms of divinely given natural law; others may see it as a human construction. Ultimately, people are justified in accepting justice as fairness if it is acceptable to them in the different wide reflective equilibria they can achieve.

If there is *general* acceptance in this way of the module within the different reasonable comprehensive views in a society, Rawls says that we have general reflective equilibrium (1995a, 141 n. 16). It is obvious that general reflective equilibrium is not itself a shared wide reflective equilibrium—except for the overlap on the module. Rawls now explicitly rejects the account of stability he offered in *Theory,* namely, that there is general convergence on a wide reflective equilibrium with comprehensive liberal commitments. On that (rejected) view, justice was a good for each person because each viewed autonomy as a particularly important good and autonomy was adequately respected by justice as fairness. In the revised view, justice is now a good for each on her own terms, which may not at all include the Kantian or Millian view of the good of autonomy, and justice is ascribed a priority over other values that reflects what is acceptable in light of those other nonpolitical values. The context and strength of this priority may thus vary from person to person, depending on their views in wide equilibrium. The emphasis that different comprehensive views give to such issues as sexual behavior or family control over moral education means that the boundary between the political and the nonpolitical varies across wide equilibria. Whatever the pressures are that lead to convergence on the module, so that an overlapping consensus is formed, they are not sufficient to force convergence on a single wide reflective equilibrium, that is, on a shared, general equilibrium.

Before turning to the question of philosophical loss, it will help to distinguish several strands of the argument about stability and to show how these elements fit together. In both *Theory* and *Liberalism,* Rawls retains the same "feasibility" condition on the acceptability of a theory of justice. Specifically, a conception of justice is feasible if it can produce a stable, well-ordered society (as compared to alternative conceptions of justice). What changes between *Theory* and *Liberalism,* as a result of taking reasonable pluralism seriously, is the way in which individuals fit justice as fairness into their overall systems of moral (and other) beliefs. In *Liberalism,* Rawls emphasizes how the key ideas in justice as fairness are present as freestanding ideas in the public culture formed by the institutions governed by that (political) conception of justice. Institutions play an educative role about the value of those ideas, and this provides opportunity and pressure for individuals with reasonable comprehensive views to elaborate those views in ways that accommodate them to the political conception, providing for overlapping consensus for the right reasons (more on this educative role later).

What is sometimes confusing is that Rawls develops another line of argument in *Liberalism* (1993, 158–67) that is aimed at showing how a broader and deeper consensus—an overlapping consensus for the right reasons—could develop from an initial narrower agreement on some constitutional procedures. Notice that this line of argument attempts to answer the question, How can we get to a (stable) convergence on an overlapping consensus if we don't start with one? That is, since we clearly lack such an overlapping consensus, how do we get there from here? But the original question behind the stability test—in both *Theory* and *Liberalism*—is, How do we stay there once we achieve a well-ordered society? How are these two different questions, or their answers, related?

I believe they are related in this way: Telling a plausible story about how we might get there from here makes it more plausible that we could stay there once we get there, since getting there is generally harder than staying there. The story about how we might develop a wider and deeper overlapping consensus should make it seem more plausible that if we were raised in a well-ordered society governed by a political conception of justice as fairness, we could maintain our commitments to giving priority to justice despite the fact of reasonable pluralism.

The reader should not be confused by the shift in questions. The question, How do we get there from here? cannot replace the original question in the stability test, How do we stay committed to a just social order, given reasonable pluralism? In *Liberalism* and in more recent writings (see 1995b), Rawls also emphasizes that there may be an overlapping consensus on certain key ideas in the democratic culture without there being agreement that, say, justice as fairness is the most reasonable interpretation of those ideas. Rawls suggests (in 1995b) that considerable stability might obtain even in such a situation, although there would also be continuing dispute about some constitutional essentials and matters of basic justice. It is arguable, for example, that the United States is in just such a situation. If there is reasonable stability under these conditions, then we might expect that stability for a well-ordered society governed by a political conception of justice as fairness might also be stable. Once again, the argument about nonideal contexts may be evidentiary for the stability argument about the ideal context.

2. Philosophical Loss?

Some people have reacted to the politicization of justice with a sense of philosophical loss. This was my own reaction, at least initially. They complain that philosophy is demoted when justice is politicized. Others have thought the approach requires a form of moral schizophrenia or, better, a form of multiple personality disorder. Justification is bifurcated: We keep a tally or ledger of reasons appropriate for justification in the public domain, and then we have a separate ledger of reasons we can use in a broader moral domain. We are divided into double bookkeepers for moral purposes, but what kind of moral integrity is there if we keep two sets of moral books? These are serious concerns.

Perhaps the sense of philosophical loss can be explicated by appealing to the metaphor about the Archimedean point with which we began. If, in the original view, philosophical argument alone could be persuasive to people with diverse views and could lead them to converge on the deep theory underlying justice as fairness, then it seemed reasonable to think that justice as fairness constituted an Archimedean point. It was not mired in the actual interests and desires of people in a specific setting, thereby avoiding the Scylla of infection by existing institutions. It was also not based on a priori or perfectionist premises, thus avoiding the Charybdis of unacceptable generality and abstraction. But if the ideas out of which the political conception of justice are constructed must already be embedded in a shared democratic culture, then why are they not "mired" in existing institutions in ways that challenge their credentials as an Archimedean point? Can we really use them to criticize the justice of existing institutions if they are the products of the very culture that produces those institutions? Can we be sure we have agreement on more than a mere compromise, a modus vivendi, or the results of historical accident or a stage of class struggle? Can we be sure our theory captures what is truly just, what anyone thinking clearly and critically could come to recognize as just, rather than what people with a particular history have been acclimated to think of as just? (In *Theory,* Rawls says little, one way or the other, about the origins of these ideas in a democratic culture; the underlying assumption seems to be that these ideas, wherever they came from, would emerge as justifiable in light of philosophical arguments [cf. Rawls 1995b, 6; quoted in section 1 of this chapter].)

Alternatively, can we really be sure there is stable agreement on the same module, the same conception of justice, if people find it acceptable for such different reasons and in light of such different considerations? How complete will the contents of the module be if there is divergence about the priority the view is given on many issues? What is it like to justify matters in the political domain solely by reference to the contents of public reason when nonpolitical values clearly have a bearing on those matters, at least as judged by some comprehensive moral views? Can people say to themselves, "Although I have fundamental values and beliefs that bear on this issue of behavior, I will refrain from raising them and consider only the reasons permitted by public reason?" Is this moral double bookkeeping a kind of multiple moral personality disorder? Perhaps Supreme Court justices can put on a public hat and refrain from introducing their nonpolitical values into their reasoning (though historically, this is not obvious), but can each of us as citizens really wear two morally distinct hats in this way?

In the politicization of justice, have we lost our grip on the notions of both justice and justification we thought we had in the earlier view? In the remainder of this chapter, I want to explore these issues in greater detail. In section 3, I begin by comparing more carefully the notion of justification in the early and late theories, and in sections 4 and 5, I consider replies to some of these questions.

3. Wide Reflective Equilibrium: Before and after Politicization

A point to emphasize at the outset is that in both early and late theories, the heart of the account of justification remains an appeal to *wide reflective equilibrium*. Details may vary about what the wide equilibria will look like, but Rawls remains committed to a broadly coherentist view of justification. Specifically, justice as fairness is justified for an individual—both before and after politicization—if it is the conception of justice that is most acceptable to her, given all her other beliefs, in wide reflective equilibrium. (I will say nothing here to clarify the notion of "coherence" except to note that it is intended to be more robust than an appeal to mere logical consistency; for example, inference to the best explanation will be crucial in much development of ethical theory, as it is in science. I also note that Rawls's commitments to constructivism fit within his appeal to a coherentist account of justification in general.)

In appealing to this coherentist view of justification in *Theory*, Rawls felt he was making justification in ethics accord with an account of justification quite broad in its use and appeal. He noted that the idea was originally cited by Goodman as an account of justification for logic, both deductive and inductive (Rawls 1971, 20). In this chapter, I do not consider the important philosophical controversies that surround this coherentist approach in general. Instead, I concentrate on how those modifications of it that result from politicization bear on the issues of philosophical loss and justificatory schizophrenia.

To assess the effects of politicization on the *contents* of wide reflective equilibrium, we should be as clear as possible about just what the justice as fairness "module" contains when we achieve general and wide equilibrium in an overlapping consensus. This module, Rawls insists, is invariant between *Theory* and *Liberalism*. Although some critics have suggested that Rawls has backed away from some of the implications of fair equality of opportunity or the difference principle, Rawls explicitly denies this interpretation. He does so with some exasperation:

> Some think the difference principle is abandoned entirely, others that I no more affirm justice as fairness than any other political conception of justice. And they do so despite the fact that early on I say that justice as fairness is held intact (modulo ["except for"] the account of stability) and affirmed as much as before in TJ. . . . If I had dropped something as central as the difference principle, I like to think I would have said so. (Rawls 1995b, 2 n. 1)

I believe the confusion in the mind of some readers arises from the fact that a political conception of justice using the same democratic ideas that justice as fairness uses might not combine them in the optimal way Rawls believes his conception achieves. Rawls says that justice as fairness is the "most" reasonable, not the only reasonable, conception based on those ideas.

The module for justice as fairness consists of the following elements: (1) the original position, with all of its constraints on knowledge and motivation; (2) the lexically ordered principles of justice that contractors choose in the original position, assuring equal basic liberties, fair equality of opportunity, and inequalities that work to the maximum advantage of those who are worst off; and (3) several key background ideas: the idea of free and equal moral agents, each having two fundamental moral powers, namely, the capacity to form and revise a conception of the good and to develop a sense of justice; the idea of society as a fair scheme of social cooperation; the idea of a well-ordered society, that is, a society effectively regulated by a public conception of justice; and a conception of procedural justice. The key background ideas are contained in the module because they provide the rationale for the specific design of the original position. This rationale for the construction of the original position must be a part of justice as fairness itself.

We come to the first important difference between the wide reflective equilibria in *Theory* and *Liberalism* when we note that the key background ideas are themselves in need of justification. We accept them, and they are justified, in light of other things we believe in wide reflective equilibrium. The full rationale for these key background ideas cannot be part of justice as fairness, for then agreement on the module would necessarily involve agreement for the same reasons in wide equilibrium. That wider agreement is exactly what the fact of reasonable pluralism, emphasized in *Liberalism,* makes politically impossible (in the foreseeable future). In *Theory,* philosophical arguments comparing alternative conceptions were presumed to lead us to accept the same background ideas for the same reasons. In *Liberalism,* justice as fairness is called a freestanding view to signal the fact that it is severed from its (full) rationale or justification, which will vary from reasonable comprehensive view to reasonable comprehensive view.

To sharpen our understanding of the change in wide reflective equilibria before and after politicization, it will help to illustrate more concretely what it means to say that a key idea, for example, that persons are free and equal, is now construed as "political" and "freestanding." It will also help to illustrate just how different wide equilibria could provide distinct rationales for the same freestanding idea. Cohen's (1994a, 1522–25) discussion of both points is remarkably clear and helpful, and I draw on it in the next three paragraphs.

A central feature of justice as fairness, captured in the use of a veil of ignorance in the original position, is the distinction between "relevant" and "irrelevant" features of persons. The veil blocks out such irrelevant features as sex, race, class position, talents, and skills and even a person's specific conception of what is good in life. In this way it models a relevant feature of persons, that they can form and revise conceptions of the good, and it blocks out an irrelevant one, that they happen to think in some particular way about what is good. In *Theory*, however, the impression is created that the boundary between relevant and irrelevant features is drawn at least partly in terms of a comprehensive liberal view, such as Kant's or Mill's. For example, the suggestion that all will view the exercise of autonomy as an intrinsic good, which appears in the discussion of the nature of the good of autonomy in the argument for congruence and stability, is plausible as a liberal claim about our "nature," and thus about what distinguishes relevant from irrelevant features.

In *Liberalism*, the same boundary is drawn, but now irrelevant or "contingent" features of persons carry no metaphysical overtones or allusions to comprehensive moral views. They simply refer to features that are not relevant to political argument, and we can tell which these are by

> systematizing and extending reasonably familiar ideas about the justification of political arrangements in a democratic society . . . we look to settled ideals and convictions about basic democratic institutions, and to settled understandings about the justification of public norms in a democratic society, and then draw the relevant-irrelevant distinction by reference to the characteristics of persons that play a role in those ideas, convictions, and understandings. (Cohen 1994a, 1523)

A feature of persons can then be called "contingent" and mean only that it is not important for political purposes, not that someone can exist without it (as Sandel 1982 seems to suggest).

In *Liberalism*, Rawls asks us to imagine an overlapping consensus of four different reasonable, comprehensive views, each of which incorporates justice as fairness though for different reasons. Cohen (1994a, 1527) suggests how three of these might endorse the idea that citizens are free in the sense that is modeled by the veil of ignorance, namely, that they are free to form and revise their conceptions of a good life and that they have an interest in establishing conditions that permit them to do so. A Kantian morality would support freedom in this sense because it calls for reflective deliberation about ends and requires us to respect people as autonomous choosers. A utilitarian concerned with the conditions that promote long-term happiness would also respect the interest we have in being able to revise our ends in life. A religious conception that endorsed free faith would accept the conception of freedom here because religious obligations cannot be fulfilled unless people genuinely are persuaded of the religious values (Cohen 1994a, 1527, cites Locke's "A Letter Concerning Toleration" as an example of this view). The rationale for the key idea is dramatically different in each wide equilibrium, but the same idea is justified for someone occupying any of these different equilibria. Saying it is justified in this way means that it is truly accepted for its fit with other deeply held values and beliefs, not simply that it is accepted as a matter of compromise or begrudging accommodation.

To summarize the observations so far, consult Table 7.1. One can see that

Table 7.1 The Contents of Wide Reflective Equilibrium in *Theory* and *Liberalism*

Theory	Liberalism
Original position; Principles of justice; Free and equal agents; Well-ordered society; Procedural justice	Original position; Principles of justice; Free and equal agents; Well-ordered society; Procedural justice
(NB: Not freestanding)	(NB: Freestanding "module")
Philosophical arguments justifying key elements of justice as fairness, including autonomy argument needed for congruence argument	Rationale for key elements of justice as fairness
(NB: Shared rationale)	(NB: Rationale specific to each wide equilibrium)
	Account of reasonableness and burdens of judgment
	Rationale for boundary between public and nonpublic; specifics of boundary
Rest of moral and religious views	Rest of moral and religious views
Considered moral judgments, all levels	Considered moral judgments, all levels

the justice as fairness module is identical in content in both *Theory* and *Liberalism*. In *Liberalism,* however, the module is called "freestanding." The first important difference in the wide reflective equilibria before and after politicization is that the rationale for the module in *Liberalism* is said to be specific to each wide reflective equilibrium. In contrast, in *Theory* the rationale is based on shared philosophical arguments, including the Kantian view of autonomy that played a role in the original argument for convergence.

The second important difference in the contents of wide equilibria in *Theory* and *Liberalism* is that in *Liberalism,* the wide equilibria contained in the overlapping consensus must each contain beliefs about the fact of reasonable pluralism, including an account of the burdens of judgment. Each thus contains an understanding and acceptance of the fact that reasonable people may disagree on fundamental moral matters and yet be reasonable in the sense that they are willing to cooperate with others on terms acceptable to others who share the same concern for cooperation. Each also accepts the idea that it is wrong to coerce people to comply with values they reasonably do not accept (cf. Cohen 1994a, 1528, 1539). In *Liberalism,* Rawls (1993, 217) argues that people should vote (at least regarding constitutional essentials and other basic questions of justice) on the basis of what public reason, not their nonpolitical values, requires. Even voting, he argues, involves a share in the coercive power of the state, and it should not be exercised in ways that involve imposing nonpolitical values that reasonable people may reject.

These beliefs about reasonable pluralism are crucial, as we shall see, to responding to the worries about philosophical loss and justificatory schizophrenia. For now, it is sufficient to note that these beliefs must be explicit within those wide reflective equilibria that form the overlapping consensus on justice as fairness in *Liberalism*. In *Theory*, in contrast, this component of wide equilibrium was not made explicit, even though Rawls was not unaware of the fact of pluralism.

Although acceptance of reasonable pluralism must show up in each wide reflective equilibrium in the overlapping consensus, there need not be, and are probably not, identical accounts of it. Someone who believes in moral truth, for example, might well accept reasonable pluralism as a practical concession, something we might in time overcome or reduce with great moral progress. Someone who believes that God has revealed the truth, but only to some, and that it takes faith to understand that truth might also accept the idea of reasonable pluralism. Such a believer might accept the fact that faith and the revelation that comes with it cannot be coerced. Someone who rejects the notion of moral truth for philosophical reasons lying elsewhere in her wide reflective equilibrium would see reasonable pluralism as a more fundamental fact of moral life.

The third crucial difference between the wide equilibria in *Liberalism* and *Theory* is the drawing, as a result of politicization, of a boundary between political and nonpolitical moral beliefs and the provision of a rationale for that boundary. From within each wide equilibrium containing justice as fairness, there must be an acceptance of a boundary between "public reason" and nonpolitical moral views and values. It is important to see that this boundary will probably be drawn in different ways by people holding different comprehensive views because of the influence of other beliefs in these wide equilibria. Differences in the conception of the burdens of judgment and reasonable pluralism, which we noted were possible, could contribute to this variation, but there are other sources of variation as well.

There are two kinds of variation possible in the way the public-nonpublic boundary is drawn. First, there may be variation in the degree and scope of priority given to political over nonpolitical values among different comprehensive views. Second, there may be variation in the response to cases where the public reason does not give determinate or clear answers. Both sorts of variation may lead people to intrude their nonpolitical values into public debate about matters of justice. Some people will see these intrusions as justifiable, others not. This suggests that the scope and content of public reason is something about which there will be reasonable disagreement and protracted controversy.

An example may help to make these points more concrete. People in different wide equilibria, each accepting justice as fairness and the political values it contains, might give different degrees of priority to some of those political values depending on nonpolitical values in the rest of their wide equilibrium. In *Wisconsin v. Yoder*, the Supreme Court ruled that the Old Order Amish were not bound by a state law requiring that children be sent to school through age fifteen. The Amish argued that their agrarian communities did not require that level of schooling and that the emphasis placed on education by the state law threatened to disrupt their community life. Suppose, for the sake of argument (and contrary to fact), that Wisconsin institutions were themselves governed by the political conception of justice as fairness and that the Amish as well generally accepted that conception, endorsing it from within their own more comprehensive moral and religious views. They might then say that *normally* they think they should comply with state laws passed in accord with that conception. This law was presumably such a law: We can even imagine that the law had been passed with an eye to securing an educational level for everyone as promoting fair equality of opportunity. In this case, the Amish are complaining that the interference with their other values of community is too great. They cannot ascribe the priority others might give to equality of opportunity over their religious scruples about a simple, agrarian life.

This example involving the Amish might not be as clear a case of nonpolitical values overriding political ones as I have described it. Freedom to practice religion is itself a political value of great importance within justice as fairness. The Amish might be construed as protesting that the state law pits two important political values against each other and that they believe the freedom to practice religion should be given more importance than it is assigned in the state law, which gives more importance to promoting equal opportunity (we may suppose). Indeed, this is how the Supreme Court decided the case: It said the harms imposed by loss of the extra education, including harms to equal opportunity, were not sufficiently immediate and beyond dispute as the kinds of harms that ordinarily are appealed to when freedom of religious practice is curtailed, for example, compulsory vaccinations of those who have religious scruples against them.

Even if, in this example, there is room within justice as fairness to decide in favor of the Amish because of a particular view about how to weigh one basic liberty against the value of equality of opportunity (and because there is no evidence the Amish children are denied knowledge of their basic rights), there is also good reason to think that the Amish would have stuck by their beliefs had the Supreme Court ruled against them. Their argument need not have been the abstract one about the relative importance of the practice of religion, which falls within the scope of public reason and is what moved the Supreme Court. Their argument could have affirmed the weight they give to the specific nonpolitical value of living the agrarian life they want to lead. This weighing of a nonpolitical value against the political value of equal opportunity would lead them to reject an argument cast solely in terms of conflicting interpretations of the weight of political values alone.

Thus far, three key differences in the contents of the wide reflective equilibria that are present in *Theory* and *Liberalism* have been noted. First, in contrast to the single rationale for the key background ideas in *Theory*, we have distinctive rationales provided by the different wide equilibria that form the overlapping consensus. Second, each wide equilibrium in overlapping consensus must contain an account of, and acceptance of, the fact of reasonable pluralism; different comprehensive views may vary in their accounts of and in their basis for acceptance of reasonable pluralism. Third, each wide equilibrium in the overlapping consensus must contain an account of the *boundary* between political and nonpolitical moral values. This account must specify how much priority to give the political over the nonpolitical values and in what contexts. These accounts, too, may vary in significant ways. That is why the metaphor of a boundary is invoked: It is not simply a question of priority being given to the political over the nonpolitical but the fact that different comprehensive views will emphasize some nonpolitical values rather than others and differ from each other in where and why the priority of the political is overridden. For the sake of completeness, Table 7.1 notes that wide equilibria in both *Theory* and *Liberalism* also include various beliefs about other moral, religious, and philosophical matters and considered moral judgments at all levels of generality.

4. Philosophical Loss: Can We Lose What We Never Had?

I noted in section 1 that the politicization of justice produced a sense of philosophical loss in some (including me). Philosophy seems to do less and to be thought capable of doing less, that is, less than some of us might have thought or hoped it was supposed to do. Philosophical argument no longer has (if it ever did) the task, or at least the expectation, of moving everyone who can think clearly and rationally about matters, regardless of their starting beliefs, to convergence on justice as fairness. Of course, philosophy still has important tasks. It may persuade those of us who accept key democratic ideas that justice as fairness is the most reasonable political conception combining them. It also plays a role within each of our comprehensive views in helping us to provide a rationale for justice as fairness (or another reasonable political conception). Indeed, as Rawls (1993, 159) emphasizes, the gaps or "looseness" in our systems of beliefs leaves room for philosophical imagination to flesh out the needed rationale. What is distinctive about Rawls's account after politicization is the major role assigned, not to philosophy, but to an institutional mechanism that, over time, helps groups with different comprehensive views to accommodate themselves to justice as fairness.

We should distinguish any sense of loss from whether there is a real loss, that is, from whether there is a real change in the task assigned philosophy before and after politicization. I think there are elements of *Theory* that suggest, or at least leave the door open, to a more robust set of expectations from philosophy and philosophical argument than is present in *Liberalism*. But I think these elements operate less at the level of insistence or commitment and more at the level of suggestion, or even less, by leaving certain hopes or expectations in place by not showing they are unrealistic. *Theory* may have encouraged a philosopher's dream, at least by leaving room for it, and the loss produced by politicization may be the reluctance to be wakened from that dream world.

One point where the suggestion of a shift in philosophical roles is strongest comes in the *role* assigned to wide reflective equilibrium before and after politicization. (In section 3, I considered the changes in the *content* of the equilibria, not their roles.) It will help to explore this in some detail. In *Theory*, contractors in the original position, operating under constraints on motivation and knowledge, select the first and second principles of justice in preference to alternative conceptions of justice, such as utilitarianism or various combinations of utilitarianism and other principles. These principles must cohere in (wide) reflective equilibrium with our considered moral judgments about the justice of cases and institutions.

This appeal to wide equilibrium is a crucial adequacy test Rawls imposes on the theory of justice. If the chosen principles do not match our considered moral judgments, we must consider revising the original position and the principles it yields until we arrive at a conception of justice that coheres in wide reflective equilibrium with our considered moral judgments. This adequacy test led Hare and others (mistakenly, I believe) to complain that the original position was "rigged" and added nothing to the process of justification (see Hare 1973; Daniels 1980). The appeal to wide reflective equilibrium as an adequacy test was iterative. Through repetition, we flesh out and refine the chosen conception of justice, making it more determinate as we go, and we show that it and its refinements are acceptable to us in wide equilibrium, that is, that we are justified in believing them. (It remained, then, to apply the feasibility test by showing that the otherwise acceptable theory was stable and did not produce relatively unacceptable strains of commitment for people who grew up in a society governed by it.)

The specific content of justice as fairness is thus made determinate through this process in which all of us are invited to participate. All of us are, in effect, put in the driver's seat for purposes of theory construction and justification. This is the philosopher's dream I alluded to earlier (and where I earlier quoted Rawls as encouraging [cf. Rawls 1995b, 2]). All of us are in this position because it is, after all, our considered moral judgments in wide reflective equilibrium that constitute the adequacy test. Indeed, in our dream, we may imagine that the philosopher's wide equilibrium can stand in as proxy for everyone's—we are just being reflectively analytic whereas others are less disciplined. In applying the test, we may make revisions not only in the construction of justice as fairness but elsewhere in our system of beliefs. We make these revisions in light of philosophical reflection on alternative views and their merits compared to the ones we begin with. This is the process through which philosophical argument will persuade us, if it can, to converge on justice as fairness in a shared wide reflective equilibrium.

Rawls nowhere says that this process will produce convergence on justice as fairness. He nowhere says that if we do not start with the basic ideas of free and equal persons or of a well-ordered society that we can be made to accept them through philosophical deliberation. Indeed, as I have already noted, he says that if we do not share those ideas, we will not find justice as fairness attractive or justified. He hoped these ideas were widely shared, but he also knew they had a moral content some might find controversial; they were clearly more robust than simple assumptions about human rationality. But the appeal to acceptability in wide equilibrium by all people willing to engage themselves in the process of theory construction and justification involved the suggestion that philosophical activity was capable of producing the needed acceptance and thus justification among all reflective persons.

There is no direct analogue to this use of wide equilibrium as an adequacy test in the politicized version of Rawls's theory. The original appeal to wide equilibrium in *Theory* had two functions: Through iteration, it made the conception determinate, and it assured us that the determinate conception counted as just by our lights, that it was justified for each of us. After politicization, there is no "we" capable of playing both roles at once. Instead, we face the diversity in comprehensive views implied by reasonable pluralism. Of necessity, the different tasks assigned the original adequacy test are divided after politicization, specifically into pro tanto justification, which we use to flesh out and make the political conception determinate and complete, and full justification, through which each of us establishes that the determinate conception is justifiable in light of our other beliefs. This shift has much to do with the sense of philosophical loss, for it takes "us" out of the philosophical driver's seat the original adequacy test suggested "we" occupied. To support my view, we must examine more carefully what Rawls says about the different forms of justification after politicization.

The original adequacy test involved finding out whether a conception of justice, such as justice as fairness, gives determinate and complete answers to questions about justice—as judged by us in wide reflective equilibrium. Pro tanto justification avoids the problem of the dissolving "us" by restricting the process of fleshing out the conception to the types of reasons and reasoning permitted in the public conception itself. It is justification that goes only so far—up to the boundaries of the political conception of justice in question. It avoids any kinds of reasons or appeals to values that come from other beliefs we hold in wide equilibrium.

Pro tanto justification allows us to see whether the conception is complete, that is, whether it gives reasonable answers to a broad range of questions about justice (Rawls 1995a, 142–43). But "reasonable answer" here does not mean, "acceptable to each of us in wide equilibrium," which was its meaning in the original adequacy test. This is true even though Rawls says that the "overall criterion of the reasonable is general and wide reflective equilibrium" (1995a, 141). Instead, a reasonable answer is one that involves a *reasonable balance* of the political values involved in this conception, as judged by the kinds of reasons and reasoning endorsed by that conception itself. From the fact that an answer is reasonable in light of these political considerations alone, it does not follow that an individual will find it reasonable in light of everything else she believes in wide equilibrium.

Rawls offers us little in the way of examples to clarify what is involved in showing that an answer is a "reasonable" or "balanced" one. His one illustration, a brief discussion of abortion, is presented in a footnote (1993, 243 n. 43) and is really offered as an illustration of what is meant by balancing values, not as a real argument about abortion. Suppose, Rawls says, that three important political values (among others) are present in a well-ordered society: "the due respect for human life, the ordered reproduction of political society over time, including the family in some form, and finally the equality of women as equal citizens." Rawls then says that "any reasonable balance" of these ideas would involve granting a woman the right to terminate pregnancy in the first trimester. Presumably, denying that right would mean giving excessive weight to one of the three values, the due respect we owe to human life, and no weight at all to the equality of women. Bringing in other nonpublic values or beliefs to justify the special weight assigned to respect for human life, for example, beliefs about the fetus having a nonoverridable right to life from the moment of conception, would clearly be departing from answers given by public reason and pro tanto justification. It is exactly these views about the beginnings of personhood that reasonable people disagree about, so insisting on one interpretation of that view to the exclusion of other public values is to act unreasonably. In this case, the failure to give a "balanced" answer that incorporates all the relevant public values stems directly from ignoring the fact that other reasonable people cannot accept the weighting involved.

Whether or not this specific example about abortion in the first trimester seems plausible, other aspects of the abortion view would quickly become problematic. Does permitting late second trimester abortion for reasons other than a threat to maternal health or life, for example, to avoid serious defects in a fetus, constitute a "reasonable balance" of these values? Does public funding of early abortion, through Medicaid or in military hospitals, constitute a necessary recognition of the equality of women, or does it involve undervaluing respect for human life by forcing those who give much greater weight to such respect to fund abortions they do not approve of? It becomes less obvious that the internal structure of the political conception Rawls described actually tells us what constitutes a reasonable balance of values in these cases. That uncertainty raises a question whether we do smuggle in our wider sense of reasonableness, derived from our considered judgments in our various wide reflective equilibria, in all of these judgments about reasonable balance, including the one Rawls takes to be settled. The answer to this question may depend on how robust and detailed the settled convictions are that arise through clear cases of the exercise of public reason.

We might think of the exercise of public reason involved in pro tanto justification as establishing a *political reflective equilibrium.* There is an equilibrium among the kinds of considerations relevant to giving reasons in, say, justice as fairness and judgments about the "reasonableness" of specific implications of the view for questions of basic justice. Any reasonable political conception of justice might yield such a political reflective equilibrium. Judgments about justice made within that political equilibrium are justified for people only pro tanto; they may be overridden in full justification once all values, not just political ones, are taken into consideration. Justification pro tanto, that is, the justification that results from being in political reflective equilibrium alone, thus falls short of full justification and it lacks the justificatory force involved in Rawls's original appeal to wide equilibrium in *Theory* as an adequacy test. Lloyd (1994) points out that even the "shallow" justification that refrains from appealing to any justifications from comprehensive views has considerable force, so that pro tanto justification will be compelling on many issues.

Consider now the second function of the original adequacy test, namely, showing that a conception of justice gives answers to questions about justice that we find acceptable in light of everything else we believe. This function is now assigned to full justification (and full justification, in turn, is crucial to establishing an overlapping consensus for the right reasons). In section 2, care was taken to sort out just what kinds of beliefs would be contained in any wide equilibrium that contained justice as fairness as a module. These wide equilibria will differ from each other in important details, even where there is overlap on important components, because of the ineliminable diversity in comprehensive views that results from the burdens of judgment. Still, as in the original adequacy test, a conception of justice is justified for individuals if it coheres in wide reflective equilibrium with all the rest of their beliefs. It is in full justification, then, that we really test the reasonableness of claims about justice—that is, their reasonableness in light of all the kinds of reasons we think are relevant, not just the political ones.

Rawls intends the notion of full justification to be perfectly general: We can imagine an individual in any time or place assessing whether a particular conception of justice fits with her other beliefs in wide equilibrium. In this regard, it resembles the adequacy test involving wide equilibrium in *Theory.* Nevertheless, the central question of *Liberalism,* as has been noted, concerns how deep a form of stability is possible. Rawls's answer, pointing to an overlapping consensus of reasonable wide reflective equilibria, thus places the discussion of full justification by appeal to reflective equilibrium in a particular context, one primarily concerned with how people raised in a society governed by a particular conception can stably adhere to it given the burdens of judgment. The stability argument presupposes that people are raised in a society governed by, say, justice as fairness: It is there as a given for them to embrace or reject. In contrast, in *Theory,* the appeal to wide equilibrium as an adequacy test is made in the context of asking, quite generally and apart from the stability test, How can we come to converge on a theory with a determinate content and accept it?

Rawls's answer in *Liberalism* to the stability question emphasizes the role of *institutions* operating over time on *groups* that share certain comprehensive views. Institutions play an "educative role," as Cohen (1994a, 1530) emphasizes. "The formation of moral-political ideas and sensibilities also proceeds less by reasoning or explicit instruction—which may be important in the formation of comprehensive moral views—than by mastering ideas and principles that are expressed in and serve to interpret these institutions" (Cohen 1994a, 1531). For example, the idea of political equality is manifest in many features of democratic institutions, explicitly in claims about equality before the law and equal civil rights but also implicitly in the way in which citizens are forced to win others to their projects in a political and market context. These practices put pressure on people holding various comprehensive views to accommodate the idea of others as equal persons and even as reasonable ones (Cohen 1994a, 1532). People become attached to ideas they become familiar with and understand through these experiences. But this attachment need not be thought of as mere indoctrination; it is reasonably viewed as the result of learning and education.

The institutional mechanism Rawls describes at once explains why some convergence is possible and why there is not full convergence on all elements of the comprehensive views (see Cohen 1994a, 1533). The institutional pressures go only so far. They put pressure on us to accommodate to the political values in the conception governing our institutions, but these pressures do not reach far enough to compel accommodation in beliefs that govern our other beliefs and the institutions that dominate the nonpublic parts of our lives. We get, then, an explanation—however anthropological it sounds—of the question why we do not have adequate forces at work to produce overall convergence, even if we get partial convergence in overlapping consensus. (Remember, this whole discussion is part of ideal theory and is intended to help us answer the original question about stability, namely, Can we maintain a motivation to comply with this conception of justice, given that we are raised under institutions governed by it? Rawls is not here explaining how we could initially produce convergence on an overlapping consensus for the right reasons.)

Since Rawls is at such pains to explain how, over time and through institutional mechanisms, the basis for accommodation of comprehensive views is achieved, it is easy to see why the *iterative* nature of the original appeal to reflective equilibrium as an adequacy test drops out of the account. No doubt, at the same time that comprehensive views accommodate themselves to a political conception there is some struggle against some of its features, and the public conception also evolves over time in response to some of that struggle. But this historical process is a far cry from the iterative role that was ascribed to the original adequacy test in *Theory*, and it is particularly far from the role ascribed to the individual seeking wide equilibrium, as opposed to groups seeking to make their political surroundings accommodate to them.

I believe the sense of philosophical loss is explained, at least in part, by this shift from a philosopher's dream, an iterative process of construction and justification involving all of us, to a social and political process in which, over time, people holding diverse views maintain an overlapping consensus on a public conception of justice. The shift may be partly an illusion created by the different problems Rawls focuses on in his earlier and later work. Further confusion may be added by the discussion of nonideal contexts (How might we get to overlapping consensus for the right reasons if we do not yet have it but only share some democratic ideas?), to which I alluded in discussing stability at the end of section 1.

In *Theory,* much of the discussion necessarily focuses on the construction of a new theory and what the process of justifying it must look like. In *Liberalism,* the focus is on the stability argument, which supposes we already have a determinate theory and are simply assessing how reasonable people with diverse views can accommodate to the conception of justice that is already determinate within their culture. If that is the basic problem *Liberalism* addresses, then it is not surprising that Rawls does not engage us in the process of theory construction in the same way he did when his project had a different central problem. Still, it is hard to see how "full justification" can play the iterative role in theory construction and justification that Rawls assigned to the original adequacy test involving wide reflective equilibrium, except over time and in the context of evolving modifications of social institutions through political disagreement, struggle, and reform. Though philosophy is not absent from that process—it plays a crucial role within and between comprehensive views in securing accommodation—it is not so clearly central as in the philosopher's dream. If philosophy can really have only that reduced role, then the sense of loss is the sorrow of waking from a pleasant dream.

We can sharpen the effect of that awakening by posing the question, Can someone be justified in rejecting reasonableness in wide reflective equilibrium? The answer seems to be "yes." That is because reasonableness is given a fairly specific content in terms of beliefs and commitments (see section 1). We are not simply asking, without equivocation, Is it reasonable to be unreasonable? Reasonable comprehensive views in wide reflective equilibrium will contain an account of the burdens of judgment and a willingness to submit matters of justice to consideration in terms of reasons that are acceptable to other reasonable people. Unreasonable people, for example, those holding views that leave no room for seeking terms of cooperation with others on grounds that others can reasonably accept, will not share these specific elements. Some members of certain fundamentalist religious sects, for example, might ascribe overriding weight to the belief that God's will should dominate human political relations. For them justice—on terms reasonable to others who are reasonable—holds no appeal at all.

How troubling is this result? We may suppose that the fundamentalist listens to reasons that fit well within his system of beliefs. We may also suppose he commits no logical fallacies, and we may even suppose that he is not epistemologically irresponsible in adhering to beliefs for which there is counterevidence he can be held responsible for taking into account, given other things he believes. Then such a person would not be justified in accepting justice as fairness (or some other reasonable political conception). But this outcome should be no more troubling to us than the fact that someone might—given a certain history, set of beliefs and experiences, and culture—be justified in believing the earth is flat or the sun orbits the earth. Neither skepticism nor relativism is an inevitable consequence of this coherence account of justification, and the fact that sound philosophical argument will not necessarily persuade all who are sufficiently reflective, regardless of their initial beliefs, is not to abandon philosophy.

There is a further analogy between the political view of justice and a position taken by some in the philosophy of science. Important features of the scientific method, it is sometimes claimed (see Boyd 1988), do not really facilitate progress in science unless a certain threshold is reached. Some "approximately true" theory must be adopted. Then, given appropriate methodological scruples, significant further progress can be made.

Certain democratic ideas constitute a similar threshold, in Rawls's view. We may not be led to them whatever our starting point by reflection and philosophical argument alone, but if we acquire them in a democratic culture, where they are embodied in our institutions, then political philosophy can help us refine them into a more reasonable, perhaps an optimally reasonable, conception of justice. And if that conception governs our well-ordered society, philosophical analysis and discussion help us to accommodate our other views, given their "looseness," to the conception. Philosophy may not be capable of leading us from the desert to a full-blown convergence on justice as fairness, as it might have appeared it was supposed to do in *Theory,* any more than scientific method could lead Robinson Crusoe to quantum mechanics, but it has not been replaced by moral anthropology either.

5. Moral Double Bookkeeping and Integrity

The politicization of justice means that we must bifurcate our justificatory practice. We must draw a line between the domain of public reason, that is, matters involving constitutional essentials and other issues of basic justice, and the rest of our moral, religious, and philosophical beliefs. Can we keep two moral ledgers in this way without threatening moral integrity? Points that have emerged in our analysis of reflective equilibrium after politicization help us to answer this question positively: There need be no threat to moral integrity. Before turning to those points, it will help to comment on the fact that there are other contexts in which we engage—fruitfully and without a loss of integrity—in analogous double bookkeeping.

In many churches and synagogues (but by no means all) there is an unspoken rule governing sermons: They may address the moral dimensions of social and political issues, but they must do so without becoming enmeshed in "politics," specifically party politics. I once asked a rabbi why he refrained from drawing the connection between his moral discussion and its implications for a particular election and the positions of the candidates. His reply was that he felt competent to explain how his religious and moral tradition contained implications for some of our social practices and policies but that "so many other factors" go into party allegiances and preferences that "intelligent, reflective people" who share the same moral views can disagree about them. He specifically mentioned the complexities of economics and political science, the difficulty of interpreting historical events, and the complexity of making judgments about the character of individual politicians.

It is worth paraphrasing his explanation in more detail. He said, "I have my carefully thought out views on those subjects, and I am sure I am right, but I would not presume to impose them on my congregation, even though I have the pulpit. Many of its most thoughtful members disagree about them, and if I tie my moral conclusions to my political ones, people whom I might influence morally will be lost to me. Some disagree with me about my interpretation of the moral tradition, but we have more common ground to carry out our discussion about such issues. These moral issues are ones we have struggled with in our families and communities for many generations, and they are debated extensively in the rabbinic literature. We may disagree, but at least we can hope for basic agreement because of our shared commitments and experiences. But politics—that's too complicated!"

Perhaps some clergy might keep politics out of their sermons solely to protect their position within their congregation. That might, at least in some instances, be a compromise that threatens moral integrity. The rationale offered by the rabbi does not threaten integrity, at least generally.

The boundary the rabbi draws between the moral and the political has some ironic contrasts with Rawls's. From within a shared tradition, supported by its own institutions over long periods of time, some moral issues will seem clear and resolvable by reference to shared assumptions whereas political ones may not. In his discussion of overlapping consensus and stability, Rawls makes the opposite point: Shared democratic institutions produce a framework for political agreement about constitutional essentials and basic matters of justice, but complexity will show up beyond the public domain. The rabbi is not restricting the political domain in the same way Rawls does, and some of the contrast in their positions derives from that fact. (For the rabbi, the political concerns all aspects of party politics, not just fundamental issues of justice.) A second ironic contrast is that Rawls is interested in protecting agreement in the domain of public reason by excluding sources of disagreement that fall outside of it whereas the rabbi is excluding "politics" in order to protect agreement in the nonpublic domain.

The main point, then, is not the differences between the boundaries that Rawls and the rabbi draw. It is the fact that in various private associations, including ones that claim significant moral authority, people draw justifactory boundaries of the sort that Rawls does and for somewhat similar reasons. The point should be familiar to all of us, since we all assume roles, professional or otherwise, in which we must distinguish our own values from the values it is appropriate to invoke given the role we must play. For example, each of us in our capacities as parents, teachers, or advisers must sometimes separate our own values from those appropriately appealed to in the context of giving advice to our children, students, advisees, or clients.

Rawls points us toward another example of boundary drawing common in our tradition: the special place we give to rules of evidence in the law (Rawls 1993, 221). We are interested in protecting the right to a fair trial, and to do so we devise a complex set of procedures for introducing and evaluating evidence in trials. The effect of these rules is that sometimes not all relevant information will be available to a jury. We are less interested in "the whole truth," however it is obtained, than we are in assuring a mechanism for fair trials. More generally, we adjust our standards of what we count as relevant authorities and procedures of reasoning to the task we have at hand in various private associations. We allow only certain authorities the power to deliberate in certain institutions, for example, in educational institutions deliberating curriculum design or in religious institutions debating a matter of doctrine. As Rawls notes, "The criteria and methods of these nonpublic reasons depend in part on how the nature (the aim and point) of each association is understood and the conditions under which it pursues its ends" (1993, 221).

Politicization should not, then, be criticized merely for drawing a boundary that bifurcates justificatory practices. We do that commonly and for good reason at many points in our lives, both in private and public contexts. The challenge to integrity must be more specific if it is to be serious, and that leads us back to some of the points that emerged in our discussion of wide reflective equilibrium.

To consider whether the boundary between public reason and nonpublic values threatens moral integrity, we must consider two cases. One case involves the situation in an overlapping consensus for the right reasons. For example, suppose that justice as fairness is a module within various wide reflective equilibria established by people with differing comprehensive views. The second case is one in which there are alternative conceptions of justice held by people who at least share some common democratic ideas but there is not yet an overlapping consensus on a shared conception. (Notice that this second case does not arise in ideal theory, where we are thinking about the original stability question. It is relevant to stability in nonideal contexts, as I noted at the end of section 1.) The analysis thus far has concentrated on the first case, and I begin with it here.

A wide reflective equilibrium that contains justice as fairness (for example) as a module must also contain three other elements that bear on the concern about a threat to integrity. The equilibrium contains a rationale for the key background ideas involved in justice as fairness. We saw how people sharing different equilibria might provide their own different justifications for thinking of people as free moral agents with an interest in conditions protecting that freedom. This means that the basic ideas involved in public reason, as defined by the shared conception of justice as fairness, are not themselves "moral compromises" begrudgingly made. The values contained in the shared conception are values for the person in wide equilibrium, and this means the person is fully justified in acting in accord with those values. Specifically, the person can say that, normally speaking, decisions made by institutions duly constituted according to justice as fairness are decisions the individual is fully justified in accepting.

The second element of the wide equilibrium is the acceptance of an account of the burdens of judgment and the reasonableness of others who may differ in their nonpublic values. This acceptance of reasonable pluralism is itself justified for each person in wide equilibrium, albeit in somewhat different ways. The effect of each person accepting reasonable pluralism is that each has respect for the kinds of reasons others can be expected to accept and those others would not accept. An element of this acceptance of reasonable pluralism is the moral belief that it is wrong to use the coercive power of the state to impose constraints on others for reasons that they can reasonably reject. If constraints—including those that result from the effects of voting— are to be imposed, they must be defensible on grounds all can reasonably accept. Because each person thus has a rationale or justification for accepting reasonable pluralism, each has a general reason for bifurcating justification in the way the public-nonpublic boundary requires. There is no threat to individual integrity if the rationale for drawing the boundary is itself ultimately justified within the agent's total system of beliefs and values.

Finally, the third element each must have in wide equilibrium is a specification of the priority each will give to public values over nonpublic ones. This boundary must reflect differences in the nonpublic values and in the specifics of the priority permitted, given the differences in the rationales for this boundary that must exist in wide equilibrium. Each might be able to say that "normally" priority will be given to the decisions made by just institutions, although how each characterizes exceptions will vary depending on features of the different comprehensive views.

Because there is variation in the rationales and in the exceptions to what is normally taken to be justifiable priority for public values, even in a stable overlapping consensus there will be ongoing disagreement on some issues. Rawls (1995a, 148–49) notes, for example, that Quakers may conscientiously object to democratic decisions to wage war, viewing that outcome of an otherwise acceptable set of institutions as warranting conscientious objection, without being forced to conclude that those democratic institutions are themselves unacceptable. The institutions may, on the whole, represent the best way to realize other Quaker values, which include a concern for basic rights and fundamental interests of other people (1995a, 149). To give another example: Someone who thinks abortion is morally wrong might accept the "balance of public reasons" that recognizes a woman's right to a first trimester abortion (see section 3) but conscientiously resist being asked to contribute resources (through public funding) to facilitate such abortions (for those on Medicaid or at military bases, for example).

Another troubling example is this one: Is permitting voluntary religious expression in the schools consistent with avoiding the "establishment" of religion? If the great majority of the students in a school shares the same religion, does this put undue pressure on those who are of different religious backgrounds or have no religious beliefs at all? One reason this type of example is troubling is that it is not clear that public reason will give an unequivocal answer. The account may not be complete with respect to all these questions. In such a case, the overlapping consensus does not preclude the intrusion of nonpublic values into the debate, and different comprehensive views will find it important for different reasons and in different degrees to intrude their own nonpublic solutions on these matters.

The permeability of the public-nonpublic boundary goes beyond these cases of incompleteness, because reasonable people ultimately must justify how much priority to give public reason and public values in their own terms. How much friction results, and how much instability is threatened, are largely empirical matters: They depend on the composition of the overlapping consensus. Since ultimate authority for how to weigh public against nonpublic values must rest with the individual and must be justifiable to her in light of all of her values, there is no general threat to integrity from the drawing of the boundary or its unevenness.

Finally, we must consider the case (in nonideal theory) in which there is an overlapping consensus on the same political conception of justice, although there may be some overlap on key democratic ideas and, thus, on some of the elements of public reason. I believe this is the situation in the United States today: There is agreement on many constitutional essentials, much less agreement on many basic questions of justice, and diverse conceptions of justice, each of which draws in its own way on important democratic ideas. For example, Rawls would argue that justice as fairness is the *most reasonable* way to combine fundamental ideas in our democratic tradition (Rawls 1995b, 2). He claims that this conception makes sense of some of our settled convictions about justice, for example, about the importance of certain basic liberties, and that it allows us to leverage those points of agreement so that we resolve remaining points of disagreement, for example, about acceptable forms of social and economic inequality (see Cohen 1989). Justice Scalia no doubt has a different conception of justice that he invokes; Justice O'Connor has yet another.

In this context, where there is less agreement on the content and limits of public reason, dispute about appropriate and inappropriate appeals to nonpublic values will be more intense and harder to resolve. Nevertheless, Rawls argues that considerable stability may result even in this situation, since each political conception that is affirmed is reasonable and all reasonable comprehensive views affirm one such conception or another (see Rawls 1995b, 2ff.). He further suggests that over time, the most reasonable conception among the family of reasonable political conceptions will form a core around which other members of the family will tend to gather "at a decreasing (or not increasing) distance" (1995b, 3). This claim about stability in a nonideal context, if it is plausible, adds weight to the claim that the most reasonable view (justice as fairness) will be stable in a well-ordered society. More effective institutional forces would be at work in the well-ordered society to educate people about the value of justice and its key ideas than in the nonideal context.

The question before us is, What threat is there to moral integrity when there is no overlapping consensus on the same political conception and each of us attempts to respect a boundary between public and nonpublic values in justifying claims about constitutional essentials and basic questions of justice? Let us suppose, as we did in the case of overlapping consensus for the right reasons, that reasonable people will include in their respective wide equilibria some account of the burdens of judgment and reasonable pluralism. Suppose that they will also include some boundary that they draw and justify in their own terms between public and nonpublic uses of reason. Compared to the case in which there is overlapping consensus on the same political conception of justice, there will be less agreement on where appeals to nonpublic values violate the boundary and where they are justifiable exceptions. Still, there is no additional threat to moral integrity in this case. The acceptance of a particular boundary between public and nonpublic values is made by each person in wide reflective equilibrium. The public-nonpublic boundary is fully justified for each person, and each has adequate reasons for respecting it. The fact that there is no consensus on the same political conception does not affect the fact that the boundary each draws in light of her own acceptance of a reasonable political conception is itself fully justified for her.

Whether or not there is overlapping consensus, then, there is no threat to moral integrity, provided people justify the drawing of a public-nonpublic boundary in ways that derive from their own views in wide equilibrium. The politicization of justice and of justification is not a threat to moral integrity. Nor does it impose unacceptable philosophical loss, even if it forces us to revise some of our expectations. Wide reflective equilibrium, and thus justification, remain alive and well after politicization.

Acknowledgments

This essay appears as Chapter 8 in Daniels 1996. I want to thank Cambridge University Press for permission to use it here. I also wish to thank Joshua Cohen, Erin Kelly, and John Rawls for extremely helpful discussions of earlier drafts of this chapter.

References

Barry, Brian. 1995. John Rawls and the Search for Stability. *Ethics* 105 (July): 874–915.

Boyd, Richard N. 1988. How to Be a Moral Realist. In *Essays on Moral Realism,* ed. Geoffrey Sayre-McCord. Ithaca, N.Y.: Cornell University Press, 181–228.

Cohen, Joshua. 1989. Democratic Equality. *Ethics* 99 (July): 727–51.

———. 1994a. A More Democratic Liberalism. *Michigan Law Review* 92, no. 6: 1506–43.

———. 1994b. Pluralism and Proceduralism. *Chicago-Kent Law Review* 69, no. 3: 589–618.

Daniels, Norman. 1979. Wide Reflective Equilibrium and Theory Acceptance in Ethics. *Journal of Philosophy* 76, no. 5: 256–82.

———. 1980. Reflective Equilibrium and Archimedean Points. *Canadian Journal of Philosophy* 10, no. 1: 83–103.

———. 1996. *Justice and Justification: Reflective Equilibrium in Theory and Practice.* New York: Cambridge University Press.

Daniels, Norman, ed. 1975. *Reading Rawls.* New York: Basic Books.

Dworkin, Ronald. 1973. The Original Position. *University of Chicago Law Review* 40, no. 3 (Spring): 500–33; reprinted in *Reading Rawls,* ed. Norman Daniels. New York: Basic Books, 1975, 16–52.

Freeman, Samuel. 1994. Political Liberalism and the Possibility of Just Democratic Constitution. *Chicago-Kent Law Review* 69, no. 3: 619–68.

Greenawalt, Kent. 1994. On Public Reason. *Chicago-Kent Law Review* 69, no. 3: 669–90.

Hare, R. M. 1973. Rawls' Theory of Justice. *Philosophical Quarterly* 23 (April): 144–55 and 23 (July): 241–51; reprinted in *Reading Rawls,* ed. Norman Daniels. New York: Basic Books, 1975, 81–107.

Lloyd, S. A. 1994. Relativizing Rawls. *Chicago-Kent Law Review* 69, no. 3: 709–36.

Rawls, John. 1971. *A Theory of Justice.* Cambridge, Mass.: Harvard University Press.

———. 1974. "Reply to Alexander and Musgrave." *Quarterly Journal of Economics* 88: 633–55.

———. 1980. Kantian Constructivism in Moral Theory. *Journal of Philosophy* 77: 515–72.

———. 1993. *Political Liberalism.* New York: Columbia University Press.

———. 1995a. Reply to Habermas. *Journal of Philosophy* 92, no. 3: 132–80.

———. 1995b. A *Theory of Justice* and *Political Liberalism* and Other Pieces: How Related? Draft of comments presented at October 1995 Santa Clara Conference on Rawls's work. Unpublished manuscript.

Sandel, Michael J. 1982. *Liberalism and the Limits of Justice.* Cambridge: Cambridge University Press.

White, Stephen. 1991. *The Unity of the Self.* Cambridge, Mass.: MIT Press.

8

ECONOMIC LIBERTIES

James W. Nickel

This chapter defends the importance of economic liberties, which, broadly described, include the liberty to buy and sell labor, to engage in independent economic activity, to hold both personal and productive property, and to buy, sell, use, and consume goods and services. I argue that these liberties are very useful to ordinary people and suggest that liberal egalitarians such as John Rawls therefore have good reasons to take these economic liberties to be among the basic liberties.[1] No claim is made, however, that economic liberties should have unbounded scopes or that their exercise cannot be regulated by law. "Private" economic transactions often have large spillovers or externalities, including negative ones, for other parties.[2] In endorsing the liberty to hire workers, for example, I don't wish to rule out legislation to protect the health and safety of workers, to prevent discrimination, to facilitate and regulate collective bargaining, or even to require some sort of industrial democracy in large enterprises.

Rawls takes only two areas of economic liberty to be basic.[3] One is free choice of occupation, which includes freedom from slavery and forced labor and freedom to choose and change one's job or profession. The other is the liberty to acquire, hold, use, and dispose of "personal property"—that is, limited holdings of property for personal rather than productive use. In Rawls's view, respect for these liberties is a matter of justice, but respect for liberties such as the freedom to sell one's labor or the freedom to start and run a business is not.

Since 1990, countries in all parts of the world, including Brazil, Peru, India, Russia, China, and Vietnam, have become much more friendly toward economic liberties for individuals and families. And theories of Third World economic development now generally put less emphasis on government-run or government-guided development and more emphasis on encouraging and providing loans to microenterprises. This historic change was driven in large measure by changed beliefs about what works, about what sorts of economic arrangements lead to development and prosperity. According to the new perspective, tapping people's energies and creativity in the economic sphere requires giving them considerable space for independent economic activity.

155

And granting such space avoids forcing independent economic activity into an underground economy. But even if we accept that economic liberties are valuable as components of the sorts of economic systems that are most conducive to prosperity, we may still wonder whether economic liberties have deeper roots.

The U.S. Supreme Court took an activist stance toward defending economic liberties during the Lochner era, but that activism died during the New Deal and has never been resurrected.[4] Whether courts should use judicial review to protect economic liberties is not my main concern. My defense of the importance of key economic liberties could serve as a central part of an argument that the Supreme Court should go back to reviewing the reasonableness of serious restrictions on economic liberties. But it doesn't by itself imply that conclusion.

In section 1 of this chapter, I explain what I mean by economic liberties, sections 2 and 3 present defenses of the importance of those liberties, section 4 explains and criticizes Rawls's position on economic liberties, and section 5 deals with how to qualify claims about economic liberties so they are not implausibly strong.

1. Basic Economic Liberties

In this section, I identify the economic liberties[5] whose importance I will defend and distinguish "dedicated" economic liberties from broader liberties that have important applications in the economic area. These liberties are described in the same broad terms that we use for other basic liberties, and thus major questions are left open, such as which occupations free choice of occupation should cover and which kinds and quantities of possessions should be protected by liberties in the area of property. In some areas these liberties overlap. It should also be noted that these liberties are bilateral in the sense that they cover, not just doing something, but also deciding not to do that thing.

It is not helpful to categorize all economic liberties under property or under freedom of contract. Economic activity can't be adequately summed up under a single category such as working, transacting, holding, or using. All four are involved, along with choices about the scope and direction of one's economic activities.[6] Since it is useful to have labels for liberties in bills of rights and lists of basic liberties, we might speak of "a right to independent economic activity" and "a right to own personal and productive property."

1.1. Dedicated Economic Liberties

There are four dedicated economic liberties.

1. *Working: Freedom to labor and use labor in production.* This is the liberty to employ one's body and time in productive activity that one has chosen or accepted, and under arrangements that one has chosen or accepted. Excluding forced labor and slavery, this category includes the freedom to sell, buy, trade, and donate labor.

2. *Transacting: Free economic activity.* This is the freedom to manage one's economic affairs at the individual and household levels and on larger scales as well. It includes the liberty to buy and sell, to make things, to save and invest, to enter into market competition, and to profit from transactions. It also includes the liberty to start, run, and shut down a business, factory, farm, or other commercial enterprise. Transacting may require specific actions such as acquiring a skill, trade, or profession; planning and making arrangements for production, including arrangements for partners, workers, tools, materials, capital, organization, and space or land; engaging individually or jointly in productive activities; displaying and advertising products; and selling products or services.

3. *Holding: Freedom in the realm of property.* This category covers legitimate ways of acquiring and holding property, using and developing property for commercial and productive purposes, and property transactions such as investing, buying, selling, trading, and giving. It also includes freedom from expropriation without due process and compensation. These freedoms apply to both personal and productive property.

4. *Using: Freedom to buy, use, and consume resources, goods, and services.* This is the liberty to make use of legitimately acquired resources for consumption and production. At the household level this liberty covers actions such as eating, drinking, inhabiting, wearing, and reading. It also covers production-related consumption such as the fuel used in a factory or the wood used in building furniture.[7]

1.2. Broader Liberties with Important Economic Applications

In addition to the "dedicated" economic liberties, several broader liberties have important applications in the economic area. These include freedom of contract, freedom of inquiry and communication, freedom to create and join organizations, and freedom of movement and residence.

2. Linkage Arguments for the Importance of Economic Liberties

In this section I defend the importance of economic liberties by showing that blocking them substantially also blocks important parts of liberties that are widely accepted as basic such as freedom of religion, freedom in the area of communication, political freedoms, freedom of association, and freedom of movement. The arguments I use might be called "linkage arguments" because they link blockage of a controversial economic liberty to the blockage of a less-controversial liberty and thus show that a person who believes the latter liberty to be important must also recognize the importance of the former.[8]

As an example of substantial restriction of economic liberties we can take the Soviet Union during the 1970s. That system obviously did not block all economic activity, but it did restrict severely the economic freedoms of ordinary people to start businesses, hire employees, and buy or lease property such as land, office space, or buildings. Ordinary people were allowed only the liberties necessary to be workers and consumers.

Linkage arguments can take strong and weak forms. Strong linkage arguments try to show that blocking one liberty directly blocks important parts of another liberty. For example, substantially blocking freedom of communication directly blocks freedom of religion because communicating about religion is a core religious activity. To succeed, these arguments require overlaps between the scopes of basic liberties. Weak linkage arguments try to show that blocking one liberty makes it more difficult to engage in the actions protected by another liberty. If a strong linkage can be shown between two liberties, then the priority of the more important member of the pair is transferred to the other liberty, or at least to part of the other liberty.[9] The arguments offered below are intended as strong linkage arguments.

2.1. Freedom of Religion

Some activities protected by freedom of religion have significant economic dimensions. Consequently, to restrict these economic activities in a wholesale way will substantially restrict freedom of religion. Consider the following things that religious groups frequently do:

- Asking people to quit their jobs in order to pursue full-time religious callings.
- Constructing buildings for religious activities.
- Starting and running religious enterprises such as churches, publishing houses, and schools.
- Hiring employees to serve as religious leaders, editors, teachers, receptionists, and janitors.
- Soliciting donations for religious causes.
- Saving, managing, and spending the funds coming from donations and the operations of the religious enterprises.

I am not, of course, suggesting that these economic dimensions of religious activity cannot be regulated, but if they are entirely or largely blocked as economic activities, religious activities will be severely limited. A political system that does not respect economic liberties tells people that they are free to have religious beliefs and follow religious practices but that they should pursue their religion in their leisure time and not let it interfere with their work, do it without property or enterprises, and do it without use or management of substantial resources. Freedom of religion is not totally demolished by this, but it is very significantly restricted, particularly in its collective dimensions.

2.2. Freedom of Communication

Many activities covered by freedom of communication have significant economic dimensions, and hence, wholesale restrictions on economic liberties substantially restrict freedom in the area of communication. Ordinary spoken communication between people does not have large economic dimensions, but other forms of communication do. Those who communicate on behalf of a cause frequently engage in activities such as the following:

- Producing and distributing printed material, which requires having access to paper, ink, editorial services, printing, and transportation.
- Employing full-time workers such as solicitors, organizers, officials, printers, secretaries, and truck drivers.
- Seeking donations and paid memberships to support communicative efforts.
- Saving, managing, and spending the funds coming from donations and memberships.

If these activities involved in large-scale communication are substantially blocked as economic activities, the result will be to block substantially the freedom to communicate. A system that grants communicative freedom but heavily restricts economic liberties tells people that they can communicate but that they should do it without offices and equipment, without starting organizations with commercial dimensions to promote a point of view, and without acquiring and using substantial resources.

2.3. Political Freedoms

Similar points apply to communication and activism on behalf of a political party or cause. Activities with a central place under political freedom frequently have significant economic dimensions, and hence, wholesale restrictions on economic liberties substantially restrict political freedoms.

- Attempts to communicate with and persuade large numbers of people are core parts of political freedoms, so all of the points made about freedom of communication also apply here.
- Political organizations and parties, like religious organizations, frequently need full-time employees, buildings, and equipment, and creating and supporting these requires soliciting, managing, and expending funds as well as buying and consuming resources.

If these political activities are substantially restricted as economic activities, the result will be to block substantially the freedom to engage in political activity through organizations and parties. A system that grants political freedom but heavily restricts economic liberties tells people that they can engage in politics but that they should do it without offices and equipment, without professional employees, without starting organizations with commercial dimensions to promote a political agenda, and without the use of substantial resources.

2.4. Freedom of Association

Central dimensions of freedom of association, such as forming, joining, and participating in social and ethnic organizations involve significant economic activities, and hence, substantial restrictions on economic liberties will limit freedom of association, particularly in its organized and large-scale dimensions. Religious association is one important form of association, so some of the links between religious activities and economic activities are also relevant here. Social organizations may be organized to promote the interests of members of a particular ethnic group or neighborhood (e.g., a retirement home mainly for Filipino Americans) or to provide opportunities for engaging in a game or activity (e.g., a jazz festival). These sorts of organizations often need to engage in activities such as:

- Renting or buying an office or facility in which the association's activities can be organized and held.
- Seeking dues-paying members to support the activities of the organization.
- Communicating with present and potential members through newsletters or other materials.
- Managing, saving, and spending funds from memberships and donations.

If a political system grants freedom of association but substantially restricts economic activities, it will find that the restriction on economic activities will also restrict important areas of freedom of association.

2.5 Freedom of Movement

Key parts of freedom of movement involve economic activity. To illustrate this point I focus on one particularly important type of movement, namely, internal or external migration to escape famine, severe poverty, persecution, and/or oppression. At the individual level, success in such a migration requires quitting one's job (if any), converting any assets one has to things that can be carried or shipped, and buying supplies. If the process of traveling is extended, survival along the way is likely to require finding places to sleep, scrounging food and water, and seeking remunerative work.[10]

If economic activities necessary to carrying out a successful migration are blocked because economic liberties are rejected, the result will be to restrict substantially the freedom to move. A political system that doesn't recognize economic liberties within some substantial range, but seeks to respect freedom of movement, will tell people they are free to move and flee but that they should do so without control over the economic resources needed for successful movement.

3. Economic Liberties and Autonomy

I suggest that economic liberties are important because economic activity, like political and intellectual activity, is an important area of human autonomy.

The ideal of autonomy holds that adults of normal intelligence and capacities should not turn over or be forced to turn over the management of their lives to other parties—even if those other parties could manage their lives better than they can. This ideal holds that people should be the authors of their own lives to a considerable degree.[11]

In appealing to autonomy to defend the importance of economic liberties I do not mean to imply that autonomy is the only consideration relevant to the justification and weight of liberties. The usefulness of general liberties in pursuing a wide variety of goals—which Joel Feinberg calls "fecundity"—is another important consideration.[12] Still another factor is the role some liberties play in preventing and remedying political and economic abuses. Liberties of political participation get some of their importance from this factor. A familiar argument claims that property held by nongovernmental agencies, including individuals, gives those agencies the ability to resist the power of government when it becomes oppressive.[13]

Rawls endorses autonomy in a limited way since within his framework the ideal of autonomy is a "perfectionist" value that some reasonable participants in society may not accept.[14] But Rawls's "political" conception of the person commits him to values that are very near relatives of autonomy in the ordinary sense. Rawls is committed to the value of developing and exercising a sense of justice and to the value of developing, exercising, and pursuing a personal conception of the good.[15] These two values cover much of the ground occupied by broader conceptions of autonomy.

Autonomy has to be realized in lives where much is already determined or constrained by nature and culture. The accidents of birth, such as who one's parents are, whether one is male or female, in which country one is born, what one's native language and culture are, and what innate talents and disabilities one has, are not open to choice. And fairness requires us to accommodate the lives, needs, desires, and choices of other people. But in spite of these limits, there is still much to choose—and life often takes surprising turns. Under severe conditions, many people will be limited to filling in the details within patterns of life that they did not choose. Under good circumstances, people can set the main directions of their lives as well as choosing the details.

The same is true in the economic area. Most people have to work and do not choose whether they are born into a family, region, or country that is rich or poor. Further, occupational choices may be limited. But even apart from deciding whether to migrate to richer areas, one can choose to pursue the occupations available and fill in the details within those occupations in various ways. The scope for choice may be limited, yet workers typically have thousands of days to put their own stamps on their jobs and to find their own particular niches. And if one has some economic liberties, one may be able to create a new occupational path to better suit oneself. The fact that economic activity is necessary to most people's survival and flourishing means that most humans engage in it and take participation and success in it to be important.

In consequence, economic activity becomes a significant area for the development and exercise of choice.

To get from the value of autonomy to a case for particular liberties we need some way to decide *which* freedoms are especially valuable to developing and exercising autonomy. We need some way of showing that economic activity is an important area for authoring one's own life. I suggest four criteria. First, freedoms are important to autonomy if they are necessary or extremely useful to being able to think, choose, and act intelligently and morally. Second, some freedoms are important to autonomy if they cover actions and decisions that have particularly intimate connections with one's body, mind, personality, and projects. Third, freedoms are very valuable to autonomy if they offer access to large-scale projects or cover decisions that structure major parts of one's life. Fourth, freedoms are important if they keep clear major paths within historically and culturally important areas of choice.

3.1. Choosing and Acting Intelligently and Morally

To be the author of one's own life, it is necessary to plan it, monitor it, discuss it, evaluate it from moral and other perspectives, and modify or reform it. Consequently, the view of basic liberties that we derive from autonomy should include the liberties of moral and rational beings such as the liberty to inquire, reflect, choose, communicate, discuss, criticize, demand, explain, apologize, negotiate, blame, forgive, and act in accordance with one's duties. These specific liberties are covered by freedom of belief and conscience, freedom of religion, freedom of communication, and freedom of association. We saw in section 2 that these basic liberties have important parts that involve economic activity and thus require economic liberties.

3.2. Intimate Connections

This criterion suggests that people should be free to control things and activities that are very close to or connect intimately with their bodies and personal identities. These liberties allow one to seek, explore, and adopt ways of living that fit the person one is and that are appropriate to the kind of life one is trying to lead. Areas of liberty covered here include sex and reproduction, the clothing one wears, food and drink, household effects like pictures and books, religious and philosophical beliefs, and how one spends one's leisure time.

One economic liberty supported by this criterion is free choice of occupation, because one's work consumes so much of one's life and so much defines who one is. And as many philosophers have noted, property that one personally uses and interacts with over an extended period of time can have a close link with one's personality and identity.[16]

3.3. Access to Large-scale and Temporally Extended Options

Joseph Raz suggests that autonomy requires an adequate range of options for choice and that adequacy requires that some of these options involve "long term pervasive consequences."[17] I would add that some of these options need to involve ambitious or demanding projects that allow us to construct complicated and extended relations with other persons, expand and test our abilities, challenge assumptions about what humans can do, and create new options for other people. Choices with long-term consequences are important to autonomy because they involve setting the direction for one's whole life, or a significant portion of it. Without these sorts of choices, one's autonomy is restricted to filling in the details. Choosing to marry and have children, for example, sets the direction for the middle portion of many people's lives. Having control over at least some of these sorts of decisions is of enormous importance to being part-author of one's own life. Choice of occupation is a structural decision in this sense, and, hence, there are strong reasons of autonomy for putting that decision in people's own hands. Some decisions about property, such as the decision to make an apartment in a certain neighborhood one's lifelong home or to make a career of farming a particular plot of land, also have this character.

Not everyone will want to try to enact a life story that is ambitious and grand, but it is important that some larger-scale choices be available to individuals and groups. Choosing to undertake an ambitious project is likely to have the long-term pervasive consequences spoken of in the previous paragraph. Further, the availability of such options allows people to try to transcend triviality and ordinariness. Economic liberties allow for the exercise of basic liberties on a larger scale by allowing groups of persons to combine their resources and act in an organized manner to achieve shared goals. Further, property rights make possible the pursuit of larger projects. By having the authority over the disposition of assets over an extended time that secure property rights give, one can plan and prepare for future projects, including larger-scale projects. Suppose, for example, that someone in a poor country wishes to build a home for his family and, over a period of years, gathers discarded building materials for this purpose. Without property rights, the materials will be available for others to use to satisfy day-to-day needs, such as the need for firewood. With secure property rights, the likelihood of being able to use in the future what one has gathered or saved is greatly increased, thereby giving greater scale to the projects that people can undertake and thus increasing their options for choice.

3.4. Historically and Culturally Important Areas of Choice

This criterion suggests that it is important to people's autonomy that they not be denied access to historically and culturally important areas of choice. Suppose that a puritanical government decided to prohibit the making and viewing of paintings and drawings. Perhaps none of the earlier criteria would explain why this would be a significant loss to at least some people's autonomy. Indeed, advocates of this prohibition could correctly point out that some people live fully autonomous lives while never engaging in these artistic activities as either participants or consumers. So we cannot claim that autonomy is impossible without the availability of these artistic activities. Nevertheless, I think we should insist that painting and drawing provide a significant area of choice and action, an area that should not be lightly closed. Even early humans engaged in such activity, and virtually all contemporary cultures have found value in it. If this area were closed off to individuals, an important area of choice and action would be lost.

Something similar is true of economic activities. Throughout history, economic activity has been central to human life. Its very necessity has made it significant. Economic struggle has been the game that nearly every human has had to play, and many people find an important source of their self-esteem in this area. This is one major reason why unemployment is generally such a bad thing.[18] The claim to freedom to engage in historically and culturally significant economic activities applies, not just at a global level, but also to particular professions or careers. The liberty to choose to pursue the life of a farmer, teacher, singer, writer, or cook draws some support from this criterion.

4. Rawls on Economic Liberties

Rawls holds that some liberties are so important they can be prescribed generally as requirements of justice. Rawls calls liberties of this sort "basic liberties" and believes they include "freedom of thought and liberty of conscience"; "the political liberties and freedom of association," "the freedoms specified by the liberty and integrity of the person" (which includes the right to hold personal property) and "the rights and liberties covered by the rule of law."[19] Rawls is opposed to including most economic liberties among the basic liberties. He recognizes the right to free choice of occupation but cuts out the freedom to hire labor for productive purposes. The freedom to engage in independent or self-organized economic activity is excluded. Property rights are recognized but restricted to personal property. I believe Rawls's view of economic liberties is too restricted and try to show that there are plenty of grounds in Rawls's theory for a ampler view of economic liberties.

4.1. Rawls's Justificatory Scheme

Rawls's root idea is that a just society is a system of fair cooperation for mutual advantage between free and equal persons (justice as fairness).[20] Rawls defends his principles of justice, including the requirement of a "fully adequate" scheme of basic liberties, by arguing that they are necessary parts of such a fair system of social cooperation.[21] To go from the abstract idea of fairness to more specific principles of justice, Rawls famously uses the idea of rational choice behind a "veil of ignorance" in what he calls "the Original Position."[22] Rational representatives of the members of society are asked to choose principles of justice that will promote their individual interests. The veil of ignorance deprives these representatives of information about themselves, thus ensuring that they will choose principles that are impartial or fair even though they choose from self-interested reasons.

Rawls claims that the rational choosers in the original position would choose to give a set of basic liberties a privileged place because these liberties are extremely valuable to anyone. In this respect, Rawls adapts the method and some of the conclusions of John Stuart Mill in *Utilitarianism,* where Mill demonstrates the great value of security to everyone and goes on to suggest that security rights are at the center of justice.[23] To defend his claim about the great value of the basic liberties, Rawls offers a theory of general human goods, which he calls "primary goods." These primary goods are intended to be sufficiently thin or uncontroversial so that people committed to different religions, ideologies, and conceptions of the good can accept and use them as a basis for political discussion and decision making. Primary goods include basic rights and liberties, freedom of movement and free choice of occupation, offices and positions of responsibility in society, income and wealth, and social conditions that promote self-respect.[24]

The account of primary goods is supported in Rawls's more recent work by a "political conception of the person." This conception, which is derived from Rawls's idea of justice as a system of cooperation for mutual advantage between free and equal persons, suggests that all persons have strong interests in being able to develop and exercise two capacities. The first of these, which Rawls calls "the first moral power," is the capacity for a sense of justice, the ability to accept and live by fair terms of social cooperation. The second moral power is the ability to form, revise, and pursue a personal conception of the good. Rawls also recognizes "intellectual powers of judgment, thought, and inference" as a third human power that is presupposed by the other two, but he doesn't seem to view the intellectual capacity alone as generating primary goods (it might, for example, be taken to show that basic education is a primary good or to provide support for intellectual liberties).[25]

The transition from the two moral powers to the list of primary goods is mediated, in Rawls's account, by three "higher-order interests." The theory goes from a political conception of the person to an account of three higher-order interests to the list (given above) of primary goods. It is because humans have three general interests that the primary goods are good for everyone.[26] The higher-order interests might also be called "fundamental interests," but Rawls does not use this term. According to Rawls, people have higher-order interests in (1) developing and exercising the capacity for a sense of justice; (2) developing and exercising the capacity to form, revise, and pursue a conception of the good; and (3) protecting and advancing one's determinate conception of the good (allowing for changes of mind) over a complete life.[27]

The third higher-order interest pertains to *realizing* one's conception of the good during one's life. It recognizes that one does not formulate a conception of one's good, or a plan for one's life, as a philosophical exercise. One exercises the second moral power at least partly as a means to accomplishing something in the world, to bringing about certain good states of affairs that one can enjoy or participate in.

4.2. Rawls's Rejection of Most Economic Liberties

The most extensive statement of Rawls's views on economic liberties is given in the following passage dealing with property: "Among the basic liberties of the person is the right to hold and to have the exclusive use of personal property. The role of this liberty is to allow a sufficient material basis for a sense of personal independence and self-respect, both of which are essential for the development and exercise of the moral powers."[28] Rawls rejects a broader conception of the right to property that includes "certain rights of acquisition and bequest, as well as the right to own means of production and natural resources" because he believes this stronger right of property is not generally "necessary for the development and exercise of the moral powers."[29]

4.3. Evaluating Rawls's Position

Rawls commits the familiar sin of treating all issues about economic liberties except free choice of employment under the heading of property. Presumably, Rawls wants to protect freedoms to buy, use, and consume resources, goods, and services for personal purposes but not for productive purposes. Whether workers can be hired for personal purposes such as cooking, cleaning, household repairs, and construction is left unclear.

As Stephen Munzer suggests, the idea that some kinds of property are more central to human welfare and flourishing than others is a sensible one.[30] But as both Munzer and Robert Nozick have noted, the contrast between personal and productive property is far from clear.[31] Nozick points out that personal property can easily be put to productive uses: Familiar examples are using one's kitchen and utensils to cook food for sale, using one's household tools to earn income as a repair person or painter, and using one's household gardening equipment to earn income as a gardener.

If personal use of an item and (thereby) a close connection with one's personality and projects is the test, property far beyond the household level is licensed. Ted Turner can probably say sincerely that he personally *uses* his large tracts of land in Montana since he hikes, drives, and rides on that land on a regular basis. Further, that land is important to one of his projects, namely, raising large herds of buffalo. As this suggests, the idea of personal use is too vague to provide a clear scale for property rights, or economic liberties more generally. Rawls seems to equate property that one personally uses with household property, but this identification fails in many cases.

I believe that Rawls is wrong in suggesting that holdings of productive property and the economic liberties identified earlier are not necessary to develop and exercise the moral powers and to satisfy the higher-order interests. As suggested earlier, the most important forms of property and economic liberty include those that are required to own and operate small and medium-sized organizations, businesses, and farms. I have two sets of arguments. The first set is based on my earlier arguments showing that a number of uncontroversial basic liberties cannot be fully enjoyed if people do not have the liberty to do things like rent or buy buildings and land, hire employees, and rent or buy printing equipment or services. Enjoying these liberties does not require that one be a captain of industry with vast holdings in land and factories, but it does require economic liberties well beyond the household level. If the uncontroversial basic liberties are necessary for the development and exercise of the moral powers, so are these more controversial economic liberties.

The second set of arguments takes us more deeply into Rawlsian philosophy. I think that it can be shown that a higher-order interest in developing and exercising one's productive capacities is already implicit in Rawls's theory of moral powers and higher-order interests. If this is so, then the primary goods will be expanded in ways that make them more supportive of economic liberties.

The easiest way to make my point is to note that the third higher-order interest, the interest in protecting and advancing one's determinate conception of the good, is among other things an interest in production, an interest in changing or rearranging the world so that it will contain more goods or better conform to one's life plan. If one finds it good to have a house or apartment, one has an interest in being able to build, buy, or rent one. If one believes it good to have a birthday cake on a family member's birthday, one has an interest in being able to bake or buy such cakes. If one finds it good to be able to worship in a cathedral, one has an interest in being able to join with others in building it or paying for its construction. And in order to be able to do these things, one has an interest in people being able to produce things like lumber, flour, and bricks. Advancing one's conception of the good often requires production by oneself and others.

Because the third higher-order interest includes an interest in access to production and the implements and materials necessary to production, we have the basis for saying that access to production and its necessities is a primary good. This primary good will support the inclusion of a larger range of economic liberties among the basic liberties. It will also support, in my opinion, the equal opportunity and economic minimum requirements in Rawls's theory, because access to production requires more than just liberty. It also requires skills and assets.

The approach just outlined could start one level deeper. Instead of starting with a higher-order interest, one could start from the view of human powers or capabilities. I believe that another power, the ability to produce goods for oneself and others, is presupposed by Rawls's root idea of a fair system of cooperation for mutual advantage. Implicit in this root idea is the notion that we will all be better-off if we cooperate under fair terms to produce and divide various useful products, goods, and services. Dividing manna from heaven is the exceptional case, not the standard one. Humans are assumed by Rawls's root idea to be producers of goods, to have productive powers. We need not say that these are *moral* powers; we can rather class them with the already recognized intellectual powers as something that is presupposed by the moral powers.[32] As I suggested earlier, there is no reason why nonmoral powers can't generate their own higher-order interests and primary goods. Since these human powers are presupposed by the moral powers, respect for the moral powers requires respect for them and the interests and goods they generate.

It might be objected that although everyone has an interest in production being done, it does not follow that everyone has a personal interest in access to production. But a representative person with normal human capacities has an interest not only in most people's developing and exercising their productive capacities but also in developing and exercising his or her own productive capacities. The situation here is analogous to the first moral power, the capacity for a sense of justice. There are good reasons to want most other people to have a sense of justice and to want to have it oneself. Reasons for developing one's own productive capacities include the following:

1. Many of the goods available to oneself over a lifetime are likely to be self-produced, or produced by participation in a cooperative enterprise.
2. Social systems of production and provision may fail, especially in particular regions or sectors, and hence if one is risk averse one will plan for this by developing back-up capacities for survival and flourishing. To flee war, famine, oppression, and religious persecution, one needs well-developed productive (and other) capacities and the freedom to exercise them.
3. In a society where most people engage in productive activity, self-respect is damaged by avoidable dependence, especially if it is total and long-term.
4. By engaging in productive endeavors with others one can enjoy goods of social union that "greatly enlarge and sustain each person's determinate good."[33]

5. Four Objections

5.1. Economic Liberties Allow
Some to Block the Liberty of Others

Although economic liberties are good for the liberty and autonomy of those who end up having money and property, perhaps these liberties are not good for the overall liberty and autonomy of those who end up having little money and property. If one is concerned about the possibility of being among the economically least favored, economic liberties are risky. They pose the danger of being dominated by the property rights, disproportionate political influence, and the purchasing power of others.

One response to this objection is that economic liberties are often very important to the poor. For example, the liberty to start and run small farms and microenterprises has kept clear the path to survival for many poor people around the world. More generally, my previous arguments show that economic liberties are important to everyone's enjoyment of basic liberties and everyone's exercise of autonomy. But this response may be insufficient by itself to overcome the objection. Perhaps economic liberties are valuable but not valuable enough to outweigh their costs and risks.

There are, however, several measures available to reduce the power over others conferred by wealth. First, one can build into one's theory of justice, and into the constitution of one's society, a requirement that rudimentary provision for basic needs be available to all who need it. Second, ample protection for basic liberties generally protects people's liberties to think, discuss, associate, protest, choose one's occupation, and move. All of these are important in protecting people's ability to understand, protest, and protect themselves against the power of the better-off. Third, the scale of holdings protected by the right to property can be limited. To protect the property rights most valuable to ordinary people one does not have to believe that respect for holdings worth billions of dollars is a requirement of justice. If we drew the line high enough to protect the holdings of small and medium-sized organizations, businesses, and farms, measures to block the accumulation of massive amounts of individual wealth could still be used if they proved workable and useful.

Fourth, measures to ensure the fair value of political liberties can be enacted. These include such things as public financing of political campaigns and limits on the size of political contributions. Fifth, a strong principle of equality of opportunity ensures that positions and offices are open to all and that efforts will be made through free public education and other means to weaken the connection between class origin and achievement.

Sixth, a principle of distributive justice can require tax policies that limit large concentrations of wealth and promote access to quality education for children and access to ownership of houses and apartments by most families. Seventh and finally, economic policies designed to avoid massive unemployment and measures to assist people during unemployment can be adopted. This would give employees not only the liberty to quit jobs but also the hope of finding other jobs and of being able to survive between jobs.[34]

I submit that this set of measures provides sufficient protection for the liberty and autonomy of those at the bottom to permit us to justify a broader range of economic liberties than the very limited set Rawls endorses. The liberty to sell one's labor need not be restricted out of concern for those with limited bargaining power, and private property can safely be allowed to extend beyond "personal" property.

5.2. Basic Liberties Do Not Permit Regulation within Their Scopes

One could be persuaded that economic liberties are important yet still hesitate about declaring them to be basic liberties because one believes that a great deal of regulation is necessary in the economic realm. After all, if economic liberties are so important, shouldn't they be near-absolute in the exceptions they allow? The objection might continue as follows: "Look, I can see declaring a general freedom of thought and belief, because efforts to regulate thoughts and beliefs coercively are almost always unjustifiable, but since you don't accept that efforts to regulate economic liberties through law are almost always unjustifiable, you shouldn't claim that liberties in this area are basic liberties."

It is a mistake, however, to think that basic liberties are immune to regulation. Within basic liberties, the freedoms of conscience, thought, and belief, with their nearly unregulated scopes, are exceptional rather than representative. Most of the liberties we find in historic bills of rights need substantial qualification and regulation. Rawls recognizes this point; he emphasizes that it is only a liberty's "central range of application" that must be unrestricted.[35]

Consider freedom of movement. First, there are regulations to make movement in the streets more efficient, such as different lanes for pedestrians, bicycles, and cars; one-way streets; and stoplights. These restrict movement but if well designed, result in greater overall ease of movement. Second, there are regulations to make movement safer, such as crosswalks, turn restrictions, and speed limits. Third, there are restrictions of entry into private property such as homes and businesses and public property such as offices and military installations that limit where one can go and stop. Fourth, there are restrictions of entry into undeveloped areas to promote environmental preservation or restoration. And finally, there are prohibitions of movements that are parts of crimes, such as interstate flight to escape prosecution.

Similar points could be made, I believe, about freedom of communication, freedom of association, and freedom of assembly and protest. It is not inconsistent to hold that economic liberties are important while prohibiting some sorts of activities in the economic sphere as crimes or misdemeanors (e.g., fraud, discrimination in hiring, operating an unsafe workplace, or eliminating competition by murder or arson).

5.3. Regulations of Basic Liberties Bear the Highest Burden of Justification

One could accept the permissibility of regulation within the scopes of basic liberties but hold that such regulations must meet an extremely high standard of justification. For example, one might believe that regulations within the scopes of basic liberties must be supported by a "compelling state interest." And one might hesitate about declaring economic liberties to be basic liberties because one does not think that such a high standard of justification is appropriate for regulations of property, conditions of employment, and economic transactions.

The problem with this objection is the falsity of its premise that any regulations within the scope of a basic liberty must be able to meet the highest standard of justification. By restricting public access to the alpine watershed of its water supply, the city of Boulder, Colorado, restricts freedom of movement, and freedom of movement is a basic liberty. If such restrictions were challenged as infringements of a basic liberty, it would not be plausible to require their justifications to meet the compelling state interest test. At most, a medium standard of justification would be appropriate.

The U.S. Supreme Court reached a similar conclusion in regard to religious freedom in *Employment Div., Dept. of Human Resources of Ore.* v. *Smith* (1990) and again in *City of Boerne* v. *Flores* (1997).[36] Religious activity, like economic activity, covers an enormous range of specific activities, and the Court has been reluctant to exempt churches from things like zoning and safety regulations or to require states to show that such regulations serve a compelling state interest and are the least restrictive means of serving that interest. Instead, the Court has come to view "the free exercise of religion" as a kind of antidiscrimination principle that protects churches only from regulations that display a discriminatory purpose or bigoted attitude. If a law is "passed because of religious bigotry," it will violate the free exercise of religion, but it will not violate that free exercise if it is merely a law "of general applicability which place[s] incidental burdens on religion."[37]

The same approach could be used for economic liberties. Regulations in the economic area would not violate economic freedom unless they displayed some sort of discriminatory intent (perhaps an intent to restrict economic liberties wholesale or to favor one company or industry over another). But the approach has some problems in the economic area. One is that the sort of discriminatory intent it should focus on is not very clear (or we could say that it is even less clear than in the case of religion). The second problem is that it does not protect against what we might call "the problem of death from a thousand small bites." Economic freedoms—like religious freedoms—can be eroded, not just by direct and intentional assaults, but also by a multitude of regulations that attempt to remedy specific problems.

5.4. Many Subareas of Economic Liberty Are Not Important Enough

The economic realm is an extremely large area of human activity; it contains thousands of specific action-types. For example, buying can be directed to thousands of goods and services. One might ask at this point whether it is really plausible to say that all of these kinds of buying are matters of basic liberty. The problem is not that some kinds of buying, such as buying children or slaves, are deeply immoral. Those can be carved out of the scope of the liberty to buy things, just as we carve human sacrifices out of the scope of freedom of religion. The problem is rather that many instances of buying—such as buying sand, or buying carrots, or buying fountain pens—just are not important enough to be basic liberties. True, people have significant liberty interests in not being blocked from buying these things. Sand, carrots, and fountain pens are things that people often find useful to be able to get through purchase. But these liberty interests are not among the most compelling or important ones. If a government blocks or heavily regulates the buying of sand, this doesn't involve anything like the degree of injustice or tyranny that is involved in blocking or heavily regulating religious beliefs. It isn't plausible to say that the freedom to buy sand is on a par with the freedom to choose one's religious or political outlook.

But it is easy to find analogous cases in the standard basic liberties. Within freedom of religion, it is important to hold religious processions in the streets on holy days, but it is usually not so important to be able to do so before 5 A.M. on those days. Within freedom of communication, it is important to be free to protest economic hardship but not so important to be free to say that it would be nice to have some sand for the children's sandbox. Within freedom of movement, it is important that one be free to move to obtain the necessities of life but not so important that one be free to make a late-night excursion to buy ice cream.

One explanation of less-important areas within the scopes of basic liberties is that when there are ample good options, access to any particular one of those options is less important. If one can hold religious processions anytime after 5 A.M. and before midnight, or if one is free to buy ice cream during the same hours, it becomes less important to be able to do those things during the middle of the night. Generally, if the next-best option is very nearly as good—as is likely to be the case when there are numerous good options— then the whole value of the liberty is not lost if one cannot get the best option. The value of the liberty attaches to a range of good options, but not to every particular one.

More broadly, there is no reason why we should expect the various subareas of basic liberties to be equally important. A useful analogy here is commercial speech, which is within the scope of freedom of expression but has lesser weight than, say, religious or political speech. The subareas of a liberty often have different levels of weight or importance. To say that a subarea is of lesser weight does not necessarily exclude it from the scope of the liberty.

Within subareas of basic liberties, we might recognize three levels of weight or importance. One is to be "basic," the highest range. A liberty can't be a basic liberty overall unless many of its subareas are basic. Perhaps the liberty to buy printing paper is basic because of its links to political and religious liberties. Another level is to be "near-basic," which is a range of high but not highest importance. Perhaps the freedom to advertise products is a near-basic liberty. The third range is "middleweight," a significant area of liberty but less important than basic or near-basic. Perhaps the liberty to buy construction materials is a middleweight liberty interest. Note, saying that a basic liberty has substantial areas that are near-basic and middleweight is different from saying that the entire liberty is near-basic or is middleweight.

Once these levels of importance are recognized, we can allow that a basic liberty can have subareas that are near-basic and middleweight. These areas will be more vulnerable to prohibition and regulation, and the highest standards of justification will be inappropriate to them. We could trim these out of the scope of the liberty, but we may want to leave them in because we believe they are significant parts of the liberty in spite of their lesser importance.

This model allows us to give a basic liberty an ample scope but not commit ourselves to saying that every part of that scope is equally important. The boundary of importance may be one of scale, as it would be if we said that small-scale economic activity is more important in terms of personal liberty than very large-scale economic activity. The boundary may be the type of activity or product, as it would be if we said that the liberty to buy books is more important than the liberty to buy sand. Or the boundary may be the context or situation, as it would be if we said that the liberty to hire juveniles is less weighty than the liberty to hire adults.

6. Conclusion

Economic liberties should be considered basic liberties because they support other basic liberties, promote realization of the ideal of autonomy, and find solid support within Rawls's justificatory framework. Accepting economic liberties as basic does not commit us to rejecting regulation within their scopes or to always holding such regulations to the highest standard of justification.

Acknowledgments

I received helpful comments on this chapter from Andrew Askland, Adrienne Chockley, Douglas Husak, Stephen Munzer, Michael Pierce, Thomas Pogge, and the participants in faculty seminars at Columbia University and the University of California, Los Angeles, Law School.

Notes

1. This chapter presupposes Rawls's conception of basic liberties and tries to expand its content by showing that key economic liberties are important enough to qualify. To say that a liberty is basic is to say that it is among the dozen or two most valuable or important liberties. It says neither that it is nonderivative or foundational nor that it is inviolable or absolute. Rawls claims that we can draw up a reasonably adequate and complete list of basic liberties and that respect for the liberties on that list is the first requirement of justice (John Rawls *A Theory of Justice* [Cambridge, Mass.: Harvard University Press, 1971], 61; John Rawls *Political Liberalism* [New York: Columbia University Press, 1993], 291). Liberties not on the list of basic liberties are not requirements of justice, but they are protected by "a general presumption against imposing legal and other restrictions on conduct without sufficient reason" (*Political Liberalism,* 292). I have recently become discontent with Rawls's conception of basic and nonbasic liberties. For an elaboration of some of the sources of this discontent, see my unpublished paper, "The Standard View of Liberty: Problems and Prospects," http://spot.Colorado.edu/~nickelj/stdvu.htm.

2. See Daniel M. Hausman, When Jack and Jill Make a Deal, in *Economic Rights,* ed. Ellen Frankel Paul, Fred D. Miller, Jr., and Jeffrey Paul (Cambridge: Cambridge University Press, 1992), 95–113. See also G. A. Cohen, Robert Nozick, and Wilt Chamberlin, How Patterns Preserve Liberty, *Erkenntnis* 11 (1977): 5–23, at 9–10.

3. *A Theory of Justice,* 61. See also, *Political Liberalism,* 298 and 338. (Unless otherwise noted, all references in this chapter to these two works are to these editions.)

4. For an account of the Lochner era, and a defense of a return to judicial defense of economic liberties, see Bernard H. Siegan, *Economic Liberties and the Constitution* (Chicago: University of Chicago Press, 1980).

5. The conception of liberties used here is largely negative. A liberty, such as liberty in the area of travel, is real when people are not blocked from traveling or staying put by prohibitions, interference, coercion, discrimination, or manipulation. A liberty consists of the absence of certain impediments to choice and action in a particular area.

In this view, social and political freedoms are concerned with some but not all impediments to action. People who are unable to leave their beds owing to illness, who have no money to spend on travel, or who cannot even imagine going somewhere distant lack the ability to travel but may nevertheless have (and indeed be exercising by staying put) freedom in the area of travel. My purpose in separating these issues from liberty is not to dismiss them. I believe that liberty ought to be supported and supplemented in various ways if liberties are to have value for everyone, if some degree of equality of opportunity is to be realized, and if the ideal of autonomy is to be achieved in most people's lives. But I do not think it is advantageous to try to squeeze all of these concerns into the idea of liberty. And I resist trying to float them all on liberty's broad tide of popular support.

6. For an alternative list, see the one used by Freedom House in its annual survey of economic freedom. The categories it uses are freedom to hold property, freedom to earn a living, freedom to operate a business, freedom to invest one's earnings, freedom to trade internationally, and freedom to participate in the market economy. See *Freedom Review* (March–April 1996): 9.

7. I recognize that environmental values may require that consumption for both personal and productive purposes be limited. But this is compatible with having a qualified freedom to use and consume.

8. Egalitarian liberals frequently argue that important liberties are not very valuable unless one has the personal and financial resources to make use of them. In consequence, they advocate redistributive schemes that try to ensure that everyone has these resources. My arguments are structurally similar. I try to show that important noneconomic liberties are not very valuable unless one has the economic liberties that are frequently needed to make use of them. These two kinds of arguments are not incompatible, and in fact they intertwine. Most of the economic liberties will not have their full value if people do not have some financial and other assets to make use of them. And the money and other resources that disadvantaged people get through redistribution will not have their full value unless they have economic liberties to make use of them.

9. For a pioneering use of linkage arguments, see Henry Shue, *Basic Rights* (Princeton, N.J.: Princeton University Press, 1980), 13–34. For criticisms and qualifications, see James W. Nickel, *Making Sense of Human Rights* (Berkeley: University of California Press, 1987), 102–5.

10. The importance of freedom of movement in avoiding starvation is discussed in James W. Nickel, A Human Rights Approach to World Hunger, in *World Hunger and Morality,* ed. William Aiken and Hugh LaFollette, 2d ed. (Upper Saddle River, N.J.: Prentice-Hall, 1996), 171–85.

11. Joseph Raz, *The Morality of Freedom* (Oxford: Clarendon Press, 1986), 369–73.

12. See Joel Feinberg, *Harm to Others* (New York: Oxford University Press, 1984), 206–14.

13. See Milton Friedman (with the assistance of Rose D. Friedman), *Capitalism and Freedom* (Chicago: University of Chicago, 1962), 15.

14. Rawls, *Political Liberalism,* 190–95. Rawls distinguishes autonomy as a political value from "the ethical autonomy" of Kant and Mill. Ethical autonomy is a perfectionist value (*Political Liberalism,* 77–78).

15. Rawls, *Political Liberalism,* 72–80.

16. For an excellent discussion of this topic, see Stephen R. Munzer, A *Theory of Property* (Cambridge: Cambridge University Press, 1990), 81–87.

17. Raz, *The Morality of Freedom,* 373–75.

18. On unemployment and self-esteem, see James W. Nickel, Is There a Human Right to Employment? *Philosophical Forum* 11 (1977): 149–70.

19. Rawls, *A Theory of Justice,* 61, and *Political Liberalism,* 291.

20. This summary is adapted from James W. Nickel, Rethinking Rawls's Theory of Liberty and Rights, *Chicago-Kent Law Review* 69 (1994): 763–85 at 764.

21. Rawls, *Political Liberalism,* 3.

22. Rawls, *A Theory of Justice,* 118–92.

23. John Stuart Mill, *Utilitarianism* (1863), chap. 5.

24. Rawls, *Political Liberalism,* 181.

25. Rawls, *Political Liberalism,* 81.

26. Rawls, *Political Liberalism,* 74.

27. Rawls, *Political Liberalism,* 74.

28. Rawls, *Political Liberalism,* 298.

29. Rawls, *Political Liberalism,* 298.

30. Munzer, *A Theory of Property,* 237.

31. Munzer, *A Theory of Property,* 237; Robert Nozick, *Anarchy, State, and Utopia* (New York: Basic Books, 1974), 162–63.

32. Rawls, *Political Liberalism,* 81.

33. Rawls, *Political Liberalism,* 320.

34. Those familiar with Rawls's work will recognize that Rawls endorses almost all of these measures. On the provision for basic needs, see his proposal that the "first principle covering the equal basic rights and liberties may easily be preceded by a lexically prior principle requiring that citizens' basic needs be met" (*Political Liberalism,* 7). See also Munzer, A *Theory of Property,* 241–47, for a plausible version of "the floor thesis." On equal basic liberties, see Rawls, *A Theory of Justice,* 64. On limits to the scale of economic liberties see Rawls, *Political Liberalism,* 298. On measures to promote the fair value of political liberties see *A Theory of Justice,* 224–28, 233–34, 277–79, and 356, and *Political Liberalism,* 327–29 and 356–63. On equal opportunity, see *A Theory of Justice,* 60–61 and 75–90. On a principle of distributive justice ("the difference principle") see *A Theory of Justice,* 60–61 and 75–83. On economic policies to minimize unemployment see *A Theory of Justice,* 87. The main area here where I disagree with Rawls is the scale of the economic liberties that ought to be protected as a requirement of justice. This issue is discussed in section 4.

35. Rawls, *Political Liberalism,* 295.

36. *Employment Div., Ore. Dept. of Human Res.* v. *Smith,* 494 U.S. 872 (1990); *City of Boerne* v. *Flores,* U.S. Supreme Court No. 95-2074, June 25, 1997.

37. Majority opinion by Justice Kennedy, *City of Boerne* v. *Flores,* U.S. Supreme Court No. 95-2074, June 25, 1997.

9

INDIVIDUAL ENTITLEMENTS IN

JUSTICE AS FAIRNESS

Claudia Card

This chapter takes up two problems regarding individual entitlement in John Rawls's theory of justice, as first presented in his book *A Theory of Justice* (1971) and later developed in *Political Liberalism* (1993). The first problem concerns the relationship between the two parts of his second main principle. The second problem concerns the idea of deserts and the relevance of both history and structure (relationships) to justice in holdings. Reflection on both was stimulated by Robert Nozick's objection in his book *Anarchy, State, and Utopia* (1974) to the very idea of distributive justice as disrespectful of individual entitlements.

1. Difference and Fair Equality of Opportunity

In *A Theory of Justice* (hereafter *Theory*), Rawls presents his two main principles of distributive justice (by contrast with retributive and corrective justice) as principles for institutions. The only principle of justice that he explicitly presents for individuals is his principle of fairness. It states what individuals are obligated to do and the conditions under which such obligations are incurred. But he does not explicitly present a principle stating to what holdings individuals are entitled. From the principle of fairness for individuals (Rawls 1971, 108–14), we may infer that individuals who have cooperated with the rules of just institutions are entitled (have a right) to other individuals' fulfillment of their obligations of fair play. But we are not offered explicitly a principle stating to what economic and social goods or services an individual is entitled.

And yet, in the second of Rawls's main principles of justice, an individual entitlement principle seems embedded. A chapter in *Theory* devoted to interpreting that principle summarizes its intent as follows: "Social and economic inequalities are to be arranged so that they are both (a) to the greatest benefit of the least advantaged and (b) attached to offices and positions open to all under conditions of fair equality of opportunity" (Rawls 1971, 83).[1] So stated, it appears that this principle might be broken down into two more specific principles (or conditions): the difference principle (a) and the principle of fair equality of opportunity (b). Although Rawls tends to refer to this entire second principle as the difference principle, the difference part of the principle is, more specifically, the part given in clause "a": that social and economic inequalities are to be so arranged that they are "to the greatest benefit of the least advantaged." "Difference" (apparently the going euphemism in economics), as used here, means "inequality." Thus, Rawls might have named this principle his "inequality principle"—only that does not have quite the right ring for a principle of justice. When I refer hereafter to "the difference principle," I will mean specifically the part given in clause "a," and I will refer to the principle as stated by Rawls with clauses "a" and "b" simply as "Rawls's second principle."

It is the fair opportunity part of Rawls's second principle (clause "b") that seems to be a principle for individuals, which distributes offices and positions, the part that states that social and economic goods are to be so arranged that they are "attached to offices and positions open to all under conditions of fair equality of opportunity." If we think of these offices and positions as holdings, the principle of fair opportunity seems to fit Nozick's category of historical individual entitlement principles. The history is an individual's history of having won an office or position as a result of having competed for it under conditions of fair equality of opportunity. Such a history, rather than, say, the possession of certain characteristics, is what entitles the individual to the position or office.

The condition of fair equality of opportunity (for short, fair opportunity) appears to have two roles in Rawls's second principle. On one hand, Rawls regards it as constraining the difference condition: "One applies the second principle by holding positions open, and then, subject to this constraint, arranges social and economic inequalities so that everyone benefits" (Rawls 1971, 61). The principle of fair opportunity, even though here stated second, appears to be lexically prior, as Rawls makes explicit a few pages later (Rawls 1971, 89). That is, its condition must be satisfied before it is permissible to go on to satisfy the condition of the difference principle. On the other hand, in addition to being said to constrain the difference principle, the principle of fair equality of opportunity is also said to be a means of incorporating pure procedural justice into the theory of justice as fairness: "It is evident that the role of the principle of fair opportunity is to insure that the system of cooperation is one of pure procedural justice. Unless it is satisfied, distributive justice could not be left to take care of itself, even within a restricted range" (Rawls 1971, 87). Pure procedural justice obtains whenever the results of a procedure are just simply because they are, in fact, the results of a just procedure actually and correctly carried out (Rawls 1971, 85). If pure procedural justice is offered by fair equality of opportunity, there is no need to be concerned from the standpoint of justice about individual entitlements as such;

we can evaluate the justice of inequalities by applying the difference principle to social classes (by way of representative persons).

These two functions of fair opportunity—that of constraining the difference principle and that of being the vehicle of pure procedural justice—are, I believe, in tension with each other. If the primary function of fair opportunity is to constrain the difference principle, as eventually it seems to be, the justice of the system of cooperation is not, in fact, purely procedural (even if individual entitlement to offices and positions is purely procedural). We are then left with the question whether there is any very meaningful way to say to what holdings individuals are entitled in the theory of justice as fairness. Or so I will argue.

The principle of fair equality of opportunity sounds like an elliptical statement of, in Nozick's terms, a historical entitlement principle, one that states what an individual must do or undergo in order to become justly entitled to certain holdings (Nozick 1974, 150–55), in this case, offices or positions to which social or economic goods are attached. If fair equality of opportunity actually did function to incorporate pure procedural justice into the theory, it would be an entitlement principle for individuals. A nonelliptical statement of that principle, so interpreted, would read something like this: An individual is entitled to an office or position to which social or economic goods are attached if that office or position is won in fair competition, understood as competition in which competitors are judged on their merits for the position and which takes place against a background of institutions designed to ensure that persons with similar talents, skills, abilities, and motivation will have similar "life-chances."[2] Such a historical entitlement principle states conditions that an individual must undergo to become entitled to an office or position in a society in which unequal benefits are attached to offices and positions.

What it means to say that benefits are *attached* to offices or positions is left vague. Authority (one of Rawls's primary social goods), for example, may partly define an office, such as the office of a judge. One's salary, on the other hand, often depends upon what one does in a position and not just upon one's occupying (holding) the position. Nor is it entirely clear what counts as an office or a position. Does being the beneficiary of a will count as a position? Does being the recipient of a gift generally count? Does being a purchaser? Administrative posts, honorary offices, and salaried positions of employment appear to be among the sorts of things Rawls has in mind, primarily the sorts of positions that provide an income. These are, at any rate, positions for which people do compete. It is less natural to think of people competing to become the recipients of gifts or to become purchasers, except in special circumstances. Administrative posts, honorary offices, and salaried positions enter into the determination of what Rawls calls "relevant social positions" in discussing the difference part of the principle and how we are to identify the least advantaged representative person. The offices or positions to which fair equality of opportunity applies, however, cannot simply be identified with the relevant social positions of the difference principle (more about this below)—a possible confusion encouraged by use of the word "position" in both cases.

Suppose that the principle of fair opportunity, understood as a historical entitlement principle for individuals, were part of Rawls's (special) conception of justice.[3] It would not be a complete entitlement principle for three reasons. First, it deals only with what Rawls calls "primary goods," those goods that anyone can be presumed to want whatever else they want, enumerated as basic rights and liberties, powers and opportunities, income and wealth, and self-respect, or the social bases thereof (Rawls 1971, 92).[4] Second, it deals only with primary goods that are attached to institutionally defined offices and positions. Third, and most important, the principle gives only one of two conditions of just entitlement. A just distribution of social and economic goods according to Rawls's theory, requires also that the difference principle be satisfied. But how does this go? Where do we begin?

Suppose we begin with the difference principle, since that part of the principle is stated first. The difference part of Rawls's second principle seems to fit Nozick's definition of a "patterned principle," although the pattern is over social classes rather than individuals: "Let us call a principle of distribution *patterned* if it specifies that a distribution is to vary along with some natural dimension, weighted sum of natural dimensions, or lexicographic ordering of natural dimensions. . . . 'Distribute according to I.Q.' is a patterned principle. . . . It is not historical, however" (Nozick 1974, 156).

Stating the difference condition of Rawls's second principle first (prior to stating the fair equality of opportunity condition), as is done in *Theory*, suggests that the social pattern generated by its application to unequally valuable offices and positions (the pattern of maximizing expectations of those who are least advantaged) is presupposed by the fairness of putting into practice the principle of equal opportunity. Were this so, the principle of fair equality of opportunity might be understood to yield a sufficient condition of entitlement to the office or position won. The idea would be that social and economic goods are first to be distributed among ("attached to") offices and positions in accordance with the difference principle and that offices and positions are then to be distributed to individuals by way of competition under conditions of fair equality of opportunity.

If the difference principle were already applied in "attaching" social and economic goods to institutionally defined offices and positions, there would be no need to be concerned about which individuals got which positions, as long as the competitions were open and conducted fairly. Thus, we would have pure procedural justice in the competition for offices and positions.

The great practical advantage of pure procedural justice is that it is no longer necessary in meeting the demands of justice to keep track of the endless variety of circumstances and the changing relative positions of particular persons. . . . It is the arrangement of the basic structure which is to be judged, and judged from a general point of view. Unless we are prepared to criticize it from the

standpoint of a relevant representative man in some particular position, we
have no complaint against it. (Rawls 1971, 87–88)

This passage suggests that Rawls relies on the idea of fair equality of opportunity in order to avoid having to be (further) concerned about individual entitlements. But it also shows how easy it can be to confuse relevant social
positions with relevantly different sorts of offices. Either relevant social positions or relevantly different sorts of offices might be thought to give the "general point of view" referred to, although they do not give the same view. I will
return to this point later.

The principle of fair equality of opportunity, as an entitlement principle
for individuals, refers (implicitly) to a procedure (or kind of procedure),
namely, competition, whereas the difference principle does not. A natural
reading of Rawls's second principle as stated in *Theory* is to take the difference
part as stating a condition to be satisfied in order that the results of competitions be just. Whether an individual were justly entitled to what was won in
fair competition when the stakes were primary goods would depend, then,
upon how the goods were distributed among the offices and positions for
which people compete, whether they were to the greatest benefit of the least
advantaged. This reading makes sense of the idea that the condition of fair
equality of opportunity brings pure procedural justice into the theory. The
idea, for example, that having the position (or office) of leader, director, or
boss who has special authority and is relieved of burdens that others have to
carry would be to the advantage of everyone in other positions (in that it
would make for a more efficient organization, enabling production of a larger
pool of goods to be distributed) seems to fit this reading: Whoever wins the
position of boss (so defined) in fair competition, then, is justly entitled to the
position with its rewards. However, there are problems with this reading.

Being to everyone's advantage means maximizing the benefits of the least
advantaged representative person. But whether that condition is met is not
determinable simply by comparing different offices. The "position" one has
as a representative of one's social class is not the same as the "position" for
which one competes under conditions of fair equality of opportunity. How
could one say, in abstraction from the results of competitions for offices and
positions, how great were the inequalities among social classes, or even whether
there were such inequalities, much less whether the greater advantages of
those who are better-off contribute to maximizing the advantages of those
who are least well-off? Rawls understands representative persons as representing different social classes, when social classes are distinguished from one
another by the size of the total expectations of primary goods of their representative members.

If offices and positions are the sorts of things they appear to be (as indicated by the examples mentioned above), individuals might be expected to
have several of them over the course of a lifetime, even several at once. In fair
competition, some people might win many favored positions while others
win few or none. Representative persons, on the other hand, represent social

classes, not offices or "positions" for which individuals compete. This is a significant change of understanding in the development of Rawls's second principle as it evolves from being conceived as applying to social practices generally in Rawls's 1958 article, "Justice as Fairness," to its being conceived during the next decade as applying to the basic structure of society. Representative persons cannot be identified with representative officeholders (with representative holders of certain kinds of offices). The most advantaged social class (or representative person) may not be identical with (represent) a class of persons who hold the most desirable positions or offices in a society. It may be, rather, identical with (represent) people who hold many desirable positions. Thus, even if president of the United States were the most desirable office in the nation, it would not follow that any holder of that office was a member of the most advantaged social class. Nor can it be assumed that the least advantaged social class is composed of those persons who occupy the least desirable positions and offices. Some persons may hold several offices, including some with little or no prestige or other benefit; others may hold none at all, at least, none for which they competed voluntarily. The least advantaged representative person in a society is a member of that class of persons whose total expectation of primary goods is lowest.

Although there is a certain arbitrariness to the drawing of class lines (Rawls 1971, 98), they cannot be assumed to coincide with lines dividing more from less desirable institutionally defined positions and offices. The results of competitions for such positions must be known—that is, we need to know the distribution of institutionally defined offices and positions, what portions of the population hold how many and what kinds—in order to identify social classes, to know what social classes there are, to know, for example, whether anyone has less than half the median income, in case one wanted to take that (as Rawls suggests we might want to do) as representing the least advantaged class. But this, of course, means that social and economic goods cannot be attached to offices and positions so as to satisfy the difference principle in abstraction from an existing distribution of offices and positions to individuals. Presumably, some social and economic goods are to be attached to offices and positions prior to individuals' competing for them. (How else are we to understand motives to compete for them?) But the lucrativeness of various offices and positions cannot be defined so as to satisfy the difference principle in any final way in advance of the competitions in which there is to be fair equality of opportunity.

This impossibility implies that one's entitlement to an office or position won in fair competition does not presuppose prior satisfaction of the difference principle. If the difference principle still remains to be satisfied after fair competitions have taken place, such competitions do not give us a very meaningful pure procedural justice, because the prize one wins in the competition is not yet well defined. Perhaps one is entitled to the position or office. But if the social and economic goods that "attach" to that office (presumably motivating the competition) are subject to modification, what is that entitlement worth?

If they actually define the office, what has one won?

The interpretation of the difference part of the principle as stating conditions under which certain competitions yield pure procedural justice thus seems wrong, or at least misleading. Rawls says that fair equality of opportunity constrains the difference principle, not that the difference principle constrains (or is presupposed by) fair equality of opportunity (Rawls 1971, 61). Thus, he goes on to say, "For the time being I shall suppose that the two parts of the second principle are lexically ordered" (Rawls 1971, 89). In other words, just as his first principle of justice is lexically prior to the second principle (must be satisfied before the second principle comes into play), the fair opportunity part of the second principle is lexically prior to the difference part.

Rawls appears to have in mind satisfying the difference principle by such means as taxing those who are more advantaged (in offices or positions they already hold) for transfer payments to those who are less advantaged in cases where possession of greater advantages by the former is not necessary to maximize benefits for the latter. Other background institutions and the idea of a "social minimum" (Rawls 1971, 274–84) are offered to illustrate the principles of justice in operation. But, then, where is there pure procedural justice? What procedure(s) have we that are characterizable independent of a criterion for judging their results, the results of which are just whatever they are? If the difference principle functioned as a constraint on fair equality of opportunity, an individual would be justly entitled to an office or a position won in fair competition. That would be pure procedural justice. But if one can be taxed on the earnings to which a position entitles one (and taxed in ways that may vary as social circumstances vary) after one has secured that position in fair competition, then it is not clear what one has won, for what one was competing, to what winning entitled one. According to the difference principle, it is unjust for some persons to have access to greater advantages than others unless this inequality is necessary to maximize expectations of the least well-off. But, then, for what does anyone have an equal opportunity? Apparently, we cannot say. But what sort of competition is that? Is it fair?

To summarize the argument thus far, on an apparently natural but inaccurate reading of Rawls's second principle, as stated in *Theory*, it seems that fair opportunity (as a vehicle of pure procedural justice) in the distribution of social and economic goods presupposes (prior) satisfaction of the difference principle with respect to the design of offices and positions to which individuals become entitled. According to the reading apparently intended, however, satisfaction of the difference principle presupposes that offices and positions are already distributed in accordance with the principle of fair equality of opportunity. We need to know how luck has treated groups of people in order to compensate the unlucky by taxing the gratuitously lucky to bring the former up to a social minimum.

Perhaps it is for this reason that in *Political Liberalism* (hereafter *Liberalism*), Rawls states the difference principle as the *second* condition of the second principle and states fair opportunity as the first condition: "Social and economic inequalities are to satisfy two conditions: first, they are to be attached to positions and offices open to all under conditions of fair equality of opportunity; and second, they are to be to the greatest benefit of the least advantaged members of society" (Rawls 1993, 6). But this seems to imply that there is really no meaningful pure procedural justice in the theory. An individual may be entitled to, at most, an office or a position. Yet the benefits attached to that office or position cannot be well defined in advance. Consequently, it may not even be clear what the office or position is.

One way to remedy this peculiar situation might be to incorporate into the idea of fair equality of opportunity some condition that would explain "the fairness" of one's entitlement independent of the difference principle, some condition that even the difference principle ought to respect. Such a condition might be a recognition of individual deserts.

2. Individual Entitlements and Deserts

In *Anarchy, State, and Utopia,* Robert Nozick argued that the original position in Rawls's theory of justice was incapable of yielding "an entitlement or historical conception of justice" (Nozick 1974, 199). In *Theory,* Rawls explicitly argued against treating deserts (as distinct from "the legitimate expectations" created by the rules of social institutions) as relevant to social justice. In *Liberalism,* deserts are not mentioned at all, so far as I can recall. Yet Rawls's second principle of justice may be revisable in an interesting way so as to acknowledge the relevance of what George Sher (1987) calls "pre-institutional" deserts, taking advantage of what even those behind "the veil of ignorance" know about human nature and society in general.

Suppose we understand a historical or entitlement conception of "justice in holdings" (to use Nozick's terminology) as being one that takes distributive justice (in Aristotle's sense, the kind of justice that corrective justice aims to restore) to be done when people have that to which they are entitled, when that to which they are entitled is determined in a fundamental way by historical principles (to be defined shortly). Historical principles might enter into the determination of entitlements in a fundamental way even if they were not sufficient by themselves to determine entitlements. The principles would be fundamental if they were not based upon or subordinate to other principles. This leaves open, however, the possibility that they may be qualifiable by other principles. A principle may be fundamental even though it is qualified by other principles that are also fundamental. This appears to be presupposed in Nozick's own views, insofar as he regards (fundamental) entitlement principles of acquisition and transfer as qualified by the Lockean proviso: that there be "enough and as good left in common for others." If, instead, we regarded principles of acquisition and transfer as qualified by Rawls's difference principle (that social and economic goods be so arranged that they are to the greatest benefit of the least advantaged), we could still have a theory to which historical entitlement principles were fundamental.

What is a historical principle of justice in holdings? Nozick says, "In contrast to end-result principles of justice, *historical principles* of justice hold that past circumstances or actions of people can create differential entitlements or differential deserts to things" (Nozick 1974, 155). Here, "differential" does not seem simply a euphemism for "unequal," although it is true that differences can be inequalities. Differential entitlements may come about by way of qualitatively different processes.

In contrast with historical principles, what Nozick calls "end-result principles"—his pejorative term for structural principles—would have us judge the justice of states of affairs in terms of the structure (or pattern) of the distribution of goods they contain in a "current time-slice" or sequence of time-slice profiles while ignoring the processes of which these states of affairs are the end results. However, in ignoring the processes, what people do or undergo, we may be ignoring what people deserve.

Nozick's position on historical principles seems to be, more precisely, that past circumstances or actions play a role that is fundamental (not derivative) but not necessarily decisive in determining differential entitlements. What they do determine decisively, if anything, appear to be certain *deserts,* which might be decisive for settling questions of entitlement in the absence of competing deserts (or other qualifications) but may not be decisive precisely because of the presence of such other considerations. The fact that I acquired a piece of land by doing certain things with it may be decisive for saying that I deserve to have it but not sufficient for concluding that I am (or should be recognized as being) *entitled* to it—because others may have done things with the same piece of land in view of which they also deserve to have it just as much as I do or even more than I do, or there may not be "enough, and as good left in common for others" (Locke 1937, 19), or there may not be any way to compensate them adequately.

Nozick does not attempt to formulate specifically any principles of justice in acquisition or transfer. From what he says in his discussion of the Lockean proviso, however, it appears that such principles would have two very different sorts of parts. One part will state what an individual must do or undergo in order to become entitled to a thing. The other part places a qualification upon the claim that an individual who participates in the requisite process is entitled to the things, not in terms of what that individual does or undergoes, but in terms of the relationship between what that individual would have and what others would have if the former were allowed to keep the thing in question. In other words, these "historical" entitlement principles are partly structural, after all. The relationship between the process parts of Nozick's principles and the Lockean proviso is similar to the relationship between Rawls's principle of fair opportunity and the difference principle (inequalities are not unjust provided that the holdings in question are obtained in such and such a manner *and* provided that the inequalities—overall?—do not exceed certain bounds). Thus, it looks as though the major differences between the theories of Nozick and Rawls with regard to justice in holdings lie in the particular historical and nonhistorical principles favored by each rather than in the contrast between a historical and a nonhistorical conception of social justice. Argument between the two theories would then proceed better by considering what can be said for and against the principles themselves, which is, of course, impossible because Nozick did not attempt to formulate his principles precisely but only to classify them by function.

Perhaps it will be objected that the Lockean proviso, unlike Rawls's difference principle, is itself a historical principle because it refers to how well-off people were *before* and "before" is a historical notion. The intent of the proviso, as Nozick interprets it, is that others are to be made no worse-off by acquisitions and transfers than they would have been had these acquisitions and transfers not occurred. He takes it that the proviso prohibits acquisitions and transfers only where compensation to others (for substantial harm or for benefits lost thereby) is impossible. If we interpret "before" historically, however, there are insuperable difficulties in the way of answering the question, Before what? Before this particular acquisition or transfer? But what if that state of affairs were already unjust owing to previous unrectified injustices? Are we then to interpret "before" as before anybody ever acquired anything? When was that? How well-off were people then? (Were they really "people"?) How are we to understand "acquiring" for the first time previous to anyone's being entitled to anything? And what does one acquire—a thing? a title?

Nozick suggests that entitlements are rights to dispose of holdings (Nozick 1974, 166). To acquire rights presupposes a legal or lawlike context in which it can hardly be the case that no one else has ever had title to anything. The epistemological, conceptual, and ethical difficulties attending a historical interpretation of the Lockean proviso seem as great as (although different from) those attending Nozick's principle of rectification, which directs that the parties wronged be made as well-off as they would have been had the wrong not been done. How could anyone determine how well-off they would have been under such a hypothetical contingency? Who knows what wrongs might have been done by others had this one not been done, what errors the victims might have committed with disastrous results, or what misfortunes they might have suffered? Is it just to the wrong*doer* to ignore such possibilities in assessing compensation due? Ironically, such a historical interpretation of the Lockean proviso would seem to make the proviso something like a historical structural principle—a category apparently not anticipated by Nozick—because it would take a historical state of affairs (the state of affairs before anyone acquired anything) as entering into the determination of entitlements independent of any processes leading to that historical state of affairs. The structure assumed by Locke seems to be that of equal access to goods held in common or perhaps not "held" at all.

As a practical way to interpret a principle of rectification, Nozick suggests that we might resort to something like Rawls's difference principle for choosing among the possible distributions of holdings that might have resulted had a past injustice not been committed. Why not similarly resort to a structural, rather than a historical, interpretation of the Lockean proviso? Such an interpretation is actually suggested by Locke's own terms: "enough and as good *left in common* for others" (Locke 1937, 19; emphasis added). This formulation suggests that others be no worse-off than they would be if everything were held in common (a structural criterion). This sounds close to, although not exactly the same as, saying that others be no worse-off than they would be if all goods were distributed equally, which—for Rawls's primary goods—is the baseline of comparison for determining how well-off representative persons are in applying Rawls's difference principle. That is, inequalities, understood as departures from a baseline of equality, are to be justifiable only on the condition that those least well-off are still better-off than they would have been under an equal distribution (or, at least, not worse-off than that).

Suppose it were granted that the most plausible interpretation of Nozick's entitlement principles is not purely historical but partly structural and only partly historical. The terms "historical entitlement principles" and "historical or entitlement conception" are, then, somewhat misleading, although useful for Nozick's purposes because it is the historical (more specifically, process) part of the principles that he wishes to emphasize and explore. Perhaps it would be less misleading to speak of historical (or process) principles of desert (than of historical entitlement principles) and more to the point to argue against Rawls that such desert principles are fundamental to what many take to be a satisfying conception of justice in holdings.

The most startling way in which Rawls's theory of justice departs from everyday thinking about justice is that it has no fundamental role for the concept of desert, independent of the "legitimate expectations" created by the rules of just institutions. Rawls explicitly rules out *moral* deserts, understood as distinct from claims or entitlements, as not even relevant to distributive social justice: "Thus the concept of moral worth is secondary to those of right and justice, and it plays no role in the substantive definition of distributive shares" (Rawls 1971, 313)[5] Some of his arguments support the view that moral desert is a problematic notion, and perhaps it is, especially the idea that a person's character can be judged as a whole and regarded as the basis of the person's deserving to be treated in certain ways or to have a certain kind of life (or to go to heaven or hell). But this is not always what people mean by deserts, even in a moral sense. Often we mean something much more specific.

Others of Rawls's arguments support more specifically the view that deserts are insufficient for (rather than irrelevant to) determining just distributions of social and economic goods. But Rawls also seems to hold the more extreme view that the natural assets that enter into the bases of desert claims (when these claims are not just "legitimate expectations" created by social institutions) are just bits of luck received in "the natural lottery" and are thus "arbitrary from a moral point of view" and that they ought, therefore, to be ignored in a theory of distributive justice, at least at the level of fundamental principles (Rawls 1971, 310–15). It is as though one's not having deserved one's natural assets, such as intelligence or a sympathetic disposition, undermines any further desert claim based on one's exercise of those assets.[6] Thus, it can come to seem that nobody really deserves anything because, ultimately, the bases of desert claims are not themselves deserved. If that is what this argument comes to, Nozick's rejoinder seems right, "It needn't be that the foundations underlying desert are themselves deserved, *all the way down*" (Nozick 1974, 225).

And yet, Rawls's reasoning makes a certain sense if we grant his idea that the natural assets that enable people to do good things are bits of luck from "the natural lottery." Desert bases are facts about the deserver. But one's luck may not seem to be a fact about oneself in the requisite sense: It neither characterizes oneself (it characterizes one's circumstances in relation to one's well-being) nor describes something that one did, something for which one can take credit. In cases where it makes sense to regard possession of natural assets as contingencies (rather than as part of the identity of the person said to "possess" them), the fact that one's possession of an asset is not in the requisite sense a fact about oneself seems an intelligible reason to find it insufficient to ground desert claims. The fact that I merely possess a natural asset may be insufficient to ground desert claims, but the fact that I use it in certain ways may not be. Even the fact that I possess the ability to use it in certain ways may be insufficient, but the fact that I actually choose to do so may not be. And if I use my assets well, I may come to deserve to have them (I may even develop potentialities that might have lain dormant), even if my coming to have them was originally just luck. Still, even if my use of natural assets were sometimes sufficient to ground desert claims, the conclusion would not follow that it was sufficient to ground entitlements.

Perhaps Rawls's theory could be revised to incorporate something like Nozick's historical entitlement principles (renamed "historical desert principles"), with the difference principle playing the role that the Lockean proviso plays in Nozick's theory. This revision would generate questions of coordination between the difference principle and the desert principles resembling the difficulties discussed in section 1 of this chapter. It may be that those problems can be resolved by according independent weights to each. In any case, I am not convinced of Nozick's claim that historical principles cannot be got out of the original position. It seems to me, rather, that the principles that can be got out of the original position are in tension with one another— a different sort of problem—as in the case of the difference principle and the principle of fair equality of opportunity, which may be understood to offer different sorts of cases for entitlement.

Nozick argues that the parties in Rawls's original position, given their prudential motivation and the veil of ignorance, would have no basis for proposing historical principles for judging distributions of goods. For no one would have a basis for thinking that any such principles would be more advantageous, according to maximin reasoning (maximizing the benefits of the least advantaged, or minimum, social position), than any others. Perhaps the idea is that giving people what they deserve has no predictable instrumental value. But the same is true of fair equality of opportunity, which acts as a constraint rather than as an instrument and serves to protect individual self-respect rather than to increase the stock of primary goods.

Consider how Rawls apparently thinks persons in the original position would argue in favor of the principle of fair equality of opportunity. Interestingly, he does not appeal to maximin reasoning on this point. Instead he argues:

> If some places were not open on a basis fair to all, those kept out would be right in feeling unjustly treated even though they benefited from the greater efforts of those who were allowed to hold them. They would be justified in their complaint . . . because they were debarred from experiencing the realization of self which comes from a skillful and devoted exercise of social duties. They would be deprived of one of the main forms of human good. (Rawls 1971, 84)

That kind of appeal to a "realization of self," which is one of the "main forms of human good," suggests an interesting way to argue for desert principles as well. The primary good here is self-respect. It can be argued that recognition of one's deserts is also important to one's self-respect, even to one's personal integrity and identity, just as recognition of oneself as politically the equal of one's peers is important to one's self-respect. Why not appeal to the realization of self that comes from being able to appropriate things by mixing one's labor with them, or even to a kind of realization of self that comes from being able to give? Appropriating might be viewed as a kind of embodiment of oneself in things. According to Emerson in his 1844 essay on gifts (1950, 403), the truest gift is a portion of oneself, by which he meant to include things one has made, for example. The point is that further reflection on human nature and character, which is open to persons in the original position, might lead the parties to propose historical principles as fundamental considerations because of their connections with self-respect, even if those considerations were not decisive by themselves for determining entitlements. Knowing the actual course of history seems no more requisite for this purpose than for other sorts of deliberations supposed to occur behind the veil.

Acknowledgments

For helpful comments and questions I thank participants in the University of Wisconsin Law and Behavioral Science seminars who heard forerunners of this chapter in the mid-1970s, my colleague Dan Hausman, and many of the graduate and undergraduate students in the Philosophy Department at the University of Wisconsin who took my courses and seminars on justice. I thank Victoria Davion for encouraging me to develop the material in its present form.

Notes

1. The first principle, which I do not discuss in this chapter, is that "each person is to have an equal right to the most extensive basic liberty compatible with a similar liberty for others" (Rawls 1971, 60). This principle, presented as lexically prior to (must be satisfied before) the second principle, is interpreted to imply that "liberty can be restricted only for the sake of liberty" (Rawls 1971, 250).

2. See Rawls 1971, 65–75, for contrast of the fair equality of opportunity conception of the openness of positions with the conception of "equally open" simply as "careers open to talents."

3. It is only for what he calls the "special conception" of justice that Rawls offers the two principles; the general conception of justice is simply the difference principle generalized to apply to all primary goods and has application only in the (early) stages of society when liberty does not have the special value that he finds it has for us (Rawls 1971, 62, 83).

4. In *Liberalism,* the primary goods are reconceptualized as "citizens' needs" (Rawls 1993, 188) and, less intuitively, as those goods essential to realizing the higher-order interests of developing one's two moral powers—the capacity for a sense of justice and the capacity for a conception of the good—as well as to realizing the third higher-order interest of developing some determinate conception of the good (not yet known behind the veil of ignorance) over a lifetime (Rawls 1993, 74–75, 81). But the enumeration of primary goods remains basically the same: "basic rights and liberties covered by the first principle of justice, freedom of movement, and free choice of occupation protected by fair equality of opportunity of the first part of the second principle, and income and wealth and the social bases of self-respect" (Rawls 1993, 76). *Liberalism* also emphasizes that this enumeration should not be thought of as complete and suggests at one point that we might wish to add to it "leisure time" (Rawls 1993, 182) and "certain mental states such as freedom from physical pain" (Rawls 1993, 183).

5. A contrasting view is developed by John Kekes (1990). Although he does not focus here on justice, Kekes defines "simple evil" as "undeserved harm," understands "desert" morally, and maintains that giving people what they deserve to be a legitimate concern of social institutions.

6. For extended arguments against this position, see Sher (1987, 22–36). His otherwise valuable discussion appears to attribute to Rawls the view that an undeserved inequality is unjust whereas Rawls's view, I believe, is that (noninstitutionally defined) deserts are simply irrelevant to justice.

References

Emerson, Ralph Waldo. 1950. *Selected Writings of Ralph Waldo Emerson.* New York: Modern Library.

Kekes, John. 1990. *Facing Evil.* Princeton, N.J.: Princeton University Press.

Locke, John. (1689) 1937. *Treatise of Civil Government and a Letter Concerning Toleration.* New York: Appleton-Century-Crofts.

Nozick, Robert. 1974. *Anarchy, State, and Utopia.* New York: Basic Books.

Rawls, John. 1958. "Justice as Fairness," *Philosophical Review* 67, no. 2 (April): 164–94.

———. 1971. *A Theory of Justice.* Cambridge, Mass.: Harvard University Press.

———. 1993. *Political Liberalism.* New York: Columbia University Press.

Sher, George. 1987. *Desert.* Princeton, N.J.: Princeton University Press.

10

Part Five

"NOT A MERE MODUS VIVENDI": THE BASES

FOR ALLEGIANCE TO THE JUST STATE

Claudia Mills

Some twenty years after the award-winning debut of William Gibson's *The Miracle Worker,* Broadway saw the production of its sequel, aptly titled *Monday After the Miracle.* This play examined the question, Once Annie Sullivan had released Helen Keller from her prison of darkness and silence, then what? What kind of a life would Helen and Annie go on to forge together? It's a wonderful title, because it invites the viewer to contemplate not only the Monday after the miracle but the Tuesday, the Wednesday . . . the endless procession of ordinary days that inevitably follow any outbreak of the extraordinary.

Political Liberalism is the Monday after the miracle of *A Theory of Justice.* The later work examines the question, Once we arrive at our principles of justice, how do we get each other to support them and live together within the framework they provide—given that we also live in a society inevitably divided by pursuit of different life goals and adherence to different systems of value? Rawls poses the question, "How is it possible for there to exist over time a just and stable society of free and equal citizens who remain profoundly divided by reasonable religious, philosophical, and moral doctrines?" (Rawls 1993, 4). If the liberal ideal of *A Theory of Justice* is going to be a viable option for us in the real world that we share, different people holding a plurality of different views are going to have to live together through the Mondays, Tuesdays, and Wednesdays of their ordinary lives. On what basis can they do this?

What Rawls is seeking is an account of the stability of liberalism that falls somewhere in between two—for him—untenable extremes. The first untenable extreme is that people support liberalism on the basis of a shared system of values, that they hold in common a collection of substantive ends which are recognizably liberal, and that they join together in endorsing political liberalism as part of a more comprehensive and far-reaching liberal moral view. Rawls rejects this possibility because of the irreducible fact of pluralism. In at least the world in which *we* live, there is and is likely always to be both widespread and deeply grounded disagreement on substantive ends. According to

Rawls, agreement on ends can be produced and maintained only through the relentless exercise of significant state coercion, an option that is foreclosed to liberals. This is the basis of Rawls's implied critique of communitarianism: "If we think of political society as a community united in affirming one and the same comprehensive doctrine, then the oppressive use of state power is necessary for political community" (Rawls 1993, 37). The other untenable model for stability that Rawls wants us to reject is that people support liberalism only as a "mere modus vivendi"—only as a crassly pragmatic tool for getting along with each other, a Hobbesian type of "compromise" that people are driven to as a reluctant means of escape from the nastiness and brutishness of survival in the absence of agreement on some rules governing our interactions.

Instead, Rawls proposes that the stability of liberalism rests on its securing the support of "an overlapping consensus" of a certain subset of our otherwise divergent comprehensive moral views. As Rawls puts it, in an overlapping consensus, "the reasonable doctrines endorse the political conception, each from its own point of view" (Rawls 1993, 134). What this means is that a more narrowly defined political liberalism can be drawn out of or derived from a range of broader, more comprehensive moral views. Person A may support political liberalism as the implication of her utilitarianism; person B may support it as the implication of his religious faith; person C may support it as the core of her less tightly organized hodgepodge of other moral commitments. Liberalism's supporters begin from different starting points, which all converge on support of liberalism. Note, however, as Rawls does, that not all roads lead to liberalism, only all "reasonable" roads. For example, religious fundamentalism does not lead there. For Rawls, "reasonable" comprehensive doctrines are those that can be held by reasonable persons, and reasonable persons are those who "stand ready to enter the public world of others and stand ready to propose, or to accept, as the case may be, fair terms of cooperation with them" (Rawls 1993, 53). These fair terms of cooperation, Rawls is arguing, will turn out to approximate his preferred version of liberalism, justice as fairness.

Rawls's project of grounding stability in an overlapping consensus has been widely—and I believe rightly—criticized. Heidi M. Hurd, reviewing *Political Liberalism* in the *Yale Law Journal,* argues that by constructing his overlapping consensus only from reasonable comprehensive doctrines, Rawls ends up preaching liberalism only to an already liberal choir: "Can one meaningfully take Rawls to be justifying liberalism when he has explicitly excluded everyone who is not a liberal from the congregation to which he is preaching?" (Hurd 1995, 822). Far from excluding only the crackpot fringe, Hurd notes that "in Rawls's sense, many of my best friends are unreasonable" (Hurd 1995, 821). And Samuel Scheffler argues that even some adherents of Rawls's own highly restricted list of reasonable doctrines would not in fact endorse justice as fairness from within their own conceptions of justice. For Rawls cites utilitarianism as an example of a reasonable comprehensive doctrine that could join in an overlapping consensus on political liberalism and yet devotes much of *A Theory of Justice* to showing the ways in which justice as fairness is in direct opposition to utilitarianism. According to Scheffler: "If utilitarianism is said to be included in the overlapping consensus on Rawls's two principles, then are we to imagine that utilitarians endorse Rawls's arguments for the rejection of utilitarianism even as they continue to affirm that view? This seems incoherent" (Scheffler 1994, 9).

Rather than adding to the chorus of objections to the notion of overlapping consensus, in this chapter I ask whether Rawls, despite the arguable failure of this notion, can nonetheless succeed in his more fundamental project of finding some way in which we can join together in giving wholehearted endorsement to liberal principles and institutions for their own sake, even if we do not and cannot participate in a shared community of values. I argue that if we look at what Rawls wants for liberalism compared to what he thinks we get from a modus vivendi, we will find that he can get what he wants more easily than he thinks. In fact, Rawls himself provides a persuasive story for how the kind of endorsement he wants for liberalism can grow out of a modus vivendi, without any invocation of an overlapping consensus. Where he goes wrong, I argue, is in overestimating the importance to stability of a shared allegiance to principles and in underestimating the importance of a shared history of living together. We may grow toward allegiance to principles *because* they allow us to live together and then, out of our shared experience of living together, develop into the kind of community that Rawls rightly believes we should cherish.

In other words, rather than starting with the miracle and then dealing with the Monday after it, we can start with the Monday of a modus vivendi and work toward the miracle of a vibrant, thriving noncommunitarian liberal community.

1. The Problem of Stability

Before we can ask whether Rawls's preferred form of liberalism, justice as fairness, is sufficiently stable, we have to ask first what stability is. Some of the answer will emerge as we proceed, but for now, let me say that what matters to Rawls is not only the fact of stability—as, say, relatively peaceable duration of a state through time—but the nature of this stability. For stability achieved at sword point or gunpoint will not satisfy the liberal.

Rawls himself poses the problem of stability in a characteristically oblique way:

> Stability involves two questions: the first is whether people who grow up under just institutions (as the political conception defines them) acquire a normally sufficient sense of justice so that they generally comply with those institutions. The second question is whether in view of the general facts that characterize a democracy's public political culture, and in particular the fact of reasonable

pluralism, the political conception can be the focus of an overlapping consensus [of reasonable comprehensive doctrines]. (Rawls 1993, 141)

The first of these two questions seems to concern our *motivation* to be just; the second, the kind of *justification* that can be offered for just institutions. Many readers (such as Hurd) have wondered, if justification is the issue, why Rawls wrote *Political Liberalism* at all, given that political liberalism was ostensibly shown to be justified by the arguments given for it in *A Theory of Justice*. (Of course, one could reply that *A Theory of Justice* has been available for over twenty-five years, and still not everyone agrees on the content of the two principles.) Let me set these questions aside. It seems to me that Rawls, in more directly accessible language, has two concerns.

The first is with the *level* of enthusiasm people will have for liberal principles and institutions. Will they endorse them grudgingly and reluctantly or warmly and wholeheartedly? The second is with the *source* of the enthusiasm people have for liberal principles and institutions. Are they endorsed only instrumentally, because they work to secure the peace, or are they endorsed *for themselves*?

The first question is largely quantitative: How *much* do people endorse these institutions? The second is qualitative: What *kind* of endorsement do they give, on what basis? These two dimensions of endorsement seem to coalesce in Jean Hampton's notion of "endorsement consent" to a political regime, which

> expresses not merely acquiescence in a political regime but also explicit approval of and support for it. A regime that receives what I call *endorsement* consent gets from its subjects not just activity that maintains it but also activity that conveys their endorsement and approval of it. . . . Beyond a kind of *attitude* toward the state, endorsement consent is a *decision* to support it because of one's determination that it is a good thing to support. By giving this form of consent, the subject conveys her respect for the state, her loyalty to it, her identification with it, and her trust in it. (Hampton 1997, 94).

Why do we want our institutions to be endorsed in this way? I read two answers in Rawls. The first is simply pragmatic: Institutions that are stable in this sense—in that they have widespread and enthusiastic support—are more likely to endure. According to Hampton, "[Endorsement] consent, if widespread, can make a state particularly robust, stable, and long-lasting" (Hampton 1997, 113). The second answer addresses, not the *duration* of our community, but its *depth*. We want to think that we live in community with persons who want to live in community with us and that we all "feel good" about our community. This is a great part of the attraction of patriotism and other particularistic loyalties generally.

Rawls seems to think that the *grounds* for endorsement of a state set upper limits to the *degree* of endorsement—in particular, that if we endorse our institutions only on instrumental grounds, only pragmatically, only because they *work,* we will end up giving them only lukewarm consent. Although I agree that the two issues, kind of endorsement and degree of endorsement, are intimately related, I disagree that instrumental endorsement cannot be wholehearted. Wholehearted endorsement of political institutions and principles, in my view, is not likely to come in the first place from the head but from the heart, not from seeing how they are related to some comprehensive moral view, but from experiencing what it is like to live by and under such principles and institutions. Thus, we should not overlook, as Rawls sometimes seems to do, the range of other resources for building a shared life: history, culture, the sheer passage of time spent in one another's company.

2. What Is a Modus Vivendi? Why Is It "Mere"?

Rawls believes that both questions of stability, how much and what kind, are answered in the wrong way by a "mere modus vivendi." I believe we can make some progress in seeing how they can be answered in the right way by first exploring why Rawls thinks a modus vivendi gets the answers wrong.

Rawls treats it as the first and "perhaps most obvious" objection to the kind of stability he is proposing for justice as fairness that "an overlapping consensus is a mere modus vivendi" (Rawls 1993, 145). Right away, then, we know that there is supposed to be something "mere" about a modus vivendi, not necessarily bad, but lesser, diminished, second-best, disappointing. Why?

Rawls first offers an answer to this question and then goes on to reject it. Accepting a political system as a mere modus vivendi "abandons the hope of political community" (Rawls 1993, 146), but "the hope of political community must indeed be abandoned, if by such a community we mean a political society united in affirming the same comprehensive doctrine. This possibility is excluded by the fact of reasonable pluralism together with the rejection of the oppressive use of state power to overcome it" (Rawls 1993, 146). If by "community" we mean the kind of community communitarians insist on, we are not going to get it, because this kind of community is impossible given the fact of irreducible pluralism combined with moral constraints upon the use of coercive state power.

So what is disappointing, then, about a mere modus vivendi? The answer (though not given explicitly by Rawls) must be that a mere modus vivendi abandons even the diminished hope of an even thinner form of political community, that it negatively affects "social concord and the moral quality of public life" (Rawls 1993, 146–47).

Rawls gives as his chief example of a modus vivendi a treaty made between two opposing states "whose national aims and interests put them at odds" (Rawls 1993, 147). Each abides by the treaty because—but only because—it is in the national interest of each to do so. "In general both states are ready to pursue their goals at the expense of the other, and should conditions change they may do so" (Rawls 1993, 147). Who would want to live together as fellow citizens, as ostensibly members of one political community, as *neighbors,* on such terms?

But note the special feature of this supposedly typical case of a modus vivendi: The parties to it are two opposing and rival *states,* not individuals, with little in common between them: no shared language, history, culture, heroes, stories that bind them together as one. Everything that two opposed states *do not* have is precisely everything that fellow citizens within a single state typically *do* have, whatever their system of political organization and whatever their further agreement or disagreement on some more specific system of values. So, two armed and potentially warring states provide an odd model for political life within a single state belonging in common to a single people. If we are asked, Do you want to live with others on the basis of a modus vivendi? and we take this as the question, Do you want to live with others as, for most of their history, France and Germany have lived together? the answer is a quick and easy "no." But to pose the question in that way is to ignore all that members of a single state have in common with each other above and beyond the character of their *political* relationship.

Rawls uses this supposedly typical case to lay out several features of a modus vivendi: "A similar background is present when we think of social consensus founded on self- or group interests, or on the outcome of political bargaining: social unity is only apparent, as its stability is contingent on circumstances remaining such as not to upset the fortunate convergence of interests" (Rawls 1993, 147). Let us look at this discussion with some care.

1. *A modus vivendi is founded on self- or group interests.* The imagined contrast here is with some interest of the larger community as a whole. But in itself, it does not seem problematic to me that each of us would be specially concerned about our own thriving, that each of us would start with caring about ourselves and about those others whom we hold dear. What other kind of interests *can* the "whole" have in a diverse, pluralistic society, given that Rawls rejects the shared ends of communitarianism?

2. *A modus vivendi is the outcome of political bargaining.* This part of the statement suggests that bargaining is somehow bad, but why? One answer, familiar to readers of *A Theory of Justice,* is that bargaining can be unfair to those in weaker bargaining positions. But if initial problems of inequality were corrected for, why would bargaining in itself be bad? It does highlight the extent to which our ends are not only distinct but opposed: In bargaining, I am trying to get as much as can for myself while giving as little as possible to you. But bargaining can nonetheless end with a hearty handshake, with each person glad to be working with the other to advance both sets of interests and glad to know that he has neither taken advantage of the other nor been taken advantage of, that the bargain, so struck, is genuinely in the interests of both parties. Now, a bargain also does suggest that each person ends up with less than he initially wanted, so the outcome is somehow second-best for each. But this is so only because each person lives in a world in which other people live, too. That each is forced in

some way to be responsive to others is not a bad thing.

Writing in the very different context of a discussion of moral psychology, Joel Kupperman notes that there are important differences between Smith's changing his behavior to avoiding hurting Jones's feelings, changing it as a compromise with Jones, and changing it as capitulation to peer pressure (Kupperman 1991, 166). For Kupperman, only the third scenario is morally problematic. In contrast, the first two scenarios show Smith as someone who "retains a clear sense of her or his own ideals, although behaving in a flexible way to maintain a friendship or family, social, or political harmony" (Kupperman 1991, 166). A compromise to accommodate how the world is—a world with other people in it—is not a compromise that is morally or, I would say, politically problematic.

It is odd that throughout *Political Liberalism* "compromise" is treated as a dirty word, as though the last thing we would ever want is (curled lip, sneering tone) a *compromise*. Rawls insists that an overlapping consensus involves "a balance of reasons as seen within each citizen's comprehensive doctrine and not a compromise compelled by circumstances" (Rawls 1993, 169). Or concerning the overlapping consensus, "No one accepts the political conception driven by political compromise" (Rawls 1993, 171). Rawls goes on to concede: "Of course acceptance depends on certain conditions. However a doctrine's adjusting its requirements to conditions such as these [limits on information, the facts of reasonable pluralism, laws of nature] is not political compromise, or giving in to brute force or unreason on the world. It's simply adjusting to the general conditions of any normal and human social world, as any political view must do" (Rawls 1993, 171).

3. *A modus vivendi makes social unity only apparent.* Here we are drawing closer to what seems to be troubling Rawls, or what his communitarian critics have convinced him he should be troubled about. For if we are going to live together with others, we do want to live with them on the basis of a deeper community. As we saw earlier when we began looking at stability, we want to feel that others feel good about living with us as we feel good about living with them, that our shared community is the object of robust enthusiasm. So the question must be, What would genuine social unity look like in a noncommunitarian state?

4. *A modus vivendi is "contingent on circumstances remaining such as not to upset the fortunate convergence of interests."* Contingency upon circumstances itself does not seem problematic. We need not think that the principles that govern our interaction would govern it in all possible worlds. It seems to me to be enough that they govern it in *our* world. But Rawls qualifies his caution about dependence on circumstances: There are circumstances, and there are circumstances. The worrisome circumstances are those that are "such as not to upset the fortunate convergence of interests" (Rawls 1993, 171.)

The relationship of our principles to circumstances is key. Consider religious toleration, Rawls's favorite example throughout *Political Liberalism*. If this is affirmed *only* because your side is not winning, then we have a modus vivendi. But what if it is affirmed only because of the circumstance of reasonable pluralism (if we would have no need or reason to affirm it in a society where we all thought and worshiped alike)? Even in such a society we might want to allow for the possibility of divergent belief, but we would certainly feel more free to legislate on the basis of one comprehensive view that was shared by all. Perhaps we are supposed to say that reasonable pluralism is more than a *contingency.* According to Rawls, it is a basic and irreducible fact of our life, but this seems to reflect the American experience of diversity growing out of several centuries of immigration from all over the world. There are many societies that are much more unified around a common core of values, societies in which toleration within the society is less important.

This suggests that while some circumstances are rooted pretty deeply in the human condition (such as Hume's circumstances of justice, to which Rawls calls attention in *A Theory of Justice,* the circumstances of moderate scarcity and limited benevolence), other circumstances (such as the circumstance of reasonable pluralism) are more variable. The problematic circumstance is the circumstance of my side currently not winning.

One reason why these features of a modus vivendi may seem problematic is that they may seem to pose a threat to stability, and so to security. Stability begins to seem only temporary and fragile, and that makes those living in such a society uneasy as they sense that the state of nature is only a failed bargain or missed compromise away.

The deeper problem for Rawls, it seems, is that we are not only afraid that we may not be able to live with each other at all on such terms—that stability of this sort is precarious and vulnerable—but that even if arrangements remain stable, they are stable in an unsatisfying way. We want more of public life than this. We want to live together on the basis of principles that we share in some stronger sense, that we endorse not only as a result of political compromise but for their own sake, that we affirm, not reluctantly and grudgingly, but wholeheartedly and with one voice. Rawls claims that one advantage of an overlapping consensus over a modus vivendi is that each different comprehensive view "supports the political conception for its own sake, or on its own merits" (Rawls 1993, 148). The interesting question here is what counts as supporting a conception of justice "for its own sake" or "on its own merits." What does that mean?

3. From Modus Vivendi to Liberal Community

It is interesting that despite his repeated disparagement of the modus vivendi, Rawls offers an encouraging discussion of how one can begin with a mere modus vivendi and nonetheless develop a more robust sense of community. For Rawls, this is a story about how we start with a modus vivendi and move to a "shallow consensus" on a liberal constitution and end up, finally, with an overlapping consensus on justice as fairness. But it's really a story about how we start with a modus vivendi and end up with *some* kind of a more robust endorsement of our principles, not because we come to see how they are situated within the network of our other moral commitments, but because we come to see that they *work,* that they do indeed provide the basis for a shared life.

Rawls briefly traces the story of how we might start with certain liberal principles of justice accepted as a mere modus vivendi, "at first reluctantly, but nevertheless as providing the only workable alternative to endless and destructive civil strife. Our question, then, is this: how might it happen that over time the initial acquiescence in a constitution satisfying these liberal principles of justice develops into a constitutional consensus in which those principles are themselves affirmed?" (Rawls 1993, 159). In reading this passage, the question we need to ask is, What is it for principles to be "affirmed"? Must they be affirmed "for their own sake," whatever that might mean, or can we affirm them because of the life they make possible? Rawls's answer seems to make room for instrumental affirmation of our principles as nonetheless legitimate: "It is possible for citizens first to appreciate the good [principles of justice] accomplish both for themselves and those they care for, as well as for society at large, and then to affirm them on this basis" (Rawls 1993, 160). Rawls concludes: "At the first stage of constitutional consensus the liberal principles of justice, initially accepted reluctantly as a modus vivendi and adopted into a constitution, tend to shift citizens' comprehensive doctrines so that they at least accept the principles of a liberal constitution" (Rawls 1993, 163).

But why bring in comprehensive doctrines at all? Why not be satisfied just with a consensus on the political conception, not based on any further philosophical argument (either that advanced in *A Theory of Justice* or that based on drawing inferences from one's existing comprehensive doctrine), but based instead on the experience of living in a just society and liking it? The problem with insisting on the overlapping consensus is that it focuses on the quality of our endorsement of the rules rather than on the quality of our shared life together. What is important is not why we endorse the rules that frame our living together but that we truly endorse them rather than, for example, merely follow them for fear of penalty.

4. Two Examples from the Nonpolitical Sphere

It may help to make sense of the transition from a modus vivendi to a thriving liberal community if we retreat from the political for a moment and trace the evolution of a true community from a modus vivendi in the nonpolitical sphere. I offer two examples that may help.

4.1 Realistic Marriage

With respect to marriage, an analogy to the modus vivendi would be the marriage of convenience: He marries her for sex, she marries him for money, both get what they want, yet neither would have married each other had it not been for the extrinsic features involved. Analogous to communitarianism is true love based on shared values and deep compatibility, when such compatibility is not accidental but based on the essential identity of the other person: I would not have loved him if he had not had these features compatible with me, but he would not have been the same person if he had not had these features. Call this romantic marriage.

Now consider something in between, a marriage that begins as a form of a modus vivendi but develops into something deeper. Call this realistic marriage. In this scenario, two people marry because they have reached (or fear soon passing) the marriageable age and are demographically "eligible"—similar age, socioeconomic class, educational level. They do not marry out of a deep passion for each other but more out of a desire to be married for marriage's sake: They would each rather have somebody than nobody. They have read Ecclesiastes: "Two are better than one. . . . For if they fall, one will lift up his fellow; but woe to him who is alone when he falls and has not another to lift him up. Again, if two lie together, they are warm; but how can one be warm alone?" (Eccles. 4:9–11). Such a marriage falls short of the romantic ideal, but while I do not see anything undesirable in the romantic ideal, it is often unavailable: Many people live their whole life without ever finding the perfect "soul mate." The inevitable paucity of perfect soulmates is analogous to the irreducible pluralism that Rawls cites in his remarks against communitarianism.

In the political case, we have not only the fact of pluralism but a liberal argument against trying to overcome pluralism: that the kind of coercive force that would be needed here would be unacceptable. One can loosely see analogous issues arising in marriage around the extent to which one can, or should, try to change the other person, to make him or her over into someone one could more easily love for his or her own sake. As in the political arena, there are clear practical limits to what attempted coercion can do to produce the right kind of shared values. (I read a lot of advice columns in women's magazines, and the chief response to those who want to reform their mates is, Good luck!)

How might a realistic marriage evolve into a marriage based on a deeper love, if not into the full-blown romantic ideal? How might it evolve into a marriage that is valued not only for the ways in which it advances the interest of each partner but for its own sake? First, over time, as the marriage is successful in terms of advancing the interests of each partner, in lifting each up when he or she falls and keeping each other warm at night, the partners experience astonished gratitude that the marriage *is* working; they savor the palpable pleasure in getting along, of developing a shared bank of memories over time and a "couple culture" of in-jokes, secrets, stored anecdotes. Each experiences gratitude to the other for his or her role in making the marriage work, as well as loyalty to the marriage itself and the terms on which they have made it possible to endure. As in the political arena, where citizens can experience loyalty both to one another and to the rules and institutions of the state they have created together, in a marriage, partners can experience loyalty to each other and to the system they have developed for resolving conflicts and deepening their relationship over the years.

At what point, then, do we move from the modus vivendi of the marriage of convenience to a deeper, love-based marriage? It may be hard to tell. But what couples do not need is any overlapping consensus on principles binding them together as much as habit, familiarity, "growing accustomed to each other's face"—the sheer weight of accumulated time spent living together.

4.2 A Professional Support Group

Now consider another example of how a smaller association might first arise as a modus vivendi and then have its members develop a deeper loyalty to their association and to the rules that govern it. I am a member of a writing group. There are eight of us, and we meet every other Monday evening at each others' homes. We are all fiction writers trying to get criticism on and support of our work with the goal of being published and, if published, well reviewed. Each of us has the primary goal that *she* will get published, be well reviewed, and go on to eternal fame and glory. Our aims are primarily and irreducibly individual. But we all realize that the best way for us to achieve our own individual goals is for us to join with others who are trying to achieve their own individual goals and work together, sharing our expertise, offering friendly criticism and advice, cheering each other through dark times. I am willing to offer these services to the others in return for their offering them to me.

When I joined the group, some six years ago, it was still in the process of formation and was working out some rules for its orderly procedure. One woman proposed the following procedures: After each person reads, the others comment on what she has read, one at a time, going in order clockwise, starting with the person to the right of the one who has read, with no one speaking twice until each person has spoken once. Some of the rest of us were dubious about the rigidity of the rules, but we did not want to disparage Claire's suggestion, so reluctantly, we agreed to go along with her plan. After all, we had to have *some* agreed-upon procedures if we were going to function as a group at all.

Years went by. The group endured. Some of us got published, some very well published; some did not. This differential achieving of our aims produced some strains in the group. But by this point, although we still all cared primarily about our own success, we had come genuinely to care about the success of others in the group, simply through years of spending time together and sharing our work and coming to value one another's support. Also, and this is the point I want to emphasize, we had come to appreciate that Claire's rules were a large part of what had kept us going as a group. Because of Claire's rules, no one member ever dominated the discussion; all members, published and unpublished, maintained a fundamental equality in the discussions that were the heart blood of our meetings.

We developed affection for the rules themselves. For their own sake? Well, again, what does that mean? Our endorsement of the rules was based first and foremost on the pragmatic consideration that *they worked.* If they had ceased to work for some reason, we would hardly have retained them out of nostalgia or mere rule worship. But because they worked, we began to feel grateful to the rules, to marvel at how well they worked, to recommend them strongly to other groups in the process of formation.

Moreover, we began to value the rules not only because they succeeded in keeping the group together but because they made visible the equality in which we stood, and wanted to stand, toward each other. I suppose we could say that we began to value their expressive function as well as their practical function. They not only worked, they worked *because* of the relationship among us that they expressed, concretely, each week.

Now, what if the rules had worked in that they kept the group together over time but did not have this added dimension of expressing the central value at the heart of our interaction? As an armchair empiricist, I am tempted to speculate that over time, rules in fact do *not* work if they do not express our central values in this way, that it is no accident that the rules *both* expressed important values *and* helped the group to endure. But I will leave that speculation to one side.

So when did our group's endorsement of the rules change from a modus vivendi to endorsement of the rules for their own sake? And precisely what transpired in the course of this change? That is hard to say. The change was gradual, almost imperceptible as it occurred. But at some point, our endorsement of the rules changed from grudging to wholehearted, and yet there was an important sense in which we continued to value the rules because they worked in the context of our particular group. If other dynamics of our group change, might our loyalty to the rules change as well? I do not know. I do not think it is dependence on circumstances that matters here. And our enthusiasm, again, is chiefly grounded in the practical success of the rules in producing stability in the group over time.

5. The Value of Stability

It is easy to underrate the value of stability, the value of sheer endurance of relationships and associations. But any one who has been married with any degree of success over any length of time knows what an achievement it is for even two human beings to get along together through the years, which is why we celebrate wedding anniversaries and cheer couples who make it to forty years, fifty, or more. The song says that breaking up is hard to do, but the truth is that breaking up is easy to do: It is staying together that is hard.

Businesses that have remained in business for as few as ten years boast of the fact in their advertising, and organizations and associations also publicize their milestones.

And states? In a way, it's easier for states to "stay together," for persons need not be as much bound together as fellow citizens of a state as they are bound together as fellow members of an association or partners in a marriage. The consequences of breaking up a state also are much more dire—as the world has seen in the breakup of the former Yugoslavia. But it is still impressive when states and forms of government do endure. I think of the self-congratulatory song from Robert Altman's bicentennial film *Nashville:* "We must be doing something right to last two hundred years."

In conclusion, let me try to highlight where I think I am agreeing with Rawls and where I think I am disagreeing with him. Rawls insists that we want support for liberalism as more than a modus vivendi and less than a communitarian style of community. I say the same. Rawls says that the right kind of support, the kind we seek, can grow out of a modus vivendi. I agree. He says the right kind of support would involve an overlapping consensus of comprehensive doctrines, and this is where he and I begin to part company. I say we need some consensus on our principles of justice, but it need not be based on their relationship to our comprehensive doctrines (in places, Rawls concedes as much). We do not need a story about how our allegiance to our principles of justice is rooted in our comprehensive doctrines but about how it is rooted in the shared experience of our life together.

It seems to me that "the new Rawls" and his communitarian critics are both making the same mistake. They both want to say that community is important (this is *not* the mistake) and that community comes fundamentally from shared principles (*this* is the mistake). According to the communitarians, this last means that we have to share comprehensive doctrines. Contrary to this view, Rawls asserts that we do not have to share comprehensive doctrines but we do need an overlapping consensus of our comprehensive doctrines. I want to say that, yes, community is important, but it comes from living together, from sharing a history and a culture and a sense of place. We then value the principles in large part because they make it possible for us to live together.

It may be that Rawls downplays allegiance to history, culture, and place and lays stress instead on shared allegiance to principles because he believes that the latter can be *voluntary* in a way that the former cannot and that social contract theories as a group seek to establish the way in which our consent to governmental authority is *free.* At one point Rawls observes that "the government's authority cannot, then, be freely accepted in the sense that the bonds of society and culture, of history and social place of origin, begin so early to shape our life and are normally so strong that the right of emigration (suitably qualified) does not suffice to making its authority free" (Rawls 1993, 222). Instead, all that we can accept *freely* are the "ideals, principles, and standards that specify our basic rights and liberties, and effectively guide and moderate the political power to which we are subject" (Rawls 1993, 222). But while history, culture, and place do not fit well with the voluntarism typical of social contract theories, they do serve well to establish the kind of stability Rawls claims to be seeking.

It is interesting, as Susan Moller Okin has noted (Okin 1994), that Rawls focuses in *Political Liberalism* almost exclusively on the example of religious toleration as a central liberal principle, one that we should come to value for its own sake and not just to avoid religious conflict. Historically, this has been an extremely important principle in the development of liberalism, but today what divides us, at least in the United States, is not first and foremost religion but race and gender and ethnicity. It is no accident that Rawls should stress religious toleration, because this is an easy example for him. We have learned—most of us have learned—to move beyond mere religious toleration to a genuine celebration of religious diversity. When I was a child attending the Methodist Church, our Sunday school teachers were forever taking us elsewhere to experience and delight in other forms of worship: the Quaker meeting, the Jewish synagogue, the Catholic Mass, the black congregation with its fervent gospel choir and frequent congregational choruses of "Amen!"

But with race we are more deeply divided in a way that our principles of justice cannot seem to overcome or perhaps even to address. When it comes to race, we live under one political system and pledge allegiance to one flag but remain deeply divided by racially and ethnically disparate cultures and histories (divisions exacerbated by grave economic disparities that all but drop out of view in *Political Liberalism*).

This suggests, in the end, a somewhat pessimistic note to my otherwise optimistic conclusion. If stability is easier to get in some ways than Rawls suggests, it is also harder. When we share a common history and culture, we can build on those to establish a political community as well. But when common history and culture are lacking, no amount of shared allegiance to political principles may be enough to bridge the gap. That may be why race continues tragically to divide a nation that fought a civil war to stay united in the principles of justice affirmed at its founding.

References

Hampton, Jean. 1997. *Political Philosophy.* Boulder, Colo: Westview Press.

Hurd, Heidi M. 1995. *Political Liberalism* (review). *Yale Law Journal* 105, no. 3: 795–824.

Kupperman, Joel. 1991. *Character.* New York: Oxford University Press.

Okin, Susan Moller. 1994. *Political Liberalism,* Justice, and Gender. *Ethics* 105, no. 1: 23–43.

Rawls, John. 1971. *A Theory of Justice.* Cambridge, Mass.: Harvard University Press.

———. 1993. *Political Liberalism.* New York: Columbia University Press.

Sheffler, Samuel. 1994. The Appeal of Political Liberalism. *Ethics* 105, no. 1: 4–22.

11

A GOOD WORD FOR A MODUS VIVENDI

Bernard P. Dauenhauer

In *Political Liberalism* (abbreviated as *PL*), John Rawls develops his conception of political justice with an eye to the stability of the political society that would adopt it. Part of the evidence that Rawls supports his theory with is evidence he draws from the history of political practice in the West. He is right, I believe, to concern himself with the society's stability, for any political order worthy of allegiance must hold promise of being stable. At bottom, stability is a necessary, even if by no means sufficient, condition for a politically just society. Rawls is right also to recognize that the evidence of history is relevant to the reasoned defense of any proposed political order.

Nonetheless, the ways that Rawls would go about ensuring stability are flawed. By demanding so much stability, they would likely turn out to threaten stability. Further, for all his use of the evidence of history, Rawls's theory remains in important respects ahistorical. But political life, whatever else it is, is thoroughly historical. Both political action and the thought that either initiates or evaluates it bear the marks of the historical context in which they are set. Attempting, as Rawls does, to construct an ideal theory that "defines a perfectly just basic structure" and that hopes thereby to provide "a necessary complement to nonideal theory without which the desire for change lacks an aim" is a mistake.[1]

To avoid instability, Rawls refuses to be satisfied with a political modus vivendi, as he conceives it. But the considerations I advance against his way of construing stability and against the impoverished view of the historical character of political thought and practice point one in the direction of granting that the sole sensible political objective is the objective of obtaining a responsible modus vivendi, but a modus vivendi conceived in an importantly different way than Rawls does. The conceptual task, then, is not to develop a theory that calls for more than a modus vivendi, it is to determine the appropriate ways of distinguishing a responsible modus vivendi from an irresponsible one. In this chapter, I confine myself to arguing that Rawls is mistaken to seek a political consensus that is more than a modus vivendi.

1. Rawlsian Stability

Let me recall three parts of Rawls's theory that bear on the matter of political stability. They are (1) the ideal of a closed political society, (2) the importance of achieving an overlapping consensus, and (3) the proposal that the discourse of the Supreme Court serve as the exemplar for exercises of public reason.

1.1. A Closed Political Society

Among what Rawls calls the fundamental ideas at play in his ideal conception of political justice is his assumption that the society in question is closed. We are, he says, to regard the society "as self-contained and as having no relations with other societies. Its members enter it only by birth and leave it only by death" (*PL*, 12). This closed society "is also conceived as existing in perpetuity: it produces and reproduces itself and its institutions and culture over generations and there is no time when it is expected to wind up its affairs" (*PL*, 18). The importance of conceiving of the society as closed is that it allows us to speak of its members as people who will lead a complete life in it. Thus, the closed society embodies "a more or less complete and self-sufficient scheme of cooperation, making room within itself for all the necessities and activities of life, from birth until death" (*PL*, 18). Rawls admits that to conceive of a society as closed is to make "a considerable abstraction," but this abstraction is justified "because it enables us to focus on certain main questions free from disturbing details" (*PL*, 12).

Rawls also admits that at some point he must try to show what the implications of his conception of political justice are for "the just relations of peoples, or the law of peoples" (*PL*, 12), but he does not do so in *Political Liberalism*. He refers us instead to his work "The Law of Peoples" in *On Human Rights: The Oxford Amnesty Lectures*.[2] But nothing he says there weakens the objections I make to *Political Liberalism,* so for present purposes I ignore it, except for its brief references to the right to emigrate.

There are at least two ways to construe Rawls's assumption that the ideal society is closed. One might take this assumption to be part of the overall normative ideal that his theory yields, or one might take it to be heuristic, adopted to make basic intrasocial relationships stand out more clearly.[3] Rawls does not say explicitly how he means us to understand this assumption, but neither of these two readings would make the assumption acceptable.

Consider the first alternative mentioned. According to this reading, the importance for Rawls's purposes of conceiving of the political society as closed would appear to be that its closure would fix the political benefits and burdens that are available for distribution and would assure the members, who remain there throughout their entire lives, that the distribution will provide them with enough benefits to lead a reasonable life of their own choice and will continue to provide similar benefits for their descendants.

But if the assumption of closure is supposed to be part of Rawls's normative ideal, the ideal has serious, irremediable defects. Consider what

Rawls intends for his ideal society to do.

> A conception of justice must specify the requisite structural principles and point to the overall direction for political action. In the absence of such an ideal form for background institutions, there is no rational basis for continuing adjusting the social process so as to preserve background justice, nor for eliminating existing injustice. Thus ideal theory, which defines a perfectly just basic structure, is a necessary complement to non-ideal theory without which the desire for change lacks aim. (*PL*, 285)

If "a perfectly just basic structure" is the structure of a closed society, then what relevance for "the overall direction of political action" could or should it have for nonideal theoretical attempts to deal with such matters of justice as political policy and practice concerning immigration or emigration, to say nothing of secession or federation? In any plausibly construed actual world of the present or foreseeable future, a crucial question of political justice is not whether a society ought to be closed or not. Rather, it is who and how many people are to be allowed to enter or leave its territory and under what terms or whether to change its borders through secession or federation. So far as I can see, if a society even aimed at becoming closed, it would be acting unjustly. Furthermore, if it sought to implement such an aim and found that it could not successfully do so, then it is quite likely that it would jeopardize its own stability. It would either have immigrants in its midst who knew themselves to be wholly unwanted, or it would force members who wanted to emigrate to remain. People who fit into either of these categories are hardly likely to be loyal to the society and its institutions.

Of course, it does not follow that a society cannot rightfully seek to control migration, but an ideal theory that has societal closure as one of its fundamental elements provides no useful guidance for dealing with issues of migration. Indeed, such a theory can be pernicious. By implying that every nonideal solution is flawed, such an ideal theory can weaken support that good solutions deserve. That is, an ideal theory can turn out to be a purported best that is, in fact, the enemy of the good.

But suppose we take the closure assumption to be heuristic. One finds some indirect evidence for doing so in Rawls's "The Law of Peoples" where he recognizes a human right to emigrate.[4] It is not implausible to think that if there is a human right to emigrate, and if some people choose to exercise it, then it cannot be counter to Rawlsian theory to have the ideally just liberal society receptive to at least some of immigrants. Therefore, the assumption of closure would not be part of the Rawlsian normative ideal. Rather, it would serve the heuristic purpose of simplifying the elements of the issue at hand.

Perhaps there have been times and places when the assumption of closure would have made intrasocial relationships stand out more clearly. Today, however, at least for political societies of any considerable size and wealth, to make such an assumption would be far more likely to lead one to see intrasocietal relationships in a distorted way. In actuality, many relationships pertinent to a society's functioning are now and for the foreseeable future relationships that involve foreign individuals or foreign states or both. Examples abound. To name just some of the obvious ones, I mention jobs, investments and savings, military defense, and environmental conditions. A model of society that oversimplifies relationships holds little promise of presenting anything but a badly distorted picture.

Not only do the distortions likely to be produced by a simplifying assumption of societal closure affect the quality of the descriptions of the relationships among the society's members, they are also likely to infect the normative assessment of those relationships. That is, a normative ideal constructed under the simplifying condition of closure is not likely to provide the "necessary complement to nonideal theory without which the desire for change lacks aim." For example, under the assumption of closure, citizens would not have to concern themselves with the preservation of their political society. Its permanence is assumed.

Interpreting closure heuristically, then, makes it no less questionable than interpreting it as normative. Unless there is some third reading of the closure assumption that has less unhappy implications, it is an unwarranted assumption.

1.2. The Importance of Achieving an Overlapping Consensus

Two of the principal merits that Rawls claims for his theory are (1) that it is realistic inasmuch as it can accommodate the existence of a multiplicity of reasonable comprehensive doctrines, not as a mere unfortunate fact but as the normal outcome of the free exercise of human reason, and (2) that it provides a basis for political stability because the consensus that it can gain can more securely sustain a society than a consensus on a mere modus vivendi could. For Rawls, a modus vivendi is nothing more than the grudging acceptance that under present circumstances one cannot compel others to live according to the tenets of his or her comprehensive doctrine. But should circumstances change, then such a person would no longer feel obliged to observe the terms of the modus vivendi. Hence, a mere modus vivendi is inherently unstable (*PL*, 144–48).

On the one hand, Rawls presents his theory as less demanding than comprehensive doctrines and therefore more capable of accommodating differences. On the other hand, because it requires more than agreement to a modus vivendi, his theory is sufficiently demanding to underpin a durable society.

For present purposes, let me dwell a little on the distinction Rawls draws between a constitutional consensus, which is, in Rawls's terminology, simply a modus vivendi, and an overlapping consensus. Consider a democratic society's political constitution. If it is supported by only a constitutional consensus, then, even though it satisfies certain liberal principles of political justice, it is not sustained by settled public conceptions of a well-ordered society and of what it is to be a person.

In a simple constitutional consensus, the constitution is supposed to establish democratic electoral procedures for moderating and mediating political rivalry. This rivalry includes not only the rivalries among classes and interests but also the rivalries among the competing versions of liberal principles. Even though there is, in such cases, agreement on certain political rights and liberties such as freedom of political speech and association and the right to vote as well as the other matters required for democratic electoral and legislative procedures, "there is disagreement among those holding liberal principles as to the more exact content and boundaries of these rights and liberties, as well as on what further rights and liberties are to be counted as basic and so merit legal if not constitutional protection" (*PL*, 159). Thus, Rawls says, a constitutional consensus is neither deep nor wide. It covers only the political procedures of democratic government and does not include the society's basic structure. As such, it remains a mere modus vivendi and is therefore insufficiently stable to underpin a durable just society.

Over time and with experience, according to Rawls, this constitutional consensus can develop, and is likely to do so, in such a way that it comes to be a significantly more stable consensus, a consensus constituted by the overlap of the several reasonable comprehensive doctrines held in the society. This overlapping consensus is deeper and wider than the constitutional consensus. It is deeper inasmuch as it demands that the political principles and ideals it holds rest on a political conception of justice that makes use of fundamental ideas of person and society as illustrated by Rawls's concept of justice as fairness. The overlapping consensus is wider than the mere constitutional consensus inasmuch as it goes beyond political principles that institute democratic procedures and includes principles covering the basic structure as a whole. Thus, the principles upheld by an overlapping consensus "also establish certain substantive rights such as liberty of conscience and freedom of thought, as well as fair opportunity and principles covering certain essential needs" (*PL*, 164).

The liberal principles that the overlapping consensus supports "meet the urgent political requirement to fix, once and for all, the content of certain political basic rights and liberties, and to assign them special priority" (*PL*, 161). Doing so removes these matters from the political agenda and establishes clearly and firmly the rules for and the scope of political deliberation and decision. Unless these matters are placed beyond the calculations of social interest or utility, Rawls argues, they will remain subject to the shifting circumstances of time and place. Furthermore, if these matters are left unsettled, the stakes of political controversy rise, and the insecurity and hostility to public life increase to dangerous levels. In sum, "The refusal to take these matters off the agenda perpetuates the deep divisions latent in society: it betrays a readiness to revive those antagonisms in the hope of gaining a more favorable position should later circumstances prove propitious" (*PL*, 161). One can readily agree that it is important for a just political society to have the stable sort of framework that constitutions provide. Constitutions should be hard to change. But it does not follow that for a political society to be just, its constitution must "fix, once and for all" any political matter. Nor does it follow that the proper goal for a constitution's framers is to express or bring about a Rawlsian overlapping consensus.

Consider a bit more closely the task of arriving at a constitutional consensus. The participants bring to this task their experiences of political controversy and rivalry, and the constitution they fashion amounts to the way they judge best to handle problems of that sort. In some respects, then, the constitution is backward looking. It is the outcome of reflection on past experience.

But, of course, a constitution is also prescriptive and therefore forward looking. In this respect, there is something inevitably experimental about it. It stands as a proposal for a way of living together that will prove to be good for everyone concerned. But who can be sure, in advance, that the experiment will be successful? Or that it could not be improved? Furthermore, because a political society always aims to perpetuate itself despite constantly changing circumstances, when could there possibly be enough evidence in favor of any specific constitutional provision under its prevailing interpretation that it could become immune to any reasonable challenge?

Given the burdens of judgment that, as Rawls points out, always weigh upon any exercise of reason, would it not be rash for any group of people to aspire to remove any matter once and for all from the political agenda? Do the burdens of judgment not require that we hold any political prescription we fashion to be always reviewable in the light of the experiences gained during the course of the time it is in force? If one were to know that the constitutional consensus he or she was asked to join was supposed to give way to an overlapping consensus that would take some matters off the agenda, would he or she not have good reason to resist joining even the constitutional consensus?

To make the likelihood of such resistance clear, consider the religiously convinced Catholic who is asked to join a constitutional consensus in support of a constitutional provision that establishes a right to the free exercise of religion. Such a person, knowing the burdens of judgment under which he or she labors, could sensibly agree to supporting the provision only if it, with the interpretations given to it in its applications, were reviewable in the light of the experience of living under it. To ask more of anyone in any matter they hold to be serious is, in effect, to ask them to ignore the burdens of judgment.

Thus, the Rawlsian demand that an overlapping consensus supersede a constitutional consensus risks threatening rather than securing society's stability. On the one hand, this demand might well discourage thoughtful people from joining even the constitutional consensus. On the other hand, if a group of people find themselves seriously disadvantaged by constitutional provisions that are held to be beyond challenge, to be fixed once and for all, then their reasons for loyalty to the society are severely strained, to say the least.

Far better than trying to fix definitively any substantive constitutional matter is to accept Claude Lefort's view that modern democracy calls on us "to replace the notion of a regime governed by laws, of a legitimate power, by the notion of a regime founded upon *the legitimacy of a debate as to what is legitimate and what is illegitimate*—a debate which is necessarily without any guarantor and without any end."[5] Reasonable citizens will not casually disrupt a constitutional consensus that sustains a generally habitable constitutional order, but they will reserve the perpetual right to inquire into that order's habitability. By allowing its citizens to make this reservation and thus to gain a hearing when they have complaints instead of being confronted with unchallengeable constitutional provisions, a society is likely to increase rather than decrease its stability.

1.3. The Supreme Court as Exemplar of Public Reason

To implement the demands of political justice as he conceives it, Rawls insists on a sharp distinction between exercises of public reason and those of the multiple nonpublic reasons. The work of public reason is, on the one hand, to give specification to the content of the two basic principles of justice and, on the other hand, to determine what ways of reasoning are proper for and what evidence is relevant to dealing with a society's fundamental issues.

The ideal of public reason holds, Rawls says,

> for citizens when they engage in political advocacy in the public forum, and thus for members of political parties and for candidates in their campaigns and for other groups who support them. It holds equally for how citizens are to vote in elections when constitutional essentials and matters of basic justice are at stake. Thus, the ideal of public reason not only governs the public discourse of elections insofar as the issues involve those fundamental questions, but also how citizens are to cast their vote on these questions. (*PL,* 215)

The Supreme Court is the branch of government in the United States that serves as the exemplar of public reason. The Court's role is to interpret the constitution and to settle the society's most fundamental political issues. In performing this task, the justices are to justify their decisions exclusively through the exercise of public reason, which can acknowledge no values other than public political values. The justices must appeal only "to the political values they think belong to the most reasonable understanding of the public conception and its political values of justice and public reason. These are values that they believe in good faith, as the duty of civility requires, that all citizens as reasonable and rational might reasonably be expected to endorse" (*PL,* 236).

Nonpublic reason, by contrast, is the kind of reason people exercise when they act, not as citizens per se, but as members of some voluntary association or organization. Through exercises of nonpublic reason, people determine which goods they will hold in esteem and which goals they will strive for (*PL,* 220–22).[6] The obvious example of an exercise of nonpublic reason is that which members of a church employ to establish norms for membership, to articulate church doctrine, and to determine what standards of conduct the doctrine calls for. Within a democratic state there is room for many nonpublic reasons, but there is only one public reason.

The Supreme Court is exemplary in matters of public reason because it is the only sort of reason that the justices, as justices, should ever use. Hence, one should never have the task of separating the justices' discourse into the parts based on public reason and those based on nonpublic reason. By contrast, when constitutional essentials and basic justice are not at stake, citizens and legislators are free to vote on the basis of nonpublic reason. Nevertheless, when they engage in public discourse about fundamental political questions, they, too, should abide by the duty to use only discourse that honors the constraints of public reason.

At least part of the reason why Rawls stresses the importance of public reason is that the constraints it places on political discourse are supposed to promote political stability. For Rawls, by properly exercising public reason, those who do so honor the values of free and public inquiry and practice the political virtues of reasonableness and civility, virtues that help to make public discussion of political questions a reasoned discussion (*PL,* 224). Failure to uphold liberal political values in dealing with a society's fundamental political issues would open the way for deep social discord and political instability (*PL,* 224–26, 241, 247). But if I can trust that the only arguments that will carry weight in fundamental matters of political justice are those I can accept as being reasonable, then I have great good reason for being satisfied with the order established on their basis.

Let me grant for the present that all the discourse of the Supreme Court should be governed by the requirements of public reason as Rawls conceives it. What I want to contest is his claim that the Court's discourse should be exemplary for the discourse of citizens and legislators when they deal with constitutional essentials and matters of basic justice. Part of my reason for challenging this claim is that making the Court's discourse exemplary in these matters is not, Rawls notwithstanding, conducive to political stability.

Consider Rawls's own discussion of the Reverend Dr. Martin Luther King, Jr.'s, invocation of religious as well as strictly political values to promote civil rights. Rawls says that when there is a deep division in society about constitutional essentials, it can be compatible with public reason for people to supplement arguments appealing to political values with others that appeal to a more comprehensive scheme of values. Those who do so would not violate the ideal of public reason "provided that they thought or on reflection would have thought (as they certainly could have thought) that the comprehensive reasons they appealed to were required to give sufficient strength to the political conception to be subsequently realized" (*PL,* 251). For King and his colleagues, invoking their religious beliefs was not unreasonable, given the prevailing conditions, because the religious beliefs they invoked "fully support the constitutional values and accord with public reason" (*PL,* 250 n. 39). It was permissible for these people to invoke these religious beliefs insofar as they did so *for the sake of* the ideal of public reason" (*PL,* 251; emphasis added). Thus, for Rawls, the propriety of their appeal to religious reasons hinged on its usefulness in providing auxiliary support for a position that was justified fundamentally on exclusively secular grounds.

There is, so far as I know, no evidence whatsoever that King and his religious supporters would agree with Rawls in matters like this. For them to accept Rawls's view would be admitting that their religious beliefs were insufficient to ground their protests against injustice. More generally, to grant Rawls's claim that basically religious arguments are permissible bases for political decisions only in matters where constitutional essentials are not at stake would be to require religious citizens to truncate the full articulation of their reasons for supporting or opposing anything that counts as one of those essentials. Such a requirement would be likely, in many instances, effectively to preclude the citizen, "the particular person she is—from engaging in moral discourse with other members of society."[7]

Religion, of course, is not the only nonpublic matter that many people find pertinent to the determination of the basic constitutional framework of their societies. Linguistic and cultural heritages are also often important. As the constitutions of democracies such as Finland, Norway, and Spain, for example, show, giving attention to these matters does not necessarily produce instability. Indeed, explicitly taking them into account seems likely to increase the society's stability.

If, as I contend, citizens in their discourse about any political matter, including constitutional essentials, need not, for stability's sake, confine their public political discourse to what would be permissible according to the norms of Rawlsian public reason, then neither should their legislative representatives be so confined. Only if their legislators' discourse can be as unfettered as their own can citizens have confidence that their views are being fully represented. Without full representation, not only do citizens have reason to resist the legislative outcomes, they also have reason to doubt that they have been fully informed about why some of their fellow citizens oppose them. This ignorance is hardly conducive to mutual comprehension and is thus destabilizing.

As I have indicated, it may well be that the Rawlsian norms of public reason should govern the discourse of the Supreme Court. The basic reason for agreeing to this is that the Court's task is to interpret and apply the constitutional provisions that are already in force. To use other considerations would amount to employing norms or principles that have not been previously enacted and promulgated. For very good reason, an unpromulgated legal provision is to be regarded as no legal provision at all.

The political discourse of citizens and their legislative representatives is oriented primarily to the future. It asks, Should we continue the legal system that we have previously established or should we change it? And if we should change it, what changes should we make? These questions are fundamentally different from those that confront the Supreme Court. The Court makes judgments on deeds that have already been done and thus is, in this sense, backward looking. The legislators and citizens make judgments about regulations for deeds not yet done. Hence, there is no good reason to take the Court's way of reasoning to be exemplary for citizens and legislators. If anything, doing so would be likely to weaken rather than strengthen stability, for citizens would have cause to worry whether the Rawlsian approach would not tend to seriously handicap their society's capacity to adapt to new exigencies.

There are good grounds, then, for holding that the Rawlsian way of promoting a society's stability as a democratic society is seriously flawed and is likely to endanger stability rather than to secure it. But further, there is another line of criticism to which these and other Rawlsian claims are subject. Generally speaking, Rawls's theory in *Political Liberalism* suffers from an inadequate reflection on the thoroughgoing historicality of everything political. It is to this line of criticism that I now turn.

2. Rawls's Inadequate Attention to Politics' Historicality

At first glance, one might think it simply a mistake to criticize *Political Liberalism* for insufficient attention to the historical character of politics. Rawls makes it clear that the version of liberalism he espouses is a response to the pluralism of moral and political values that have come to be a permanent feature of life in the West since the era of the Protestant Reformation. He recognizes, for example, that even though his political conception of justice covers the constitutional essentials and matters of basic justice, "it has little to say about many economic and social issues that legislative bodies must regularly consider. To resolve these more particular and detailed issues it is often more reasonable to go beyond the political conception and the values its principles express, and to invoke nonpolitical values that such a view does not include" (*PL*, 230). The nonpolitical values that may be invoked in these matters may indeed, Rawls agrees, be historically specific and thus gain their force from their particular historical contexts.

Similarly, as I have already mentioned briefly, Rawls grants that it is likely a society's members' experience of living together that enables them to arrive first at a constitutional consensus and then at an overlapping consensus. For example, he explicitly asks, "How might it happen that *over time* the initial acquiescence in a constitution satisfying liberal principles of justice develops into a constitutional consensus in which those principles themselves are affirmed?" (*PL*, 159; emphasis added). After responding, Rawls again explicitly considers how the constitutional consensus might become an overlapping consensus, claiming that "gradually, as the success of political cooperation continues, citizens gain increasing trust and confidence in one another. This is all we need say in reply to the objection that the idea of overlapping consensus is utopian" (*PL*, 168).

These examples, and there are others, are enough to show that Rawls has not totally disregarded temporal and historical considerations in developing his theory. But, or so I claim, he has failed to give sufficient attention to the radical historicality of all political norms and the practice they govern. More specifically, he fails to appreciate that all political principles and norms, even those that we may now cherish most unreservedly, not only have been learned over time but, precisely because they are historical, are constantly subject to reconsideration in the light of material and cultural changes in the circumstances affecting political life, changes that are always likely and whose specific characteristics are never wholly predictable.

To make my case, I consider several mutually related aspects of Rawls's discussion of constitutional essentials. I consider, first, the way Rawls's ideal theory would have the democratic constitution deal with religion and religious discourse; second, the role that Rawls would have the Supreme Court play in the process of amending the constitution; and third, the distinction Rawls draws between different sorts of constitutional essentials.

2.1. The Democratic Constitution and Religion

Rawls's version of political liberalism calls for constitutional provisions that bar religious considerations from influencing basic political institutional arrangements as well as for constitutional neutrality concerning religious belief and practice. Though Rawls does not say so in so many words, the tradition of political practice that serves as the model for his position on religion and politics is that which finds expression in the First Amendment of the U.S Constitution. But Rawls does not confine the applicability of his theory to the United States. It is, in principle, a theory that claims to serve as the ideal that all democratic politics should aim to satisfy.

Given all the available historical evidence, I surely agree that the First Amendment has been, is now, and will for the foreseeable future be a superb political response to the religious pluralism found in the United States. But it does not follow that unless the substance of the First Amendment is embodied in other democratic constitutions they are defective and ought to be changed. Consider some of the provisions of the constitution of the kingdom of Norway.

> *Article 2.* All inhabitants of the Realm shall have the right to free exercise of their religion. The Evangelical-Lutheran religion shall remain the official religion of the State. The inhabitants professing it are bound to bring up their children in the same.

> *Article 4.* The King shall at all times profess the Evangelical-Lutheran religion, and uphold and protect the same.

> *Article 12.* The King himself chooses a Council from among Norwegian citizens who are entitled to vote. This council shall consist of a Prime Minister and at least seven other members. More than half the number of the Members of the Council of State shall profess the official religion of the State.[8]

As the examples of Finland, Great Britain, and Iceland show, Norway is not the only democratic state that has an established state religion while at the same time providing for the religious freedom of all citizens.

These constitutions obviously reflect their people's history. But, so far as I can tell, the Rawlsian adherent would have to claim that until these states disestablished their churches they were seriously defective, partially unjust democracies. That claim would apparently rest either on the contention that the history of the United States and its constitutional outcomes ought to serve as normative for other democratic states or on the contention that the reflection provoked by the history of the United States has been able to develop an ideal that now has validity independent of that or any other history. Rawls himself apparently adopts the latter, strongly ahistorical, path when he says, "The idea of right and just constitutions and basic laws is always ascertained by the most reasonable political conception of justice and not by the result of an actual political process" (*PL,* 233).

Far better, I contend, is the view that democratic political constitutions and each of their provisions, about religion or anything else, both originate in relatively specific historical circumstances and find their legitimacy in the acceptance they gain from the citizenry in the course of unfettered open debate. This view applies both to the original constitutional document and to all proposed or adopted amendments to it. It also applies to judicial interpretations of the constitution.[9] Rawls himself sometimes seems to admit this, as when he says: "The constitution is not what the Court says it is. Rather it is what the people acting constitutionally allow the Court to say it is" (*PL,* 237). But as will appear later, he fails to draw the full consequences from this admission of the people's role in legitimating the constitution or its interpretation. To see this failure, consider the role that Rawls would have the U.S. Supreme Court play in the process of amending the constitution.

2.2. The Supreme Court and Constitutional Amendments

In explicating the Supreme Court's role as exemplar of public reason Rawls says: "The Court's role as the highest judicial interpreter of the constitution supposes that the political conception judges hold and their views of constitutional essentials locate the central range of the basic freedoms in more or less the same place. In these cases at least its decisions succeed in settling the *most fundamental* political questions" (*PL,* 237; emphasis added). Rawls then goes on to ask whether the Court could count as invalid any constitutional amendment that met the constitutionally prescribed way of amending it, in the United States an amendment that satisfied the requirements of Article 5. Must, for example, the Court accept an amendment that would repeal the First Amendment and instead "make a particular religion the state religion with all the consequences of that" (*PL,* 238)? Rawls answers that such an amendment would amount to a complete breakdown of the constitution, indeed a revolution. Therefore, it would not be a valid amendment, and the Court should declare its invalidity (*PL,* 238–39).

Rawls's position asks us to believe that some group of people, for example Supreme Court justices, reasoning in a certain way—here, exercising Rawlsian public reason—can arrive at timelessly valid legal and political norms. These are norms that, however dependent their recognition was on historical factors, are now set in stone. They become substantive parts of the political society, and no procedures for constitutionally amending them could be valid.[10]

Even if in some ontology it were the case that there are such unalterable constitutive parts that if one of these parts of society A were to change, then it would cease to be society A and would become society A', it is hard to see the political relevance of such a conception. The people involved would remain the same. The historical record of actual political societies shows us ebbs and flows in the quality of their practices. The quality of the principles and norms that governs a society's practice cannot be assessed independent of that practice and its outcomes. Full assessment, then, is always after the fact. And usually the assessment is open to revision.

I grant that the historical record does show us political principles and norms to be avoided at all costs. Any principle that would authorize genocide is of this sort. But I know of no political principle that is unqualifiedly valid, so settled that it is immune to reasonable challenge. As Maurice Merleau-Ponty noted, history gives errors to avoid but no definitive truths to embrace.[11] Because politics is historical through and through, there are no final political truths. The importance of this point for assessing Rawls's theory becomes even clearer if one considers from another angle than that discussed earlier the distinction Rawls makes between different sorts of constitutional essentials.

2.3. Rawlsian Constitutional Essentials

Constitutional essentials, according to Rawls, are of two sorts. A just liberal constitution must contain fundamental principles that specify the general structure of government and the political process. It must also make explicit the equal basic rights and liberties of citizens. Thus, a constitution must delineate and allocate the legislative, executive, and judicial powers, and it must acknowledge that legislative majorities must respect such rights as "the right to vote and participate in politics, liberty of conscience, freedom of thought and association, as well as the protections of the rule of law" (*PL*, 227).

Rawls recognizes that constitutional essentials of the first sort, namely, those that establish the structure of government and the political process, can be specified in a number of different ways. For example, one liberal political society might adopt a presidential form of government while another adopts a parliamentary or cabinet form of government. But the second sort of constitutional essentials, those dealing with basic rights and liberties, can be specified in but one way, "modulo relatively small variations" (*PL*, 228). Liberty of conscience and freedom of association, and the political rights of freedom of speech, voting, and running for office, are characterized in more or less the same manner in all free regimes (*PL*, 228).

Rawls goes on to distinguish the principles of justice that specify the equal basic rights and liberties of citizens from those that regulate basic matters of distributive justice such as equality of opportunity and social and economic inequalities. It is easier to tell whether the former principles are realized than it is to tell whether the latter are. Whether the former are realized is more or less visible in the constitutional arrangements and how they can be seen to work in practice. But whether the aims of the principles covering social and economic inequalities are realized is far more difficult to ascertain. These matters are nearly always open to wide differences of reasonable opinion; they rest on complicated inferences and intuitive judgments that require us to assess complex social and economic information about topics that are poorly understood (*PL,* 229).

Because some constitutional essentials can, with relatively small variations, be specified in only one way, one can readily tell whether a constitution contains them. When they are present and when the body of citizens ratifies them, then these essentials are fixed once and for all. These essentials ensure that citizens, being free and independent, enact ordinary laws in a fixed way. Through these fixed procedures, the people can express "their reasoned democratic will, and indeed without these procedures they can have no such will" (*PL,* 232). My criticism of this part of Rawls's theory does not imply criticism of any particular constitutional provision. Rather, it is directed at Rawls's claims about the clarity and unalterability of constitutional provisions.

Consider, in the light of Rawls's claims, the free speech provisions of the Norwegian and French constitutions. Article 100 of the Norwegian Constitution says:

> There shall be liberty of the Press. No person may be punished for any writing, whatever its contents, which he has caused to be printed or published, unless he wilfully and manifestly has either himself shown or incited others to disobedience to the laws, contempt of religion, morality or the constitutional powers, or resistance to their orders, or has made false and defamatory accusations against anyone. Everyone shall be free to speak his mind frankly on the administration of the State and on any subject whatsoever.[12]

One has reason to ask a number of questions about this article. For example, does it declare two freedoms, one of the press and one of speech, or only one? Does the free speech provision have the same restrictions as the freedom of the press provision seems to have? What counts as proscribed resistance to constitutional powers? And, not of least importance, what amendments of Article 100 would be permissible in light of Article 112's prohibition against constitutional amendments that would "alter the spirit of the Constitution"? Further, there is the crucial question for Rawls's theory, namely, is it visible on the face of Article 100 whether it is equivalent to the free speech provisions in the First Amendment of the U.S. Constitution?[13]

The French Constitution's free speech provisions give rise to similar issues. Its provisions are more complex to state. First, the Preamble of the present constitution, the Constitution of 4 October 1958, says, "The French people solemnly proclaim their attachment to the Rights of Man and to the principles of national sovereignty as defined by the Declaration of 1789, reaffirmed and amplified by the Preamble to the Constitution of 1946."[14] The Preamble of the Constitution of 27 October 1946 said: "The French people proclaim anew that every human being, without distinction of race, religion or creed, possesses inalienable and sacred rights. They solemnly reaffirm the rights and freedoms of man and the citizen as set forth in the Declaration of Rights of 1789, and the fundamental principles recognized by the laws of the Republic."[15] The Declaration of the Rights of Man and of the Citizen said: "Article 10: No one is to be importuned because of his opinions, even religious ones, provided their manifestation does not disturb the public law established by law. Article 11: Free communication of ideas and opinions is one of the most precious of the rights of man. Consequently, every citizen may speak, write and print freely: yet he may have to answer for the abuse of that liberty in the cases determined by law."[16]

I am ignorant of the history of both Norwegian and French constitutional interpretation, but it seems evident that questions like those I raise can be answered only by considering that history, a history that is still unfolding. For example, in early September 1996, serious French political figures argued that French constitutional principles would not stand in the way of legally punishing Jean-Marie Le Pen and the French National Party he leads for his racist speeches. Similarly, there is a history of interpretation of the U.S. First Amendment. There is no good reason to think that any of these histories are or should be at an end.

One learns several things from these examples. First, to know what a constitutional provision amounts to in practice and, hence, its actual meaning and political significance, one must know the history of its interpretation. No provision is self-interpreting. Second, the history of the interpretation of a principle is never finished and is, in principle, unable to be finished. And third, particular constitutional provisions are regularly interpreted in the light of other constitutional provisions and their interpretations. No particular provision, with its interpretation, is a closed topic. Therefore, Rawls's ambition to have some constitutional essentials settled once and for all and thus taken off the agenda of political deliberation and debate is misplaced.

It is truer to the historical character of all human doings, including political doings, to admit that no political document, constitutions or others, can or should be definitive. They are all responses to some particular set of circumstances. Inasmuch as they claim to be reasonable prescriptions for future conduct, they are always subject to the test of how the people who live by them fare. If experience shows the prescriptions to be wanting, then the document should be changed.

Constitutions are, of course, documents of exceptional importance. They claim to capture a people's sense of themselves as members of a durable political society. They do, or should, embody the society's twin political objectives, namely, stability and survival, on the one hand and political concord and justice on the other. Framers and ratifiers of constitutions rightly seek to give them the preeminence they need to retain their force through all foreseeable circumstances.

Nevertheless, framers and ratifiers are not omniscient. Neither is any interpreter. No one can justifiably claim to have the final word. They can all only reasonably claim that they articulate a modus vivendi that is good for now and for the foreseeable future. They can reasonably ask no more of their fellow citizens than they join in what Rawls calls a constitutional consensus. To ask for an overlapping consensus is to ask for more than a prudent person should give.

3. Conclusion

Rawls's rejection of a modus vivendi as insufficient for a stable, just society rests in part on how he understands the term. For him, a modus vivendi is, in the words of the *Oxford English Dictionary,* "a working arrangement between contending parties, *pending the settlement of matters in debate*" (emphasis added). He fears, not without reason, that those who accept such an arrangement would constantly be looking for a settlement of matters on *other* terms than those involved in the working agreement. Hence, their consent to the modus vivendi would be inherently unstable.

But there is a more generous sense of "modus vivendi," one taken from Donald Davidson and inscribed in Webster's *Third International Dictionary.* According to this definition, a modus vivendi is "an arrangement between two nations or groups that effects a workable compromise on issues in dispute without permanently settling them." Nothing in this latter definition suggests that a modus vivendi is only temporary, pending something permanent. A populace that is properly attentive to the pervasive historicality of everything political would have no reason to think that it or anyone else can devise definitive solutions to political questions. To the extent that a constitution has proved its worth by the history of stability, justice, and concord its people have lived in according to its prescriptions, it gains in evidence that it deserves acceptance.

But we have no good reason to believe that there will ever be a definitively stable, just, and harmonious society. Therefore, the presumption in favor of a constitution or any of its parts can never become so strong that it is beyond reasonable contestation. To demand that citizens accede to a Rawlsian overlapping consensus is not only conceptually unwarranted. Because this demand would refuse to countenance a challenge that might be politically successful, it would be actually destabilizing. Those who are free to challenge a constitution have reason to be loyal to a society that provides this freedom. Those who find themselves politically thwarted by political provisions that are treated as unchallengeable have significantly less reason to be loyal.

Although I cannot claim to have definitively refuted Rawls's theory, I have given solid, mutually supporting reasons for not adopting it. These reasons, instead, lead us to conclude that the proper objective of every democratic constitution is to prove its worth, and that of its several provisions, in the course of its application to ever-changing historical circumstances. Even the most explicit constitutional provision, if it is reasonable, is at bottom a question. It amounts to asking citizens, You find that living according to this prescription is conducive to political stability, justice, and concord, don't you?

To deny the fundamentally interrogative character of any legal principle or norm, inasmuch as the denial rules out contestation, verges on the despotic. Though Rawls is right to concern himself with political stability, a properly conceived modus vivendi that achieves a Rawlsianesque constitutional consensus is the appropriate arrangement for a democratic polity that is stable and aspires to justice and concord.

Notes

1. John Rawls, *Political Liberalism* (New York: Columbia University Press, 1993), 285; hereafter, page references to this edition appear in parentheses in the body of the text, preceded by *PL*. The case against Rawls that I make is, in general terms, instructed by Michael Walzer, Philosophy and Democracy, *Political Theory* 29, no. 3 (August 1981): 379–99, and Hannah Arendt, Philosophy and Politics, *Social Research* 57, no. 1 (Spring 1990): 75–103.

2. John Rawls, The Law of Peoples, in *On Human Rights: The Oxford Amnesty Lectures 1993*, ed. Stephen Shute and Susan Hurley (New York: Basic Books, 1993), 41–82. For critiques of this work, see Stanley Hoffmann, Dreams of a Just World, *New York Review of Books*, 42, no. 17, 2 November 1995, 52–56, and Bernard Dauenhauer, *Citizenship in a Fragile World* (Lanham, Md.: Rowman & Littlefield, 1996).

3. Clark Wolf's comments on an earlier draft of this chapter drew my attention to this distinction.

4. See Rawls, The Law of Peoples, 63 and 68.

5. Claude Lefort, *Democracy and Political Theory*, trans. David Macey (Minneapolis: University of Minnesota Press, 1988), 39.

6. Rawls emphasizes that "the public vs. the nonpublic distinction is not the distinction between public and private. The latter I ignore; there is no such thing as a private reason" (*PL*, 220 n. 7).

7. Michael J. Perry, *Morality, Politics, and Law: A Bicentennial Essay* (New York: Oxford University Press, 1988), 72–73.

8. The Constitution of the Kingdom of Norway, informational document produced for the Ministry of Foreign Affairs by NORINFORM, November 1992.

9. On the historical character of judicial constitutional interpretation, see the brief but instructive remarks of former U.S. Supreme Court Justice William J. Brennan, Jr., in What the Constitution Requires, *New York Times,* 28 April 1996, E13, where he says: "Our Constitution is a charter of human rights, dignity and self-determination. I approached my responsibility of interpreting it as a 20th-century American, for the genius of the Constitution rests not in any static meaning it may have had in a world dead and gone but in its evolving character." I would add that there can be no guarantee that this evolution is necessarily progressive in the light of any atemporal criterion.

10. As Rawls recognizes, Bruce Ackerman denies that an unamendable Bill of Rights is compatible with the U.S. Constitution. See Ackerman's *We the People,* vol. 1 (Cambridge, Mass.: Harvard University Press, 1991), 308–22.

11. Maurice Merleau-Ponty, *Adventures of the Dialectic,* trans. Joseph Bien (Evanston, Ill.: Northwestern University Press, 1973), 28.

12. Constitution of the Kingdom of Norway.

13. Articles 10, 20, and 21 of the Norwegian Constitution cover subject matter much like that of Article 100 and the First Amendment. One can raise comparable questions about them.

14. *The French Constitution,* bilingual ed. (Paris: Ministere des Affaires Etrangeres, 1995), 5.

15. *French Constitution,* 63.

16. *French Constitution,* 59.

12

A MERE MODUS VIVENDI?

Scott Hershovitz

The project of John Rawls's *Political Liberalism* (1996, abbreviated as *PL* 1996) is to articulate how it is possible for people with different reasonable comprehensive doctrines to live in a stable democratic society. It is possible to imagine a different project Rawls might have undertaken—he might have tried to articulate how it would be possible for people with radically diverse and sometimes opposed comprehensive doctrines to live in a stable democratic society. The main difference between the two projects is the inclusion of the concept of reasonableness in the former. The concept of reasonableness serves in *Political Liberalism* as a sieve through which the adherents of comprehensive doctrines that would not be amenable to the creation of a stable democratic society (Nazis and the such) are eliminated from consideration. Many have found Rawls's use of reasonableness problematic for, if not downright offensive to, some of the groups labeled unreasonable under his definition. This might lead one to wonder why Rawls did not adopt the latter, more inclusive project. It seems that part of the reason Rawls did not adopt that project is because he believes it to be impossible. For Rawls, stability must be stability for the right reasons, which means that it must be the result of an overlapping consensus. An overlapping consensus, Rawls argues, will only be possible amongst the adherents of reasonable comprehensive doctrines.

In this chapter, I argue that Rawls could have taken up the more ambitious project described in the second question. I argue that Rawls's demand that stability be stability for the right reasons is motivated by the belief that a modus vivendi, or balance of power, cannot provide enduring stability. I then challenge this belief, arguing that Rawls grossly underestimates the power of a modus vivendi, and conclude that the power of modus vivendi arrangements makes the latter project feasible and allows one to circumvent the concept of reasonableness in articulating the basis for stability in a democratic society.

1. The Demand for Stability for the Right Reasons

Rawls says early on in *Political Liberalism* that when he uses the word "stability," he intends for the reader to interpret it always as "stability for the right reasons." What is the difference? The word "stability" alone might refer to situations brought about as a modus vivendi, a balance of power. For example, the Cold War represented a period of great stability in the relationship between the United States and the Soviet Union and indeed is taken by many to have been a great stabilizing force on global politics in general. The stability was the result of a balance of power; neither side was confident that its military capability could provide it hegemony over the other. Each side pursued a doctrine of mutual assured destruction in order to deter aggression from the other. Mutual assured destruction provided good reason throughout the Cold War for each side to seek to avoid conflict with the other, and a remarkable stability resulted given the animosity between the parties.

The stability in the relationship between the United States and the Soviet Union was not, however, stability for the right reasons. A situation in which there is stability for the right reasons, according to Rawls, is a situation in which "the reasons for which citizens act include those given by the account of justice they affirm" (*PL* 1996, xlii). Applying this definition to Cold War stability, we can see that stability for the right reasons would have existed if both sides had acted in a manner aimed at avoiding conflict because the principles they accepted demanded this of them. Clearly, fear of mutual assured destruction does not constitute a principled reason for acting.

The mechanism for achieving stability for the right reasons is the overlapping consensus on a political conception of justice that Rawls believes will develop among people affirming reasonable comprehensive doctrines. Since citizens will all affirm the same political conception of justice, their society will be stable, and this stability will rest on their acting in accord with principles they accept as opposed to their calculus of a balance of power. Thus, the overlapping consensus provides for stability for the right reasons. Yet, none of this explains why stability for the right reasons is considered superior to or more desirable than stability of different forms, particularly the modus vivendi.

Rawls's reason for requiring stability for the right reasons as opposed to accepting a modus vivendi rests on his belief that a modus vivendi cannot provide enduring stability:

> A typical use of the phrase "modus vivendi" is to characterize a treaty between two states whose national aims and interests keep them at odds. In negotiating a treaty each state would be wise and prudent to make sure that the agreement proposed represents an equilibrium point: that is, that the terms and conditions of the treaty are drawn up in such a way that it is public knowledge that it is not advantageous for either state to violate it. The treaty will then be adhered to because doing so is regarded by each as in its national interest, including its interest in a reputation as a state that honors treaties. But in general, both states are ready to pursue their goals at the expense of the other, and should conditions change they may do so. This background highlights the way in which a treaty is a mere modus vivendi. (*PL* 1996, 147)

Rawls uses the word "mere" in characterizing a modus vivendi because he sees such a situation as necessarily tenuous. As soon as one side has more power than another, we are to expect that it will violate the pact, as its accordance with the pact was motivated only by self-interest. Since that self-interest now demands that it be violated, we should expect that side to do so. Further, a stable democratic regime cannot be the result of a modus vivendi, because "a similar background is present when we think of social consensus founded on self- or group interests, or on the outcome of political bargaining: social unity is only apparent, as its stability is contingent on circumstances remaining such as not to upset the fortunate convergence of interests" (*PL* 1996, 147).

Since the modus vivendi cannot provide stability, Rawls argues, we must demand stability of a different sort, stability for the right reasons. This type of stability corrects the defects of the mere modus vivendi because supporters of a political conception of justice that is the object of an overlapping consensus "will not withdraw their support of it should the relative strength of their view [comprehensive doctrine] in society increase and eventually become dominant" (*PL* 1996, 148). Such stability is to be preferred, Rawls tells us, because it does not "depend on happenstance and a balance of relative forces" (*PL* 1996, 148).

It is important to note that the desire to have stability for the right reasons is a significant part of the motivation for the inclusion of the concept of reasonableness in Rawls's work. He finds stability for the right reasons by appealing to a political conception of justice, which is the object of an overlapping consensus among people affirming different comprehensive doctrines. The only way such a consensus can develop is if the comprehensive doctrines in question are reasonable ones. If we can show that stability for the right reasons is not necessary or not superior to stability through the mere modus vivendi, then the notion of reasonableness will not be necessary to account for how a democratic society can be stable. This will not mean that the concept of reasonableness can be dropped entirely from Rawls's project, as it plays other roles. However, if the concept of reasonableness is not essential for stability, Rawls can pursue the second, broader project outlined earlier, which given its greater inclusiveness is a more desirable project.

2. A Mere Modus Vivendi?

As I have already shown, the direction Rawls's project takes in *Political Liberalism* is partly motivated by his belief that a modus vivendi cannot provide an enduring stability in which we could have confidence. This view is not unique to Rawls. In "Theory and Practice," Immanuel Kant wrote, "For a permanent peace by means of a so-called *European Balance of Power* is a pure illusion, like Swift's story of the house which the builder had constructed in such perfect harmony with all the laws of equilibrium that it collapsed as soon as a sparrow alighted on it" (Kant 1970, 92). Kant, too, feared that the slightest change in circumstance—a sparrow landing on the house—might possibly destroy a modus vivendi, and thus he was unwilling to rely upon a peace secured through a balance of power.

I maintain that Rawls, and Kant as well, have severely underestimated the power of a modus vivendi as a means for securing an enduring stability that is tolerant of even significant change in circumstance. Part of the reason Rawls goes astray in assessing the merits of a modus vivendi is that his example, a treaty among two nations, is a poor one. It is true that reflection on world history teaches us that treaties are often broken when one party believes it has sufficient power to dominate another. Further, nothing in the construct of most treaties prevents this; there are no third-party enforcement mechanisms in most treaties, and while there may be some monitoring provisions, parties to a treaty rarely cede any sovereignty to others. Two reasons, however, make the choice of treaties a bad case on which to test the merits of a modus vivendi in providing for enduring stability.

First, it is odd to consider treaties between nations as the relevant example of a modus vivendi when the project Rawls is engaged in is accounting for domestic stability among people affirming diverse comprehensive doctrines. It seems that there might be relevant differences in the efficacy of a modus vivendi for providing stability among people in a nation as opposed to providing stability between nations. Indeed, I argue that a modus vivendi can provide a great deal of stability within a nation. Second, treaties normally represent a very simple type of modus vivendi. They usually take the form of agreements and, as noted earlier, often have no enforcement mechanisms. There are, however, more complex types of modus vivendi arrangements, and these may provide for a considerably more enduring stability than treaties do. In this section, I present the conditions under which a suitably complex modus vivendi could provide for enduring stability, using the form of the U.S. government as my exemplar.

It is possible to construct a modus vivendi in which the coercive power of the state is fractured to such an extent that the prospects for any single group within society consolidating enough power to topple the agreement approach zero. It will be rational for members of a society to enter into such a modus vivendi if the following conditions hold: (1) the current situation represents a balance of power; (2) the future is uncertain enough that no group is sure of, or has a strong expectation of, being able dominate other groups; and (3) the situation in which one's group is dominated is viewed as so offensive that one is willing to sacrifice the possibility of dominating other groups in order to avoid it. If these conditions are met, a society is likely to develop a stable modus vivendi, which may or may not reflect liberal principles. For example, if all the groups involved share a common religion, religious liberty is unlikely to be a part of the modus vivendi. However, when the society is sufficiently pluralistic, the features of the modus vivendi that will be chosen will likely reflect liberal ideals and incorporate basic rights, equality, and toleration. Thus, sufficient pluralism can be added as a fourth condition for producing a stable modus vivendi of the liberal variety.

The fracturing of power can be brought about through the creative use of institutional arrangements that exploit human nature. The most obvious method for fracturing power is instituting a government with a separation of powers. In the United States, the legislative, executive, and judicial branches of government all exercise power over a different arena, and total control of government decision making is denied unless one power manages to gain control of all branches. Further, the duties of each branch of government are set up with the notion that each branch should check and balance the power of the other branches. Mechanisms such as the executive veto; Senate confirmation of judges, ambassadors, and presidential advisers; and judicial review guard against the consolidation of power by any particular societal group.

The protections do not end with the separation of powers and checks and balances, however. The rules of Congress are designed to prevent and slow change and to magnify the power of minority groups through the use of procedural maneuvers such as the filibuster and the senatorial hold. The War Powers Act and the power of the purse sharply limit the ability of the executive to prosecute a war without the agreement of congressional leaders. The federal nature of the U.S. government, with powers divided between the states and the federal government, further compounds the difficulty for one group to consolidate power. The lifetime appointment of the justices of the Supreme Court guarantees an inertia in the nation's highest judicial body that is aimed at preventing quick and radical change. Even the oft-ridiculed electoral college protects against the passions of the electorate, for instead of winning a majority of voters, a candidate must secure a majority in a sufficient number of different states in order to be elected.

The list is by no means exhaustive of the features of the U.S. system of government that are designed to make it a stable modus vivendi. Ingenious institutional designs are present at all levels of government, and this is no accident. The delegates to the constitutional convention conceived of their task as creating a form of government that would protect all citizens, especially members of minority groups, against the abusive use of the power of the state. They believed that by fracturing power and by wisely arranging the powers of the state, they could produce an enduring stable democracy that respected the right of minorities. Nowhere is this belief more evident than in *Federalist 51,* written by James Madison.

> But the great security against a gradual concentration of the several powers in the same department consists in giving those who administer each department the necessary constitutional means and personal motives to resist encroachments of others. The provision for defense must in this, as in all other cases, be made commensurate with the danger of attack. Ambition must be made to counteract ambition. The interest of the man must be connected with the constitutional rights of the place. It may be a reflection on human nature that such

devices should be necessary to control the abuses of government. But what is government itself but the greatest of all reflections on human nature. If men were angels, no government would be necessary. If angels were to govern men, neither external nor internal controls on government would be necessary. In framing a government which is to be administered by men over men, the great difficulty lies in this: you must first enable the government to control the governed; and in the next place oblige it to control itself. A dependance on the people is, no doubt, the primary control on government; but experience has taught mankind of the necessity of auxiliary precautions.

This policy of supplying by opposite and rival interests, the defect of better motives, might be traced through the whole of human affairs, private as well as public. We see it particularly displayed in all the subordinate distributions of power, where the constant aim is to divide and arrange the several offices in such a manner as that each may be check on the other—that the private interest of every individual may be a sentinel over the public rights. These inventions of prudence cannot be less requisite in the distribution of the powers of the state. (Madison 1961, 322)

Madison's passage strikingly illustrates the extent to which he viewed the construction of the constitution as the construction of a modus vivendi. Whereas Rawls bases his stability on citizens' endorsing the same political conception of justice and acting accordingly, Madison is unwilling to rely on the good intentions of citizens. His view of human nature may be cynical, but it engenders the desire to construct a system of government that will protect against the abuse of power should those Rawls would term "unreasonable" gain office. Rawls relies on an overlapping consensus for stability; Madison relies on ambition. Madison presents a more pragmatic view than does Rawls, and it seems not only that his idea of providing for stability through a well-constructed modus vivendi is possible but that it may well be superior to Rawls's attempt to provide for stability.

Imagine how difficult it would be for any particular group in the United States to consolidate power in a manner that would allow it undermine the liberal form of the government. A majority of seats, a significant majority, would have to be won in both houses of Congress. The presidency would have to be won by winning majorities in enough states to win a majority of the electoral college. Such control over the executive and judicial branch would need to last long enough to reshape the composition of the federal judiciary. Additionally, majorities in state legislatures and a mass of governorships and state attorney generalships would have to be won. Career bureaucrats would have to be replaced, as would career military leaders. Juries would need to be sympathetic to the group aspiring to totalitarian control. The difficulty of accomplishing all of these goals is mind-boggling, and the prospect for holding such a coalition together if one did develop are equally daunting. Many have complained about the inertia with which the U.S. government acts and changes, but it was designed this way intentionally.

The founders of this nation entered into a modus vivendi that is so well-constructed it is self-perpetuating. In the intervening years, there have been many changes in the relative fortunes of the groups that were party to the original agreements, but the prospects of any group's gaining enough power to topple the arrangement approach zero. The situation is at least as stable as the one Rawls articulates. If any one group achieved the goals above, they would certainly have the power to enforce adherence to their own comprehensive doctrine under the situation Rawls articulates and would do so if they were not reasonable. If Nazism gained enough power to wreck the American system of government, the Rawlsian overlapping consensus would provide no protection. It may be true that conflicts will be less frequent in a society that has an overlapping consensus, but if conflicts arise with unreasonable groups, such a society would be less able to cope than a society founded in a well-constructed modus vivendi.

Further, pluralism plays a strikingly different role in the accounts provided by Rawls and Madison. For Rawls, the difficulty is to articulate how it is that a pluralistic society can be stable, and he has this challenge because his conception of stability rests on citizens' affirming the same political conception of justice. For Madison on the other hand, pluralism presents no difficulty; he sees it as another safeguard against the abuse of government:

> It is of great importance in a republic not only to guard the society against the oppression of its rulers, but to guard one part of the society against the injustice of the other part. Different interests necessarily exist in different classes of citizens. If a majority be united by a common interest, the rights of the minority will be insecure. There are but two methods of providing against this evil: the one by creating a will in the community independent of the majority—that is, of the society itself; the other, by comprehending in the society so many separate descriptions of citizens as will render an unjust combination of a majority of the whole very improbable. (Madison 1961, 324)

The first method Madison highlights in that passage seems akin to the development of an overlapping consensus such as Rawls's. But he adds a second method as well: The society should be so diverse that the generation of an unjust majority is exceedingly unlikely. Diversity enhances the effects of the checks and balances; homogeneity is to be feared. Madison might very well be concerned about a situation in which all citizens affirmed the same political conception of justice, even if that conception were liberal.

3. Rawls's Constitutional Consensus

Rawls might object that the United States is not a pure modus vivendi situation, arguing either that there is some degree of consensus on a political conception of justice or, alternatively, that some middle point exists. *Political Liberalism* includes a discussion of a constitutional consensus as just such a middle point between a modus vivendi arrangement and an overlapping consensus on a political conception of justice. Rawls says that a constitutional consensus exists when "principles are accepted simply as principles and not grounded in certain ideas of society and person of a political conception, much less a shared public conception" (*PL* 1996, 158). Thus, various principles, such as a principle of due process or freedom of the press may be accepted widely, even though there is no further consensus on a conception of justice.

Rawls views the constitutional consensus as a link in the chain of progression toward an overlapping consensus on a political conception of justice. He hypothesizes that one way in which an overlapping consensus could develop is for a modus vivendi reflecting liberal principles to first come into existence. He argues that living under such a modus vivendi might engender acceptance of the principles it reflects, thus producing a constitutional consensus. Further, Rawls argues that a constitutional consensus might ultimately give rise to an overlapping consensus. I grant Rawls that this chain of events seems possible and perhaps even probable if the initial modus vivendi is well-formed and reflects liberal principles. I depart with Rawls on the degree of stability the society can have if it never progresses from the first stage and on the source of stability if it completes the progression.

As I have already argued, a modus vivendi can provide stability without even a constitutional consensus if it is well constructed. Madison does not appeal to a general acceptance of liberal principles to ground stability; he appeals to the institutional arrangement of the government, the self-interest of citizens, and the diversity of the society. Further, the United States today more closely approximates a modus vivendi than it does a society with either an overlapping or a constitutional consensus.

Certainly, we do not have an overlapping consensus on a political conception of justice. Many Americans do not affirm the political conception of justice embodied in the U.S. Constitution, Bill of Rights, and Declaration of Independence. Examples abound in which the structure of the U.S. government has prevented encroachment upon the liberties of the citizens by government officials who fall into this category. A majority of Alabama voters elected fundamentalist Fob James governor, and he has attempted to do away with many religious freedoms in the state. James even declared at one point that decisions of the Supreme Court did not apply in Alabama. But the federal structure of the government and the process of judicial review have prevented James from encroaching on religious liberty even though a significant majority of the voters in his state support his efforts to do so.

Further, the United States may not even have a constitutional consensus. Many Americans, perhaps even a majority, are not committed to respecting the freedoms articulated in the Bill of Rights. There are consistent calls for government censorship that violates the freedom of speech from many different quarters in society, and some of the groups calling for censorship are by no means small in number or on the fringe of society. Further, many in American society are willing to abandon the establishment clause in the First Amendment in order to have government support for their religion in a variety of ways. Despite the lack of commitment to the principles in the Bill of Rights, the liberties are respected to a great degree. I submit that this stability is the result of the ingenious construction of the government and the fragmentation of powers and exemplifies the power of a modus vivendi to provide stability. We can conclude two things: First, neither a constitutional consensus nor an overlapping consensus is a prerequisite for stability, as a modus vivendi will suffice; and second, even if a constitutional consensus or an overlapping consensus does exist, the modus vivendi structure of a society provides a greater degree of stability than would be available otherwise.

It may be that Rawls would concede the second point. At times, he refers to the separation of powers indicating that he supports such an arrangement. However, one of the deficiencies of *Political Liberalism* is that Rawls spends very little time articulating what institutional frameworks the society he envisions should have. If Madison is correct that the arrangement of powers in institutions has a significant impact on the degree to which the rights of citizens are respected, then the structure of democratic institutions is a question of central importance. Rawls's discussion of the matter is lacking.

4. Reassessing Rawls's Project

Rawls's underestimation of the power of a modus vivendi to provide for enduring stability leads him to demand that stability be stability for the right reasons, or stability based on an overlapping consensus among the reasonable members of society on a political conception of justice. The demand for stability for the right reasons leads Rawls to restrict his question to how reasonable groups can coexist in a stable democratic society. However, the articulation of a well-constructed modus vivendi, using many of the features of the American system of government and perhaps many other institutional arrangements as well, allows one to circumvent the use of the concept of reasonableness in providing for stability. When the appropriate background conditions necessary to make it rational for members of society to accept such an arrangement are present, the ball is set in motion. Once the agreement is in place, even significant changes in the relative positions of the parties will make it unlikely that the agreement will lose its force. We can reasonably expect to achieve an enduring stability without labeling and excluding some groups as unreasonable.

At the beginning of this chapter, I articulated two potential projects Rawls might have undertaken in *Political Liberalism.* He attempted to describe how people affirming different reasonable comprehensive doctrines could live together in a stable democratic society. Rawls could have dropped the concept of reasonable from the formulation of his project and described how people affirming radically different comprehensive doctrines could live together in a stable democratic society.[1] After all, a well-constructed modus vivendi can tolerate Nazis as well as Jews and Amish as well as atheists without sacrificing stability. The second project is more ambitious, more inclusive, and more useful for the situations developing democracies encounter. It is time to give the modus vivendi its due and to explore and exploit its ability to provide stability.

Notes

1. Reasonableness would not be dropped entirely from Rawls's project, as it plays other roles. For example, nothing said in this chapter reduces the need for the concept of reasonableness in articulating the liberal principle of legitimacy.

References

Kant, Immanuel. 1970. On the Common Saying: "This May Be True in Theory but It Does Not Apply in Practice." In *Kant's Political Writings,* edited by Hans Reiss. Cambridge: Cambridge University Press, 61–92.

Madison, James. 1961. Federalist No. 51. In *The Federalist Papers,* edited by Clinton Rossiter. New York: Mentor, 320–25.

Rawls, John. 1996. *Political Liberalism.* Paperback edition. New York: Columbia University Press.

13

RAWLS VERSUS UTILITARIANISM IN THE

LIGHT OF *POLITICAL LIBERALISM*

Richard J. Arneson

The critique of utilitarianism forms a crucial subplot in the complex analysis of social justice that John Rawls develops in his first book, *A Theory of Justice* (abbreviated as *TJ*).[1] The weaknesses of utilitarianism indicate the need for an alternative theory, and at many stages of the argument the test for the adequacy of the new theory that Rawls elaborates is whether it can be demonstrated to be superior to the utilitarian rival. The account of social justice shifts in the transition to Rawls's second great book, *Political Liberalism* (abbreviated as *PL*).[2] The account of what is wrong with utilitarianism undergoes revision as well.

In this chapter, I examine both the initial critique of utilitarianism and its transformation in Rawls's later writings. To anticipate my conclusion, Rawls's proposal that we should maximin rather than maximize leads to an interesting standoff. The argument for maximin is not compelling, but straight additive maximization of the utilitarian sort is revealed to be merely one possible function among many, any of which (for all we know) correct morality might instruct us to maximize. Rawls further urges that utilitarianism goes astray in taking "the maximandum," the thing to be maximized, to be utility rather than primary social goods. The argument for primary social goods is not compelling, but it does not follow that utility alone is to be maximized. The espousal of the ideal of legitimacy in *Political Liberalism* does not affect these conclusions, and the arguments advanced to support that ideal are either diversionary or beg the question with respect to the debate between utilitarianism and Rawlsian justice as fairness.

For purposes of this exercise, *utilitarianism* may be understood as the doctrine that an institutional arrangement, a social policy, or an individual action is morally right just in case it is the one that, compared to the available alternatives, maximizes utility. Rawls assumes that justice is the overriding, preeminent part of the morality of institutions, so he formulates the doctrine in this way: "Society is rightly ordered, and therefore just, when its major institutions are arranged so as to achieve the greatest net balance of satisfactions summed over all the individuals belonging to it" (*TJ*, 22). He understands utility (human welfare) as the satisfaction of rational desire.

1. Taking Rights Seriously

Perhaps the animating philosophical idea in *A Theory of Justice* is that utilitarianism does not take rights seriously, and that not taking rights seriously is a grave defect, so we need a theory of justice that better fits our core convictions about ways people must not be treated. Slavery is morally wrong because it violates fundamental moral rights of the persons who are enslaved. Suppression of speech intended to persuade that concerns public affairs and how people might best conduct their lives is morally wrong, at least when the ground for suppression is the prospect of harm that might be caused via the audience's understanding of the speech. If the fundamental moral requirement were to maximize human welfare, then it would seem that whether or not slavery and suppression that violates the core of freedom of expression are morally wrong would depend on the outcome of complex and uncertain empirical calculation about which policies work best over the long run to achieve the utilitarian aim. Rawls observes that our convictions regarding slavery and freedom of expression are not tentatively and uncertainly held, and not held on the basis that utilitarianism posits.

Even if a utilitarian theory conjoined to a complex set of plausible empirical claims could support the positions that slavery and violation of freedom of expression are morally wrong, utilitarianism is in tension with the strength of our moral conviction in these matters and seems not to capture our intuitive grounds for these convictions. These concern individual rights. Hence, we need a theory of rights, a genuine theory of justice, that makes sense of our core convictions about individual rights and extends these core judgments to controversial cases in a plausible way.

Reply: In a utilitarian moral system, individual rights, if present at all, will be derived from the single fundamental aim of utility or welfare maximization. Roughly, the idea is that the recognition and protection of individual rights better promote the utilitarian goal than alternative practices, policies, and acts. Rights function to simplify and coordinate decision making among imperfectly informed individuals of limited reasoning powers and limited altruism. If we were to eschew rights and directly apply the test of utility on each occasion of acting or implementing social policies, the results would predictably be less successful, from the standpoint of utility maximization, than the results of instituting and promoting the recognition of rights. Recognition of rights involves proclaiming their moral importance and socializing and training individuals to give extra weight to rights that impinge on their practical deliberations than to their own fallible utility calculations when these conflict with rights. In this sense, a utilitarian theory can take rights seriously without assigning rights any nonderivative moral significance.

The utilitarian will also note that the commonsense agreement that rights are uncontroversially decisive determinants of what we ought to do is in a sense illusory. Many rights appear uncontroversial when they are stated vaguely and at a high level of abstraction, so that the practical implications for social policy of acceptance of these abstract rights are highly uncertain. Take freedom of expression, for example. Almost everyone is for free speech, but this appearance of unanimity quickly dissolves if we ask what a right to free speech is supposed to entail in a host of complex circumstances. It does not follow that there is no way to proceed except by appeal to utility, as John Stuart Mill argues, but the claim that embracing utilitarianism would force us to regard what are really simple and obvious moral truths as contingent and uncertain matters is misleading.

2. The Separateness of Persons

Rawls urges that utilitarianism "does not take seriously the distinction between persons" (*TJ*, 27). The objection is that utilitarianism extends to interpersonal conflicts of interest, a rule of maximizing aggregate benefit that is morally unproblematic when what is at issue is conflict between a person's interests at earlier and later times of his life. Prudence dictates accepting a smaller pain now to avoid a larger pain at a later time, and utilitarian maximization dictates imposing on one person a smaller pain in order to avoid a larger pain for another person. But in the intrapersonal case, Jones now is compensated by the gain to the same Jones later whereas in the interpersonal case, a loss imposed on Smith is not compensated by greater benefits that accrue to other persons. This last formulation might suggest that Rawls intends to assert the principle that there should be no sacrifice imposed on one individual for the benefit of others unless the individual who suffers the imposition is compensated. But to mention an example described by Philippa Foot, we may leave a row of beautiful shade trees standing along a roadway even though we know that in the long run, some individuals who do not voluntarily consent to bear this risk will be killed in a roadway crash and that they would have lived but for the presence of the trees. Surely, not all such imposition of risk is morally forbidden whatever the ratio of cost imposed to gains secured.

It is better to regard Rawls as making the point that the utilitarian principle is indifferent to the distribution of utility across persons. Utilitarianism bids us to do whatever maximizes the aggregate of utility regardless of the different distributions of utility the alternative actions we might take would achieve. But the distribution of utility across persons is morally significant, so it is a flaw that utilitarianism would have the decision about what should be done vary only with the utility total that different acts could achieve.

3. Primary Social Goods Not Utility

Rawls's rejection of utilitarianism is structurally complex. He embraces two views of justice, a general conception that is supposed to be valid at all times and a special conception that is valid under modern social conditions. For now, I focus on the general conception. It holds that the major institutions of society should be set so as to make the worst-off representative person as well-off as possible, with benefits measured in terms of primary social goods—goods distributable by society that a rational person would want more rather than fewer of, whatever else she wants. Rawlsian justice so conceived differs from utilitarianism in two respects: We are to maximin rather than maximize, and the basis of interpersonal comparison for social justice is primary social goods, not utility. Consider the latter difference.

In later writings, Rawls refines the definition of *primary social good,* and for simplicity, the discussion in this chapter employs the refined notion. According to it, these goods are ones that would be wanted by any rational person who seeks to develop and exercise her moral powers to cooperate with others on fair terms and to develop and reflectively adjust a conception of her final ends, as well as seeking means to satisfy whatever final ends she has.

The comparison of a primary goods standard and a utility standard varies with one's conception of utility. One conception identifies utility with rational preference satisfaction—satisfaction of preferences that would withstand rational scrutiny. Another conception identifies utility with objectively valuable goods, goods that appear on an "objective list" and are valuable for a person independent of the subjective attitudes she has toward them. For my purposes, the differences between these conceptions of utility do not matter. In both views, utility is not to be identified with happiness or any other quality of experience. Nor is it identified with simple desire satisfaction.

Use of a primary goods standard in a theory of justice involves a division of moral responsibility between society and individual. Society is responsible for securing fair shares of liberties and other primary goods to individuals. Given this fair background, each individual is responsible for developing a set of final ends and a plan of life to achieve them and for organizing her own life to satisfy the plan. The individual is responsible for these aspects of her life in the sense that any deficits in the outcomes she reaches do not trigger further claims for compensation by society. Society is obligated to provide fair shares of resources to individuals, not to secure them any guaranteed level of quality of life or utility. Citizens are viewed as competent to set their own ends and live their lives as they choose. A primary goods standard also insulates citizens, who together constitute society, from the open-ended, perhaps excessive, obligations to others that would be a feature of a social justice regime in which society was obligated to ensure a desirable quality of outcomes after resources were used. For example, people who have developed expensive needs are not thereby entitled to more resources than people who have chosen a life in which their needs are modest.

The theme of responsibility that Rawls's discussions link to a primary goods standard does not succeed in justifying that standard. Suppose we accept the plausible idea that a theory of social justice involves a fair division of responsibility between society and individual, which will yield the result that sometimes individuals behave in a faulty self-damaging manner for which they alone, and not society, should bear the costs, and that sometimes individuals choose in a substantially voluntary way to pursue some end other than their own well-being and any resultant individual well-being deficit they suffer should not trigger further claims for compensation by society. This acceptance of personal responsibility is fully compatible with the rejection of a primary goods standard of interpersonal comparison. We might instead link personal responsibility to a utility-based approach by holding that distributive justice requires that individuals have a fair share of opportunity for utility (well-being) over the course of their lives.

To a first approximation, one has an opportunity for a good provided that if one chooses the good, one obtains it. To develop this sketch of a principle into a workable principle, one would have to specify under what circumstances one enjoys a fair share of opportunities. One factor here will be the cost of providing an opportunity to an individual that consists of lost opportunities for others. If the cost of providing me the opportunity for an apple is that ten people lose the opportunity for an orchard, the cost is probably too high. Another factor is that other things being equal, if one has little opportunity for utility as measured by the highest level of utility one can reach if one chooses prudently, then providing increments of opportunity to the person who is poor in opportunities is morally more valuable than providing the same-sized increments to those who are already rich in opportunities. A third factor is that the idea of fair shares should take into account provision over the course of an individual's life, not just the sum of opportunities at one moment or from now on. If I squandered my opportunities when I was young, there may be nothing unfair in the circumstance that my opportunities now that I am old are small compared to those of people who husbanded their opportunities wisely. A fourth factor is that one may forfeit one's claim to opportunities in whole or in part by morally wrongful action and especially by illegal acts chosen so that one is responsible for them.

Another factor is that one may have an opportunity for a benefit in the sense that if one chooses it, one gets it, yet one may fail to choose it either because one has substandard choosing ability or because one fails to exercise such ability as one has through no fault of one's own. As an example of a nonculpable failure to exercise, suppose that you and I both have the ability to choose prudently with respect to personal savings and investment decisions but that exercising this ability is fun for you and excruciatingly painful for me. For this reason, opportunity as defined previously is not quite the notion we need to specify a fair opportunity for utility principle. The relevant issue is what level of utility one would reach if one did as well as could reasonably be expected, given one's choice-making deficiencies.

An opportunity for a utility standard evidently differs in theory and in practice from a primary goods standard. Two individuals may have different abilities, given by nature or nurture, for transforming primary goods into utility. With the identical allotment of primary goods, the two individuals will have very different opportunities for utility. One is legless, the other has two good legs; one suffers from chronic severe headaches, one does not. Also, individuals may have different abilities to perceive the good and to select genuinely worthwhile final ends. Again, with the same bundles of primary goods, two individuals with different value-setting and choice-making abilities will have very different life prospects. Moreover, all of these differences that influence people's capacities to transform resources into utility can occur through no fault of the individuals who end up disadvantaged in these respects. To reiterate the main point: Acceptance of appropriate norms of personal responsibility does not per se supply any reasons for rejecting a utility-based standard of interpersonal comparison, qualified by personal responsibility, in favor of a resource-oriented conception such as a primary goods standard.

My defense of utility as a standard of interpersonal comparison for the theory of justice has not so far addressed the question of how to defend a particular standard of utility or human well-being—one that is selected nonarbitrarily from rivals, enables one to make the cardinal interpersonal comparisons that principles of justice in the utilitarian family will require, and coheres with our considered judgments in reflective equilibrium. My own belief is that the best conception of utility will not identify it with fulfillment of the individual's actual preferences, aims, or plan of life. These subjective attitudes and ends can fail to track what is truly valuable, so an objective ideal of utility is needed (whether this would turn out to be a rational preference satisfaction theory or an "objective list" theory or something else is a task for another occasion).

The defender of a Rawlsian primary goods standard might interject a skeptical response at this point: The utility-based conceptions of justice are nonstarters because no satisfactory standard of interpersonal comparison for the purpose can be developed. In *A Theory of Justice,* Rawls does not emphasize the difficulties about interpersonal comparison and indicates that the superiority of justice as fairness lies along some other dimension. The interpersonal comparison problem is no doubt significant, though in my judgment, it is not insoluble. Here I wish to make a more limited point: Rawls has his own unsolved difficulties with interpersonal comparison, so living in a glass house, he is poorly placed to be throwing stones at utilitarian windows.

According to Rawls, there are several primary social goods. Some of these qualify as basic liberties and are thus treated within the equal liberty principle, which is accorded strict priority within Rawls's system. But this leaves several primary goods other than basic liberties, and in order to apply the difference principle, which requires that the expectations of these primary goods be maximized for the worst-off class of persons, we need an index of these goods, a way of determining, for any disparate bundles of these goods, which contain more primary goods overall. If one bundle containing various amounts of various primary goods can be matched with another bundle that contains more of each of these distinct primary goods, then the second bundle dominates the first and unambiguously contains more primary goods overall. But for the many cases in which dominance does not hold, we need an index.

I do not see how an individual's bundle of primary goods can be assessed except in terms of the extent to which those goods enable the individual to satisfy her preferences, or to fulfill some given objective conception of the good, and neither of these ways of assessment provides a measure that is consistent with Rawls's strategy of argument and core assumptions.

To my knowledge, the only serious discussion of the index problem for primary goods is in John Roemer's *Theories of Distributive Justice*.[3] In that work, Roemer asserts that the index problem admits of a solution, but his proposed solution compromises Rawls's avoidance of utility-based measures and causes Rawls's principles to unravel, so this is not a friendly construal of Rawls that could be used to defend his position against a utilitarian critic. Without pressing this issue further, at the very least there is a problem here that the defender of a primary goods standard would need to solve, and has not solved to date, if the primary goods approach to justice comparison issues is to be a viable position.

4. Maximin Not Maximize

Rawls's general conception of justice holds that the basic structure of society should be arranged so as to maximize the long-run expectation of primary goods for the group of members of society that is worst-off in this respect. As noted earlier, one important aspect of this principle is its use of primary social goods rather than utility to measure the condition of individuals for purposes of social justice. Another crucial aspect of the doctrine is the imperative to maximin, to make the worst position in society as tolerable as possible.

A straight maximizing doctrine such as utilitarianism that bids us to arrange society so as to maximize the aggregate sum of benefits enjoyed by persons yields different implications than a maximin principle in situations in which the latter's strong tilt in favor of the worst-off looks attractive. We can imagine a world in which utilitarianism would require taking away large and important benefits from a small number of the very worst-off, driving them to the wall as it were, in order to yield trivial benefits for a very large number of persons who are already enjoying an extremely high level of benefits. We are asked to take the corn from the serfs to add one more layer of frosting to the desserts of the very rich. Here a revulsion against maximizing the aggregate sum of benefits is reasonable.

But there are cases and cases. A maximin principle is entirely insensitive to the numbers of the worst-off who gain or lose, by comparison with the numbers of the other members of society who might be asked to sacrifice for the benefit of the worst-off. Maximin is also utterly insensitive to the amount of benefit that is gained or lost by the worst-off, by comparison with the amount that others stand to lose. This means that maximin would prefer the outcome in which a single worst-off person gains a penny's worth of benefit at the cost of the loss of thousands of dollars for each of thousands of the better-off. A maximin rule introduces a strict lexical priority for the interests of the worst-off, however slight, when they conflict with the interests, however great, of the next worst-off. Lexical priority relations among moral values are strong medicine and perhaps are very rarely, if ever, justifiable. They are especially difficult to justify if the value given lexically lower priority really has value at all. In the context of the distribution of social benefits as assessed by social justice principles, lexical priority for the worst-off is implausibly extreme.

Rawls has an interesting response to this obvious objection. He asserts that maximin is not a good choice rule in general but makes sense in the special context of choice of principles regulating the basic terms of social cooperation. And it makes sense despite yielding implausible implications in some possible cases because these implausible cases are never actually confronted in this-worldly distributive justice conflicts. The scenario in which we can gain a penny for a single worst-off person at the cost of huge losses for huge numbers of the already better-off individuals is simply unrealistic. Hence, maximin is acceptable as a this-worldly principle of social justice, even if it is not acceptable as a moral principle to govern all possible worlds.[4]

This conclusion invites two further objections. First, it is simply untrue that plausible this-worldly scenarios cannot be imagined in which we could face a choice of very small gains for the worst-off at the cost of very large losses for the better-off. Consider public education policy viewed as a mechanism for enhancing the job and income prospects of low-skilled persons. We could spend more money on the least skilled and less on the more skilled, and we could continue doing this even if the further gains from further educational resources deployed on the least skilled produced marginal increments in the labor market and entrepreneurial market prospects of this disadvantaged group. The least natively skilled, in the absence of special education, may well be poor transformers of educational resources into enhanced skill levels, and even if there is a range within which extra education for the worst-off produces significant gains, maximin requires us to keep transferring resources to the worst-off until further expenditures produce no extra gains at all. At this point, the curve that plots expenditures versus benefits in terms of enhanced skills might be unfavorably steep. I do not believe that maximin provides a plausible guide to an egalitarian, socially progressive public education norm.

One might object that at some point, rather than moving more educational resources to the education of the worst-off we should instead expand the education of the talented, who will then move into productive slots in the economy, and the extra productivity their extra education generates can be partly captured for the worst-off in the form of a tax and transfer policy. But first of all, this depends on the trade-off in an index of primary goods between the good of extra income and the good of enhanced chances of getting hired at better jobs. The latter good is gained by increased education but not by a tax and transfer policy.

More fundamentally, a tax and transfer policy that gives lexical priority to producing gains for the worst-off can itself, if pushed to the limit as the principle requires it must be, eventually be generating very tiny gains for the worst-off that are secured by very large losses suffered by the better-off.

Rawls's criticism of utilitarianism commits him to a standard of adequacy for proposed moral principles that the maximin principle, given his own account of its merits, cannot meet. Recall that Rawls has objected that even if it turns out that utilitarianism in the actual circumstances we face or are likely to face would imply policies of respect for individual rights that we find acceptable, utilitarianism would still be delivering the right answers for the wrong reasons. The utilitarian defense of rights such as the right to freedom of speech does not fit the actual reasons that, on reflection, we take to be the reasons that underlie our affirmation of such rights. The test of adequacy that utilitarianism cannot meet is agreement with our considered moral convictions, including among those convictions our reasons for believing why the policies we support for actual circumstances are right. To put the point another way, utilitarianism as applied to issues of individual rights fails a test of counterfactual stability: Even if utilitarianism delivers plausible answers in actual and likely circumstances, we can imagine possible, even if improbable, circumstances in which we would continue to find that our reasons for supporting free speech are fully in play even though utilitarianism would recommend the suppression of free speech.

By the same token, the maximin principle is unacceptable as a principle of justice if it yields implications for policy in many possible situations that we would, on reflection, judge to be unjustifiable even if it yields policy judgments we mostly agree with in actual and likely circumstances. Here the critique of utilitarianism comes to haunt Rawls. The weapons he turns against utilitarianism, to some degree successfully, can be deployed with success against the maximin principle and perhaps other principles he favors.

5. The General and the Special Conception

At this point it will be helpful to introduce a distinction that Rawls draws between the general and the special conception of justice. The general conception is supposed to hold true throughout human history. It specifies that institutions are just when over the long term the primary social goods holdings that accrue to the worst-off social group are as great as possible. The special conception of justice is intended to apply only to modern societies that are sufficiently wealthy so that it is possible for all citizens to exercise the basic liberties. The special conception asserts that (1) "each person has an equal claim to a fully adequate scheme of equal basic rights and liberties" and (2) "social and economic inequalities are to satisfy two conditions: first, they are to be attached to positions and offices open to all under conditions of fair equality of opportunity; second, they are to be to the greatest benefit of the least advantaged members of society" (*PL,* 6).

The "basic liberties" of the "equal liberty principle" consist of a list of civil liberties such as the right to vote and stand for office in free elections and the right to freedom of speech and assembly. Fair equality of opportunity requires that institutions be arranged so that any two persons in society with the same native talent and the same ambition should have the same prospects for success in competitions that confer above-average levels of primary social goods other than basic liberties. The second part of the second principle is known as the difference principle. Rawls specifies that the equal liberty principle has strict lexical priority over the second principle and the equal opportunity clause of the second principle has strict lexical priority over the difference principle. One principle has strict lexical priority over another when one must bring about satisfaction of the first to the greatest possible extent and devote resources to implementing the second principle only insofar as doing so does not lessen at all the extent to which the first principle is satisfied.

One might view these principles as implicit in the public culture of modern democratic societies, where maintaining equal civil liberties is commonly regarded as especially important and deserving special priority. We should not be willing to trade civil liberties for increased economic wealth, for example. Rawls presses this intuition to its logical limit by assigning strict lexical priority to the equal liberty principle. Another firm conviction in modern diverse democracies is that all citizens, regardless of their race, creed, or sex or similar differences, are entitled to equal protection of the laws. Again, Rawls presses this antidiscrimination norm to the limit by asserting fair equality of opportunity, the requirement that nothing but native talent and individual ambition should affect one's success in competition for social positions that confer special advantages. Another, perhaps less widely held, conviction is that society should take steps to offset the outcomes of competitive markets to ensure decent life prospects for all members of society, even the least talented. Rawls again presses this help-the-needy intuition to the limit by proposing that institutions should be set so that the group that is worst-off by the measure of primary goods holdings is made as well-off as possible.

If one shares these core social democratic convictions, one might object that Rawls carries them too far or ignores other values that should have countervailing weight in policy choice, but one cannot object that Rawls is halfhearted in his embrace of them or tepid in his espousal. He requires that these democratic egalitarian values, properly ordered, be implemented to the greatest possible extent.

This characterization invites an objection. Strict lexical priority relations are supposed to govern the elements in Rawls's system, so that concern for equal basic liberties trumps concern for all else, concern for fair equality of opportunity trumps the difference principle, and according to the latter principle, achieving a benefit no matter how tiny for the worst-off trumps the achievement no matter how large for any other group. All of these lexical priority relations turn out to be implausible when one contemplates them. I have already remarked on the implausibility of the maximin idea that the difference principle expresses. To take another example, we would not judge a society that did worse than another on the score of basic liberties even by a very slight amount to be necessarily less just overall than a society that does slightly better with respect to civil liberties no matter how dreadful its comparative record with respect to other justice values. But the lexical ordering of Rawls's principles of justice with the equal basic liberty principle in first place enforces the contrary judgment.

It is not clear how seriously Rawls expects us to take his stipulated lexical priorities. He offers the idea in a tentative and provisional spirit (*TJ*, 45), but he is led to a tentative assertion of lexically ordered principles because he believes that a fully successful rival to a utilitarian theory of justice must be a genuine theory in the sense of a set of principles that, by themselves, determine what should be done without the need for further ad hoc moral judgment, given any specification of the factual circumstances in which the principles are to be applied. Mill, in his essay on *Utilitarianism,* had asserted this completeness requirement as a condition of adequacy for a candidate moral theory. Mill believed that utilitarianism satisfied this adequacy condition and that this fact gave the utilitarian doctrine a leg up on its competitors.[5] One might then hold that if Rawls's lexical priority relations are deemed unacceptable, then his justice as fairness conception minus the lexical priorities does not constitute a genuine theory of justice and cannot, then, win the competition against utilitarianism. After all, it is said that you cannot beat a theory except with another theory.

This point does not seriously undercut Rawls's criticisms of utilitarianism. If Rawlsian arguments convince us that utilitarianism cannot do justice to our considered moral judgments after reflection, then even if we are unsure exactly what principles should be substituted for utilitarianism, this uncertainty does not weaken the force of the negative case against that doctrine. The position thus reached will be unstable pending the elaboration of a set of principles that match our considered judgments, and the possibility remains that if no such superior set of principles is ever forthcoming, our initial confidence that the negative case against utilitarianism is compelling might have to be revisited. But we can know that a doctrine must be wrong without yet perceiving a replacement doctrine that is correct.

6. Original Position Arguments

The critique of utilitarianism and the defense of the conception of justice Rawls calls "justice as fairness" are developed on two separate fronts. On the one side, Rawls presents considerations that show the intuitive plausibility of the principles he favors over the utilitarian rival he rejects. The principles of justice are presented as plausible in themselves and as recommending policies that, after reflection, we will come to embrace. On another front, Rawls argues that his favored principles of justice would be chosen over alternatives that prominently include utilitarianism in a special choice situation that is supposed to collect and express our judgments about fair procedures for choosing moral principles. This is the celebrated and vexed original position argument.

The core idea of the original position is that parties choosing principles which are then imagined to regulate the society they will inhabit, and choosing on a basis of self-interest in ignorance of all particular facts about themselves (they are stipulated to know only general facts about the world given by physical and social science), would choose Rawlsian principles of justice. Rawls mainly argues that the parties in his original position would choose his favored principles rather than a version of utilitarianism that calls for maximizing the average level of utility in society over the long run. The original position in Rawls's hands is a complex construction. To some extent it is designed with a view to producing as output principles we find intuitively plausible, and to this extent the device showcases conclusions already reached and does not involve independent argument for those conclusions. But to some extent Rawls believes that the choice situation he constructs collects intuitions about fair procedures for choice of principles and fair procedures for securing agreement that have a justifying force independent of our preexisting moral judgments about the principles that might emerge as the outcome of the procedure.

Here I want to register dissent. I do not believe that we have any moral intuitions about fair procedures at the level of abstraction at which Rawls is working. We do not have any ideas about fair procedures for choosing moral principles. The best procedure is whatever is most likely to lead to the choice of principles that make sense. Rawls suggests that it is appropriate to place the agents in the original position under a thick veil of ignorance, which deprives them of information that might be used to bias the choice of principles. But this claim gets things back to front. Since we have antecedent strong opinions that moral principles should not favor individuals of any particular sex, race, or religion, we do not want the original position structured in such a way as to render it likely that principles expressing bias of this sort would be chosen. Any weak views we might have about how the artificial choice situation of the original position should be designed are entirely determined by strong preexisting views about the appropriate content of the principles to be chosen. I would say that, in general, our notions of fair procedures are subordinate to our convictions about the outcomes that we think it fair for the procedures to reach—fair procedures in general are those most likely reliably to lead to outcomes that are fair. Whether this is correct or incorrect, it seems hard to deny that we do not have intuitions about procedural fairness when the procedure we are talking about is supposed to be picking fundamental moral principles to serve as a standard of social justice.

Despite my skepticism about the original position project, it is worthwhile looking briefly at the arguments Rawls deploys there against utilitarianism, for they may shed light on the character of his opposition to utilitarianism and help us decide to what extent Rawls's criticisms of that doctrine suffice to exhibit his favored principles as morally compelling. Rawls stipulates that the parties in the original position, knowing no particular facts about themselves, including their desires and aims, are motivated to gain primary social goods for themselves. So the issue that is salient in the original position is not primary social goods versus utility but, rather, maximin versus maximize. If the parties prefer more primary social goods to fewer, and know that once the veil of ignorance is lifted they could be anyone in society in any social position, one might suppose they would choose a principle that bids society to maximize the level of primary social goods per person over the long run. Maximizing the average level would be the best one could do to maximize one's own individual level if one were entirely ignorant of the person one might turn out to be in the society to be regulated by the principles one is choosing. This line of argument for maximizing the average is what Rawls sets himself to rebut.

At this point we might stand back and ask what power this derivation of maximizing-the-average would have to justify a view such as average utilitarianism in the face of objections that maximizing the sum of benefits ignores our moral concern for fair distribution of benefits. Suppose it were the case, contrary to Rawls's intention, that the original position he designed relentlessly yielded the conclusion that the parties would pick a principle of maximizing-the-average. What then? I would say this result would have no justifying power whatsoever against the initial pre-original-position claim that a single-minded focus on the average benefit level incorrectly leaves out of account the genuine moral significance of fair distribution. These intuitions about fair distribution (just by themselves) would lead us to embrace some distribution-sensitive welfarist consequentialism rather than the average utilitarian variant of welfarism. Being told that self-interested parties choosing under extreme ignorance would pay no heed to issues of fair distribution and would choose a principle of maximizing-the-average to regulate a society they would inhabit should not cause us to doubt our beliefs in the significance of fair distribution for a moment. After all, the parties in the original position are given no concerns that would make them pay heed to fair distribution. Their ignorance is not ours.

If, despite these objections, we proceed further into the original position labyrinth, we find that Rawls is concerned to remove the air of implausibility that attaches to the lexical priority aspect of the maximin principle. This principle asserts that we should at all costs bring about the best possible outcome for the very worst-off. As we have already indicated, and as Rawls is fully aware, this means that we should prefer to gain an extra penny for the worst-off rather than gain instead any amount of benefit, however large, for any number of better-off persons. Rawls says that maximin is not in general an acceptable principle of rational choice but becomes that when three conditions are met, and these three conditions are satisfied to a high degree in the special circumstances of the original position. The conditions are, one, knowledge of probabilities is unavailable, so one cannot estimate the chances of ending up in the worst-off position or any other; two, "the person choosing has a conception of the good such that he cares very little, if anything, for what he might gain above the minimum stipend that he can, in fact, be sure of by following the maximin rule" (*TJ*, 154); and three, the principles competing with maximin may produce outcomes that one finds unacceptable.

The second condition seems straightforwardly not to obtain in the original position if the general facts about nature and society to which the parties have access include facts about the normal range of human motivation. In fact, humans in their everyday behavior are not extremely risk averse but normally make such choices as, for example, to drive across town, risking slightly a violent death in a car accident, in order to get a fancy loaf of bread when one could have obtained less fancy bread, with no such risk of death, at a store near one's house. People generally care a lot about being able to obtain ambitious life goals that require large amounts of resources to fulfill. There is an unclarity here, because in the original position, not knowing what society one belongs to or the level of economic development of that society, one cannot estimate what level of primary goods the adoption of the maximin rule would guarantee in the actual society one would inhabit. But even if we assume that the level of economic development and wealth is high, the point remains that humans as we know them do attach considerable value to obtaining very large holdings of resources that are far above what maximin could be thought likely to guarantee.

The third point taken by itself does not seem to motivate choice of maximin but, rather, something like a disaster avoidance principle that would have society organize itself so as to get as large a proportion of its population as possible over some threshold level of resource provision deemed necessary for a decent existence. This disaster avoidance rule would require transferring resources from worse-off groups in society to the best-off, when only the best-off can be raised over the threshold of minimal decency. Whatever the attraction or lack of attraction of such a principle, it is not to be confused with maximin.

The first point, the unavailability of information about the probability that one will end up in one or another social position, is simply stipulated to hold in the original position. We must then ask what the justification is for that stipulation. Suppose that the choice of maximizing-the-average benefit level in certain circumstances might entail a social order in which a tiny number of people lead lives of excruciating misery. If in the original position we knew that the chances of becoming one of these unfortunates was extremely small, we might find the prospect of ending up in a better social position sufficiently attractive to render choice of the average rule a good bet despite the possibility of a disastrous outcome for oneself. Ruling out probability information in the original position rules out this sort of reasoning.

If one had an antecedent conviction that making the condition of the least advantaged person in society as advantageous as possible was the paramount consideration for social justice, and that no amount of benefit, however large, to any number of other people, however huge, could overbalance this consideration, we could justify the Rawlsian stipulation regarding lack of information about probabilities. But so understood, the acceptability of excluding such probability information assumes a prior conviction of the moral correctness of the maximin rule as a principle of social justice, and so does not offer independent support for maximin. By the same token, our antecedent conviction that maximin is an extreme rule that does not permit balancing and trade-offs of benefits and losses among worse-off and better-off within a distribution-sensitive scheme that we, on reflection, would endorse is not impugned in the slightest by the abstract reasoning of the parties in the hypothetical original position as designed by Rawls.

7. Political Liberalism

Beginning about 1985, Rawls reconceives the project of constructing a theory of justice.[6] He tells his readers that his starting point is a recognition that his theory as originally presented fails to solve the problem of stability. The problem emerges if we imagine that the institutions of a society are made to conform fully to Rawlsian principles of justice. Now Rawls notes the fact of pluralism, that in the absence of unjustifiable state tyranny, reasonable citizens of a society under modern conditions will continue to embrace different and opposed general and comprehensive ethical doctrines. This pluralism is a permanent feature of modern society, not a temporary phenomenon. An ethical doctrine is fully comprehensive when it embraces all values and virtues and general when it applies to a wide range of subjects. Many religions aspire to be general and comprehensive, as does the utilitarian moral philosophy. Given pluralism, the citizens of a society that fully implements Rawlsian justice would not tend over time to accept its justification, Rawls's partially comprehensive theory of justice. This means that an ideal of legitimacy is violated that holds that the uses of state coercion in a community should be in accordance with moral principles that each member of the community, if she were reasonable, would accept. A satisfactory theory of justice fulfills legitimacy, so Rawls concludes that his doctrine of justice as fairness is unsatisfactory and stands in need of revision.

At this point it might seem that Rawls has painted himself into a corner. If the conditions of modern society, absent unjust tyranny, spawn continuous and unending reasonable disagreement about morals, and if an adequate theory of justice must be capable of being implemented so as to attract unanimous assent from all reasonable persons affected by it, then it looks as though an adequate theory of justice is impossible. Rawls has an ingenious solution. What is needed is a political conception of justice that does not aim to be a comprehensive doctrine of any sort but, rather, a doctrine of fair terms of cooperation to regulate major social institutions that is designed to bypass intractable ethical, religious, and philosophical controversies. A political conception of justice suitable for a constitutional democracy with stable pluralism of belief among its citizens seeks to define fair terms of cooperation for the circumstances we face, including the fact of pluralism itself. A successful political conception will be one that can attract an overlapping consensus of the reasonable comprehensive views held by the members of the society. In this scenario, all reasonable citizens agree to the basic terms of social cooperation, though they do so from different and opposed moral standpoints.

That an overlapping consensus of this sort is possible for us, Rawls holds, reflects favorable contingencies. The history of constitutional democracy shows that its basic features can attract wide support. A political conception of justice draws upon commonsense ideals that are latent in the public culture of constitutional democracy and develops those ideals into a system that can order and guide our judgments and be acceptable to all after due reflection.

By a happy coincidence, according to Rawls, it turns out that the conception of justice espoused in *A Theory of Justice,* though not designed to be a political conception of justice that can become the focus of an overlapping consensus, is in fact suitable to this role. In justice as fairness, a solution to the problem of devising fair terms of cooperation is solved by representing persons as fair and equal and determining what such persons would choose as fair terms of cooperation in an original position. *Political Liberalism* adds a twist to this account. The ideal of a free and equal, rational and reasonable person is now to be embraced by persons as a political ideal, a way they wish to be conceived for the purposes of settling basic rights in a diverse democracy. It is supposed to be fully compatible with embracing this Kantian ideal of the person as a political ideal that in private life one regards oneself quite differently. As a private member of society, I may regard myself as forming my beliefs by deferring to religious authority and unable to imagine myself as renouncing my core beliefs. This is compatible with also holding that as a citizen, I regard myself as free to choose new beliefs and values, and I hold that if I were to renounce my present faith, my rights and responsibilities set by social justice norms should remain the same.

Rawls has an attractive answer to the concern that in a society divided by permanent disagreement about what ultimately matters, purported norms of justice will express the values of the citizens who happen to gain political power and will amount to an imposition of some people's values on others who reject them. A related concern is that only a skeptic can be a liberal with respect to issues of toleration. Someone who really believes that salvation is all-important and can be gained only through his church, or that saving the planet for the benefit of all beings who inhabit it is an absolute duty and requires an ascetic lifestyle, cannot without hypocrisy assent to a political regime in which people are free to behave in ways that promote damnation or planetary ruin. The answers to both concerns proceed from acceptance of a legitimacy ideal. In politics, the legitimacy ideal requires that the coercive use of state power should not be deployed on individuals on the basis of moral principles that they reasonably reject. In the conduct of life, the legitimacy ideal requires that one act toward others only on the basis of moral principles they cannot reasonably reject. The legitimacy ideal can be regarded as an expression of a Kantian norm of respect for persons.

An argument against basing public policy of a diverse society on utilitarianism or any principle in the family of utilitarian views waits just around the corner. Like any comprehensive moral or religious doctrine, utilitarianism will inevitably be controversial. Many persons will reasonably reject it. Hence, any attempt to advance utilitarianism as a political conception of justice would be sectarian; it would amount to imposing a set of ultimate values on people who reasonably reject it. Basing state policy on utilitarianism or entrenching utilitarianism into the constitution of a democratic society as the foundational value would be akin to establishment of religion. No more than Buddhism, Roman Catholicism, or any other comprehensive doctrine should utilitarianism be advanced for the role of political conception of justice.

One signal that something is amiss in the overlapping consensus story that Rawls tells is his account of the problem of stability. He envisages moral argument aimed at finding the best account of social justice that is responsive to the problem of arriving at fair terms of cooperation among persons with diverse beliefs. The next stage of the argument is to try to determine as best we can whether this candidate conception of justice could be implemented in a modern society so as to attract, over time, the unanimous or nearly unanimous agreement of reasonable members of society living under this regime. This is the legitimacy ideal. If it cannot be met, this shows the candidate conception of justice is unsatisfactory and must be rethought. A satisfactory political conception of justice must be capable of becoming the focus of an overlapping consensus including all of the reasonable comprehensive doctrines with adherents in the society.

One might suppose that if the candidate conception by assumption is the one that after full critical reflection is best supported by moral reasons, then reasonable members of society must support it. If they did not, they would show themselves to be unreasonable after all. So it is hard to see how stage two of Rawls's argument, addressing the supposed problem of stability, can be other than irrelevant.

It turns out that "the best reasons" that hold sway at stage one of the argument need not be the same "best reasons" that hold sway at stage two. For one thing, the overlapping consensus that Rawls deems necessary is intended to sweep broadly and include the major traditions of ethical thought that attract allegiance in modern democracies. To this end, the notion of the "reasonable" pitches its requirements at a modest level. A reasonable individual in this modest sense has a disposition to justice, an effective desire to cooperate with others on fair terms acceptable to all. The reasonable individual is specified as also having the capacity to form and act on a conception of the good. The reasonable individual is further specified as one who accepts the fact that fully reasonable people (reasonable by this same conception) may fail to agree on substantive moral principles, given what Rawls calls "the burdens of judgment" (factors that may lead individuals to hold stable conflicting views but that do not tend to impugn the rationality of any of the parties to these disagreements). Rawls finally stipulates that if a reasonable person embraces a comprehensive doctrine, this will be a reasonable doctrine, that is, "one that covers the major religious, philosophical, and moral aspects of human life in a more or less consistent and coherent manner" (*PL*, 59).

By now it should be evident that the *Political Liberalism* argument misfires. To recapitulate: It is proposed that a legitimate government is one that acts only on the basis of principles that all reasonable citizens accept. A legitimate government cannot, then, be one that imposes a state religion on all citizens even though some citizens reasonably reject the state religion. But any government that affirms any comprehensive moral doctrine as the basis of its policies cannot be legitimate, because some reasonable citizens will reject any comprehensive doctrine such as utilitarianism. Add to this the premise that no society can be just whose government is illegitimate, and we have a quick argument to the effect that the norm that forbids liberal governments from enforcing a state religion equally forbids the enforcement of any secular comprehensive moral doctrine such as utilitarianism. If advanced as a fundamental principle of justice, utilitarianism is irredeemably sectarian. Call this "the argument from legitimacy."

This argument ushers utilitarianism out the front door but allows entry at the back door. Even if the argument from legitimacy were sound, all that it would rule out would be the adoption of the comprehensive moral doctrine of utilitarianism as the fundamental principle of justice. But for all that has been said so far, we could propose a simple noncomprehensive version of utilitarianism as a candidate political conception of justice. We might assert that given the intractability of disagreement about morals, a society can do no better than to adopt policies that count welfare improvements to any citizen as equally valuable and strive to maximize the sum of the welfare of all citizens. I doubt that this repackaging of utilitarianism as a stripped-down political conception of justice would succeed, so I shall not follow this line further. Since Rawls has set the requirements for qualifying as "reasonable" very low, the constraint that a legitimate social order must be acceptable to all reasonable persons becomes correspondingly constraining, to the point that one wonders whether any very substantive morality—utilitarianism or any other—could satisfy the constraint. It surely becomes immediately a doubtful proposition that Rawls's justice as fairness could pass this demanding legitimacy test.

More important is this: Rawls deliberately sets the requirement of "reasonable" at a low level, so that one can be fully reasonable in Rawls's sense when embracing moral doctrines on the basis of errors in reasoning or other cognitive failures. But, then, acceptance of the legitimacy ideal carries a moral cost. There are the fully reasonable doctrines that would be embraced as acceptable options by persons after ideal critical deliberation while making no cognitive errors. There is the different set of moral doctrines that would be embraced by all persons in a society who are "reasonable" in the special undemanding Rawlsian sense. But why is it morally better for society to be governed by the latter moral views of justice rather than the former? The views of justice acceptable to all, reasonable and unreasonable, are likely to be thin gruel. At least there are aspects of justice that would be affirmed by all fully reasonable persons that would be rejected by some Rawlsian-reasonable persons. We can choose between achieving legitimacy to a greater degree or justice to a greater degree. I see no reason not to opt unequivocally for justice given the way that the legitimacy ideal has been constructed.

If there are competing visions of social justice in a society, and if one assumes that any one can be fully implemented, it is morally better that the one be implemented that is superior as a theory of justice, best supported by the balance of moral reasons all things considered. If more than one conception ties for best, then one of the best conceptions should be implemented.

The idea that the same principle of state legitimacy that rules out the imposition of an established religion also rules out the organization of society according to a secular moral doctrine such as utilitarianism turns out to be a nonstarter. The legitimacy ideal should be rejected because it is warped by the Rawlsian insistence on a least-common-denominator notion of what qualifies a person as "reasonable" for purposes of deciding when one's nonacceptance of a proposed norm of social justice is reasonable or not.

This leaves us back where we started before the introduction of the special arguments of *Political Liberalism.* Nothing of what I have said in this connection undermines the sound criticism of utilitarianism that we have discovered in Rawls's earlier writings, but the issue remains what theory of justice is best supported by the balance of moral reasons, rather than what theory of justice could command unanimous assent among well-meaning but variously reasonable and confused and ignorant members of society.

8. The Epistemic Asymmetry between the Good and the Right

A deep feature of Rawls's views that shapes his thoroughgoing rejection of utilitarianism is his conviction that "principles of justice are objective and interpersonally recognizable in a way that conceptions of the good are not."[7] This conviction leads him to sweep aside not only utilitarianism but any view that takes the fundamental idea of justice to be achieving a fair distribution of opportunity for genuinely good, choice-worthy lives for people. In *Political Liberalism,* the focus of Rawls's skepticism on this point shifts and targets comprehensive conceptions of morality rather than specifically conceptions of human good. But Rawls does believe that despite pluralism of belief about morals, we can, in the end, if we are reasonable, agree on what is fair but not on what is good and worthwhile in human life.

The method of reflective equilibrium that Rawls recommends for determining what ethical claims are acceptable does not suggest a reason for supposing that reasoned agreement about the good cannot form part of the moral consensus of a just society. Rawls in effect proposes a coherence test for the acceptability of ethical claims. The claims we should accept are those we are disposed to believe after thorough critical scrutiny of pertinent arguments with full information, and we can imagine an ideally extended version of this process and conceive of rational ethical claims as those we would affirm in ideal reflective equilibrium. No doubt we now are far from the position of ideal reflective equilibrium, so assertions about ethics must for now be tentative. But this is as true of our judgments about what is fair and just as of our judgments about what is good and choice worthy.

No doubt, also, if we glance around a modern democratic society we will notice all manner of disagreement about fundamental ethical matters. But this disagreement spans disagreement about what is fair as much as disagreement about what is good. Moreover, some of this disagreement about the right and the good alike is rooted in ignorance, prejudice, confused reasoning, and other forms of inattention to reasons and an incapacity to grasp them. The class of ethical claims that are in fact controverted is larger than the class of claims that are in fact controversial. To reiterate: In our present primitive state of development of ethical science, we have no reason to accept an epistemic asymmetry between the good and the right, much less to make such an assumed asymmetry a core doctrine of the theory of justice.

In passing, I should note that the idea that rational agents in communication with each other can end up in stable disagreement about what is true seems likely to prove incoherent under examination. If you believe that fish is good food and the difference principle is unfair and I believe initially that fish is not good food and the difference principle is fair, then when we share our reasons, the alternatives would seem to be that we rationally agree or we fail fully to appreciate the force of the reasons in play (we are not, then, fully rational agents). How could I continue to believe that my beliefs on the good and the right are uniquely correct in the face of your continued disbelief and my inability to articulate reasons that compel belief by both of us? If we say your experiences have led you to one conclusion and me to another, but we cannot extract any statable reasons from our experiences, how can I think my experience has epistemic significance? How can my experience rationalize my claims when I see that the epistemic situation is symmetric and that you can make a parallel claim? Although this issue needs more discussion, my sense is that I must retract my claim to knowledge in the face of your claim, and you must do the same. If you have reason to believe fish is good food and I have comparable reasons to affirm beef as choice worthy, the tentative conclusion should be that there are equally cogent considerations to find fish and beef choice worthy, so perhaps either is good.[8]

Rawls raises the question why it is that the free institutions of a liberal society lead to reasonable pluralism of belief as opposed to reasonable agreement in belief. In ethical matters and the conduct of life we experience pluralism, whereas, says Rawls, we find reasonable agreement in the domain of natural science.

This contrast between reasonable pluralism in ethics and reasonable agreement in science is ill-posed. Scientific agreement is agreement among a rather small cadre of trained experts. Within the general population of a modern democracy all manner of bizarre and superstitious and metaphysical beliefs about empirical matters flourish. Throughout most of human history even this agreement about broad theoretical empirical claims did not exist even among a small elite of trained experts. If a modern democracy bases its policies on scientific views about the causal structure of the world, society is not relying on an uncontroversial consensus but is imposing expert views on a largely unbelieving lay public. This practice does not violate the Kantian injunction against imposing on people on the basis of claims they could reasonably reject. It is not treating someone disrespectfully to treat him according to standards that he does not actually accept but would if he were fully rational. This holds true whether the standards in question are empirical or normative.

Rawls interprets the Kantian requirement concerning reasonable reject-ability in an overly strict way. He regards it as a necessary condition for an acceptable theory of justice that it should become the object of a consensus that includes all reasonable members of society. According to Rawls, the con-cept of a *reasonable person* that is appropriate for the theory of justice should aim to be inclusive. A reasonable person, according to Rawls, wants to coop-erate with others on fair terms and has a capacity for a conception of the good. But, then, a reasonable person's conception of the good can be based on confusions of reasoning or ignorance of fact. The reasonable person's con-ception of the good might be based on adding two plus two and getting the answer five.

My surmise about what has gone wrong here is that Rawls wants the idea of the reasonable person to be tightly linked to the doctrine of toleration. I'm skeptical about the link. I have little doubt that many religious doctrines, maybe most, perhaps all, attract adherents on unreasonable grounds and that significantly better grounds for the doctrines are not to be found. The reason for tolerating, say, fundamentalist Christian belief is that interference is likely to do more harm than good. This tends to be so, among other reasons, be-cause any popular sect's unreasonable doctrines tend to have few bad conse-quences in practice, since most religions, however unreasoned their basic te-nets, counsel prudence, not imprudence, in the affairs of life. One should also mention the general case for freedom of speech—that toleration even of manifestly unreasonable speech creates a freewheeling context of inquiry that is more favorable to social progress in the long run.

If the set of reasonable beliefs about the good is restricted, appropriately, to the beliefs that are well supported by reasons, the extent of intractable disagreement about the good lessens and the reasonable pluralism of belief that remains does not preclude the aspiration to construct a consensus on a substantial doctrine of the good that will partly determine the content of a reasonable doctrine of justice for modern democratic society.

9. Conclusion

This review of Rawls's critique of utilitarianism has reached a mixed verdict. Rawls's opposition to the idea that justice consists of maximizing aggregate human well-being is sound, but his rebound to the maximin ideal gives ex-cessive priority to gains for the very worst-off and does not allow for the incorporation of sensible ideas about personal responsibility into a distribu-tion-sensitive consequentialism. His suggestion that justice should be con-cerned with the distribution of resources, the primary social goods, rather than with utility (individual well-being) strikes me as incorrect. The themes

of pluralism and diversity of belief in modern democracies that have preoc-
cupied Rawls in his recent writings on justice do nothing to alter these ver-
dicts. The issue of how the theory of social justice should, as it were, split the
difference between John Stuart Mill and Immanuel Kant remains wide open.

Notes

1. John Rawls, *A Theory of Justice* (Cambridge, Mass.: Harvard University Press, 1971).
Further page references to this work are given in parentheses in the text.

2. John Rawls, *Political Liberalism,* pbk. ed. (New York: Columbia University Press,
1996). Further page references to this work are given in parentheses in the text.

3. John E. Roemer, *Theories of Distributive Justice* (Cambridge, Mass.: Harvard University
Press, 1996), 165–72 and the references there cited.

4. For interesting further defense of maximin, see Joshua Cohen, Democratic Equality,
Ethics 99, no. 4 (July 1989): 727–51.

5. John Stuart Mill, *Utilitarianism,* in *Collected Works,* vol. 10, ed. J. M. Robson (Toronto:
University of Toronto Press, 1969), 206–7. The work was originally published in 1861.

6. See John Rawls, Justice as Fairness: Political not Metaphysical, *Philosophy and Public
Affairs* 14, no. 3 (1985): 223–51.

7. Quoted from Thomas Nagel, Rawls on Justice, *Philosophical Review* 82, no. 2 (April
1973): 220–34; see 228.

8. See Charles Larmore, *The Morals of Modernity* (Cambridge: Cambridge University
Press, 1995), for an opposed view.

14

JUSTICE BEYOND DESIRES?

Christoph Fehige

Justice, some of us believe, is a matter of fulfilling people's desires. John Rawls disagrees. His justice deals in "primary goods", not in desire fulfillment. I propose to look at a handful of objections that Rawls raises against the desire-based view, and to ask whether they are sound. So we will witness *some* moves concerning *one* question of normative ethics, the question of "the currency of justice".

The chapter begins with thumbnail sketches of the two doctrines in question: of the desire-based view (also known as preference-justice or preferentialism) in section 1, and of Rawls's principles in section 2. Sections 3 to 7 present the controversy.

1. Preference-Justice

1.1 The Basic Idea

What ought to be the case is what people want to be the case, says preference-justice. Preference-justice is based on two claims. First, the good, the right, and the just are determined solely by what is good *for* people, by their benefit, happiness, interests, utility, or welfare. One world cannot be better than another without being better for somebody. This type of claim is known as welfarism. Second, the answer to the question what is good *for* a person must, in the end, reside in that person herself; it is a matter of her *own* preferences (desires, wants, wishes) and their satisfaction. The idea is that by giving her X we benefit her if, and only if, in some suitable subjective sense of these words, she "gets something out of it", and that desire fulfillment *is* the suitable sense.

From those two premises, preference-justice follows. For if the good is a matter of "good for", and "good for" a matter of preference satisfaction, then the good itself is a matter of preference satisfaction. In other words, preferentialism is welfarism coupled with a specific notion of welfare: welfare as preference satisfaction. In order for something to be good *for* Fritz, that something must correspond to a wish he has, has had, or will have; and in order to be good simpliciter, it must be related that way to *somebody*.

Views like preferentialism go back a long way. Recall Kant on what morality demands of each of us: other people's "ends", he says, "must [...] be also, as far as possible, *my* ends"[1]. Routes that lead, or have been thought to lead, into such doctrines depart from autonomy, universalizability and the Golden Rule, moral sentiments and intuitions, the meaning of the moral words, from sympathy, and from affinities between rationality and morals.

1.2 Some Clarifications

Obviously, not any old notion of preference will do. In order for it to bear the weight they put on its shoulders, preferentialists *craft* a notion of desire—with considerable care. Failure to take this into account can cause confusion, and can lead opponents of preferentialism to criticize and reject a straw man rather than the real thing. Let me mention four important features of the pertinent notions of desire and desire fulfillment, and avert some possible misunderstandings along the way.

Desire and pleasure. We stipulate, following Kant and others, that everybody wants, pro tanto, to spend the time he's conscious as pleasantly as possible. There are, I think, independent reasons to take the concepts of preference and pleasure to be linked in this way, but that is another issue. Suffice it to say that the stipulation saves the preferentialist from having to mention "pleasure and the absence of pain", which no doubt *are* a part of welfare, separately.[2] It makes sure that desire fulfillment includes that part—the hedonic part. Notice that nothing serious hinges on this stipulation; it is a trivial device to unify our terminology. We could as well do without it and say instead that both preferences and pleasure count.

With the stipulation in place, the fact that some states of affairs that we wished for end up disappointing us is no argument against preferentialism. Such a state of affairs, call it *p*, has satisfied one desire (the desire that *p*—if there really was such a desire, and not just a desire to get pleasure out of *p*), and in that respect it was good; but it has also frustrated another desire (the desire to spend one's conscious time pleasantly), and in that respect, the preferentialist agrees, it was bad. We can also see now why the preferentialist can do justice to the value of, say, pleasant surprises: by being pleasant, they answer a standing desire.

Implicit desires. That a person desires something is not supposed to imply that she desires it consciously; only that, *if* (under proper conditions) she fully represented it to herself, correctly and completely and vividly, she *would* desire it consciously.[3] In the sense indicated by this conditional there can be desires that are purely implicit.

We tie welfare and morality to implicit desires because, if we consulted just the explicit ones, we would run into problems. It is, for instance, not clear how many explicit desires we have at all: how often do we go to the trouble of fully representing something? Furthermore, which thoughts find their way into our consciousness is rather contingent; and those that do are often the petty ones, having to do with waiters, traffic lights, or phone numbers. A notion of welfare should not be at the mercy of trifles, with our deepest concerns playing second fiddle at most. The appeal to implicit preferences—to how we *would* feel about things *if* we thought about them—gets the priorities right.

Intrinsic desires. Words like "desire" or "prefer" are meant to refer, unless otherwise stated, to intrinsic preferences—that is to say, to preferences not for mere means to other ends. One effect of this is that we exclude desires that are derived from false beliefs. If a person desires, say, to fly to Alaska just because she wants to see pineapple plantations and believes she will find them there, then the Alaska desire, doxastically contaminated as it is, has no moral grip on us.

Frustration and satisfaction. If we say that a preference or desire is frustrated or satisfied or fulfilled, we do not imply that the preferrer's consciousness is affected thereby; only that what he has wished for is the case. Since one can desire states of affairs that have nothing to do with one's own consciousness, preferentialism differs markedly from hedonism. It does, for instance, respect death-bed promises. You do not just have obligations, as hedonists would have us think, to make the moribund feel good by making him believe that his desire will be fulfilled. You have obligations to fulfill his desires.

1.3 A Restatement

We have come to know the impetus of preferentialism (section 1.1) and begun to explain the relevant notion of preference (1.2). Let me end this sketch with a more orderly presentation of the doctrine.

Preference-justice, as has become clear by now, is not one particular, complete theory of justice; it is the doctrine that any such theory should satisfy certain conditions. More precisely, the preferentialist subscribes to three claims —or, since it might be wiser to define a position by family resemblance, to something very much like them. Here they are.

(1) Every preference counts. That is to say, given any preference, its satisfaction would, pro tanto, be a good thing. In William James's much-quoted words:

> "Take any demand, however slight, which any creature, however weak, may make. Ought it not, for its own sole sake, to be satisfied? If not, prove why not. The only possible kind of proof you could adduce would be the exhibition of another creature who should make a demand that ran the other way."

(2) Only preferences count. As William James continues, "The *only* possible reason there can be why any phenomenon ought to exist is that such a phenomenon actually is desired." It follows that, if we knew a world's fulfillment profile—i.e., if we had complete information as to who desires what and when and how strongly, and which of these desiderata come true—, then we would have all the facts we need in order to evaluate that world.[4]

(3) Push-pin can be as good as poetry.[5] This slogan is meant to say that, in themselves, differences in the objects of preference make no moral difference. Any two worlds whose fulfillment profiles differ just with respect to the desiderata are equally good.

Condition (3), also known as the "condition of neutrality", reflects an important aspect of the preferentialist's view that "good for" is concerned with a subjective magnitude. It is the preferredness that matters, and if it is only preferredness that bestows value on objects in the first place, then it doesn't matter whether these are poems or games of push-pin (or whatever else). That is part of the preferentialist's conception of equality: every preference is equal, and of tolerance: *chacun à sa façon.*

What about justice? We have to find the most adequate moral theory that entails claims (1) to (3) or something very similar. For any two fulfillment profiles, the theory will tell us which of the two is better than the other, or that the two of them are equally good. *Just* worlds are worlds with optimal fulfillment profiles; just societies are societies in just worlds; and, to anticipate a Rawlsian term, just "basic structures" of societies are the basic structures of just societies. Feasibility constraints, including those that arise from other people's denial of preferentialism,[6] are dealt with by applying the same chain of definitions to constrained feasible sets: just worlds, given what's feasible, are the worlds with the best fulfillment profiles *of all the feasible worlds*; and so on.

Our sketch doesn't, and for today's purposes shouldn't, state what ought to happen in the case of conflicting preferences. Should the strongest preferences win? Should we satisfy the preferences of those who, all in all, have less preference satisfaction than others? Are there such things as utility functions, and would an adequate principle of aggregation refer to them?

Various answers have been given within preference-based ethics.[7] Utilitarianism, which asks us to maximize the total amount of preference satisfaction, regardless of its distribution and with no special concern for those who are badly off, is just one of them. Yet the discussion tends to focus on the special case. The step from the rejection of utilitarianism to the rejection of preference-justice, or straight to the acceptance of Rawls-justice, is often hasty, to say the least. Whoever, following Rawls, "rejects the idea of comparing *and maximising* satisfaction in questions of justice"[8] will have to consider comparing without maximizing before he can close the file on comparing. And while objections to utilitarianism are understandable, it is much harder to see why an adequate morality should, or could, depart from preferentialism.

2. Rawls-Justice

Let us now turn to John Rawls's theory; I present the briefest of outlines here, and more as we go along. Rawls asks what it is for the " 'basic structure' of a modern constitutional democracy" to be just. By the "basic structure" he means "the way in which the major social institutions fit into one system. These institutions assign fundamental rights and duties, and by working together they influence the division of advantages which arise through social cooperation. "[9]

What does, for such a structure, the question of justice amount to? What is it we're after? A theory of justice, says Rawls, has the practical task of reconciling people whose values differ. However, trying to talk them out of their differences would be hopeless—a situation he calls "the fact of pluralism". We had better see whether people happen to share at least *some* values and whether these suffice for a consensus on how to run a society.[10]

Thus, Rawls turns to values that are already floating around in our political culture. These values, he suggests, can be expressed as follows: the basic structure of society is just if it is of a type that a certain kind of rational person would in a certain hypothetical choice situation opt for. The choice situation he employs for these purposes is the famous "original position". Prominent among its carefully designed features is a device with a significant preferentialist pedigree: the "veil of ignorance", i.e. the fact that there are many things the choosers don't know. Most notably, they don't know which role they themselves would have to play in the society governed by the principles they choose.[11]

Rawls then tries to show what type of basic structure would be chosen, and, thus, what type is just. The choosers, he says, would require that the basic structure conform—in other words, the basic structure is just if it conforms—to the following principles, with principle 1 taking priority over principle 2, and 2.a over 2.b:

"1. Each person has an equal right to a fully adequate scheme of equal basic rights and liberties which is compatible with a similar scheme for all.
2. Social and economic inequalities are to satisfy two conditions.
2.a They must be attached to offices and positions open to all under conditions of fair equality of opportunity; and
2.b they must be to the greatest benefit of the least advantaged members of society."[12]

As it stands, this criterion of justice doesn't tell us much, for at crucial points it employs *further* normative concepts. After all, every conception of justice will want to be "fair" and "adequate—the question is, What *is* fair and adequate? Fleshing out the principles, says Rawls,

"requires specifications [...] [that] assign weights to certain of the primary goods[,] and citizens' fair shares of these goods are specified by an index which uses these weights. The primary goods may be characterized under five headings as follows:

(a) First, the basic liberties as given by a list, for example: freedom of thought and liberty of conscience; freedom of association; and the freedom defined by the liberty and integrity of the person as well as by the rule of law; and finally the political liberties;

(b) Second, freedom of movement and choice of occupation against a background of diverse opportunities;

(c) Third, powers and prerogatives of offices and positions of responsibility, particularly those in the main political and economic institutions;

(d) Fourth, income and wealth;

(e) Finally, the social bases of self-respect."

Given Rawls's principles 1 and 2, and the priorities among and within them, every citizen will "have the same equal basic liberties and enjoy fair equality of opportunity"—see the items under (a) and (b), protected by principle 1. "The only permissible difference among citizens is their share of the primary goods in (c), (d) and (e)"—governed by principle 2. This is, as Rawls calls it, "justice as fairness".[13]

3. Preference Satisfaction: Too Hard to Specify, and Too Rarely Endorsed?

What reasons does Rawls adduce against preference-justice? We can skip all those objections that are clearly addressed to only some forms of it. To utilitarianism, for instance. It may well be that, unlike utilitarianism and some of its relatives, we should secure, if possible, a minimum level of well-being for everybody, give at least some weight to equality in the distribution, look after those who are worst off, or whatever. But, as noted towards the end of section 1.3, such anti-utilitarian requirements can be, and have been, met *within* preference-based ethics.

The discussion includes some objections, however, which, though put forward by Rawls on special occasions—say, when he criticizes utilitarianism, or a "principle of restricted utility", or the system of "equal proportionate satisfaction"[14]—, have, and may be suspected to be intended to have, a more general ring: the ring of anti-welfarism or anti-preferentialism. Where the general ring is sufficiently obvious, the arguments will simply be treated as general ones.

At times we shall travel within sight of roads that have been traveled before—by welfare-theorists and utilitarians over the ages, by critics of John Rawls's writings, and, most notably, by Richard Arneson, in his papers on primary goods, distributive subjectivism, and preference formation.

3.1 Definiteness

Rawls says, on various occasions, that he must introduce "primary goods" in order to have any chance of getting "a definite result" out of the "original position" at all.[15]

Two brief points at the outset. First, Rawls's remark assumes that *his* principles *are* blessed with the virtue of definiteness. This is a big assumption, and we will briefly return to it in section 3.2. Second: if Rawls's remark were true, we could ask whether it doesn't constitute an argument against the "original position" rather than for "primary goods". Rawls's "original position" is quite a baroque construction, with numerous premises, some of which are decidedly on the vague side. How plausible, and how "definite", is *it*? Has it not lost much of the clarity and intuitive appeal of its preferentialist ancestors?[16]

Be this as it may—*in* the "original position", what problem of definiteness would preferences raise? It is not a problem of definiteness that perhaps the parties just don't want preference satisfaction, or that Rawls has destined them to want other things along with it. (Though at least the latter *is* a problem; see below, section 4.3.) As Rawls seems to see it, the problem of definiteness, or one such problem, is rather that, even to the extent that the parties wanted preference satisfaction, they would just not know enough about the preferences—and preference changes and opportunities of preference changes and possibilities of preference satisfaction—that would come up.

But then why don't they choose a principle of desire fulfillment whose wording and acceptance do not presuppose any of this knowledge? They could rank the logically possible fulfillment profiles and opt for the principle that the best feasible profile ("best" according to the ranking) ought to be brought about. In order to make sure that their choice remains an impartial one, we would of course continue to require, with John Rawls, that they choose a principle that makes no mention of particular individuals, or that was in some other way insensitive to the distribution of identities.[17] And the principle could still characterize the "basic structure" of society: the basic structure ought to be of the type that makes sure, or has the best prospects of making sure, that the best feasible fulfillment profile is realized.

In fact, if the choosers are, as Rawls tells us, means-ends rational with respect to their later yet unknown purposes, a principle of this type is the obvious choice. Such a chooser will either believe an option to be, all things told, the best bet *in view of her future desires*, or she won't choose it. Therefore, *any* choice she makes—no matter how general the issue or how small her knowledge of facts, identities, and desires to come—will be based entirely on considerations of desire fulfillment, and can thus be expressed entirely in those terms.[18]

Perhaps Rawls takes preferentialist criteria to lack definiteness in that they are, in a certain sense, *conditional*. After all, there will be, if preferentialism is right, a great number of things that are forbidden as long as they have certain consequences, and permitted as long as they have certain others.

That, however, will hold for any sane conception of morality, including any sane conception of political morality. Pouring water out of your window is fine if nobody gets wet, and not so fine otherwise; driving fast, or a traffic code that permits people to drive fast, is fine if no-one gets hurt, and not so fine otherwise. Et cetera. Furthermore, there is not exactly a dearth of conditional structures in Rawls's own theory. His second principle of justice is explicitly conditional. And rights and liberties are implicitly conditional; to say that you have a right to something is roughly equivalent to saying: it ought to be the case that, *if* you want (or try) to have (or do or bring about) that something, then you can (or, at any rate, nobody will interfere). Similarly for liberties.[19] Conditionality, then, cannot be the problem.

If conditionality as such does not impugn definiteness, perhaps conditionality *on mental states* does? Probably not. First, because there is nothing particularly indefinite about, say, being in pain or desiring something. Second, conditionality upon mental states is again a feature of *every* sane conception of morality, preferentialist or not; for who wants to say that people's pleasure and pain and preferences do not count at all? Third, mental states are again something we find in Rawls-justice, too. Not only because rights and liberties in general imply an appeal to mental states (see previous paragraph), but also because, even if not all of them did, some of the items on Rawls's list certainly do: the liberty of conscience, for instance, and the integrity of the person. And in rare and memorable moments of Benthamism, Rawls is even prepared to consider freedom from pain as a candidate for a "primary good".[20] We may conclude that the reference to mental states, too, is not, at least cannot consistently be, the problem he is driving at.

Something else is enigmatic. There are several preferentialist theories that Rawls criticizes on moral grounds, pointing out in gruesome detail what he believes they would, in certain circumstances, require us to do: hold slaves, persecute minorities, give all our resources to a few enthusiastic astronomers, etc.[21] Surely the theories can't be that indefinite if they're definite enough for that.

Of course, there may be a usage in which the word "definite" *means* "not couched in terms of satisfied preferences". But if this is the usage, then the statement that we need "primary goods" in order to get a definite result just *means* that we need them in order to get away from preference talk. It doesn't mention a *reason* for getting away from preference talk.

3.2 Verification

Another problem with utility, says Rawls, is that we would "require a workable public interpersonal measure to identify it" and that

> " [t]he difficulties with [...] utility on this count are substantial. Uncertainty is likely to increase disputes and mistrust for much the same reason that unclear and ambiguous principles do [...]."

The point now is not that an orectic criterion, including any interpersonal comparisons it might require, is badly defined,[22] but that it is hard to verify. Applying it will therefore be difficult and costly—costly, as the reference to disputes and mistrust reminds us, even from a moral point of view.

But this argument doesn't work. For one thing, many preferences, and strengths of preferences, can be diagnosed beyond reasonable doubt. Second, it is, to say the least, an open question whether the remaining, difficult cases are more numerous or more difficult than those involved in talk of "primary goods", or of "liberties", or of "fully adequate schemes" of these.[23] For what is included in a fully adequate scheme (and with what weight), and what is not, and how do we—consensually, without "disputes and mistrust"—find out? And, as was mentioned in section 3.1, at least some of Rawls's "primary goods" have to do with mental states, too, and are thus, with respect to verification, in the same boat as preferences. Rawls shouldn't include freedom from pain (and the like) among his "primary goods" to make them look adequate while blaming *others* who talk of freedom from pain (and the like) for dealing in goods that are hard to observe.

Third, even if Rawlsian "primary goods" were more manageable than utility, we could work with two levels of principles. We could consistently be, on the one hand, preferentialists when doing political philosophy and when wondering what the laws ought to achieve (and why), and, on the other hand, write and apply laws that do not even mention preferences. Notoriously, there may be sound general reasons for a two-level structure of this type.[24] And if everybody knows about it and nobody is cheated, it is unobjectionable.

Fourth, remember that Rawls is a "publicist"; that is to say, he insists that the principles of justice, and the reasoning that led to them, be publicly known. This request is hardly compatible with the objection we are currently considering, viz. an objection from application costs. For the general form of such an objection is this: "Let us grant, for the sake of the argument, that principle X correctly *characterizes* the good or the right. But its public use wouldn't *promote* the good or the right."[25] Now, a publicist would not want us to hide *that* argument from the public either. However, if we don't, and if therefore the public knows that X correctly characterizes the good or the right, then how can its members fail to base their moral reasoning, in political as well as other matters, at bottom, on X? Given X's alleged practical weakness, we might hope and suggest that, for quick reference, they adopt some other principles. But once they see that X is correct we cannot stop them from judging things, more or less directly, in the light of X.

Fifth, last, and most important: verification problems need verification answers. As Rawls puts it very aptly, in another context, "It is irrational to advance one end rather than another simply because it can be more accurately estimated."[26] Absolutely. So we cannot give moral authority to "primary goods" just because sometimes the impact things have on desire fulfillment is hard to figure out. Compare this to other areas of life: we do not get into a habit of going by hearsay just because sometimes the truth is hard to figure out.

In the preferentialist's eyes, relying on an index of "primary goods" is arbitrary unless there is a warranted hope for the procedure to approximate the results that are best in terms of desire fulfillment. Without that hope, there is no reason to believe that the distribution of "primary goods" is a matter of justice. Having sometimes to guess what will best serve a principle is one thing. Having the guesswork replace the principle is another.

3.3 Popularity

Rawls also objects that preference-justice would not be able to gain large-scale support. This, he thinks, is bad news for a political philosophy.[27]

However, Rawls has simply not shown, or come anywhere near showing, that preferentialism's prospects of getting support *are* worse than those of *his* principles.[28] And, more importantly, let us be careful not to overrate general endorsement. It would be nice for a theory of justice to have support, but there is no straightforward argument from lack of support to lack of adequacy. After all, majorities can be dumb and immoral. We shouldn't try to humor them when thinking about norms—only when marketing our norms.

This is not to say that we may disregard other people, whose views and interests may diverge radically from ours. Indeed, we mustn't. Part of our values is that we count everybody for one, nobody for more than one.[29] But it is one thing to have democratic values, and quite another to be democratic about what values one has.

Neither is it to say that considerations of stability, intimately connected with those of support, should play no role in our moral practice. They had better play a large role; they too had better make us, to some extent, tolerant. An armed rebellion, for instance, involves pain and inconvenience on both sides, which is itself a large moral drawback; it follows that we ought hardly ever to pursue our moral goals in ways that would stir up those who don't share them. This is one more type of reason, though less direct and noble than the one we embraced in the previous paragraph, why we ought not to ride rough-shod over people with a different view. But, once again, it only means that we have moral reasons to give others a say; not that we have reasons to give them a moral say.

The picture that emerges—the picture of diversity, support, and tolerance—is this. The fact of moral pluralism resembles the fact of bad weather. Bad weather ought to influence our actions, and some trips it ought to make us cancel. But it needn't impair the fact that we desire these trips, and that we *would* go on a picnic if the weather were *not* as bad as it is.

The same goes for justice. It is a sufficient response to the "fact of pluralism" that our fellow-citizens have *moral* standing. We take them into account, especially their interests, no matter how different from ours; doing so will often mean giving in to them, making moral sacrifices. However, giving them *meta-ethical* standing—polling them as to what the norms of political justice themselves should look like—is implausible. It is also unnecessary and dangerous. The expression "public reason" may not qualify as an oxymoron, but it's not far off.[30] What is public need not be reason (and often isn't), and what is reason need not be public (and often isn't). The quest for support should shape our actions; it should not shape our values.

Two objections to these remarks are worth addressing. One of them says: our observation that majorities can commit moral howlers might miss the point, since Rawls aims at a consensus among *reasonable* people—doesn't that make all the difference?[31]

It does make a difference: it shifts the problem elsewhere. For whom do we count as reasonable? If "reasonable" is supposed to perform the job of fending off the immoral, a whole lot of moral substance will have to be packed into it in the first place. And the more moral substance we pack into "reasonable", the less clear it is that reasonable people will reject preferentialism. To say that they will is then no longer an argument against preferentialism; only a roundabout way of claiming, not showing, that preferentialism is wrong.

The second objection says that, if society is to be liberal,

> "the state can no more act to maximize the fulfillment of citizens' rational preferences, or wants (as in utilitarianism), [...] or to advance human excellence, or the values of perfection (as in perfectionism), than it can act to advance Catholicism or Protestantism, or any other religion. None of these views of the meaning, value, and purpose of human life, as specified by the corresponding comprehensive religious or philosophical conceptions of the good, are affirmed by citizens generally, and so the pursuit of any of them through basic institutions gives political society a sectarian character. "[32]

But one of the items in the first sentence is, other than the sentence claims, *not* like the others. The objection holds that, if preferentialism had few followers, then ipso facto a society based on preferentialist principles would be illiberal. This is wrong. Preferentialism is a paradigm of liberalism. It is, recall the remarks from section 1.3, "chacun à sa façon"—in its purest form. No other doctrine takes the idea of neutrality, the idea that one woman's meat is another woman's poison, as seriously as preference-justice does. If preferentialism lacked support, this would show, not that preferentialism is illiberal, but that liberalism lacks support.

4. Priorities—and a Glimpse of the Background

4.1 Who Rules the Roost?

Rawls complains that for the preferentialist many important things will have priority under some circumstances only and that these circumstances needn't always hold. It is easy to think of scenarios, though perhaps less easy to think of realistic ones, in which the preferentialist would want to violate, say, somebody's "basic liberties" in order to optimize preference satisfaction. Thus, preference-justice might fail to protect what ought to be protected.[33]

Remarks like these, however, *assume* anti-preferentialism; they do not *support* it. To what degree certain liberties are accountable to the standard of preference satisfaction is the very issue between the preferentialist and the Rawlsian. The issue is hardly settled by *announcing* that the preferentialist got it wrong. The preferentialist could announce, vice versa, that the allegedly overriding importance of certain particular items is an error, or at the very least a mystery, in Rawls's principles: Rawls runs the risk of securing what isn't worth securing, and of sacrificing what ought to be secured.[34]

Furthermore, it is wrong to say that the preferentialist *relies* on certain facts to validate, in conjunction with the preferentialist values, the "basic liberties" or some such items.[35] He does not. While the preferentialist happens to think that frequently, given his values, the facts *will* validate the "liberties", he also thinks that nothing hinges on this. Whenever they don't validate them, this does not embarrass him. It simply reflects the moral authority of preference satisfaction over particular "goods". Of course the director should take over when the deputies would go astray.

Perhaps this is also the right place to look at Rawls's concession that the index of "primary goods" is flexible. It needn't be fixed once and for all, he says, but can be formed in the course of time[36]—how does that sound to the preferentialist? Not very comforting. The more protean the index, the less Rawls-justice tells us. Rawls's readers and the parties in the "original position" would have to buy a pig in a poke. The *creatio continua* would be fine if it traced desire fulfillment, but that, Rawls explains in no uncertain terms, is not intended.[37] So there's little hope for the preferences. That the index changes is at best useless, at worst frightening, if it doesn't change in the right way.

4.2 Either—Or

At times the issue—desire fulfillment or "primary goods"?—looks not so much like a dissent between Rawls and the preferentialist as a dissent *in Rawls*: is his theory, with respect to the pecking-order between preferences and "primary goods", consistent? The question has already arisen in section 3, and will arise several more times.

One telling example is Rawls's argument why the choosers in the "original position" would favor a principle that gives priority, inter alia, to the liberty of conscience. It might be asked, he says, why the choosers, instead of opting for this priority, wouldn't allow for trade-offs. Imagine an alternative principle that, when many people could become very happy if the religion of just a few people were repressed, permitted repression. For the choosers in the "original position", wouldn't such a principle be the "better bet"? Rawls replies: "If the parties were to gamble in this way, they would show that they [...] did not know what a religious, philosophical, or moral conviction *was*."[38]

Thus, in Rawls's usage the predicate "religious conviction" *entails* that nobody would want to abjure their religious conviction, not for all the tea in China. It is, in this usage, analytically true—true of *words* like "faith"—that people have a lexicographical preference for their faith over tea (or money, or whatever). And *because* people have this preference, says Rawls, principles will be chosen that respect the priority.

However, if this argument from lexicographical preferredness works at all, it will work across the board. Principles will be chosen according to which *whatever* is lexicographically preferred gets lexicographical protection.[39] Why not admit this, then? Friends of "primary goods" can't have it both ways, and they should face up to that fact. Either preferences don't have authority in matters of justice—in which case Rawls cannot employ arguments like the one we have just seen him employ. Or they do have authority—in which case the principles of justice had better say so.

4.3 "Moral Powers"

The plan was to discuss explicit objections to preference-justice. Even so, we should take a moment to leave the individual objections aside and glimpse, as far as it can be made out, the root of the dissent: where in Rawls's doctrine do the "primary goods", and the absolute priority of some of them over the others, come from? As we know, a significant part of the answer is that they get chosen in the "original position".

But beware—the *particular* "goods" get chosen because Rawls has equipped the choosers with *particular* preferences. He has equipped them with "highest-order interests" to cultivate what he decides to call their "moral powers":

> "The first power is the capacity for an effective sense of justice, that is, the capacity to understand, to apply and to act from (and not merely in accordance with) the principles of justice. The second moral power is the capacity to form, to revise, and rationally to pursue a conception of the good. *Corresponding to the moral powers, moral persons are said to be moved by two highest-order interests to realize and exercise these powers.* [...] [T]he parties [of the "original position"] are simply trying to guarantee and to advance the requisite conditions for exercising [...] [these] powers. "[40]

Now, to say that the right thing is the thing that friends of goods A, B, and C would choose is, first and foremost, to say that the right things *are* goods A, B, and C. The "original position" has degenerated into a labeling machine. The moralist puts in "highest-order interests" at his discretion, and the machine declares them to be highest-order moral priorities. Little of import is going on here.

What we're left with is an axiological bottom-line: John Rawls wants to live in a society in which people understand (apply, etc.) the principles of justice and in which they revise and rationally pursue a conception of the good; these two things are more important to him than anything else. And the "primary goods" are not, as Rawls would sometimes have us believe, "all-purpose means"[41]. They are, to a considerable extent, special-purpose means; the special purposes include the understanding of justice and the revision of one's values.

So we have once again arrived at the gulf between the preferentialist and the Rawlsian. The problem is not the appeal to second-order preferences as such: if only they were sufficiently neutral! A second-order preference, say, to lead a life with as little preference frustration as possible—whatever the particular first-order preferences may turn out to be—would do fine. It might even amount, more or less, to the third interest Rawls says his "moral persons" have, viz. a "higher-order interest in protecting and advancing their conception of the good as best as they can". However, by making this only one high-order interest among several, and also by saying that this higher-order interest is "subordinate" to the other two,[42] which are high*est*-order, Rawls celebrates *some* interests. In doing so, he violates the neutrality condition (clause 3 of the creed we presented in section 1.3), and thus the preferentialist's ideals of fairness and tolerance. In that sense, Rawls's system is really on the other side: the "chacun à *ma* façon"-side.

While any violations of neutrality are hard to accept, the particular ones Rawls has in mind do not make the task easier. Thus, with "highest-order interest" no. 1, i.e. the interest to understand etc. the principles of justice, Rawls's morality turns intentionalist; whether people *think* the right thing is held to be of moral importance.

But why? Other things being equal, people could just as well conform to the old-fashioned ideal of a mother: few principles, lots of warmth; they could also "become as little children", or as "the fowls of the air", or the "lilies of the field"—to quote just a few prominent suggestions.[43] There is, I submit, no intrinsic point in *understanding* the good or the right, and in acting *from* it. Good thinking can, on occasion, serve the good or the right, but it doesn't constitute it. What counts are the consequences, not the motives, and certainly not the IQ.

As an illustration, suppose that we could choose between two societies: in the first, the citizens are deeply unhappy but cultivate their sense of justice; in the second, they are deeply happy but do *not* cultivate their sense of justice. Now, if we really gave top priority to the cultivation of the sense of justice, we would have to favor the first of these societies over the second—that is, misery over happiness. This would be absurd. And things would not get significantly less absurd if we said that the cultivating, by being just one of the top priorities (with happiness itself among the others), cannot outweigh *everything*. It could still outweigh a lot, including a lot of misery, and that is highly implausible.

The emphasis on things other than the interests of the affected parties is also why the mentally handicapped, the seriously ill, and animals play no role, or at best a rather awkward one, in Rawls's political ethics. Say that Mary falls severely ill and needs costly medical treatment. Why should society give it to her? Because she is suffering? Because she does not want to die? Because her children are suffering with her and do not want to lose her? Wrong, says Rawls: "The aim is to restore people [...] so that once again they are fully cooperating members of society."

Is that what we want to say? Is that our "considered judgment", "after due reflection"?[44] Gloomy prospects for those patients who would love to be saved, but will not be able to function, or to cultivate their "moral powers", afterwards. No life-support for those, e.g., who will no longer be able to understand the principles of justice?

A few words also on the second "highest-order interest". It includes, among other things, a praise of revisions. This, too, I find hard to join in. I have no intrinsic objection to people simply *having* values.[45]

To be sure, it is in a person's own best interest, and thus ought to be the case, that, *if* she wants to revise her values, she can and does; and similarly that, *if* revising her values leads to a fulfillment profile that is better for her (better in terms of desire fulfillment), she can and does revise them. But these two "ought"s and their implications are fully looked after by an interest in one's own good, where they are, as they ought to be, on a par with other considerations about one's own good. In order to adequately protect them, we need no extra clause about revisions.

Notice that Rawls goes further in two respects.[46] One is that via "highest-order interest" no. 2 he ascribes *intrinsic* importance not just to the possibility, but to the *exercise* of revisions. This is implausible. Little Dorrit, for example, is *never* going either to question or to change her own conception of the good, and what is wrong with her?[47]

And Rawls assigns *top* importance to revisability. This is also implausible. Some of the best things in life require decisions that are not revisable. To live is to forsake possibilities, to pass points of no return. A person who gives high priority to revisability—mostly choosing the course that will commit her least, mostly "keeping her options open"—is an unlikely candidate for a moral ideal.

Ulysses, in order to listen to the sirens, has himself tied to the mast. He gives orders that his future orders be ignored, thus choosing, autonomously and rationally, to reduce revisability to zero. We hope for him that the coup works, and are glad to read that it does. Our lives abound with such structures, large and small.[48] Obviously, some things are worth some very basic liberties. Even if revisability were a special good, it surely wouldn't have lexicographical, or even high, priority over other goods. And if it doesn't, an argument for the lexicographical priority of "basic liberties" over other goods cannot be grounded in it.

Is it really the case, then, that "we *want* people to care about their liberties and opportunities in order to realize" Rawls's two powers, and that "we think they [including Little Dorrit?] show a lack of self-respect and weakness of character in not doing so"?[49] Fellow-citizens, somebody is preaching one particular life-style and pushing it at the cost of others. He can't be a liberal.

5. Expensive Tastes

Rawls frequently mentions "expensive tastes" as a problem for the preferentialist. Given some of its connotations, the word "taste" may not be a happy choice. It suggests that the mental states in question either, some way or other, fall short of being preferences in the full-fledged sense (in which case, however, the preferentialist wouldn't want to count them in either, so Rawls would be carrying coals to Newcastle) or are preferences we are permitted to ignore (which, however, is the moral claim that is at issue, and should therefore not be entailed, or insinuated, by the choice of words).

The examples Rawls adduces include people who "have a strong desire to study quasars with powerful radio telescopes", people who desire "going on pilgrimages to distant places or building magnificent cathedrals or temples", and people who "are distraught without expensive wines and exotic dishes"[50]. Preferentialists, Rawls seems to think, are committed to fulfilling these desires—whereas if we talk of "primary goods" instead, we can simply leave Chablis, St. Peter's, and telescopes off the list, and thus render justice immune to the special claims of connoisseurs, popes, scientists, and the like.

However, that the items can be left off the list is no good reason for *having* a list. Forcing a village of miserable serfs to build, say, a château or a radio telescope for their local potentate is a revolting idea anyway. Even utilitarianism says so, not to mention those systems of preference-justice, gestured at towards the end of section 1.3, that work with minimum levels of utility or with other equality constraints. To see this, just look at the preferences of the hundreds of serfs and at those of their starving children.[51] Where, then, *is* the scandal in the preferentialist treatment of "expensive tastes"?

But would not, an objector might insist, preferentialists "require society to skew the allocation of resources in an extreme way in favor of the person interested in quasars"?[52] Yes and no. In never-never land, where the non-astronomers simply don't mind parting with their money and time, nothing is wrong with transferring these resources to the astronomer who would be sad without them. It would be wrong not to. But in life as it is, people have their own projects and do mind very strongly giving up their money and time; thus, the preferentialist will tend to decree, like Rawls, that they ought *not* to be asked to do so. To say that all preferences, including expensive ones, *count* is not to say that when the counting is over expensive preferences will *win*. In fact, "expensive" already entails that their chances of winning are slim. For it *means* that there are lots of competing considerations on the other side of the scales.

Neither should we forget the person who has the costly preference: what about *her* rights and *her* welfare? What would permit us to leave them out of the picture? Surely what these situations call for is a weighing, not an ignoring, of claims.

Rawls is worried that taking into account "expensive tastes" would be "socially divisive", almost "a receipt for [...] civil strife".[53] But first of all, as was pointed out in section 3.3, preferentialism entails lots of reasons against hubbub. Second, even if it didn't, the objection would be incomplete. If taking into account expensive preferences caused riots, then the preferences thereby frustrated would still have to be weighed against the others. We cannot just assume that conflict must be avoided; we must look at the moral costs of the avoidance.[54] Third, we have seen that taking costly preferences into account the way preferentialism does is far less demanding than Rawls seems to think. And finally, what about his own theory? There are some rights or liberties that Rawls does not just honor but kowtows to.[55] Their lexical priority makes them *infinitely* expensive—is that *not* an incentive for civil strife?

Next, Rawls sees the danger that people would cheat, and would pretend to have expensive desires that in fact they don't have.[56] But deception is a special case of the verification problem, which we covered at length in section 3.2. And the problem arises for other goods as well. Hiding money is at least as easy as hiding preferences.

Even if people don't cheat, Rawls says, they could feel encouraged to

> "*develop* [...] costly conceptions of the good in order to shift the distribution of the means of satisfaction in their direction, if only to protect themselves against exorbitant claims of others."

However, counting expensive preferences doesn't lead to exorbitant claims. It may lead to claims, but so does every conception of justice, Rawls's included. And *developing* costly preferences in order to get the means of their satisfaction is foolish.[57] It's like borrowing money for the *sole* purpose of returning it. That's not a way of coming out ahead.

It doesn't help that Rawls never gives us a general characterization of "expensive tastes". When we endeavor to fully understand his objection, and to figure out the scope of his ban, including the decisive features that are supposed to justify the ban, the censor forces us to speculate. The best we can do is recall his examples, quoted at the beginning of this section, and try to extrapolate from them.

So let us see. Should justice ignore these preferences because they are strong? This suggestion is too macabre to deserve discussion. Should justice ignore them because they are unusual? This can't be right either—especially if we're still talking about strong ones. Should justice ignore them because their satisfaction would require that other people have lots of frustrated preferences, or have to give up lots of their "primary goods"? Hardly, for how could that make it right to not even *take into account* some of the preferences involved (especially some of the strong ones)? To be sure, problems of justice arise when we can't give everything to everybody. These are times for adjudicating, and also for deciding, unavoidably, against some preferences—but not for plugging our ears. And, once again, remember that Rawls himself cultivates "goods" that can cost other people a fortune; he does so, unlike the preferentialist, without even checking whether they are worth anything in the eyes of their recipients.

Here's another idea: should justice ignore these preferences because they can easily be changed?[58] However, it is not at all clear from the Rawlsian examples that they can be changed any more easily than others, which the Rawlsian index protects. Furthermore, *whenever* preferences get into each other's way and a collision can be avoided or ended, without too much trouble, by removing some of them, they ought to be removed and not, at the cost of others, satisfied. But that is fully acknowledged by the preferentialist, and can, as section 7 will show in some more detail, easily be expressed in his framework. And it holds true of *every* preference, not just of expensive ones and not just of preferences for specific items that fail to get Rawls's approval.

At this stage, one might be tempted to probe further. Should justice ignore these preferences because preferences are morally irrelevant anyway? But even if the "because"-clause were plausible (a big "if"), it would amount to the admission that there *is* no argument from "expensive tastes". That "expensive tastes" should be discounted would be taken to follow from anti-preferentialism, rather than to support it. Any other suggestions? Should justice ignore these preferences because their content is not on the index of "primary goods"? It is about time we stopped. Once again: the objection from "expensive tastes" was supposed to give us one of the *reasons* to turn away from preference satisfaction to "primary goods" as the currency of justice. Such a reason should hardly invoke the *premiss* that "primary goods" are what justice is all about.

6. Preferences with an Unfair Genesis

Rawls, like others, has objected to preference-justice on the grounds that preferences can have an unfair genesis. This is why they are a poor guide for morals, and this is why we should specify people's needs in some other way.[59]

If, for instance, you have no wish to own a house, then this may have been caused by conditions that are themselves unjust. Say you're destitute, and so are your parents and friends and neighbors, and that's the way it has been as long as you can remember. This has shaped you; it has made owning a house "unthinkable" for you, has prevented or stifled, not frustrated, the desire to own a house. If that is why the preference has never, or hardly ever, existed in you, and if today you still live in a trailer park, whereas a rich man has a weak preference to own yet another house—should we really give, as preference-justice seems to imply, the house to him rather than to you?

Notice a parallel. The argument is, in a sense, an anti-preferentialist variety of the argument that "voluntary" agreements can have moral authority only if they have been reached in fair bargaining situations. They must be "truly voluntary".[60] A contract doesn't morally bind you, if, say, signing it was your only way to avoid starvation. In both these cases—house and starvation—an unfair genesis is supposed to deprive an item of its moral authority: a preference pattern in the one case, a promise in the other.

Returning to the real-estate example, let me begin with a preliminary observation. The point the example is trying to establish is compatible with allowing preferences, and in a sense preferences only, to have substantial moral weight. For the challenge, supposing it was one, could be met by appealing to the preferences people *would* have under certain, perhaps morally less problematic, circumstances. Nothing here propels us away from preferences and on to "primary goods". Even if the example worked, it would suggest a modification, not a rejection, of preferentialism.[61]

Anyway, it does *not* work. Recall, from section 1.2, that we are studying a brand of preferentialism in which hedonic happiness, too, counts. "Pleasure and the absence of pain" have always been seen as a part of welfare, and we have built this into our preferentialism by stipulating that people desire, roughly speaking and among other things, their own pleasure. (As I have pointed out we could just as well do without that stipulation and say instead that both desire fulfillment and pleasure count.)

Bearing this in mind, let us ask who should get the house. The preferentialist replies as follows:

> There are preferentialist reasons to make you hedonically happy. *If* giving you a house neither contributes to your hedonic happiness nor satisfies, directly or indirectly, any other preference, then there is indeed no moral reason to give you the house. (But who on earth would want to deny *that*?) *If*, however, it makes you hedonically happy or satisfies, directly or indirectly, another preference, then there *is* a moral reason to give you the house.

Thus, the preferentialist says what we all want to say. Of course, *aggregational* principles will still have to be applied in the second case (where your receiving the house would make you happy or satisfy another preference), since the rich man, too, wants to own the house. As to aggregation, we can choose—remember the end of section 1.3—from the vast range of preferentialist options, including, e.g., moral priority for the worst off. It is sad that Rawls decides to burke most of these systems, by just not putting them on the menu that the parties in the "original position" can choose from.[62] At any rate, preferentialism itself is merely a claim about what counts—about the currency of justice. That's the claim the unfair-genesis objection was supposed to discredit, and that's the claim that stands vindicated.

Four more remarks may be in order. First, some authors seem to be concerned with the problem that the deprived and repressed may not dare to *articulate* their wishes.[63] It is indeed vital for the preferentialist to bear this in mind whenever he endeavors to establish the facts his morality responds to. As an objection, however, the problem is a special version of the objection from verification, which was discussed in sections 3.2 and 5. Notice, incidentally, that the objection, or at least what most of the objectors want to make of it, presupposes significant knowledge on their part of the unarticulated wishes; but, obviously, when that knowledge is available, the objection doesn't get off the ground.

Second, we should bear in mind from section 1.2 that we're talking about *intrinsic* preferences. If you merely fail to want the house in a sense of "wanting" that implies "deeming attainable", then that is not an absence of a preference in the preferentialist's sense of "preference".

Third, preferentialists look at *implicit* desires. This point was also mentioned in section 1.2, and here becomes relevant as follows. According to some critics, the fact that deprivation might narrow down your *imagination* gets preference-justice into trouble.[64] But it doesn't. Preference-justice guarantees, just as the critics think it should be guaranteed, that this kind of fact can have no moral impact whatsoever. For, if your poverty prevents you from even imagining that you own a house, this doesn't imply that you do not desire, in the sense of "desire" relevant for the preferentialist calculus, to own a house. What preferentialists go by is how you would feel *if* you imagined it, not whether you do imagine it.

Since many of the preferentialist moves in this section admonish us, one way or another, not to rush into the judgement that a certain preference fails to exist, a critic would be right to remind us in return that, in the house story as I told it, at least one preference, the one for the house itself, does indeed not exist. Although I have already given the main reason why this shouldn't worry us, I would like to add a brief general word on "missing" preferences. It should not be thought that the worship of preference satisfaction entails indifference between the existence of one preference pattern and that of another. Quite the contrary: since some preference patterns are more conducive to satisfaction than others, friends of preference satisfaction will take an enormous interest in the creation of the right patterns. (A little more on this below, in section 7.) And of course, as parents know, creating the right pattern will sometimes involve giving you something that you didn't want ex ante, but get to want ex post.

If *all* this is understood, why should we believe, with John Rawls, that "needs are different from desires, wishes, and likings"[65]?

7. Changes of Preference

7.1 Fickleness

The final objection to be considered concerns changes of preference. It is one of those objections, mentioned towards the beginning of section 3, that Rawls addresses to one particular brand of preferentialism, in this case utilitarianism, but that he could just as well have raised against the other brands.

Utilitarianism, Rawls criticizes, will ask citizens

> "to adjust and revise their final ends and desires, and to modify their traits of character and to reshape their realised abilities [...]."

Utilitarians have to see citizens as "passive carriers of desires", as "bare persons", ready to "consider any new convictions and aims, and even to abandon attachments and loyalties" when doing so is required by their conception of justice. These observations, Rawls says, "suffice to illustrate the contrast between utilitarianism and justice as fairness".[66]

What contrast? Reprogramming is precisely what Rawls himself prescribes. Defending "primary goods" against the reproach that they might diverge radically from desiderata, and thus be morally off the mark, he says that his doctrine "relies on a capacity to assume responsibility for our ends"; he assumes

> "citizens to stand apart from conceptions of the good and to survey and assess their various final ends; indeed this must be done whenever these ends conflict with the principles of justice, for in that case they must be revised."[67]

What are we to make of this? If Rawls can say this, why can't Sidgwick? It is true that Rawls professes to exempt *some* preferences from the scythe of justice.[68] This exemption, however, cannot make the decisive difference. First, because it is still true of Rawls, too, that he will subject many a deep and strong preference to revision, since many a deep and strong preference could, in certain realistic circumstances, be fulfilled only if Rawls-justice were violated; consider, for instance, a mother's ardent wish that her son, the robber, be spared from going to prison. Second, because the form, too, of the exemption confirms the *tu quoque*.[69] For Rawls says that people should revise only those desires whose fulfillment would conflict with justice. The utilitarian believes the same—the only question being what justice is. There is no *extra* dissent here with respect to the question whether justice can, to a considerable extent, boss around preferences.

It seems, then, that Rawls's views on preference changes are themselves prone to change—depending on whether he is defending his own theory or attacking others.

7.2 Preference Changes in Rawls's Defense of "Primary Goods"

We have encountered a tension in Rawls's position on preference changes: he decries utilitarianism for requesting them, but requests them himself when it suits him. Let us now look a little more closely at the second of these moves—that is, at Rawls's own appeal to preference changes in his defense of "primary goods".

First, and perhaps most significant, isn't that appeal peculiar? Doesn't it suggest that, if the preferences could not be changed, the "primary goods" would be inadequate—and thus, that preferences have the last word after all? But if they do, why not say so straightaway, in the principles of justice? Why switch to "primary goods"?

Second, feasibility: deciding to desire, or bringing about a change in one's desires, is not always possible. It will not do to reply that the choosers in the "original position" had a strong preference for revisability and will therefore have secured it.[70] Even if this were one of the more plausible premises of the "original position" (we have seen in section 4.3 that it is not), the "therefore" would be too quick; for no matter how strongly the choosers prefer, their choices won't bring about the impossible. Thus, for every desire that Rawls wants to be changed, he would have to show that it *can* be changed. And since for him the praise of revisability has to do with autonomy,[71] not every form of change will satisfy him; think of brainwashings, drugs, or television. So it would have to be shown not just that the changes can be brought about, but that they can be brought about autonomously, in whatever sense of "autonomous" that Rawls may have in mind.

Third, even if I *can* change certain preferences I have, will I want to? Remember from section 7.1 that quite a few of the preferences Rawls requires us to change will be deep and strong. Against other criteria of justice he adduces what he calls the "strains of commitment": people in the "original position" choose no principle that they believe might require so much of them that they won't comply.[72] But wouldn't preference changes of the type Rawls requests themselves be such strains, and rather heavy ones?

The previous three points connect to a fourth one. For in as far as preferences have moral authority even according to Rawls (see the first point), but sometimes cannot, or cannot in the right way, or will not, be changed to correlate with "primary goods" (see the second and the third points), justice in terms of "primary goods" will violate even the moral authority Rawls himself grants to preferences. Over and above injustice, inconsistency threatens.

Finally, whoever demands revisions of preferences must tell us which of the conflicting parties he wants to change, and *why* that party rather than another. Where preferences clash, who is the victim, who the culprit?

Say the pope wants me to do a handstand, I don't feel like doing one, and both of us could revise our preferences—which of us would Rawls ask to revise? To claim that the index of "primary goods" will answer such questions (for instance, by including a basic liberty to stand on one's feet) would only be passing the buck: how do we justify the index? From there, it can be passed further, via the "original position" or some such device, to a hypothetical individual rational choice. But what then? Rational choice as such, even behind a "veil of ignorance", will give us results conditional on the strength of the conflicting preferences (see above, section 3.1), and this is not what Rawls wants. His only chance of getting results in non-preferential terms is to *equip* the morally relevant hypothetical choosers with *specific* preferences (see above, section 4.3). This, however, gets us nowhere near a moral argument. It's just a moral verdict.

7.3 Reasonable Changes

Rawls's ideas about preference changes, including the anti-preferentialist moves he is trying to make, are flawed—in numerous ways and sometimes to the degree of inconsistency. That has been the upshot of sections 7.1 and 7.2.

Contrast that diagnosis with the preferentialist stand on these issues. Our decisions, political and private, will bring into existence certain preferences as opposed to others. Some of the decisions—think of procreation, famine relief, or schooling—will do so on a grand scale. "[H]ow can we judge", Mill is quite right to ask,

> "in what manner many an action will affect even the worldly interests of ourselves and others, unless we take in, as part of the question, its influence on the regulation of our, or their, affections and desires?"[73]

Morality must indeed be sensitive to that dimension; it must take into account preference *dynamics*, and preferentialism does. In their society and family and own life, preferentialists will aim at the existence of satisfiable preferences—to be exact, of co-satisfiable preferences. For the more co-satisfiability there is, the less frustration there has to be. Of course, they will bear in mind that some frustrations pave the way to satisfaction. However, owing to the condition of neutrality—a condition of equality and tolerance— they will *not* discriminate on grounds of content.

In short, if and only if the best feasible fulfillment profile requires changes of preference, these changes ought to be effected. All the preferentialist wants is a preferentialist reason for them.

8. Conclusion

Desire fulfillment, says the preferentialist, is the alpha and omega of justice. John Rawls denies this, and we have looked at his major objections.

The objections have been defused. Doing so required little or no appeal to moral intuitions. Some objections vanished as soon as preferentialism was properly understood. Others turned out to be based on double standards, with Rawls considering the mote in his brother's eye, but not the mote, or beam, in his own. And quite a few backfired, raising serious doubts about the consistency of Rawls's doctrine. To be sure, the fact that the objections have been defused does not settle the issue: there are other arguments for and against preference satisfaction and its rivals. Still, preferentialism does emerge strengthened.

Let us have a parting look, not at the particular objections, but at the general issue. What counts, we preferentialists hold, is not things, but how people relate to them. It is not *just* to give one loaf of bread each to a being that has no desire to eat and to a being that would love to survive but needs two loaves in order to do so; ditto in matters that are less specific, or less dramatic, or both. Rawls-justice, I submit as others have submitted before me, does not sufficiently respect this.

If, as Rawls suggests, our principles of justice talk of particular "goods", we are bound to get into trouble: in which sense are they goods, and how do we know? What happens when they diverge from the things people desire and the things that make people happy? Worse still, what happens when they diverge and the relevant preferences should not, or even cannot, be changed?

If, vice versa, we start with preferences, and make the goods accountable to them, we get a story that makes sense: the search for the best feasible fulfillment profile. In that story, people get what they want—and will be asked to revise their preferences when this is both good and possible.

Preferentialism has a simple old truth on its side. Perhaps we can re-open our eyes to it. Means receive their life from ends. Being preferred, or being conducive to what is preferred, is precisely what *turns* things into goods. If our principles of justice lose sight of this, we might as well play blind man's buff.

Acknowledgements

For critical discussions I'm grateful to Ulla Wessels; furthermore, to Chris Abbey, Richard Hare, Wilfried Hinsch, Georg Meggle, Elijah Millgram, Clark

Wolf, and to the participants of the conference "Zur Idee des politischen Liberalismus", held in Bad Homburg, Germany, in July 1992. Thanks are also due to the Center for Philosophy of Science, University of Pittsburgh, where I started writing an ancestor of this chapter back in 1992; to the *Deutsche Forschungsgemeinschaft (DFG)* for supporting the research project "Was zählt?"; and, finally, to the *Alexander von Humboldt Stiftung* and to Stanford University, for two productive years in California.

I should also acknowledge this chapter's relation to Fehige 1997, where the battle between the desire camp and the Rawlsian camp was on the agenda as well. I have there traced the dissent—its reasons, scope, and implications—through the various levels, old and new, of Rawls's system: his aims (political), his method (intuitionist), the quest for consensus, the "original position", the "ideal of the moral person", and others.

Notes

Arabic or Roman numerals not marked as page numbers and not used to indicate years are numbers of parts, chapters, or sections; "-B" means "towards the beginning", "-E" means "towards the end".

1. Kant 1785, p. 430. For more on preferences and their role in ethics, see Fehige/ Wessels 1998, esp. the introduction; large portions of the literature can be explored with the help of the structured bibliography in the same volume.

2. The expression "pleasure and the absence of pain" is Mill's, from 1861, II-B; similarly Bentham 1789, I. For the relation to desires, see e.g. Kant 1785, pp. 399, 415f, 1788, pp. 43 and 45 ("Anmerkung II"-B), as well as Singer 1979, p. 131.

3. The "proper conditions" include that she is sober, not too agitated by other issues, etc.; preferentialisms can differ with respect to the details. See also below, section 6. For appeals to counterfactual conditionals in this and related contexts, see Arneson 1990a, pp. 162–4, 1994, Brandt 1970, 1979, VI, 1998, Lewis 1989, esp. pp. 121–6, Railton 1986, p. 16, Sidgwick 1874, pp. 110–12, Smith 1984.

4. Both quotations are from James 1891, p. 149, emphasis added. Recall the remark on desire and pleasure from section 1.2; against that background, claim (1) includes, and claim (2) doesn't exclude, hedonic happiness (that is, feeling good).

5. Bentham, notoriously the source of this slogan, was, just as notoriously, concerned with pleasure, not preference satisfaction: "Prejudice apart, the game of push-pin is of equal value with the arts and sciences of music and poetry. If the game of push-pin furnish more pleasure, it is more valuable than either." (1825, p. 253.) For the "condition of neutrality" see e.g., via the entry "neutrality" in the index, Sen 1970.

6. From, in Rawls's words, the "fact of pluralism"—see below, section 2; ditto for more on the "basic structure".

7. See Blackorby/Donaldson 1977, Foster 1985, Kutschera 1982, 4.3, Parfit 1991 , Sen 1973, 1982, 1992 (with numerous further references on p. 93), Temkin 1993, Trapp 1992, 2.

8. SUPG IV-E, emphasis added. Lyons, see 1972-B, is one of many who assume utilitarianism to be Rawls's main rival. Rawls's own tendency to ignore preferentialist alternatives to utilitarianism will come up again, see the introduction to section 3 (including note 14, with references to his discussions of utilitarianism and to other people's critique of

that discussion) and the remarks on aggregation in section 6.

9. SUPG II-B; the previous quotation ("'basic structure' of a modern constitutional democracy") is from JFPM I-B. More on the "basic structure" in *TJ* 2, BSS (correspondingly *PL* VIII), and *PL* I.2.1; see also Fehige 1997, 3.3 and pp. 317–19.

10. For the "fact of pluralism", see e.g. IOC, pp. 424, and *PL* I.6.2; as to how it should shape a theory of justice and the search for it, see KCMT, first lect., I, JFPM If, and *PL* I.6. The issues are also discussed in Fehige 1997, 3.1–3.3; and below, in section 3.3.

11. On the "original position", see *TJ* 4 and III, BLP IV (correspondingly *PL* VIII.4), JFR 6 and III, *PL* I.4; for its preferentialist ancestors and relatives, see below, note 16. Rawls's version is criticized e.g. in Fehige 1997, 3.2, and Hare 1983. More on the "certain kind of person" who chooses: below, in section 4.3.

12. BLP I-B (correspondingly *PL* VIII.1-B); for the quotation I replaced "First, they" with "2.a They" and "second," with "2.b". See also SUPG II-B and *PL* I.1.1. The changes compared to the wording in *TJ* are motivated and explained in BLP (correspondingly *PL* VIII).

13. The label "justice as fairness" comes up throughout, see JF, JFPM, and the indexes of *TJ* and *PL*. It is not too helpful (in much the same way as the label "true justice" wouldn't be), since, as I have already mentioned, *most* theories of justice would claim to capture the ideal of fairness.

The previous three quotations are from SUPG II-B; for "primary goods", see also *TJ* 15, KCMT, first lect., IV, PRIG IIIf, and *PL* V.3f. Critical discussions can be found in Alexander/ Schwarzschild 1987, III.A, Arneson 1990a and b, Arrow 1973, III.1, Fehige 1997, 3.4f, Schwartz 1972/73, and Sen 1980, 3.

14. I shouldn't get side-tracked into exploring or discussing these systems here. Notice two things, however. First, the second of the three Rawls has to invent before dismantling it; second, the last two are unusually bizarre proposals. As I have remarked earlier (section 1.3-E) and will remark again (section 6, paragraph on aggregation), Rawls seems to have little interest in discussing intelligent preferentialist alternatives to utilitarianism.

For Rawls's discussion of utilitarianism, see e.g. JF 6f, *TJ*, 5f, 27f, 30, and pp. viif, SUPG VI–VIII, and JFR 27–33 (parts of this discussion are criticized in Fehige 1997, 3.6, Hare 1983, Lyons 1972, Narveson 1982); for his discussion of the "principle of restricted utility", *TJ* 49 and JFR 34–8; and for his discussion of "equal proportionate satisfaction", FG VII (cf. Arneson 1990b, pp. 434f).

15. KCMT, first lect., IV, and *PL* II.3; similarly FG I and BLP, p. 21 (correspondingly *PL*, p. 307).

16. Such as Vickrey 1945 and Harsanyi 1953; Pattanaik 1968 and Sen 1970, 9.3-B, are instructive guides to the pre-*TJ* literature. For other more or less preferentialist versions, or thoughts on the matter, see Arrow 1973, II, Fehige 1995, 2-E, Hare 1981, p. 129, Harsanyi 1975 and 1977, I.4, Kutschera 1995, pp. 67–70 (and Hare's response in the same volume), Resnik 1987, 2.

17. Cf.*TJ*, p. 131, and Hare 1981, esp. p. 21.

18. Not surprisingly, this is also what happens in preferentialist versions of the "original position"; see above, the references in note 16, and cf. below, in section 4.2, the discussion of Rawls's more or less preferentialist argument for the liberty of conscience as well as, in section 4.3, the discussion of Rawls's first "highest-order interest". For the choosers' means-ends rationality, see *TJ* 25 and VII.

19. Explications of rights in terms of preferences or interests can be found in the writings of Bentham, Feinberg, Frey, Godwin, Hare (e.g. 1981, 9), Hutcheson, Lyons, MacCormick, Nelson, Raz, Sumner, and Tooley; parts of this tradition are pointed out in Waldron 1984, pp. 9–11 of the introduction. As to *liberty* in this sense, see e.g. Hobbes's well-known dictum that a free man "is he that [...] is not hindered to do what he has a will to do." (1651, XXI-B.) Similarly Mill 1859, p. 226.

Some would say that the conditional I've sketched should be a counterfactual one, for the reasons pointed out by Isaiah Berlin (1958, III-B, 1963/64, pp. 191–3, 1969, pp. xxxviii–xl) and many others. If this were so, it would only strengthen the point I've been making. Since counterfactual conditionals are even harder to check than those in the indicative mood, the violation or nonviolation of counterfactual-based rights and liberties, too, would be even harder to check. More on conditionality below, in section 4.1.

20. PRIG III-E, *PL* V.3.4.

21. See the references and discussions in Fehige 1997, 3.6; and below, sections 4.1-B and 5-B.

22. Rawls says that, as far as interpersonal comparisons of utility are concerned, he does not want to rest his case on *conceptual* problems (*TJ*, 15-B and p. 321). It is not quite clear how these remarks fit in with his objections from a lack of definiteness; be this as it may, definiteness itself is a point we have already discussed in section 3.1. The quotations are from JFR 38.1.

23. Cf. Alexander/Schwarzschild 1987, III.A, Arneson 1990b, IV, on the indexing problem, Fehige 1997, pp. 334, 358–60. A similar question applies to Rawls's complaint that preferentialist arguments would have to be "complicated" (*TJ* 26-E). Surely Rawls's readers, especially those who have had a try at fleshing out or applying his principles, must be surprised to hear him employ that objection; Wolff 1977, I-B, talks of the "labyrinthine complexities" of Rawls's system.

24. Cf. Hare 1981, 3, Parfit 1989, I, Sidgwick 1874, IV.IVf. As Mill puts it, "Those who adopt utility as a standard can seldom apply it truly except through the secondary principles; those who reject it, generally do no more than erect those secondary principles into first principles." (1838, p. 111.)

25. Whoever would not grant what is granted here would no longer make an argument from application (and only such arguments are now at issue), but one from other alleged inadequacies of X. As to Rawls's "publicity condition", see *TJ* 23 and *PL* II.4.

26. *TJ* 15-B.

27. For the general point, see e.g. JFPM II-E and DPOC IV; for its application to utilitarianism in particular, *TJ*, 29 and p. 145. Notice also that the seemingly anti-utilitarian arguments e.g. in SUPG are really arguments against the possibility of a "*well-ordered* [which in Rawls's terminology means, roughly speaking, consensual] utilitarian society" with a "*shared* highest-order preference function" (VII-B, emphasis added). See also the discussion in Fehige 1997, 3.1–3.3, as well as the reflections on validity vs. stability and on acceptability vs. acceptance in Habermas 1995, p. 122; and cf. above, section 2-B, and below, section 5 (on civil strife).

28. Especially not for the type of support he envisages: the support of people who fully understand competing doctrines of justice (see e.g. JFR 35.1 and the first "highest-order interest", on which more below, in section 4.3) and who support the public conception not just as a modus vivendi (see IOC III, *PL* IV.3, V.5.4, and again the said "highest-order interest"). And despite what Rawls seems to think, the "strains of commitment", including those of compensation, do not make the prospects of preferentialism any dimmer than those of Rawls-justice—see Nagel 1973, p. 13; and below, the remarks on civil strife (in section 5) and on the costs of preference changes (in section 7.2, which also contains references and a brief explanation of "strains of commitments").

29. Bentham, as quoted in Mill 1861, V-E.

30. For Rawls's ideas on "public reason", see *PL* VI and my sketchy remarks above, in section 2-B.

31. As to "reasonable" and related expressions, see *TJ* 4, 9, KCMT, pp. 305f, JFPM, pp. 393f, *PL* I.6.2, II.1.2, II.3, III.7.4, IV.3.1, VI, and index (*s.v.* "reflective equilibrium" and "due reflection"), as well as RH, pp. 139, 148, 153. Fehige 1997, esp. 3.1, and Hare 1983-B discuss some of the problems in more detail.

32. PRIG III (similarly and correspondingly *PL* V.3.2).

33. FG 6f, *TJ*, pp. 156, 160, 262f, in RLT clause (c) of the reply to Lyons, RAM, p. 239, and SUPG VII-E; cf. above, section 3.1-E, and, earlier on in the same section, the remarks on conditionality.

34. Schwartz 1972/73 argues and illustrates this point, as do Alexander/Schwarzschild 1987, III.A, and Sen 1980, 3.

35. "It is characteristic of utilitarianism that it leaves so much to arguments from general facts. The utilitarian tends to meet objections by holding that the laws of society and of human nature rule out the cases offensive to our considered judgments." (*TJ* 26-E.)

36. RAM IV-E, SUPG, p. 369, BLP, p. 48 (correspondingly *PL*, p. 333), and JFR 50.

37. "Desires and wants, however intense, are not by themselves reasons in matters of justice. The fact that we have a compelling desire does not argue for the propriety of its satisfaction any more than the strength of a conviction argues for its truth." (SUPG V-B.) See also FG 6f (esp. p. 70), *TJ*, 15-E and pp. 260–2, KCMT, first lect., IV-E, second lect., III, SUPG II-E, IV-E, BLP, p. 22 (correspondingly *PL*, p. 308), JFPM, p. 407, PRIG IIIf, and *PL* I.5.4, V.3.2, V.4.1, V.4.3.

38. BLP, p. 26 (correspondingly *PL*, p. 311), emphasis added; similarly JFPM, p. 405, and JFR 29.4-B, 30.1.

39. As in the preferentialist system discussed in Fehige 1995, involving a non-Archimedean concept of utility; see also the remarks on the protection of minorities in Fehige 1997, 3.6.

40. KCMT, first lect., IV-B, emphasis added. See also SRMC, p. 228, again emphasis added: the parties "think of themselves as beings who can choose and revise their final ends and who *must* preserve their liberties in these matters. [...] Since the two principles secure these conditions, they must be chosen." Similarly BLP, pp. 27f (correspondingly *PL*, pp. 313f).

"Moral persons" are already mentioned in *TJ* (see the index), but play a less central role there; on this important change see KCMT, first lect., I-B, second lect., IV-B, SUPG III, BLP III (correspondingly *PL* VIII.3), JFR 15, and *PL* I.5. That an interest is of a "high order" means, in Rawls's usage, not (or not just) that other interests are in its scope, but that it has "great strength" or "great rational weight"; I follow this usage for the sake of the argument.

41. BLP, p. 22 (correspondingly, *PL*, p. 307), similarly *TJ*, p. 93; for references that show how radically "primary goods" are *not* intended to be all-purpose means, see above, note 37. That the "highest-order interests" select the "primary goods" is made very clear e.g. in KCMT, first lect., IV; see also my previous note. Some of the criticism I will raise in this section resembles that of Arneson 1990b, II.

42. The quotations in this paragraph are from KCMT, first lect., IV-B (see also *PL* II.5.2). In parts of *PL* Rawls speaks of high*er*-order interests only, which might mean that the subordinateness is gone; obviously, this move leaves the objection unaffected.

43. Matthew 18:3f, 6:26, 6:28; a splendid plea for such an ideal is Schlick 1927, esp. pp. 349f. Intentionalism is a crucial premiss for Rawls. In his system, (1) intentionalism plus (2) the "fact of pluralism" generate (3) tolerance: since now, in the "original position", the parties (1) want that later they support the principles of justice (intentionalism), and (2) know that later many different moralities will be in the air (the "fact of pluralism"), (3) they choose principles of justice compatible with lots of moralities (tolerance).

44. For these and similar expressions, and the important role they play in Rawls's theory, see the references above, in note 31. The previous quotation, about restoring people, is from *PL* V.3.5. For Rawls's struggle with the issue of health care, see also SRMC, p. 227, RAM III, note, KCMT, second lect., III-E, and SUPG IV-B.

45. The following paragraphs, together with section 3.1 above, imply a critique not just of Rawls, but also of the influential argument in Buchanan 1975, II.

46. This is clear from the long quotation at the beginning of this section and also from

SRMC, p. 228, and BLP, pp. 27f (correspondingly *PL*, pp. 313f).

47. In BLP V-E (correspondingly *PL* VIII.5-E) Rawls writes that "many persons may not examine their acquired beliefs and ends but take them on faith [...]. They are not to be criticized for this [...]." But they *are* heavily criticized ("insulted" might be the better word) by Rawls—see, for example, the statements I quote in the final paragraph of this section. Worse still, they are discriminated against, since the principles of justice are designed for, and justified with permanent reference to, the interest of the other kind of people, who *do* want to examine their ends. The non-examiners pay for the examiners' liberties.

48. More on such structures, including numerous further references, in Elster 1979, II.

49. KCMT, first lect., IV-E.

50. The three quotations are from FG VII-B, BLP, p. 44 (correspondingly *PL*, p. 329), and SUPG IV-B, where the words "expensive tastes", too, can be found. Dworkin (1981, II-B and VIII) also presents the objection from "expensive tastes". Cf. the slaveholders in FG 6f, the critical remarks in Arrow 1973, III.1-E, and the relevant passage in Hausman/ McPherson 1996, 6.3.2. Arneson 1990a, "Seventh Objection", discusses the same problem; his and my discussions, I hope, supplement each other nicely.

51. There is, incidentally, a reasonably reliable procedure to establish that one person's real-life preference for survival is stronger than another person's (say, the potentate's) real-life preference for a château: very roughly speaking, we could check whether the potentate would rather survive *without* the château or starve *in* the château. The issue raised here is that of "extended preferences"; cf. the discussion in Broome 1998 and the reply by Rudolf Schüßler in the same volume, as well as their references to the *loci classici*, esp. to the writings of Arrow and Harsanyi. See also Hare 1981, 7.

52. FG, p. 282.

53. BLP, p. 44 (correspondingly *PL*, pp. 329f).

54. See Fehige 1997, 3.1f; and above, section 3.3.

55. See the priority of his principle 1 over his principle 2, mentioned above, in section 2. On this problem, cf. Arrow 1973, II, Harsanyi 1975, 3 and postscript, Nagel 1973, p. 13, Narveson 1982, p. 132; and above, sections 4.2 and 4.3-E.

56. FG VII-B.

57. Cf. Fehige 1998, esp. 1. Though introduced for different purposes, the drug example in Parfit 1984, p. 497, illustrates the point. Remember that the extra *fun* of having fulfilled extra desires is another issue; it counts as the fulfillment of a different, existing, standing desire for pleasure, and does thus not argue for the intrinsic value of fulfilled extra desires; see above, section 1.2, and below, section 6. The quotation is from FG VII-B, emphasis added.

58. A *leitmotiv* in Rawls's writings on "primary goods" and related issues; see below, the references in notes 67 and 70.

59. See Rawls's remarks that "we want to go behind de facto preferences generated by given conditions" (*TJ*, p. 155; similarly JF, p. 66), and that a "free person is not only one who has final ends which he is free to pursue or to reject, but also one whose original allegiance and continued devotion to these ends are formed under conditions that are free." (SRMC, p. 228.) Similarly *TJ*, p. 88, BSS IVf (correspondingly *PL* VII.4f), Elster 1983, III, Hausman/ McPherson 1996, 6.3-E, Hinsch 1995, V, Nussbaum 1990, pp. 213–16, Marx 1844, Rousseau 1755, pp. 181f, 192f, 214, Sen 1985a, pp. 21f, 1985b, pp. 191, 197, 1986, p. 178, 1987, p. 11, 1990, pp. 127f, and some of the sources these authors refer to. See also the discussion in Arneson 1990a and 1994 and the essays (especially the one by Lawrence Haworth) in Christman 1989. On "primary goods" as the specification of citizens' "needs", see e.g. PRIG IV-E and *PL* V.4.2.

60. Cf. JF, p. 66, BSS IV-B (correspondingly *PL* VII.4-B) and Gauthier 1986, IV.3.2 and VII.

61. Arneson 1990a, "Second Objection", points this out and pleads for such a modification;

see also Arneson 1994 and Nussbaum 1990, note 32. Remember (from the remarks on implicit desires in section 1.3, esp. note 3) that the preferentialist's conditional contains a reference to "proper conditions" anyway. The more strictly we interpret this expression, the less need there will be for a modification in view of the unfair-genesis objection.

62. See *TJ* 21; and cf. above, section 1.3-E and note 14.

63. See Nussbaum 1990, p. 215, reporting Chen's reports on polls among women in Bangladesh.

64. This seems to be the main worry in Nussbaum 1990, pp. 213f.

65. SUPG V-E; similarly FG-E and JFPM, p. 407.

66. The quotations are from SUPG, VI-E and pp. 369, 382f; Wessels 1998, note 57, contains many further references, to authors other than Rawls. On these issues, see also Arneson 1990a, "Third Objection" and "Fourth Objection", and 1990b, III; some of the moves presented here are anticipated there.

67. The two quotations are from SUPG, p. 369, and KCMT, second lect., III-B; similarly RAM III-E, BSS VIII-E (correspondingly *PL* VII.8-E), and *PL* V.3-E; see also below, the references in note 70.

68. See e.g. KCMT, second lect., III.

69. See the long quotation that lies behind us (on citizens' standing apart from their conceptions of the good) and Rawls's idea of "admissible conceptions of the good", SUPG I-B and PRIG III (correspondingly *PL* V.3), as well as his principle that "justice draws the limit", in the introduction to PRIG (correspondingly introduction to *PL* V).

70. See *PL* I.5.4, V.3.6-E; and above, the references in note 67.

71. More precisely, with "moral personality", which itself has to do with autonomy; see KCMT, first lect., IV-E, *PL* II.5; and above, section 4.3.

72. For Rawls's position, see *TJ*, 29-B and p. 145; more on the "strains of commitment" in RAM VI. Again, Nagel's argument in 1973, p. 13, resembles the one given here.

73. Mill 1838, p. 98. See also the symposium on possible preferences, esp. its introduction, in Fehige/Wessels 1998.

References

Alexander, Larry, and Maimon Schwarzschild. 1987. Liberalism, Neutrality, and Equality of Welfare vs. Equality of Resources. *Philosophy and Public Affairs* 16, pp. 85–110.

Arneson, Richard J. 1990a. Liberalism, Distributive Subjectivism, and Equal Opportunity of Welfare. *Philosophy and Public Affairs* 19, pp. 158–94.

———. 1990b. Primary Goods Reconsidered. *Noûs* 24, pp. 429–54.

———. 1994. Autonomy and Preference Formation. In Coleman/Buchanan 1994, pp. 42–75.

Arrow, Kenneth J. 1973. Some Ordinalist-Utilitarian Notes on Rawls's Theory of Justice. *Journal of Philosophy* 70, pp. 245–63.

Bentham, Jeremy. 1789. *An Introduction to the Principles of Morals and Legislation.* London 1970: Methuen.

———. 1825. *The Rationale of Reward.* In vol. 2 of *The Works of Jeremy Bentham.* Edinburgh 1838–43: W. Tait.

Berlin, Isaiah. 1958. Two Concepts of Liberty. In Berlin 1969, pp. 118–72.

———. 1963/64. "From Hope and Fear Set Free". In Berlin 1979, pp. 173–98.

———. 1969. *Four Essays on Liberty.* Oxford: Oxford University Press.

———. 1979. *Concepts and Categories.* New York: Viking Press.

Blackorby, Charles, and David Donaldson. 1977. Utility vs. Equity: Some Plausible Quasi-Orderings. *Journal of Public Economics* 7, pp. 365–81.

Brandt, Richard B. 1970. Rational Desires. In Brandt 1992, pp. 38–56.

———. 1979. *A Theory of the Good and the Right*. Oxford: Oxford University Press.

———. 1992. *Morality, Utilitarianism, and Rights*. Cambridge: Cambridge University Press.

———. 1998. The Rational Criticism of Preferences. In Fehige/Wessels 1998, pp. 63–77.

Broome, John. 1998. Extended Preferences. In Fehige/Wessels 1998, pp. 271–87.

Buchanan, Allen. 1975. Revisability and Rational Choice. *Canadian Journal of Philosophy* 5, pp. 395–408.

Christman, John, ed. *The Inner Citadel*. Oxford 1989: Oxford University Press.

Coleman, Jules, and Allen Buchanan, eds. 1994. *In Harm's Way*. Cambridge: Cambridge University Press.

Daniels, Norman, ed. 1989. *Reading Rawls*. Stanford: Stanford University Press.

Douglass, R. Bruce, Gerald M. Mara, and Henry S. Richardson, eds. 1990. *Liberalism and the Good*. New York: Routledge.

Dworkin, Ronald. 1981. What Is Equality? Part I: Equality of Welfare. *Philosophy and Public Affairs* 10, pp. 185–246.

Elster, Jon. 1979. *Ulysses and the Sirens*. Second, revised edition. Cambridge 1984: Cambridge University Press.

———. 1983. *Sour Grapes*. Cambridge: Cambridge University Press.

Fehige, Christoph. 1995. Das große Unglück der kleineren Zahl. In Fehige/Meggle 1995, vol. 2, pp. 139–75.

———. 1997. Rawls und Präferenzen. In Hinsch 1997, pp. 304–79.

———. 1998. A Pareto Principle for Possible People. In Fehige/Wessels 1998, pp. 508–43.

—and Georg Meggle, eds. 1995. *Zum moralischen Denken*. Frankfurt a. M.: Suhrkamp.

—and Ulla Wessels, eds. 1998. *Preferences*. Berlin: de Gruyter.

Foster, James E. 1985. Inequality Measurement. In Young 1985, pp. 31–68.

Gauthier, David. 1986. *Morals by Agreement*. Oxford: Oxford University Press.

Goldman, Alvin I., and Jaegwon Kim, eds. 1978. *Values and Morals*. Dordrecht: Reidel.

Guhan, S., and Manu Shroff, eds. 1986. *Essays on Economic Progress and Welfare*. Delhi: Oxford University Press.

Habermas, Jürgen. 1995. Reconciliation through the Public Use of Reason: Remarks on John Rawls's Political Liberalism. *Journal of Philosophy* 92, pp. 109–31.

Hare, Richard. 1981. *Moral Thinking*. Oxford: Oxford University Press.

———. 1983. Rawls' Theory of Justice. In Daniels 1989, pp. 81–107.

Harsanyi, John C. 1953. Cardinal Utility in Welfare Economics and in the Theory of Risk-Taking. In Harsanyi 1976, pp. 3–5.

———. 1975. Can the Maximin Principle Serve as a Basis for Morality? A Critique of John Rawls's Theory. In Harsanyi 1976, pp. 37–63.

———. 1976. *Essays on Ethics, Social Behaviour and Scientific Explanation*. Dordrecht: Reidel.

———. 1977. *Rational Behavior and Bargaining Equilibrium in Games and Social Situations*. Cambridge: Cambridge University Press.

Hausman, Daniel, and Michael S. McPherson. 1996. *Economic Analysis and Moral Philosophy*. Cambridge 1996: Cambridge University Press.

Hinsch, Wilfried. 1995. Präferenzen im moralischen Denken. In Fehige/Meggle 1995, vol. 2, pp. 87–112.

———. ed. 1997. *Zur Idee des politischen Liberalismus*. Frankfurt a. M.: Suhrkamp.

Hobbes, Thomas. 1651. *Leviathan*. Indianapolis 1994: Hackett.

James, William. 1891. The Moral Philosopher and the Moral Life. In James 1897, pp. 141–62.

———.1897. *The Will to Believe and Other Essays in Popular Philosophy*. Cambridge, Mass., 1979: Harvard University Press.

Kant, Immanuel. 1785. *Grundlegung zur Metaphysik der Sitten.* In *Kant's gesammelte Schriften,* ed. by the Royal Prussian Academy, vol. 4. Berlin 1911: G. Reimer. Quoted from H. J. Paton's translation, but with the page numbers of the academy edition.

———. 1788. *Kritik der praktischen Vernunft.* In *Kant's gesammelte Schriften,* ed. by the Royal Prussian Academy, vol. 5. Berlin 1908: G. Reimer.

von Kutschera, Franz. 1982. *Grundlagen der Ethik.* Berlin: de Gruyter.

———. 1995. Drei Versuche einer rationalen Begründung der Ethik: Singer, Hare, Gewirth. In Fehige/Meggle 1995, vol. 1, pp. 54–67.

Lewis, David. 1989. Dispositional Theories of Value. *Proceedings of the Aristotelian Society, Supplementary Volume* 63, pp. 113–37.

Lyons, David. 1972. Rawls versus Utilitarianism. *Journal of Philosophy* 69, pp. 535–45.

Marx, Karl. 1844. Privateigentum und Bedürfnisse. (Title chosen by the editors of the *Gesamtausgabe.*) In: Karl Marx, Friedrich Engels, *Gesamtausgabe,* vol 1.2. Berlin 1982: Dietz, pp. 418–23.

McMurrin, Sterlin, ed. 1983. *The Tanner Lectures on Human Values 1982.* Salt Lake City: University of Utah Press.

Mill, John Stuart. 1838. Bentham. In the *Collected Works of John Stuart Mill,* vol. 10. Toronto 1969: University of Toronto Press, pp. 75–115.

———. 1859. *On Liberty.* In the *Collected Works of John Stuart Mill,* vol. 18. Toronto 1977: University of Toronto Press.

———. 1861. *Utilitarianism.* In the *Collected Works of John Stuart Mill,* vol. 10. Toronto 1969: University of Toronto Press.

Miller, Harlan B., and William H. Williams, eds. 1982. *The Limits of Utilitarianism.* Minneapolis: University of Minnesota Press.

Nagel, Thomas. 1973. Rawls on Justice. In Daniels 1989, pp. 1–16.

Narveson, Jan. 1982. Rawls and Utilitarianism. In Miller/Williams 1982, pp. 128–43.

Nussbaum, Martha. 1990. Aristotelian Social Democracy. In Douglass et al. 1990, pp. 203–52.

Parfit, Derek. 1984. *Reasons and Persons.* Edition with revisions from 1985 and 1987. Oxford 1989: Oxford University Press.

———. *Equality or Priority?* (The 1991 Lindley Lecture at the University of Kansas.) Lawrence, Kansas, 1991: University of Kansas.

Pattanaik, Prasanta K. 1968. Risk, Impersonality and the Social Welfare Function. *Journal of Political Economy* 76, pp. 1152–69.

Pieper, Annemarie, ed. 1992. *Geschichte der neueren Ethik,* vol. 2. Tübingen: A. Francke.

Railton, Peter. 1986. Facts and Values. *Philosophical Topics* 14, pp. 5–31.

Rawls, John. JF. Justice as Fairness. In Rawls 1999, pp. 47–72.

———. *TJ. A Theory of Justice.* Cambridge, Mass., 1971: Harvard University Press.

———. RLT. Reply to Lyons and Teitelman. *Journal of Philosophy* 69 (1972), pp. 556 f.

———. SRMC. Some Reasons for the Maximin Criterion. In Rawls 1999, pp. 225–31. Paper first publ. in 1974.

———. RAM. Reply to Alexander and Musgrave. In Rawls 1999, pp. 232–53. Paper first publ. in 1974.

———. FG. Fairness to Goodness. In Rawls 1999, pp. 267–85. Paper first publ. in 1975.

———. BSS. The Basic Structure as Subject. In Goldman/Kim 1978, pp. 47–71.

———. KCMT. Kantian Constructivism in Moral Theory. In Rawls 1999, pp. 303–58. Paper first publ. in 1980.

———. SUPG. Social Unity and Primary Goods. In Rawls 1999, pp. 359–87. Paper first publ. in 1982.

———. BLP. The Basic Liberties and their Priority. In McMurrin 1983, pp. 3–87.

———. JFPM. Justice as Fairness: Political Not Metaphysical. In Rawls 1999, pp. 388–414. Paper first publ. in 1985.

————. IOC. The Idea of an Overlapping Consensus. In Rawls 1999, pp. 421–48. Paper first publ. in 1987.

————. PRIG. The Priority of Right and Ideas of the Good. In Rawls 1999, pp. 449–72. Paper first publ. in 1988.

————. DPOC. The Domain of the Political and Overlapping Consensus. In Rawls 1999, pp. 473–96. Paper first publ. in 1989.

————. JFR. Justice as Fairness: A Restatement. Typescript. Cambridge, Mass., 1990.

————. PL. *Political Liberalism*. New York 1993: Columbia University Press.

————. RH. Reply to Habermas. *Journal of Philosophy* 92 (1995), pp. 132–80.

————. 1999. *Collected Papers*. Cambridge, Mass.: Harvard University Press.

Resnik, Michael D. 1987. *Choices*. Minneapolis: University of Minnesota Press.

Rousseau, Jean-Jacques. 1755. *Disours sur l'origine et les fondements de l'inégalité*. In *Œuvres complètes*, vol. 3. Paris 1964: Gallimard.

Schlick, Moritz. 1927. Vom Sinn des Lebens. *Symposion* 1, pp. 331–54.

Schwartz, Adina. 1972/73. Moral Neutrality and Primary Goods. *Ethics* 83, pp. 294–307.

Sen, Amartya K. 1970. *Collective Choice and Social Welfare*. San Francisco: Holden-Day.

————. 1973. *On Economic Inequality*. Expanded edition. Oxford 1997: Oxford University Press.

————. 1980. Equality of What? In Sen 1982, pp. 353–69.

————. 1982. *Choice, Welfare and Measurement*. Oxford: Basil Blackwell.

————. 1985a. *Commodities and Capabilities*. Amsterdam: North-Holland.

————. 1985b. Well-Being, Agency and Freedom. *Journal of Philosophy* 82, pp. 169–221.

————. 1986. The Concept of Well-Being. In Guhan/Shroff 1986, pp. 174–92.

————. 1987. *The Standard of Living*. Cambridge: Cambridge University Press.

————. 1990. Gender and Cooperative Conflicts. In Tinker 1990, pp. 123–49.

————. 1992. *Inequality Reexamined*. Oxford: Oxford University Press.

—and Bernard Williams (eds.). 1982. *Utilitarianism and Beyond*. Cambridge: Cambridge University Press.

Sidgwick, Henry. 1874. *The Methods of Ethics*. Seventh edition. London 1907: Macmillan.

Singer, Peter. 1979. *Practical Ethics*. Second edition. Cambridge 1993: Cambridge University Press.

Smith, Michael. 1984. *The Moral Problem*. Oxford: Basil Blackwell.

Temkin, Larry S. 1993. *Inequality*. Oxford: Oxford University Press.

Tinker, Irene, ed. 1990. *Persistent Inequalities*. Oxford: Oxford University Press.

Trapp, Rainer W. 1992. Interessenaggregationsethik. In Pieper 1992, pp. 303–46.

Vickrey, William S. 1945. Measuring Marginal Utility by Reactions to Risk. *Econometrica* 13, pp. 319–33.

Waldron, Jeremy, ed. 1984. *Theories of Rights*. Oxford: Oxford University Press.

Wessels, Ulla. 1998. Procreation. In Fehige/Wessels 1998, pp. 429–70.

Wolff, Robert Paul. 1977. *Understanding Rawls*. Princeton: Princeton University Press.

Young, H. Peyton, ed. 1985. *Fair Allocation*. Providence, Rhode Island: American Mathematical Society. Vol. 33 of *Proceedings of Symposia in Applied Mathematics*.

INDEX

ABOUT THE AUTHORS

Richard J. Arneson is professor of philosophy at the University of California, San Diego, where he was department chair from 1992–1996. Recently he has held a variety of visiting appointments at the University of California, Davis; the University of Cergy-Pontoise; Yale University; and Australian National University. He works on social and political philosophy with an emphasis on contemporary theories of justice. He has written more than fifty essays in these fields and currently is working on a book on personal responsibility and egalitarian justice.

Samantha Brennan is associate professor of philosophy at the University of Western Ontario. She has written on thresholds for rights, paternalism, feminist ethics, and feminist criticisms of rights, as well as on the badness of death and the right not to be killed. Her articles have appeared in *American Philosophical Quarterly, The Canadian Journal of Philosophy, The Journal of Social Philosophy, The Southern Journal of Philosophy, Ethics,* and *Social Theory and Practice.* With Tracy Isaacs and Michael Milde, Brennan edited *New Canadian Perspectives in Ethics and Political Philosophy* (1997). Brennan is also an editor of *The Canadian Journal of Philosophy.* Her current research includes work on children's rights and family justice (with Robert Noggle) and ongoing work on the nature and structure of moral rights. Brennan's work is funded by the Social Sciences and Humanities Research Council of Canada.

Allen Buchanan is professor of philosophy at the University of Arizona. He lectures and publishes mainly in bioethics and political philosophy. He is the author of over one hundred articles and the following books: *Marx and Justice: The Radical Critique of Liberalism* (1982), *Ethics, Efficiency, and the Market* (1985), *Deciding for Others: The Ethics of Surrogate Decision Making* with Dan W. Brock (1989), and *Secession: The Morality of Political Divorce from Fort Sumter to Lithuania and Quebec* (1991). He served as staff philosopher for the President's Commission on Medical Ethics, where he was a principal author of the commission's two book-length reports on ethical issues in genetics (1983). As staff-consultant for the U.S. Advisory Committee on Human Radiation Experiments, Buchanan authored the ethical framework chapter for the committee's *Final Report* (1995). He currently serves as a member of the Advisory Council for Human Genome Research, which advises the director of the Human Genome Research Institute on goals and funding priorities for genomic research. Buchanan is also author (with Dan W. Brock, Norman Daniels, and Daniel Wikler) of a book on ethical issues in genetic intervention, forthcoming from Cambridge University Press.

Claudia Card is professor of philosophy at the University of Wisconsin. She is the author of *The Unnatural Lottery: Character and Moral Luck* (1995) and the editor of *On Feminist Ethics and Politics* (1999), *Adventures in Lesbian Philosophy* (1994), and *Feminist Ethics* (1991). She is currently writing a book on the concept of evil.

Roger Crisp is fellow and tutor in philosophy at St. Anne's College, Oxford. He is the author of *Mill on Utilitarianism* (1997) and editor of *Utilitas*. He is a member of the Analysis Committee (U.K.), which is responsible for publication of the journals *Analysis, Philosophical Books,* and the *Analysis Trust.*

Norman Daniels, Goldwaite Professor at Tufts University, has written widely in the philosophy of science, ethics, political philosophy, and health policy. His more recent books include *Just Health Care* (1985), *Am I My Parents' Keeper?* (1988), *Seeking Fair Treatment* (1994), *Benchmarks of Fairness for Health Care Reform* with Don Light and Ron Caplan (1996), *Justice and Justification* (1996), and *From Chance to Choice: Genetics and Justice* with Allen Buchanan, Dan Brock, and Dan Wikler (in press).

Bernard P. Dauenhauer is professor emeritus of philosophy at the University of Georgia. Among his books are *Citizenship in a Fragile World* (1996) and *Paul Ricoeur: The Promise and Risk of Politics* (1998).

Victoria Davion is associate professor of philosophy at the University of Georgia and faculty affiliate in the Environmental Ethics Certificate Program. Davion specializes in feminist philosophy, ethical theory, applied ethics, and social and political philosophy. She has published articles in a variety of journals such as *Hypatia, Social Theory and Practice*, and *The Journal of Social Philosophy.* She is the founding and current editor of *Ethics and the Environment.*

Christoph Fehige received his doctoral degree in philosophy from the Westfälische Wilhelms-Universität in Münster. He has worked at the Universities of Münster, Saarbrücken, Uppsala, and Leipzig, has visited at the University of Pittsburgh, and currently is a visiting scholar at Stanford University. Fehige has written on desire, welfare, and practical reason; on deontic logic and the rational foundation of ethics; and on political philosophy and the value of life. He is coeditor of *Zum moralischen Denken* (Frankfurt a.M. 1995), *Preferences* (Berlin 1998), and *Der Sinn des Lebens* (Munich 1999).

Marilyn Friedman teaches philosophy at Washington University in St. Louis. She has published numerous articles in ethics, social philosophy, and feminist theory. Her books include *What Are Friends For? Feminist Perspectives on Personal Relationships and Moral Theory* (1993); *Political Correctness: For and Against* (1995) with Jan Narveson; and three coedited collections—

Feminism and Community (1995); *Mind and Morals: Essays on Ethics and Cognitive Science* (1996); and *Rights and Reason: Essays in Honor of Carl Wellman.*

Scott Hershovitz holds an M.A. in philosophy from the University of Georgia. He is a Rhodes Scholar reading for the D.Phil. in jurisprudence at Oxford University.

Dale Jamieson is Henry R. Luce Professor in Human Dimensions of Global Change at Carleton College, adjunct scientist in the Environmental and Societal Impacts Group at the National Center for Atmospheric Research, and adjunct professor at Sunshine Coast University College, Maroochydore, Australia. For twenty years he taught at the University of Colorado, Boulder, receiving both the Dean's and the Chancellor's awards for research in the social sciences and the humanities. He regularly teaches courses in ethics, environmental philosophy, environmental justice, philosophy of biology and mind, and global change. Jamieson is the author of more than sixty articles and book chapters, is editor or coeditor of six books, is associate editor of *Science, Technology and Human Values*, and serves on editorial boards of several journals. He recently edited *Singer and His Critics* (1999). He is completing a book on the philosophical dimensions of global environmental change and editing the *Companion to Environmental Philosophy* (Blackwell, forthcoming). His research is funded by the Ethics and Values Studies Program of the National Science Foundation, the U.S. Environmental Protection Agency, and the National Endowment for the Humanities.

Claudia Mills is associate professor of philosophy at the University of Colorado, Boulder, and director of its Center for Values and Social Policy. She writes on a wide range of topics in social and political philosophy and applied ethics and is also the author of many children's books.

James W. Nickel is professor of philosophy at the University of Colorado, Boulder, where he has taught since 1982. Nickel specializes in ethics, political philosophy, and philosophy of law. He is the author of *Making Sense of Human Rights* (1987). Recent publications include "Group Agency and Group Rights" in *Ethnicity and Group Rights* (Ian Shapiro and Will Kymlick, editors, 1997) and "The Liberty Dimension of Historic and Contemporary Segregation" in *Law and Philosophy* (1997).

Robert Noggle is assistant professor of philosophy at Central Michigan University. He has written on neo-Kantian ethics, personal autonomy, manipulative actions, moral motivation, and value theory. His articles have appeared in *American Philosophical Quarterly, The Canadian Journal of Philosophy, Philosophical Studies, The Southern Journal of Philosophy,* and *Social Theory and Practice.* In addition to ongoing work with Samantha Brennan on the moral status of children, his current research focuses on moral theory and the role that claims about the nature of persons play in the construction and justification of moral theories.

James P. Sterba is professor of philosophy at the University of Notre Dame, where he teaches moral and political philosophy. He has written more than 150 articles and published 16 books, including *How to Make People Just* (1988),

Contemporary Ethics (1989), *Feminist Philosophies* (2nd edition, edited with Janet A. Kourany and Rosemarie Tong, 1999), *Morality in Practice* (5th edition, 1994), and *Justice for Here and Now* (1998). He is past president of the International Society for Social and Legal Philosophy, the American section; past president of Concerned Philosophers for Peace; and past president of the North American Society for Social Philosophy. He has lectured widely in the United States, Europe, and the Far East.

Clark Wolf is associate professor of philosophy at the University of Georgia. His papers have appeared in numerous collections and journals, and he is currently writing a book on intergenerational justice.